NEXT YEAR I WILL KNOW MORE

NEXT YEAR I WILL KNOW MORE

Literacy and Identity among Young Orthodox Women in Israel

TAMAR EL-OR

TRANSLATED BY HAIM WATZMAN

WAYNE STATE UNIVERSITY PRESS   DETROIT

06 05 04 03 02   5 4 3 2 1

Library of Congress Cataloging-in-Publication Data

El-Or, Tamar.
[Be-Fesaòh ha-ba. English]
Next year I will know more : literacy and identity among young
Orthodox women in Israel / Tamar El-Or ; translated by Haim Watzman.
p. cm. — (Raphael Patai series in Jewish folklore and
anthropology)
Includes bibliographical references and index.
ISBN 0-8143-2772-9
1. Jewish religious education of women — Israel. 2. Women religious
Zionists — Israel — Social conditions. 3. Women religious
Zionists — Israel — Interviews. 4. Orthodox Judaism — Israel. 5.
Feminism — Religious aspects — Judaism. I. Title. II. Series.
BM85.I8 E5313 2001
305.48'892405694 — dc21
2001004173

♾ The paper used in this publication meets the minimum requirements of
the American National Standard for Information Sciences—Permanence
of Paper for Printed Library Materials, ANSI Z39.48-1984.

Grateful acknowledgment is made to the Mary Dickey Masterton
Fund for financial assistance in the publication of this volume.

In memory of my beloved mother, Yona Freiman (Opatowski-Daum)

How could it be that I'd know next Pesach exactly
what I knew about the holiday last Pesach?

Miri K., Midrasha student

~

CONTENTS

~

TRANSLATOR'S NOTE—
A NARRATIVE GLOSSARY

THIS BOOK WAS WRITTEN BY a nonreligious Israeli anthropologist, who immersed herself in a subculture that is one part of a larger, but still minority, Israeli subculture. The larger subculture is the religious Zionist community, and the sub-subculture is that group of women who, by acquiring religious literacy, are on the cutting edge of the religious Zionist community. In its Hebrew version, the book is aimed at an Israeli public which has some familiarity with the religious Zionist subculture. The English version cannot assume that its readership will understand the context—neither of the religious Zionist subculture nor of the general Israeli culture in which it is embedded.

This narrative glossary is intended to provide the reader with some general background and explain a number of terms and concepts that appear throughout the book. It is not, of course, intended to be an exhaustive survey of Israeli culture, and, in aiming for simplicity, it at times makes generalizations to which knowledgeable people may take exception. It is meant to do no more than provide some context and serve as a ready reference for the reader.

Religious Zionism was the movement founded within the larger Zionist movement by those who sought to integrate orthodox Jewish religion with the Jewish national movement, in keeping with the teachings of thinkers such as of Rabbi Zvi Kalisher (1795–1874) and Rabbi Yehuda Alkalai (1798–1878). The organized religious Zionist movement was called the *Mizrahi,* which in pre-state Palestine established a network of schools and social services that served its public and consolidated it into a unified community. The religious Zionist community is colloquially referred to as the *knitted kipa* (pl. *kipot*) community (a *kipa* is the skullcap that religious Jewish boys and men wear) because these patterned *kipot* have become a distinguishing mark of the religious Zionist community. (Another religious garment worn by boys and men is *tzitzit*, a four-cornered piece of cloth worn under the shirt; to each corner is attached, as Jewish law requires, a set of braided fringes.)

Originally, most orthodox religious leaders rejected the attempt to take political and military action to establish a Jewish state, seeing this as a rebellion against God's will. Religious Jews who rejected Zionism, and who adhered in general to a more rigid form of orthodox observance that rejected modern influences, came to be called "ultra-orthodox" Jews, or *haredim* (sing. and adj.: *haredi*); the *haredim* are themselves divided into two major groups, the *Hasidim*, who adhere to a more spiritually oriented theology centered around a charismatic leader, and the *Lithuanians* (or *Misnagdim*), who tend to emphasize rationalism and intellectual study. In popular Israeli parlance, the *haredim* are sometimes referred to as *black*, because that is the color they generally dress in. Most *haredi* girls and young women attend schools that are part of the *Beit Ya'akov* system. While *haredi* Judaism was for a long time largely a phenomenon among *Ashkenazim*—Jews whose origins lie in Eastern and Central Europe—recent years have seen the creation of a *haredi* movement among *Sephardi* or *Oriental* Jews, those whose origins are in the Islamic world.

The life history of the average Israeli religious Zionist is fairly standard. The educational and social institutions created by the Mizrahi are still largely in place, some as community institutions, other as institutions of the state. The religious Zionist child is generally enrolled in a *state-religious school,* a public school that integrates secular and religious studies. Such schools may be coed, single gender, or enroll both boys and girls but in separate classes or seated separately in the same classroom. In fourth grade the young religious Zionist will generally join *Bnei Akiva,* the religious Zionist youth movement. While there are some coed religious Zionist secondary schools, in general elementary school graduates enter separate gender frameworks. Boys go to a boys' high school or a *high school yeshiva,* a boarding school with an emphasis on religious studies but which also teaches secular subjects according to the public school curriculum. For boys, religious studies are pursued in the traditional framework of the *havruta*—

two boys studying as partners, usually in a *beit midrash,* a large hall equipped with sacred texts where pairs of boys and men study together. Girls may attend a girls' high school: an *ulpanit,* which is a semiprivate school with more religious studies; or an *ulpana,* a boarding school. Religious men and women who want to pursue university studies may choose to do so at Bar-Ilan University, an institution established by the religious Zionist community as a place where secular and religious studies would be combined. While Bar-Ilan is a public university open to all, and although a majority of its students are not religious, it still retains more of a religious character than other Israeli universities.

After secondary school boys go into the army. Many attend a *yeshivat hesder,* a framework that allows them to integrate further religious studies with military service. While Israeli law mandates the conscription of women as well, it also—controversially—grants exemption to women who declare that they cannot serve for religious reasons. *Haredi* women do not serve at all; some religious Zionist girls serve in the army, but most take the exemption and instead perform *National Service*—one or two years of voluntary community service. A man who wishes to continue to study full-time after marriage will attend a framework called a *kolel.*

An orthodox Jew's life is governed by Jewish law or *halacha* (pl. *halachot,* adj. *halachic*), which sets out how a Jew is to observe God's commandments and precepts, the *mitzvot* (sing. *mitzvah*). These observances cover every area of life, but a number of them, including many of those performed in public, are incumbent only on men. For the most part, the observances from which women are exempt are those classified as "positive time-dependent" observances—those that require a given observance (as opposed to those that are in the form of a prohibition) be performed at a specific time of the day or year. The logic is that women, who are occupied with caring for children, are not free to commit themselves to such observances. The extent to which this logic is applicable today is one of the issues debated by the women in the classes Dr. El-Or observed.

One central area of religious Jewish life in which there are many positive time-related observances is prayer, especially public prayer in the synagogue. For example, a religious Jew is required to pray three times a day—in the morning, afternoon, and evening; the morning and evening prayers include recitation of the *shma* prayer. For morning prayers, the religious male wears *tefillin,* phylacteries worn on the head and left arm, and a *tallit,* a four-cornered and fringed prayer shawl. Three times a week the morning prayers include a public reading from the *Torah* scroll, kept in the *ark* in every synagogue. Worshipers are honored by being given *aliyot* (sing. *aliya*)—by being called up to recite the blessing over the reading of the Torah.

One important central observance is the Sabbath, or *Shabbat*. Shabbat observance is governed by a large number of halachot that prescribe what must, may, and may not be done on this day. One element of Shabbat observance is *kiddush*, a special blessing of the Sabbath recited over a cup of wine in the evening and in the morning. One central holiday is *Pesach*, or Passover, the holiday celebrating the Exodus from Egypt. Since every single trace of leavened food must be removed from the home before the holiday, pre-Pesach cleaning is a major task for every religious Zionist housewife. Another day of observance mentioned in the book is *Tisha B'Av*, the fast day that commemorates the destruction of the First and Second Temples.

The women in this book are concerned both with the fact that they are not obligated to observe many mitzvot that men are and with special mitzvot or strictures that apply particularly to women. Among these is the rabbinical prohibition against women giving testimony or serving as judges in religious courts. Another is *nida*, the law that declares that a woman is impure during her menstrual period and for a week thereafter. During this period she and her husband may not have sexual relations and must avoid physical contact.

Women in this community dress in accordance with the rules of modesty laid down by Jewish law. There is, however, a fairly wide spectrum of dress based on varying interpretations of those standards. On the more conservative end women will wear long sleeves below the elbow and long skirts and dresses; pants are forbidden. On the more liberal end of the Zionist religious community women will wear short sleeves, skirts at knee-length or even somewhat above, and even pants (though generally loose-fitting pants with a specifically female cut). Jewish law enjoins married women to cover their hair, but again there is a wide variation in practice. On the more conservative end wigs or kerchiefs that cover all the hair are preferred. On the more liberal end a hat or kerchief that leaves some hair exposed may be used. Hats and kerchiefs were less accepted socially by the previous generation, which is why a number of the young women who appear in this book remark that their mothers, though religious, did not cover their hair.

One of the major Jewish observances is the study of Jewish religious texts. The highest form of learning is *Torah le-shma*, meaning religious study for its own sake, rather than for any practical purpose. The works studied include the Torah (the Five Books of Moses; the term "Torah" is sometimes used to refer to religious knowledge generally), the Bible, and their commentators (one of these, *Rashi*, is commonly studied beginning in elementary school). Other works are those produced by Jewish sages and rabbis over the ages. The most important of these is the *Talmud*, a compendium of discussions, debates, and stories by the sages and rabbis of the first through fifth centuries of the common era. The Talmud contains the *Mishna* and the *Gemara;* in colloquial Hebrew the term "Gemara" is often used to refer to the Talmud as a whole. The narrative sections of the Talmud are called the *aggadah* (pl. *aggadot*). Other narratives or homilies written by the sages are included in the *midrashim* (sing. *midrash*). Jewish religious scholars have also produced writings on theology and philosophy, the best known being *Maimonides*, a medieval Jewish philosopher and rabbi. Some such works have gained special status in the religious Zionist community, among them the *Maharal*, written by a late medieval rabbi who lived in Prague, and the *Kuzari*, by Yehuda Ha-Levy.

A more recent rabbi and scholar who became the spiritual father of religious Zionism is Rabbi Avraham Yitzhak Hakohen Kook (sometimes called simply "Rav Kook"), who was appointed the first chief rabbi of Palestine by the British. Rabbi Kook viewed the return of the Jews to the Holy Land as a stage toward the coming of the Messiah and the reestablishment of the Temple, and he claimed that even nonreligious Zionists who were helping build the Jewish state were doing God's work. Rabbi Kook's writings are central texts for the religious Zionists, and the yeshiva he founded, Merkaz Ha-Rav, became a central religious Zionist institution; nearly all of today's religious Zionist leaders studied there or at affiliated institutions. (I would like to thank Dr. Moshe Halbertal for helping me translate the selections from Rabbi Kook's works that appear in this book.)

Since religious Zionists believe that political and historic developments in modern Israel have religious significance, they are very politically involved and aware. Dr. El-Or's ethnographic work was done at a critical historical-political moment for this community.

The religious Zionists, under the aegis of their political framework, the *National Religious Party,* have been members of nearly every government coalition since Israel was founded. Up until 1967 the party tended to take a moderate line on domestic and foreign policy and generally restricted its activity to religious issues. But the Six Day War in 1967, when Israel occupied the West Bank, Golan Heights, and Sinai Peninsula, was seen by many religious Zionist leaders—in particular, by Rabbi Zvi Yehuda Kook, Rabbi Kook's son—to be another watershed in the messianic process. With Israel's acquisition of these territories, which included key sites associated with ancient Jewish history, Israel became Greater Israel, and the religious Zionists became its most enthusiastic proponents.

A group of younger men and women assumed the leadership of the National Religious Party and of other religious Zionist institutions. They also set up *Gush Emunim,* an organization devoted to establishing Israeli settlements in the occupied territories. Young members of the religious Zionist community were brought up to believe that they were at the vanguard of a messianic movement that would lead to a State of Israel that embraced its ancient boundaries and in which all Jews would return to their faith. The 1977 accession of the right-wing nationalist party, *Likud,* with which the National Religious Party was allied, was seen as further proof of the divine hand behind this process.

When the *Labor* party, led by Yitzhak Rabin, won the 1992 election and set up a government with the left-wing peace party, *Meretz,* the religious Zionists underwent both a religious and theological crisis. God's will seemed to have been stymied, and the community groped for an explanation. When Rabin entered negotiations with Palestinian leader Yasser Arafat and signed the Oslo accords, which handed sacred Jewish territory over to the Palestinians, the community found itself at a critical point. This was not helped by the fact that Rabin and many of his supporters made frequent and often tactless statements that led the religious Zionists to feel they were being pushed outside the normative Israeli community.

In November 1995 Rabin was assassinated by a religious Zionist student from Bar-Ilan University, precipitating a further crisis in the religious Zionist community and in the country as a whole. It is against this background that Dr. El-Or analyzes the changing literacy of religious Zionist women.

HW

~

PRELUDE:
THE CYPRESSES IN MAGDIEL

THE CYPRESSES IN MAGDIEL ARE tall ones, the survivors of old towns. Their gray-green loftiness proclaims the pride of the first settlers. Standing on the marches of old orange groves, they lead from the main road to the houses, marking the school, the old post office, the playing field, the cemetery.

The cypresses planted by Magdiel-born Yehezekel Daum when he moved to Ramat Magshimim on the Golan Heights are shorter and less slender. He planted them in two rows leading from the central path along the sidewalk to the door of his house, just as his grandfather had done at the handsome old house in Magdiel. Rabbi Yehezkel Daum died at a young age, in the summer of 1993.

While still in the immediate shock of grieving for this well-loved man, his family had to decide where he should be buried. His grandfather, grandmother, father, uncles, and aunts all lay in the Magdiel cemetery, on the Sharon plain north of Tel Aviv. The cemetery at Hispin on the Golan plateau had only a handful of graves, and an air of uncertainty hung over them. In the end, the funeral ceremony took place on the Golan.

When I paid a condolence call I found myself in a home buzzing with people. In the awkwardness of the moment I was pressed into a corner; afterward, very slowly, I approached Yehezkel's mother and sisters, who were sitting, as Jewish laws of mourning prescribe, low, close to the floor.

"Those cypresses," his mother said, "they are his Magdiel. You understand, for him the Golan Heights and Ramat Magshimim are like the Sharon Plain and Magdiel for us. The deep mud that was here when they arrived, the delicate seedlings they planted—that was simply his Magdiel."

Clearly, his mother, knowing that I come from the nonreligious, left-wing, big city side of the family, was guessing—correctly—that the decision to bury Yehezkel on the Golan raised some serious questions for me. After all, I am among those Israelis who believe that the Golan Heights will eventually have to be ceded to Syria in the framework of a peace treaty—putting Yehezkel's grave in a foreign country. By comparing Ramat Magshimim to Magdiel, was his mother deliberately translating the family's decision into language she thought would be more pleasing to me or that would keep me from completing my train of thought? Or was it she herself who needed to make the comparison, to make it easier for her to accept the separation and distance her grandchildren had imposed on her?

Yehezkel Daum's grandfather, who was also my mother's grandfather, had six children: two daughters and four sons. He himself was an early member of the Mizrahi movement, a religious Zionist who in 1924 picked up his family and took them from Warsaw to Magdiel. One of his daughters (following her husband) and one of his sons (following his wife) continued along the religious Zionist road. The others, with the exception of one of the grandchildren, drifted away from it. Yehezkel and his sisters grew up in one of the two religious families.

I loved to spend long days in the yards in Magdiel, where my mother's uncles and aunts lived side by side. The orthodox Sabbath observance of one of those homes did not seem exceptional, given that the other two homes were also traditional, though not orthodox. Miriam and Yonit, who were about my age even though they were the children of my mother's uncles, were wonderful companions for long walks and games, for climbing the citrus and loquat trees and smoking forbidden cigarette butts behind the henhouses. From Miriam I learned that you have to wait until three stars have appeared on Saturday night before you can collect the eggs, and she taught me some girls' versions of dirty jokes, too. From nonreligious Yonit I learned the morning prayers that she said in her religious public school, because the village had no other elementary school. Magdiel was for me an "other" place, because of its slow tempo and because it was so different from the neighborhood where I grew up on the edge of the big city.

As time went on, my visits became less frequent and the distances grew. Children's games were replaced by politics and life decisions, fashions and images that colored old ties and friendships. Nothing remained simple or self-evident. The private history of the Daum family, and its division into many biographies, is one example of the divergence so common in Israeli society, one that put Miriam and me on either side of social, ideological, and political barriers.

The work of this book took me back to Miriam's "field." I chose to study the women's seminary—from here on out I will call it as its students do, in Hebrew, the Midrasha[1]—at Bar-Ilan University because it lies at the crossroads of religious and women's literacy that is my field of study. But the fact that at one of our family weddings I pored over the class schedule with Miriam in order to choose classes worth observing and studying, and that I made use of her name and that of her brother to gain my foothold at the Midrasha, is part of the same research path.

Study of the home ground,[2] and not just of distant and foreign cultures, has become the order of the day in contemporary anthropology. In this work the home is not a sociological metaphor but a real home. In such a home, communication becomes a charged discourse, one that reflects and refracts both their private and public lives.

I attended a memorial service for my Uncle Shlomo at the Magdiel cemetery not long after the Oslo peace talks had become an established fact. "Did you hear?" Miriam asked. "They said today on Arutz Sheva [a radio station associated with the right wing of the religious Zionist movement] that our army no longer deserves to be called the Israel Defense Force because it isn't defending us any more." "I didn't hear that," I whispered to her. "I haven't the slightest idea where Arutz Sheva is on the radio dial."

At the end of the ceremony, some of the participants stopped to view other graves, seeking to instill in their children knowledge of the family tree and the tradition of visiting the departed. Those children visiting a cemetery for the first time gazed at their parents as if to find out what level of sorrow and interest they were supposed to express. At the gate, next to the faucets provided for the ritual hand-washing religious law requires upon leaving a cemetery, Miriam looked at me with her green eyes and said: "Forget politics. Have you gone to sit in on the classes at the Midrasha that I recommended?" "I went to some of them," I answered. "So, how are they?" "It's a long story," I replied.

I can begin far from the cypresses of Magdiel, folding the beginning into the envelope that arrived from the Midrasha at Bar-Ilan University. Within it I found a sheet of paper made to look like yellowing parchment notifying me of the opening of a program for graduates of the Midrasha that would begin in 5753—that is, the 1992–93 academic year. The studies would be intensive:

six hours on Tuesdays from the afternoon until eight in the evening, including two, two-hour classes and two hours of study in *havruta*—that is,
independent study with a partner. I looked at the yellow parchment, the
curlicued heading, and the list of courses on offer, and tried to figure out
how such an invitation had reached me. I refused to give myself over to the
feeling that fate had mailed me a field of anthropological study, but it was
hard to avoid that thought. The letter came just when I was on the verge
of deciding on a topic for a new research project, and I had been considering a look at one of the seminaries that offer religious studies for women
after they complete their military or alternate national service. This field of
inquiry had suggested itself after my study on the link between knowledge
and gender among ultra-orthodox (*haredi*) women.[3] The program I held
before me fit my expectations so well that it was hard to relate to it disin-
terestedly. It promised a concentrated day of study that included women
studying Gemara (Talmud) in the traditional way. There was also a class
in Bible and in the writings of Rabbi Kook,[4] and all this in the company
of graduates of the Midrasha. My great luck, I quickly understood, was a
product of the Midrasha's computer, which had me listed as having taken,
in 1987–88, a course in Hasidism, in the framework of my Ph.D. studies.

I suddenly recalled a forgotten scene. I was standing by the door of the director of the Midrasha, waiting for a personal interview with Rabbi Yitzhak
Cohen. For the first time in my life as a student I was being interviewed
to decide whether to permit or deny me participation in a course. I had
registered for a class that appeared in the university catalogue, a course that
required the approval of the director of the Midrasha. The memory became
clearer and more components appeared. There was a new building, alive
with young women, no men, a small and stuffy office, two office workers,
one of them wearing a wig, and a long line of women waiting to speak with
the director.

My turn arrived when the door opened and a young woman came out.
I recalled brown curls, a long skirt of Indian fabric, and a large backpack.
She smiled at the man sitting out of my sight and promised to pass on the
regards he had asked her to convey. Inside the room I found myself facing a
large desk, behind which a man with a black and white beard sat on a high-
backed chair. There were a few pictures on the walls, and a vase with fresh
flowers. Within the space of a few minutes, tactfully and indirectly, the rabbi
made it clear to me that this place, where young Jewish women study, was
not for me: "It won't be right for you. The class isn't on the level of a doctoral
student. You won't get much out of it. It's not a historical or philosophical

class on Hasidism. It's something else." I left his room with no intention of returning.

On my way out I took another look at the corridor leading from the offices to the classrooms, at the profusion of women filling it to overflowing, and at the glass-enclosed foyer facing the path. At home I crossed the class off my schedule, but, as it later turned out, the computer had not done likewise. In its memory, one Tamar El-Or had registered as a student, had graduated from the Midrasha three years later, and now, five years later, was being invited for another talk with the rabbi.

I returned to Rabbi Cohen's room hoping for a positive answer this time. I enlisted my new status of scholar, and dropped the names of family members he knew. I was happy to hear that he had read my newly published book. Rabbi Cohen made inquiries about the nature of my interest in the graduate program and listened to me talk vaguely about wanting to study both Torah and the women studying it. He understood, I think, that I wanted to join the women in order to observe them. When we parted, he summed up my motives as follows: "I won't stop anyone who wants to study Judaism." What had been denied me as a student at the university turned out to be surprisingly easy to get as a scholar.

During the three years I spent in the Midrasha, and in my visits after I completed my principal fieldwork, I received a warm reception and cooperation from Rabbi Cohen. When I took one of the classes he taught himself, we had conversations in his office in which I asked questions and shared my thoughts, preliminary analyses, and critiques. His receptiveness, and the very real and non-patronizing assistance he gave me, were not things I took for granted. The approachability of the students, instructors, librarians, and office staff was a surprise and a delight; I have never stopped wondering why they cooperated with me.

This is the place to thank Rabbi Yitzhak Cohen for allowing me to pursue this research. I am also grateful to the teachers of the classes I observed, to the young women in whose company I studied, and to those of them whom I interviewed.

I would also like to thank Ora, who joined me when I began conducting my interviews and whom the reader will meet in the book itself. The names of some of the teachers and students I interviewed have been changed at their request.

The initial work on this book was done at the Center for Advanced Judaic Studies at the University of Pennsylvania in Philadelphia. I am grateful to the Center's directors for choosing me as a member of a literacy research group in 1995–1996. The Center for Judaic Studies brought me together with outstanding colleagues and created a work atmosphere that was both challenging and supportive. A Fulbright grant I received made my stay in the U.S. both possible and pleasurable. The other parts of the book were written during the course of my ongoing work at the Hebrew University of Jerusalem, with the aid of The Shein Center for Social Science Research. I would also like to thank my colleagues and students in the Department of Sociology and Anthropology, who listened and responded to different parts of this work, with special gratitude going to Gideon Aran and Tal Kohavi. Additional thanks goes to Gideon Kunda of Tel Aviv University.

The bridge between the Hebrew and English versions of this book was made by the editor of this series, Prof. Dan Ben Amos. My thanks to him, to Arthur Evans and Kathryn Wildfong of Wayne State University Press, and to copyeditor Sandra Williamson for their excellent work.

Special thanks goes to my translator, Haim Watzman, who embarked on a second journey with me, and to Nita Schechet, who helped me find my way past additional barriers between the two languages.

My motives for choosing to study the corner of Zionism at the intersection of knowledge, gender, and religion are complex. They include a natural continuity with my studies of *haredi* women, an invitation whose source was a computer error, and a family biography that in the course of a generation created boundary lines within my own home. To these reasons was added a vague realization that this is not the time to search far afield for objects of research, that things are happening at this heavily traveled intersection, that study among religious women is now in a critical period. The field and research work produced findings that point not only to a critical and interesting period but to a real revolution. During my years of observation, research, and writing (1992–97), I followed the beginning of a revolution in real time, and this book, in its modest way, will endeavor to portray that.

The central claim of this study is that the spreading practice of intensive Judaic studies among women in the religious Zionist community is a revolutionary phenomenon that will, within a short time, bring about a profound transformation in orthodox Judaism. Its source lies in a change in the relations between genders and in the construction of gender identities of the members of the community, but its influence is sweeping. Before us is a feminist literacy revolution that is bringing about theological and halachic (Jewish legal) changes. These changes will not be traumatic because they are taking place gradually and along with a continual institutional metamorphosis. They will make the community more religious and more feminist. More religious because it will contain more people—that is, women—who know Torah, and more women who believe and observe the mitzvot (commandments and precepts). More feminist because of the desire to de-emphasize the gender of the female believer to enable her full participation in the life of the community. On the verge of the twentieth century, religious Zionism shaped itself as an orthodox Jewish movement that decided to link itself with the Zionist enterprise. This decision required social courage and halachic creativity. At the turn of that same century, the religious Zionist community faces a no less serious effort to incorporate changes in the system of gender relations into the orthodox way of life.

The tracking of this revolution in this book covers a limited corner and a bounded period of time. It focuses on one out of many places, and on a specific community of women within the whole. What is presented is a partial view of the process as a whole, deriving from the nature of anthropological work, with all its strengths and its limitations.

The book is divided into four parts: Part I: The Research Site and Methods; Part II: Next Pesach—Biographies of Students and Their Analysis; Part III: Dialogues on Torah Study and the Constitution of Identity; Part IV: Anthropology and Literacy—From Critique to Participation.

PART I: THE RESEARCH SITE AND METHODS

The first chapter of this section deals with the extent and nature of the demand for midrashot. It provides a short history of the institutions that offer intensive Judaic studies for young women high school graduates, and it surveys the various midrashot, their curricula, and the ideology of literacy that guides them. At the center is the women's seminary at Bar-Ilan University, the Midrasha, including a comparison of the 1992–93 curriculum with that of 1997–98. This chapter presents, in a general way, the link between knowledge and gender, a subject discussed in depth in other chapters.

Chapter 2 is methodological. At its core is the question of fieldwork as "home work"—that is, the question of conducting research on a proximate community that is tangential at many points to the researcher's society. Power relations, the representation of others in the scholarly text, the production of the text, and its status as a sociological and political space are presented via ethnographic segments made up of edited selections from the researcher's field log and diary. These segments enable the translation of general methodological questions into their unique context: 1. the observation of the religious Zionist community in the period of the center-left Labor-Meretz government of 1992–95 and of the advance of the peace process; 2. the analysis of the material and the composition of the greater part of the book in the years 1995–97, under the influence of the assassination of Prime Minister Yitzhak Rabin and the subsequent change of government in Israel.

Part II: Next Pesach — Biographies of Students and Their Analysis

Chapter 3, the first chapter in this section, presents six literacy biographies, stories edited from recorded interviews in which the subject was asked to describe her history as a student, with an emphasis on her experience in Jewish studies. Chapter 4 analyzes these interviews and others according to themes that emerged as central topics in the interviews themselves.

Part III: Dialogues on Torah Study and the Constitution of Identity

In this section readers are invited to enter the Midrasha's classrooms and listen in on dialogues between students, teachers, and texts. These dialogues are presented as a critical and incisive negotiating process, linking Torah study to the construction of the students' identities. The research material here focuses on three central features of identity: motherhood, nationalism, and religiosity.

Part IV: Anthropology and Literacy — From Critique to Participation

The concluding section is largely theoretical, although it also contains ethnographic segments taken from the field log. It integrates literacy as a topic of study and anthropology as a scientific discipline. The location of this chapter at the end of the book is meant to make the work more readable. Readers interested in the field of literacy should skip to this section whenever they choose.

I

THE RESEARCH SITE AND METHODS

1

$\backsim$

THE DEMAND FOR MIDRASHOT

AS I WRITE THESE LINES, it is reasonable to assume that somewhere in Israel people are working to establish a new seminary for religious study for young Jewish women. The founders will necessarily be doing some serious thinking about the institution's character. Should this new midrasha be designed along the lines of the *hesder* yeshiva, a men's seminary that combines traditional religious studies with military service (for most women this would be alternative national community service rather than military service), or should it be a real yeshiva, in which students are required to free themselves of all other obligations and "to slay themselves in the sanctuary of the Torah" for a year or two? It could be a less demanding midrasha that offers afternoon and evening courses. Such a program would attract older women who would come for two or three hours a week. The promotional material and registration forms would show young women seated in a circle on a green lawn, with pines or cypresses in the background, and behind them low buildings with shingled roofs. The catalogue describing the courses might have more pictures, perhaps of two young women standing on a grassy path holding folio-sized volumes of Talmud, and others leaning over a similar volume's open pages. Or it might show a teacher, her hair covered with a kerchief, facing a classroom full of women, and another sitting on a chair, surrounded by a young audience seated cross-legged on the grass.

Such pictures greeted me when I leafed through the material sent to me by several midrashot. At the beginning of October 1996 I received a list of nine of them from the Torah Education Branch of the Ministry of Education. At my request, the list comprised only midrashot that serve young Israeli women from the religious Zionist camp who are interested solely in sacred studies. It did not include *haredi* (ultra-orthodox) institutions or institutions for women who had recently become religious. The women's Midrasha at Bar-Ilan University was not included in the list, perhaps because it has no independent status. Nor did the list include other institutions in which there are frameworks for sacred studies for women, either because they had not been accredited by the Torah Education Branch or because they did not fit my specific criteria.

The fact that I received material about these religious institutions from a government official in the Ministry of Education is evidence of the integration of religion and the state in Israel. Religious education is offered by the state in the framework of a system of religious public schools (called the state-religious system). While officially public and nonpartisan, this system is largely a continuation of the community school system run by the religious Zionist community's political arm, the Mizrahi (now the National Religious Party), during the period before Israel's independence. This public school system has always been run, with a large measure of autonomy, by officials closely associated with the National Religious Party and the religious Zionist community. The party and community have also exercised a great deal of influence over education in the nonreligious system. In fact, between 1977 and 1999 (but not including 1992–96, the years during which this research was done), the minister of education has been a representative of the National Religious Party.[1]

State-religious schools differ from Israel's nonreligious public schools in a number of important ways. First, while many state-religious elementary schools enroll both boys and girls, some are single sex; others have separate classes for boys and girls or seat them separately in the classroom. Second, in addition to the normal general subjects of study, the curriculum devotes a large number of class hours to studies, which generally differ for boys and girls, especially after elementary school.

Most religious Zionist secondary schools are segregated by gender. The flagships of the community's secondary education are the high school yeshivot for boys and the *ulpanot* for girls. These are boarding schools offering intensive religious Zionist education and sacred studies, but also general studies toward the national high school graduation exam. Boys devote some six to seven hours a day to sacred studies, girls two to three hours. The disparate number of hours is not the only gender distinction in sacred studies.

THE DEMAND FOR MIDRASHOT

The content of these studies differs for boys and girls, as do teaching and study methods. Boys devote the major part of their energies to the study of Gemara (Talmud), while girls specialize in the reading of midrash, Jewish philosophy, and in *midot,* that is, values of character and behavior. There are also non-boarding *ulpanot* (called "ulpaniot," sing. "ulpanit") and religious high schools for boys and girls, especially in the larger cities. While these non-boarding schools have historically tended to have less status in the religious Zionist community than the high school yeshivot and *ulpanot,* in recent years there has been increasing demand for this kind of framework. The formal education system is complemented by the religious Zionist youth movement Bnei Akiva, which by the end of the 1990s had become the largest Israeli youth movement, with some 70,000 members belonging to 375 branches around the country.

Formally, a two-year term of mandatory military service is incumbent on all Israeli women. Girls who identify themselves as religious may, however, obtain an exemption. While the religious Zionist community and its rabbis generally maintain that military service is inappropriate for girls, the community expects its girls to volunteer for alternative national community service out of uniform and has established several organizations that provide such a framework. This National Service is the next step on the path taken by most *ulpana* graduates. (A minority of religious Zionist girls choose to serve in the army. The army refuses to provide data on the number of soldiers who are religious girls; the estimates are that between five and ten percent of the girls who enlist every year are religious.) Most girls do one year of National Service, but many stay for two years, equating it with the length of mandatory military service for women. In Part II of this book, readers will hear the young women at the Bar-Ilan Midrasha address the different images of "one-year" and "two-year" girls.

Upon completing National Service, most young religious Zionist women pursue postsecondary studies. It is here that this book encounters them. At this point they are continuing along the path the community has laid out for them, yet they are already more independent, no longer under close educational supervision, choosing a wide variety of specializations.

In recent years there has been a growing tendency for these young women to include, at this juncture, a period of intensive sacred studies at a midrasha. These studies reinforce what they have already learned, but also open before them new fields of knowledge previously denied them. This is in fact a continuation and reshaping of the revolution in women's education begun by Sarah Schenirer, who established, in 1917 in Krakow, Poland, the Beit Ya'akov system of girls' schools.[2] The dispensation allowing religious women to pursue sacred studies has been reinterpreted many times since by different generations of learners and teachers, in dynamic social and political contexts.

The first midrasha to offer intensive Jewish religious studies for women, Bruria,[3] was founded in 1977. It was established at the initiative of Rabbi Haim Brovender, in cooperation with Mrs. Malka Bina. This midrasha sought to respond to a growing demand among women who were searching out a way for themselves in the world of orthodox Judaism. Most of these women, like the founders, came from English-speaking countries. There can be no doubt that Bruria College was the seed from which the phenomenon of women's midrashot grew. It was a pioneering institution that formulated a revolutionary curriculum for women. Later, Mrs. Bina left Bruria and established Matan, the Torah Center for Women. Both these institutions were influences on the establishment of the Nishmat Midrasha. All three were initially based on a large core of pupils and teachers from English-speaking countries. In these countries, the economic, social, and political roles of women were changing, and this inevitably had an impact on the orthodox Jewish communities there. One result was the creation of a demand for frameworks for sacred studies for women, including the study of Gemara (Talmud) *al ha-seder*[4] and in *havruta,* just as in the traditional male yeshiva. The innovation began far from the religious Zionist establishment in Israel, and it took time to work its way in, first at the margins, then into the center. This literacy revolution in religious education for women has proceeded in parallel with the general progress of feminism in Israel. Both have been influenced by individuals and groups who have brought with them feminist thinking from the West.[5]

The link between local and English-speaking women, the common paths they traced through women's learning and their different directions are well illustrated in the biographies of two central figures in this process: Nurit Fried and Esti Rosenberg. Nurit Fried grew up in a *haredi* home in Haifa and was educated in the Beit Ya'akov school system. A sense of personal and ideological unease led her into the religious Zionist camp. Esti Rosenberg is the daughter of Rabbi Aharon Lichtenstein and Dr. Tova Soleveitchik. Rosenberg brought with her from the U. S. a tradition of linking the academy and religion, and benefited from family support and encouragement for her religious studies.[6] These two women, perceived as having picked up the torch of advanced sacred studies for women, traveled a long way together at Bruria and are now proceeding along different paths. Fried, director of the Institute for the Training of Rabbinic Advocates, under the sponsorship of Midreshet Lindenbaum (the former Bruria), chooses her words carefully in explaining the process of which she is a part. Rosenberg, who wishes to extend the boundaries of the process further, left Lindenbaum and began (in 1997) working to establish a midrasha more similar to a *hesder* yeshiva at Kibbutz Migdal Oz in Gush Etzion, south of Jerusalem.

Literacy was the first and central arena in which feminist trends were processed, whether or not they were explicitly designated as such. In other words, the feminist spirit that blew into the religious community from the outside, and similar trends that were taking place within the religious community, ripened toward action and change at the site of education for young women. At the same time additional changes took place, on the levels of the individual and the community, touching on the lives of women: acquisition of higher education, integration into the labor market, reorganization of the division of roles between the sexes within the family, participation in political activity, and so on. But the matter of literacy was and remains the first site in which changes have been taking place regarding the life of a woman as a religious person, as a member of a "believing and practicing" society.

The field of study and knowledge is the weak link in the chain separating the world of women from the world of men. It is the link that the feminist-religious process has latched onto, straining it to the breaking point. Sites of knowledge, argue critical and pedagogical sociologists, are sites of power. They construct and reproduce the social structure on an ongoing basis and so prevent radical change. This is no less the case in an open and democratic society.[7]

Jewish religious and *haredi* societies are exceptional test cases. Religious-halachic knowledge forms the primary power center in the organization of the daily life of religious Jewish individuals and communities. It is the material from which the imperative conceptual, moral, political, and ideological fabric is woven. This knowledge lies in the hands of "knowing men": *talmidei hahamim* (religious scholars), teachers, rabbis, *dayanim* (religious court judges), *poskim* (authorities who make rulings on halachic questions), and spiritual guides. Orthodox communities of all types have been operated and have operated from within and through it. Religious-halachic knowledge has become a central sociological asset, one that characterizes different religious communities and distinguishes between them and non-religious communities. The choice made by *haredi* communities (and, following them, all orthodox communities) to place study at the center of contemporary existence has raised the status of the "knowing man" to a supreme one.[8] This move has turned the site of knowledge into a paradoxical region—a place in which, on the one hand, the orthodox community wishes to structure and preserve itself and, on the other, the place in which the most significant changes in its life are occurring. These changes involve the community's spiritual-theological and national political[9] existence, as well as its gender definitions.

This work shows that it is not possible to obstruct a Jew, neither a man nor a woman, who wants to know. Making study the generator of contemporary Jewish experience, the activity that sets a religious Jew apart from a secular one, that distinguishes a "good Jew" from other Jews, required the spread of this knowledge among and within all believing communities. The banal statement that knowledge is power and that social change derives from the force of education takes on special meaning in the religious world. This is because religious study openly seeks to preserve, not to change. In this way religious study receives a connotation of preservation and distinction along with that of broadening the circle of knowers, both male and female. The gatekeepers of the site of study cannot easily turn away those who seek to enter.[10]

The request to participate in what has been marked by the "knowing men" as a central activity of the community puts these men in a problematic position, since it turns them into collaborators, willing or unwilling, in bringing women into the circle of knowing participants.

Rabbi Avraham Yosef Wolf, founder of the *haredi* Beit Ya'akov College for girls in the largely *haredi* town of Bnei Brak, described his initiative with the following paradoxical statement: "If we succeed in instilling in our girl students that the purpose of their studies is to aspire to emulate our matriarchs, who did not study, then we have succeeded in educating our daughters."[11] This paradox, the attempt to "educate to ignorance," is not absent from religious Zionist discourse, but it is becoming more and more untenable. The rapid growth of women's midrashot demonstrates the great transformation that has taken place in the field of Jewish literacy in women's lives, and the changes that the new place of women are generating in the religious Zionist world.

Social and historical research seeks to examine the pace and quality of the movement toward the gates as well as what is taking place within the site of study. This book focuses on a limited angle, in a given time, and one arena. Nevertheless, a close acquaintance with this test case can illuminate a process in which women are seeking a place of their own in the world of knowledge that determines so many facets of their lives, a place from which they can go on to make further changes.

WHERE, HOW MANY, AND WHAT

The portrait of sacred studies for women crafted in this chapter is a mosaic composed of the spectrum of curricula that were sent to me by the midrashot and information gleaned from the answers their directors gave to a short questionnaire I sent them. The mosaic has been enriched by a special issue of the periodical *Mar'ot: A National Magazine for the National Service Girl and the Young Religious Woman,* which devoted its issue of May–June 1997 to the subject of Torah studies for women and the status of women. The prominent parts of the mosaic mark the inclinations, orientations, and literacy approaches of the midrashot. Given the multiplicity of the midrashot, and the fact that they are becoming institutionalized features of the religious Zionist community, each of them is impelled to establish a unique profile. Each evolves a special character, in keeping with its institutional relationship (association with a yeshiva or with other Torah study institutions, geographical location, and so on) and its director, and this character enables it to compete in a constantly expanding cultural marketplace.

In the questionnaires I sent to the midrashot I asked for, among other things, information on three issues that elucidate the midrasha's character and direction. These are the study of Gemara *al ha-seder;* the existence of separate programs for the study of *Torah le-shma* (the study of Torah for its own sake—not for a specific purpose, such as teacher training or earning a degree) involving an intensive year of study preceding, during, or after national or military service; and the institution's declaration of purpose. The first of these is a content element—inclusion of Gemera *al ha-seder* in the curriculum declares the midrasha's intention of taking possession of an asset heretofore considered exclusively male. The second element is structural and biographical. The third is ideological.

Responses to the questionnaire are recorded in Table 1, which does not include the Midrasha at Bar-Ilan University, whose literacy portrait will be presented separately. Study of Gemara: Four of the twelve midrashot set themselves the goal of providing their students with basic and in-depth knowledge of Gemara. This has become, over time, one of the most important defining characteristics of the women's midrasha as an institution. The candidates, their families, and their teachers in high school or *ulpana*

TABLE 1. Midrashot for Women

NAME	LOCATION AND DATE OF FOUNDING	NUMBER AND AGE OF STUDENTS	GEMARA STUDY	INTENSIVE STUDY PROGRAM	DIRECTOR AND MISSION STATEMENT
Lindenbaum (Bruria)	Jerusalem, 1977 (as Bruria), since 1986 as Midreshet Lindenbaum	82 Israeli women in National Service, 30 in intensive program	Yes, a great deal, and *al ha-seder*	"Tushia," a program that integrates studies with service along the model of a *hesder yeshiva* plus sacred studies *le-shma*	Ohad Tehar-Lev: 1. Deepening the spiritual world and service of God through understanding and in-depth study. 2. Independent ability to approach any text. Building an independent generation in the service of God.
Matan— Torah Institute for Women	Jerusalem, Ra'anana, 1988	Some 800 students of all ages in part-time programs, about 30 in intensive study program for young women	Yes, a great deal, and *al ha-seder*	"Matmidot," year-long program for students who devote themselves full-time to sacred studies.	Malka Bina: To understand, become knowledgeable, to obtain tools for the study of all texts through intellectual honesty. Training ground for young women destined to take leadership roles in education and research.
Nishmat – High Midrasha for Sacred Studies for Women	Jerusalem, 1990	Students of all ages, from both Israel and overseas, on an advanced level. About 15 in intensive program	Yes, and *al ha-seder*	Full intensive program	Hannah Henkin: Love of Torah, ability to study independently, spiritual development, awe of heaven, lovingkindness, involvement in Israeli society and the state.

	Location, Year	Students	Study type	Program	Founder and Goals
The Religious Kibbutz Movement	Kibbutz Ein Ha-Natziv, 1986	50 young women before or after military or National Service, and women of all ages; about 30 in full-time program	Yes, and *al ha-seder*	Full program for young women before or after military or National Service. Option of integrating service and study	Rachel Keren: Establishment of a stratum of scholarly women with a critical viewpoint based on the fundamentals of faith and commitment to halacha, through a process of gaining and internalizing deeper knowledge and choosing it deliberately as a way of life.
Shuva	Ofra, 1984	About 120 students of different ages, including 50 young women in the full-time program	Partial study, by subject matter	An intensive program for young women	Rivka Shapira: To instill knowledge that will create a holistic worldview. To develop spiritual tools in order to cope with Western culture. Integration of the Torah world with modernity.
Yi'ud	Ofra, 1995	15 young women prior to National Service	Some, by subject matter	An intensive year of study that requires a year of teaching afterwards	Ya'akov Shapira: Creation of a cadre for teaching sacred studies (especially oral law) in *secular* schools.
Orot	Elkana, 1980	About 12 young women in the full-time program and another 50 in various courses	Yes, some *al ha-seder*, most by subject matter	An intensive *Torah le-shma* program	Ari Shevet: *Torah le-shma* with an in-depth spirituality, especially in faith and good character.

continued

TABLE 1. *Continued*

NAME	LOCATION AND DATE OF FOUNDING	NUMBER AND AGE OF STUDENTS	GEMARA STUDY	INTENSIVE STUDY PROGRAM	DIRECTOR AND MISSION STATEMENT
Shevut Rachel	Shevut Rachel, Samaria, 1995	12 young women before or after National Service	Very little, according to subject matter	One-year intensive program	Segula Melet: To help the girls build themselves a personal and religious worldview. To integrate intellectual studies and emotional life.
Nov	Nov, Golan Heights, 1995	About 20 young women in a full-time program and 50 part-time students	Some, according to subject matter	One-year intensive program	Rabbi Hai Babad: Preparation for integration into the life of a modern state. Help in constructing a worldview and identity.
Aviv	Tel Aviv, 1996	About 35, of whom 20 are in the full-time program, before and after National Service	Some, *al ha-seder*	One-year intensive program and part-time programs	Rabbi Yair Ben-Shitrit: Instilling Torah and faith in the heart of the Tel Aviv metropolitan area. To build personality through the clarification and fundamental study of religious and Torah worlds.
Reishit	Moshav Ma'on, southern Mt. Hebron	30, after military or National Service	Some, not *al ha-seder*	One-year intensive program with the option of continuing for a degree in art education	Shlomit Stoskin: Development of creativity that is devoted to the sacred. A holistic nurturing of the creative spirit (plastic arts, writing) through deep study and personal experience.

Midreshet Ha-Rova	Old City, Jerusalem, 1993	About 50 young women	Some, by subject matter	One-year intensive program	Ohad Tirosh: To deepen students' Torah world and consolidate their personalities, in the light of the heritage of Rabbi Kook.
Migdal Oz	Kibbutz Midgal Oz, Gush Etzion, 1997	About 40 students after National Service or military service	Yes, and *al ha-seder*	Option of integration with National Service or military service and university studies. One-year intensive program	Esti Rosenberg: To build a generation of scholarly women who view study as a serious and deep personal process as well as an engine for living a life of contributing to the Jewish people.

know: "That's a midrasha where they learn a lot of Gemara." Gemara is still not the dominant subject in the curriculum and does not approach the central position it takes in a men's yeshiva. Nevertheless, at Matan, Nishmat, Lindenbaum, and Ein Ha-Natziv young women study Gemara more than at any other place. Most of the students come to the midrashot without any prior knowledge of Gemara study, and they must devote an extended period of time to cracking the Talmudic code—the structure of the page, the Aramaic language, abbreviations and key words, cross references, and so on. Only after this stage are they ready to advance into methodical study under a tutor, alone, and in *havruta*. Abstention from enhanced study of Gemara is an important characteristic of the give-and-take conducted by the midrashot with their applicants and with the community. On the one hand, it is no longer possible to avoid Gemara study across the board; on the other, designating Gemara study as a preferred and important goal has not yet won sweeping support. For this reason, the eight other Midrashot take an approach similar to that expressed to me by Segula Melet, director of Midreshet Shvut Rachel: "Yes, we teach them what a page of Gemara is and how to approach it, but we teach little Gemara, only subjects that touch on them, on their lives."

Negotiations over the quantity and quality of Gemara instruction constitute a central axis for decoding the nature of the literacy now offered to women. It is a "male axis," since the male literacy world has marked it as a collection of texts central to Judaism. Both a policing discourse(what and how much women are permitted to know) and a critical discourse (what the important texts are and what Jewish literacy is—in other words, the hierarchy of sacred texts) are conducted around this axis. The mass entrance of a new community of learning women has shaken both these types of discourse and given them new content. Women studying Gemara blur the boundaries between knowers and laywomen. Learned women who refuse to study Gemara, or those who claim, after some Gemara study, that they find it uninteresting and not of primary importance—not a text that brings empowerment—challenge the dominant male order of knowledge. There can be no doubt that each type of discourse is dependent on the other, since only the entry of women into the group of knowers, or its margins, allows development of critical discussion of the supreme importance of Gemara. This means that only midrashot that allow methodical study of Gemara will produce literate and critical women who at a later stage might develop a questioning discourse on the male world of knowledge. These two types of discourse (the governing and the critical) are parallel to the feminist-liberal and feminist-essentialist types of discourse. The first seeks to interpolate women into all areas of male dominance while for all intents and purposes recognizing or accepting these areas as "important," whereas the second seeks to exploit women's "otherness" in order to produce an alternative scale of values.

In the Torah world (as in the secular literacy world) this struggle is also described in terms of "emotion and mind." The (male) mind is bound to halachic texts, while (female) emotion is bound to aggadah (narrative texts in the Talmud and other Rabbinic works), *mussar* (ethical writings), the Bible, and Jewish philosophy. As Ohad Tehar-Lev of Midreshet Lindenbaum says:

> Women search more for spiritual meaning in study [of Gemara]. They are not satisfied, as the men are, with cold, intellectual, Briskish [the city of Brisk, Lithuania, serves here as a characterization of intellectual study] study. At the beginning, women's Torah study was really an imitation of rigid, intellectual "male" learning. Now we are trying to create a "women's" Torah study and the chemistry of the two types of study will certainly create a new synthesis. It may well be that in the next stage there will be a joint *beit midrash*. But beyond this, as a man who teaches Torah to women, I already see the synthesis being created in me. The synthesis can be created in a body of written works [to be composed by people associated with these programs]. The moment such a body of women's work is created and men are exposed to it, a synthesis will be created.[12]

Depicting the differences between men and women's study as being a consequence of mind and emotion is to offer essentialist reasons for these differences. However, the second part of Tehar Lev's statement challenges the claim that men and women learn differently because of qualitative differences between them that express themselves in the mechanisms that shape the man-woman, mind-emotion binary discourse. The statement that there is men's study and women's study, when taken together with the segregation of the sexes during the act of learning, reconstruct these dichotomies. Encounter, dialogue, and the broadening of the act of learning beyond the gender of the learners[13] creates new and nonbinary fields of learning, or a synthesis, in Tehar Lev's words. Encounters that induce the collapse of these dichotomies are still few in number, and they take place with a man teaching women, and learning women developing critical stances toward the text. In the future, Tehar Lev predicts, when women express their creative and critical power in writing, these spaces will open up to all readers.

TORAH LE-SHMA

All the midrashot listed above offer young women at least one intensive year of study, involving between forty and sixty hours of study a week. The women study from morning to night, on weekdays, holidays, and Shabbat. Adding an additional year of study to the life tracks of young women is not a small matter. Beyond its significance for literacy it carries biographical meaning. Young religious Zionist women generally pursue postsecondary education. During these years most of them marry and some of them become mothers. Lengthening the period of study before or after national or military service, and before commencing postsecondary studies, stretches their youth moratorium and postpones marriage and children. This year constitutes an important component in the "curriculum vitae" of young women, and it has an effect on the matchmaking discourse. As I conducted my interviews with students at the Bar-Ilan Midrasha, I noted that Ora (a Midrasha student who interviewed some of the women for me) made a point of asking her subjects whether they had performed one or two years of National Service. A girl's decision to enlist in the army or in National Service, like the decision to serve one year or two, constitutes a declaration of intent to herself and to those around her.[14] With the expansion of the midrashot phenomenon, a new element has been added to the "curriculum vitae" of a young religious Zionist woman—whether she pursued or did not pursue a year of *Torah le-shma*. The current curricula of the different midrashot display a trend toward adding a year of exclusive religious study to a framework that provides practical benefits. This will change the significance of the year and turn it into part of a remunerative course of study. Some midrashot are attempting to gain recognition from one of the religious teachers colleges, or from the Open University (an accredited Israeli nontraditional distance-learning institution). Others, such as Ye'ud in Ofra, offer a two-year track in which the first year is devoted to general religious studies and especially to the instruction of Talmud and rabbinic texts in secular schools, while in the second year the students serve as teachers in these schools.

The curricula described above make it possible to track the character of the midrashot. Those that continue to offer an intensive year of *Torah le-shma* will be marked as literacy avant-gardes. It appears that the direction this avant-garde will aim for is the creation of a cadre of scholarly women engaged in study and research who will serve as teachers in the midrashot. The midrasha being established at Kibbutz Migdal Oz in Gush Etzion by Esti Rosenberg plans to offer a five-year program, including National Service, along the lines of a *hesder* yeshiva.

In 1993, in one of the first interviews I conducted at the Bar-Ilan Midrasha, one of the students told me: "I wanted to study for a year at Matan or Nishmat. I was dying to do that. But those girls seemed a little, well, weird. They have a reputation for being freaks, and that scared me and certainly my parents. You know that everyone expects you to keep going, to get married, and that [those midrashot] make a kind of weird impression." Now, at the end of 1997, there is an ongoing discussion of the connection between women's studies and their family lives (some of which will be presented in part II of this book). But the "weird girl" label is disappearing, to the point that in some circles study at a midrasha is perceived as a desirable, even requisite, sociological marker, a bonus point in a woman's "life chronicle."

Those involved in the midrasha phenomenon describe their growth as a "revolution from below," a change that began on the margins, was initially rejected by the establishment, but which now has penetrated its heart because of the growing number of ordinary women from the religious Zionist community who are joining it. In order to complete a broad portrait of this feminist literacy revolution before going into details, it is instructive to listen to the declared intentions of midrashot directors, educators, teachers, and founders. They formulate their pedagogical ideology in the midrashot's publicity material, as part of the negotiations they conduct among themselves, with their community, and with the society around them.

DECLARED GOALS

The four "Gemara midrashot," that is, those which devote a sizable portion of their programs to Talmud study, offer, in their declarations of purpose, similar components with different emphases. The most notable components in their declarations are: deepening the students' spiritual world; worshiping God through understanding; choice; in-depth study, the development of an independent ability to approach texts; and the acquisition of tools for all types of learning. The more innovative expressions receive different shadings at the different midrashot: at Lindenbaum, building an

independent generation of women in the service of God; at Matan, a training ground for young women who will fill roles in leadership, teaching, and
research; at Nishmat, the ability to engage in independent study with awe of
heaven and loving-kindness, and involvement in Israeli society for the benefit of the country. The Religious Kibbutz Movement Midrasha is the only
one to use the word "critical"—the establishment of a stratum of scholarly
women with a critical point of view.

An examination of the declarations of these four midrashot shows that
they do not conceive of study as *Torah le-shma*—that is, they see sacred
studies as a means to an end—but they could also be understood to be
redefining the concept of *Torah le-shma*. A woman who devotes herself to
in-depth study (even if she does not receive academic or other credit for
it—that is, *Torah le-shma*) is supposed to be part of a new and revolutionary
generation that will transform what it is to be a religious woman, as well as
the nature of the community in which she lives. In these declarations there
is a call to promote personal and gender independence in the service of God,
in the study of texts, and in the construction of spiritual identity. The young
woman is supposed to act within her new identity and to use it to nourish
her life, the life of her family, and those of her community and society. Generation after generation of graduates, ten to thirty young women in each
institution each year, are all meant to join a heterogeneous cadre of women
"knowers" working privately or in an organized way to realize the revolution
that everyone sees but only a few call by name. Most of the other midrashot
prefer to keep their distance from this revolutionary pole and to revolve
around it in more familiar and less threatening orbits. On the other hand,
they cannot afford not to participate. Therefore, the declarations characterizing the other midrashot center on the concepts of *hashkafa* (meaning
worldview and religious outlook) and "spirituality," both key terms in the
philosophy of Rabbi Kook that indicate the clear influence of the spirit of
the Merkaz Ha-Rav Yeshiva.[15] These concepts are generally interwoven with
the phrase "preparation for integration into modern society."

Midreshet Shuva: development of spiritual tools in order to cope with
Western culture. Nov: help in building a *hashkafa* before setting out in life.
Shvut Rachel: help in constructing a personal and religious *hashkafa*. In
these midrashot, it would seem, ideology is a kind of defense and prophylac-
tic. The young girl going off to National Service, or to her life as an adult, is
perceived as a person who needs her spiritual and religious world strength-
ened so that she can survive as a believing woman. As a pupil, what she
gets most is personal attention. The studies are supposed to help her build

her world and to strengthen her spirituality and faith. She is perceived as deficient, as weak and vulnerable, as one who needs to be filled.[16] Empowerment of the student is not presented in these midrashot (as it is in the "Gemara midrashot") as a stage in building a generation of knowing, creative, and perhaps even critical women who influence the community from within. Instead, the student's empowerment is presented as part of building a defense against the "outside." The women's studies are presented as part of a system of preserving the community and not as a step toward changing it. While the educators are interested in young women, the women as individuals are not their main concern. It is the community, its survivability and its influence on surrounding society that are portrayed as the supreme goal, and the women become soldiers in the service of this objective.

There can be no doubt that the entire religious Zionist community is preoccupied with these issues. Its existence as a vital and dominant part of the Israeli collective lies at the foundation of its existential ideology. Nevertheless, it is interesting to examine how each midrasha assimilates this principle into its pedagogy. Such an examination elucidates significant differences in the revolutionary process of women's education. It points to an educational axis at whose innovative end lies instruction directed at establishing a generation of knowing women, and at whose conservative end lies instruction directed at defending women from external society. From the vantage point of the sociology of education such an examination makes possible the elucidation of an additional subject: the power of educators and the declared ideology in the educational process itself. It is possible to see if, and especially how, the negotiation between learners and teachers over the results of the educational process is conducted.

THE WOMEN'S MIDRASHA AT BAR-ILAN UNIVERSITY

My fieldwork at the Women's Midrasha at Bar-Ilan University is a fascinating test case. At the beginning of my research, I would have put this midrasha close to the conservative pole. The motives for its establishment, its declared ideology, curriculum, and faculty clearly indicated a pedagogical institution meant to defend its students and to recreate a generation of half-knowing women in the religious Zionist community. My observations in the Midrasha have revealed penetrating negotiations among the students themselves, between them and the texts they study, and between them and their teachers. This negotiation within the Midrasha, in light of parallel events in other midrashot, has moved the Midrasha away from the conservative side.

The Women's Midrasha at Bar-Ilan was established in 1976. The primary motive for its establishment was a desire to preserve a separate educational-religious framework for religious girls in the university. Bar-Ilan, the only university in Israel with an orthodox religious orientation, provides an encounter between secular and religious students, Jews and Arabs, women and men.[17] This encounter is a first opportunity, for most of the religious student public, to devote themselves solely to professional studies in the framework of a mixed society. A young woman arriving at the university to study, for example, chemistry, finds herself, for the first time in her literacy history, studying solely academic subjects in a society that is mixed in gender, religious orientation, and national affiliation. While she is also required to take Jewish studies—a requirement imposed on all students at Bar-Ilan—this requirement can be met in a large lecture hall in which a religious professor teaches, say, the philosophy of Maimonides to a mixed audience of men and women, religious and secular, Jews and Arabs.

For this reason the university has worked along two parallel tracks. Some of the required Jewish studies are open only to graduates of the religious-educational system. These classes ostensibly require prior knowledge of Judaism and are directed at those committed to a religious life style. They are taught to men and women separately, and secular students cannot enroll in them. In addition, the university has established two institutions that are not subject to the academic system (since the required courses in Judaism are given by the academic departments)—a higher yeshiva and *kolel* for men (a *kolel* is a study framework for married men) and the Midrasha for women. These institutions accept religious students through a selection process; most of those accepted receive a financial aid stipend. They are exempt from the courses in Judaism required of all the other students. In this way, these institutions circumvent the diversity that the university declares is one of its guiding principles. Both institutions function even if the academic campus is on strike, and there is constant and immanent tension between academic and religious literacies. Students at the Midrasha devote more time to their Jewish studies than the minimum that the university requires. Attendance is mandatory, and students must meet course requirements (a paper or examination), but grades are not given. Scholarly-academic studies and Torah studies are thus woven into a web in which they intermingle, yet are kept separate, on the same campus. This problematic set of relations will be analyzed in Part III.

The Midrasha serves the young women as a kind of home on campus. Within and around it they are likely to find many friends and acquaintances—former schoolmates, former companions from their chapter of the religious Zionist youth movement, Bnei Akiva, or acquaintances from National Service. In 1985 the Midrasha moved into a new building built especially for it. In addition to classrooms, it also has a synagogue, library, and cafeteria that draw many of the students, who take advantage of these public areas both for their intended purpose and as social meeting places.

Many women prefer to spend their free time between classes in the cafeteria, alone or with friends. During the first years of this research the cafeteria was run by the students themselves. They would make themselves pita bread sandwiches, take a drink from the refrigerator, and pour themselves coffee, leave some coins in a jar, and settle into the easy chairs scattered around the room. During the course of my years of observation the cafeteria was handed over to professional management but did not lose its homey atmosphere. A girl who has run out of supplies for the *kipa* she is knitting can find a nice selection of yarn there; she can also purchase socks if she needs them; there is an occasional hat bazaar (hats being an important fashion accessory for the married religious woman, who is required to keep her hair covered), and copies of the day's newspapers are scattered over the tables.

The library, which contains religious and associated books, is a popular place to study, prepare assignments, conduct intimate whispered conversations, and to work in *havruta*. Since 1995 the library has also served as the home for the *beit midrash* program. The lawn around the Midrasha, and between it and the men's *kolel*, is a busy meeting area, a place in which the religious esthetic is clear. There are more long skirts and more *kipot* here than on the rest of the campus. Young couples meet there at the end of a day of studies, before going home, and groups of young women gather there to chat and to survey the field—who has arrived, who has left, what's new and interesting. If you've just gotten back from a weekend at home and don't have time to get to the dorm, you can just put down your heavy backpack in the Midrasha, with all the gear you need until next Shabbat, and run off to class. As one of the students told me: "There will always be someone to watch the stuff for me, and if there isn't, you can leave it in the office. If I'm sad and I don't have anyone to talk to, I go by the Midrasha, there's bound to be some friend of mine there. I've never been let down. You know what, I even like the bathroom there better."

This home is meant to serve as an anchor for women in the transitional period between youth and adulthood. Between the years 1992–96 I was able to follow the protective efforts of the workers in this home and to identify what elements were threatening it. I was able to observe the revolution in real time, the feminist revolution coming from below, with the conscious and unconscious, hesitant cooperation of the educators. This observation will begin with an examination of the Midrasha's curriculum and will, in the following chapters, proceed to look at the classrooms, the texts, the voices of the teachers, and the voices of the students.

THE CURRICULUM AT THE BAR-ILAN WOMEN'S MIDRASHA, 1993–98

A look back at the 1992–93 academic year, the first in which I conducted my observations, shows sixty-four classes being offered to the Midrasha's students.

Courses are traditionally divided into four fields of knowledge (as they are in the mandatory Jewish studies program at Bar-Ilan, according to the classic division of sacred studies within the religious Zionist community): Jewish philosophy, Bible, oral law (Mishna, Gemara, and other parts of the rabbinic literature), and halacha (religious law). The 1992–93 catalogue offers seventeen classes in Jewish philosophy, twenty-seven in Bible, ten in oral law, and ten in halacha. The program for graduates that I joined followed a similar model: a class on the philosophy of Rabbi Kook (Jewish philosophy), a reading of the book of Genesis (Bible), and a class in legal rulings (halacha). The division of the world of Jewish knowledge into these fields is apparently linked to the broadening of the circle of male and female students and the transfer of activities from traditional yeshivot to newer institutions, such as university departments, secular schools, religious girls' schools, high school yeshivot, and midrashot.

The connection between the teaching institution, the division into fields of knowledge, and their hierarchy are interesting subjects in and of themselves, but they will not be addressed here.[18] However, one example that gives an idea of the complexity of this connection is the existence of two academic departments that teach oral law at Bar-Ilan. One is the Talmud department, in which there is an overwhelming male majority in the faculty and a large male majority among the students (although there is a growing female presence). The second is the oral law department, in which only women are enrolled. The entry of women into the world of learning, and the extension of Gemara study beyond the yeshiva, have produced new definitions of old texts, meant to mark the position of the students and their institutions of study.

Of the twenty teachers at the Midrasha in 1992–93, three were women. Not one taught oral law. One of them taught Jewish philosophy, one Bible, and the third taught a course that fell into the halacha category and which was a class in laws applying to women's lives and their status in the community.

A look at the 1997–98 academic year shows that over five years the number of course offerings grew. The 1997–98 catalogue offers seventy-four classes, as opposed to fifty-four in 1992–93, and two more women have been added to the faculty. It is difficult, nevertheless, to discern any curricular change. The structural division is the same, and the distribution of the courses among the categories is similar to that of 1992–93.

A significant change has taken place outside the Midrasha's central curriculum through the establishment of two new programs. The first is a program for training women as rabbinic advocates (legal counsels who can represent clients before rabbinic courts), and the second is the *beit midrash* program. Neither of these programs is included in this research, since they were launched after completion of my fieldwork. However, an outside view of their establishment and of their curricula is sufficient to attest to a huge change, and to point to the way in which it has been realized.

Most of the women studying at the Midrasha will not, in 1997–98, be exposed to literacy changes. More than a thousand of them, those enrolled in the central program, will hear what their sisters heard five, or seven, or even ten years ago. But at the margins of the Midrasha, in the two prestigious programs at whose gates many applicants are knocking but to which only a hundred or so are accepted, innovative literacy events of major importance are taking place. These two programs were born of a response to growing pressure from applicants and as an attempt by the Midrasha to be a player in the field of contemporary Torah instruction for women, as a way of competing with the new midrashot. Their establishment within, but outside, the framework allows the Midrasha to keep up with the midrashot at the forefront while preserving its own conservative character. The program for rabbinic advocates, which began in the 1995–96 academic year, is the only program of its type outside the one run by Midreshet Lindenbaum in Jerusalem. The advocates' halachic training and their social role are innovations that may be interpreted in different ways.[19]

The establishment of the *beit midrash* program is in a way an expansion of the class for advanced students given by the Midrasha's director. This expansion of a class into an entire framework of study was a response to ongoing pressure from students who were demanding more classes of this kind, including intensive Gemara studies like those given in the competing midrashot. The two programs are thus responses by a central institution to pressure "from below and around."

The institution is careful to select students for these programs in a very stringent and careful way, and there are very strict requirements. Students study for twenty hours a week (six more than students at the Midrasha) in addition to their regular university classes. Students in the rabbinical advocate program study twenty-two hours a week, over three long days, culminating in a difficult battery of examinations administered by the Ministry of Religious Affairs.

The selection and supervision of the students in the special programs make it possible to teach them things not included in the general program—Gemara *al ha-seder,* many hours of study in *havruta,* and halachic legal texts. Under these circumstances, a generation of knowledgeable women is being produced at the Bar-Ilan Midrasha, while the surrounding community does not directly sense the transformation in literacy that is taking place within it. Most of the students are still exposed to a conservative literacy experience, one that grows out of the existing relation within the religious Zionist community between knowledge and gender, between one's gender and the quality and quantity of one's religious knowledge.

KNOWLEDGE AND GENDER

Among the seventy courses offered at the Midrasha in 1994–95 (as in 1997–98), two-thirds were in the categories of Jewish philosophy, Bible, and halacha. There were only ten classes in the category of oral law. Most of the courses were thus in frameworks that had been open to women students for some time.

Only fourteen had titles specifically relating to women. Four of these were in Bible: "Four Matriarchs and Seven Prophetesses," "The Book of Ruth," "The Five Megillot" (the books of the Song of Songs, Ruth, Lamentations, Ecclesiastes, and Esther), and Psalms (the courses in Ruth and the Five Megillot were not offered in 1997–98). While the titles of the last two courses do not include women protagonists, the Psalms have long been considered "women's" texts because of their poetic and spiritual nature and because they do not contain laws and commandments, which are men's

provenance. Eight of the courses in the category of halacha were also specifically directed at women students. These included classes in laws relating to
dietary practices in the home, modesty in dress, Shabbat, law and morals
in the family, the woman and her commandments, and so on. The oral law
classes included two in Gemara (beginners and advanced) which are borderline in subject matter. On the one hand, they do not appear under the
heading "Gemara" or "Talmud," but instead shelter under the conservative
classification of oral law. (Literally, of course, the term is synonymous with
Talmud or Gemara, but within the religious community the connotation
of oral law is Talmud for women; the term is also used in nonreligious elementary schools.) On the other hand, these classes are meant to provide
young women with an elementary ability to study a page of Gemara, thus
removing them from the position of merely studying oral law. The other
two courses were in the classic arena of study for women, one of them being
on aggadah (the narrative as opposed to legal texts in the Gemara) and the
other on the Midrash Aggadah on the Book of Esther, another primarily
narrative rabbinical text.

The actual encounter between the students and the world of religious
knowledge creates constant friction between their gender affiliation and
the subjects studied. First, they are sitting in a class made up entirely of
young women, within an exclusively women's Midrasha. They face, in general, a male teacher. Among the twenty-five instructors who taught at the
Midrasha in 1994–95 there were just three women, only one of whom had a
Ph.D. In 1997–98, as noted, two more women joined the teaching staff, and
one of the veterans completed her Ph.D.

Examination of the subjects these women taught shows that, with one
exception—the teacher of halacha and family ethics—they all teach general
classes with a notably academic orientation. With the exception of the class
in halacha and ethics, all the classes that deal directly with gender and identity are taught by male rabbis. The result is that direct Torah dialogue about
gender questions is largely navigated by men, while most of the women who
teach prefer to immerse themselves in academic Torah study. For example, Dr. Ruth Ben-Meir describes her class as follows: "*Drash* and *Pshat*[20]
in Biblical Interpretation—a presentation of the different interpretive approaches of the sages to the Bible and their definition; understanding the development of interpretive methods among the central commentators of the
Middle Ages including their comparative study." Rabbanit[21] Nehama Ariel
and Mrs. Osnat Braverman, who have recently joined the Midrasha's faculty, also offer scholarly courses that do not necessarily touch on questions

of religion and gender. The female faculty members at the Midrasha are certainly qualified to serve both as teachers of specific academic subjects and as educators in the broader sense—figures who convey an educational message and serve as role models. Yet these women teachers largely restrict themselves to academic roles. The Midrasha at Bar-Ilan still has no figure who integrates her professional-scholarly training with educational activity directed specifically at matters of identity and gender.

The literacy history of the students shows that their studies have been gendered throughout their lives. Their entire learning experience has been imbedded in a distinct Jewish and gender identity prior to their first class at the Midrasha. When the words come, they are words aimed directly at these women. They are taught as girls are taught. Girls are taught to love God and his people, to be moral and modest—and definitely also to think. Girls may be taught subjects that cannot be taught to boys. For this reason, midrashot for women and high schools for girls serve as a refuge for creative male teachers who seek to make new connections between, for example, literature and art and sacred studies. Dr. Admiel Kosman, a poet, taught a class at the Midrasha called "Judaism and Art." It is hard to conceive of a yeshiva offering such a class. Rabbi Ari Shevet, who heads Orot, the women's *Torah le-shma beit midrash* in Elkana, presents himself as, among other things, a composer and singer of Jewish soul music. In one of the photographs used to advertise the midrasha he is shown sitting among his women students, next to a table laden with books, and holding a guitar.[22] The status of women as learners of a "different" type allows them to be exposed to freer and more creative teaching. Still, in parallel, women are also exposed to summarizing and generalizing instruction that does not acquaint them with the primary texts on which it is based, and whose main direction is pedagogical (this will be discussed in the following chapters).

The form of instruction for women is a hybrid that has turned into a genre. It is a pedagogy that has been stitched together from Enlightenment modes of instruction (school, class, a single teacher, frontal teaching, a written text in the background, the teacher's oral text echoing in the classroom, homework, tests, and so on), and from more traditional modes (explication, preaching, studying in *havruta*, rote, cross-referencing, discomfort with the idea of giving examinations and grades, and so on). This collage, also found in other teaching sites, has largely been assembled according to the students' gender. It is teaching which is unmistakably for girls, for women.

The learning experience of women is enveloped in a male presence, since it is men who instruct the women. The Bar-Ilan Midrasha's director and his deputy are men, as are most of the faculty. All texts studied were written, interpreted, decoded, and studied by men. In rare cases there are bibliographical references to woman scholars, but these will never be feminist scholars of the Bible, the Midrash, Jewish philosophy, or Gemara—even though there is flourishing feminist study in these areas, including among orthodox women scholars.[23]

On the other side of the Midrasha's front lawn lies the men's *kolel,* where the women's brothers occupy themselves with the male version of sacred studies. The Midrasha's proximity to the *kolel* links the women students to the Jewish literacy act, as distinguished from the campus's academic studies. The women do not enter the *kolel;* only the building's upper floor is open to them, and from there they can view certain classes or events. Likewise, men steer clear of the Midrasha. A sign in the cafeteria asks the students not to invite members of the opposite sex to eat there. Nevertheless, boyfriends, brothers, husbands, and fathers penetrate the space between the women students' hands as they knit *kippot,* exchange work methods and patterns, and tell, in low voices, about the preferences of those slated to get the *kippot*—the preferred colors and sizes of what has become the symbol of the religious Zionist community—a symbol borne on men's heads but created by the labor of women.

THE DEMAND FOR MIDRASHOT—CONCLUSION

Those who have given thought to the phenomenon of increasing and spreading Torah study among religious women have been concerned largely with a single question: What for? Why should religious women, whether *haredi* or modern, want to enter into the demanding process of study, when it is hardly clear what empowerment and benefit they will gain from it? Why should women make such great efforts and invest so much time in order to obtain knowledge that was long kept from them, when the orthodox system in which they live allows them only restricted use of this knowledge because of their gender?

Most studies identify the motive as a kind of balancing act,[24] a way to harmonize the modern secular world and the religious world. From this perspective, women study Torah in order to close the gap between their broad general knowledge and their limited Torah knowledge. It is seen as compensation for their inferior social-public position within orthodoxy, a position which has become all the more glaringly obvious in the face of their growing equality in the labor market and in the civil sphere. The demand to know, to know more, to discover new texts, to attain the ability to read, decode, interpret, and criticize these texts, and the less vocal desire to observe religious rituals such as the public reading of the Torah and public prayer, become, in these explanations, a "need." Educators speak of women's "need" to balance their knowledge of, say, physics with theological achievements. The students themselves (as will be shown below) also speak of a "need," of a desire to resolve contradictions at the interface between their civil and professional lives and their religious lives.

But these explanations, which partially illuminate the phenomenon of the demand for women's midrashot, are not sufficient. Although it is reasonable that women acting in this arena have "needs," it would be a mistake to leave the analysis of these needs in the functionalist field, where every social activity is directed at reinstating a harmony that has been disturbed. The activity of women's study is indeed described in the field in which it occurs as an unavoidable act of balance, but in fact its direction is revolutionary. The pursuit of Torah knowledge by religious women—said to be aimed at uniting, harmonizing, and balancing—actually establishes a new and different social situation. This situation does not solve the problems from which it emerged—instead it exacerbates them. Since the phenomenon of new education for women derives from the tension between the religious world and the modern secular world, this education will not resolve that tension but will instead organize it in a new and different way.

This new situation, which this book addresses, is similar to other social situations generated by feminist revolutions. Its uniqueness, however, lies in two points. First, there is an immanent opposition between the fundamental values of feminism and orthodox Jewish mores (which is not the case in the relation between democracy and feminism). Second, religious feminism is connected to the personal and intimate level of the worship of God. The matter of private faith and the existence of a transcendental force, and the labor of recognizing, loving, and obeying this force have public, national, and political dimensions in the Jewish religion. However, the longing to have a women's minyan, to read the Torah in public, to study and teach Gemara, and to take part in the process of halachic decision making, needs to encompass not only the gatekeepers of orthodoxy; it must first transcend the private level. Here new ways must be paved for the service of heaven (as opposed to, say, work in a lawyer's office) that stand in contradiction to the personal, family, and public memory of that same service.[25] This additional issue of the holiness and intimacy of faith broadens this women's revolution and sets it apart from other feminist revolutions.

The voices describing this change will be presented in the second part of this book. Prior to that, however, the next chapter will present the methodology; the mode of listening, observation, and dialogue used in this work; and the power relations produced in the research field.

2

~

FIELDWORK AS HOMEWORK

"The boundaries between the field and the home are blurred; sites of research (what used to be the field out there) and sites of writing (what used to be remote observation, far away from home, from here) blend together. There is still home."

Lavie and Swedenburg, 1995, p. 67–68

SMADAR LAVIE AND TED SWEDENBURG addressed this blurring of boundaries between the research field and the home site in an essay on time dimensions and cultural boundaries. Their discussion, which appraises the current power of anthropology to shift between time and culture realms, summarizes and promotes discussion about the studied "other(s)" out there and the I/us writing about them at home.

Lavie and Swedenburg endeavor to turn anthropological research itself into a field—a realm between these worlds and within them. They assert that traditional anthropology, which actively created the other, partly to enhance the figure of the (white, European) writer, can now switch roles. Potentially it can become a twilight zone between and within the boundaries of time and culture, and fashion itself as a "blooming site of criticism and resistance." This possibility depends upon doing "homework" instead of "fieldwork," in a move that weaves field and home into a single fabric, no longer allowing a distinction between here and there, but rather contributing to undermining the home disrupting its tranquility. Thus the focal point is the home, the cultural realm within which the researcher lives and works. Her work must be done at home, but it is not work at home, but rather work about home.

From its inception, Israeli anthropology has tended to perform most of its research at home rather than in remote societies. Mass immigration to Israel and the institutionalization of its absorption provided culture researchers with an extensive field of research at home. Researchers were mostly Ashkenazi in origin, and they studied Oriental Jews. Their work contained criticism of the absorbing establishment and its handling of the various ethnic groups, but they simultaneously re-labeled the different social groups, reaffirming their "otherness."[1]

This new homework, as Lavie and Swedenburg present it, is aimed at the home's centers of power (even if it is performed at its margins), to what they dub "the citadel": the academy, courts, museums, business world, industry, politics, and so on. Such work undermines the foundations of the home. It damages its uniform color, destroys its confidence, and presents it as a non-melting pot of invented identities. The role of anthropology is to expose the processes by which these identities are created and "map new geographies and histories of identity."[2]

This chapter endeavors to describe and analyze the fieldwork at the Bar-Ilan Midrasha as homework; as a research-oriented move taken within the researcher's national Israeli-Jewish home, as a work of writing and deciphering aimed at the heart of this home.

The first part of the chapter—"Home Map"—focuses mainly on observation. It contains ethnographic sections attesting to the place of both subjects and researcher. It is an opportunity to discuss the positionality of the participants, to reveal attitudes from which the material sustaining the research was produced, and to start recognizing the boundaries of the home.

The second part—"Peace at Home"—is dedicated to the writing process; that is, to the production of anthropological knowledge. It depicts a kind of game of tag, in which the writer wishes to draw farther away from home in order to write about it, while at the same time home pursues her, lying in wait for her insights. The attempt to understand the rules of the game by writing about the Midrasha is also an attempt to learn about the nature of the national home.

The chapter ends with an analysis of Prime Minister Yitzhak Rabin's assassination, which happened while I was writing the first draft of the book. The fact that the murder was committed by a student of the Men's Kolel (the Midrasha's twin institute) and the Faculty of Law at Bar-Ilan University brings the discussion about the "home" to its peak.

HOME MAP

THE PATH TO THE MIDRASHA IS CLEAR—
THE RESEARCHER'S PLACE

Hannahle drove her green Alfa Romeo with a light hand. She was leaning slightly forward, as if she wanted to know what was going on right under the car's nose. From my position in the back seat I saw her in a whole new light. As a driver I tend to look at people over my right shoulder, or gaze at my kids in the back seat through the rear view mirror. Now, with my leg in a cast, the back seat of my chaperone's car had become a new site for me. The Bar-Ilan University security guard gave us a hard time. He went over and over the list of temporary entry permits without finding ours. Behind us, drivers with permanent permits honked their horns in irritation; this helped the guard find the permit for the green Alfa, and we glided past the checkpoint and right into the campus. The first left turn brought us to the parking area in front of the Midrasha. The parking spaces were all taken by now, a shady spot was out of the question, and the two parking spaces reserved for the disabled were occupied. Hannahle parked on the sidewalk. I handed her the improvised sign I had made, announcing my temporary handicap, and, my mobility gradually improving, I pulled myself out of the car supported by my crutches. (The outfits I adopted for my visits to the Midrasha were incredibly well-suited for a woman with a leg in a cast. Fortunately, maxi skirts were back in fashion that year.)

The path leading from the parking lot to the Midrasha's door ascends like a ramp. On either side there is a low stone wall, usually populated by students who have come out for a bite to eat, to talk, to knit in the wintry sun, to wait for someone, or to hide in the crowd. Now it took longer than the usual two minutes to negotiate this exposed path. In any case I always had the feeling they were looking at me. Someone older, dressed in clothes which seem okay but aren't really. The women sitting on the fence and standing on the lawn in small groups, methodically turning their heads toward the path, do not remember me from high school, the *ulpana*, the youth movement, or National Service. We never hitchhiked together to settlements in the West Bank, nor have we ever met at weddings or in demonstrations; I am neither a sister, nor a sister-in-law, nor a mother of anyone they know. My visibility on this short gangway was even more dramatic this time due to the crutches and the accompaniment of pretty Hannahle, who, beyond her wish to help me and her interest in the lessons, was also glad for the opportunity to show off her impressive collection of hats.

The way into the Midrasha was clear, the glass door, as usual, open, and at the end of the route I dropped into one of the single chairs scattered around the sides of the class, lifting my cast onto another chair with a sigh.

Having spent more than a semester studying with these students, I located a few familiar faces inside the classroom, this time welcoming me with a smile.

"Well, when will they take off your cast?"

"Lucky for you it is not really hot yet. I remember I had an arm cast once during the summer. It was a nightmare."

Sitting on the chair next to me was Miri. She had recently gotten married and now wore a kerchief. The lock of hair on her forehead was somewhat moist. Unlike most of the others, who meticulously matched their head covering to their outfits, Miri seemingly grabbed the first kerchief that came to hand each morning. (Married students sometimes added a colorful, ornamental band, reminiscent of the Arab *akal*, lending them a Canaanite appearance; some put their hair in a knitted hairnet or adorned themselves with fashionable hats.) From the whispers we exchanged during previous lessons, I learned that Miri was pursuing an M.A. in Talmud and was older than most of the others.

She looked at me with her green eyes and said: "I don't want to poke my nose into anything, but if you need a ride home, I live in Tel Aviv, and I can take you, no problem."

"Thanks," I answered, "really, but it's okay. As you can see, my friend Hannahle accompanies me regularly. I have a feeling she'll want to keep coming with me even when I can resume driving. But since you're already being so nice to me, could I ask another favor of you?"

Miri gave a little smile, and I took advantage of this, the longest conversation we had during the six months we had been sitting side by side, to ask her: "Would you give me your phone number? I'd like to interview some girls from the class about your studies here. I'm a student, but I'm also doing research about what goes on here and. . . ."

"Yes, I know," she replied. "I figured that out from the very first lesson."

I recalled that first class session with Dr. Yael Weiss, the first of the three courses I took in the graduate program. I had walked into the big, illuminated room on the ground floor, looking for that hidden corner from which you can view the entire class while still feeling concealed. The Midrasha's new and modern furniture was made up of long connected desks with swivel chairs attached to them, arranged in two columns that left an aisle in the middle. Additional chairs, used during crowded sessions, were scattered along the walls. These were highly popular even when there were free seats; the swivel chairs had not been good choices—they cramped one's legs and restricted movement. I chose a place for myself at the back of the classroom, put my straw bag next to me, and began observing and counting: twenty-six women excluding myself, five with head coverings, hats, berets, knitted kerchiefs. No wigs.[3] There was one other woman, in addition to me, who

looked secular. Except for the two of us and an older religious woman, all
the students were in their early twenties. I began to wonder whether this was
really a graduate program. The students around me did not look like they
could have graduated from the Midrasha a few years ago and had now come
back to "recharge their batteries."

Dr. Yael Weiss entered the classroom two minutes late. A big, tall woman,
dressed in a purple skirt and a flowery shirt, her head was covered by a
purple kerchief which hung down to her forehead, hiding all her hair. Her
legs were clothed in opaque nylon stockings, and she was wearing sandals.
She put on her glasses, greeted the participants, and smiled at the girls she
already knew. When she took out the list of students, I shrank in my chair,
assuming for some reason that although I had registered and paid my fees,
my name would not be on the list. I listen to the names of the other students
attentively, trying to learn something from the list.

"Averbuch, Efrat!"

"Here."

"Isar, Shira!"

"Here."

"Oh. Hello Shira, *Mazal Tov.*" (Shira smiled shyly, lowering her head and
thanking her quietly).

"Iluz, Rachel!"

"Here."

"El-Or, Tamar!"

"Here." (I said it quietly, hoping no one would look at me. As it was, I
felt like my age and my bare head were sharply distinguishing me from the
group, despite my long skirt.)

"Oh, hello there. I just finished reading your book. I heard you lecture
about it at the Van Leer Institute this week—I thought I'd go."

That's it, I told myself, I'm doomed from the start. I felt as if all the girls
were looking at me, and I was relieved when she moved on to the next name.

"Birenberg, Naomi!"

"Here."

Miri must have kept Yael Weiss's remark in mind, but she had said nothing
about it until I made my request for an interview. Many others had perhaps
forgotten about it or had paid no attention to it to begin with. Nevertheless, my presence at the Midrasha throughout my three years of studies was
certainly characterized by the tension between anonymity and conspicuousness.

The Midrasha is an open, yet supervised, public place. Admission is based on classifications of gender, age, and religiousness. The full-time students are young, religious women who have passed the entrance interview with the Midrasha director. Occasionally, however, some older or less religious women slip in, getting on the list through the graduate program or the Bar-Ilan staff. For example, a senior citizen kibbutz member from the Jordan Valley selected the Midrasha as a place to pursue Jewish studies. The permission I was granted to conduct research in the Midrasha can be attributed to the fact that the place is part of a public university, that the religious Zionist community is neither closed nor cloistered, but mainly to the consent of the rabbi who served as the institution's director.

From that moment on, my visibility as a researcher fluctuated between conspicuousness resulting from my age, style of clothing, and communal foreignness on the one hand, and an indifference demonstrated by most of the students with regard to my presence, on the other. Participating in classes of twenty to seventy students was convenient for observation and recording purposes. With two or three exceptions, I did not participate in discussions nor ask questions; my voice was not heard, nor did I express my opinions in public. If a student or two sitting next to me greeted me with a smile, it was a pleasant surprise. It would be hard to say that I made friends there. My sense of anonymous visibility accompanied me throughout my stay, and the regular greetings on which I could count were those of the Midrasha principal, the assistant principal, and the office and library staff. A time critical for me, both personally and professionally, seems to have been registered by my subjects as a blurred sketch of someone who hung out there; some researcher who studied with them in *havruta* for a while and hardly ever opened her mouth, or somebody they would hardly remember, even if they tried.

For a small minority (forty out of 1,300), things were a little different. These women agreed to be interviewed, and they allowed me to conduct long and personal conversations with them, which are presented in part II of this book. The fact that Miri remembered the first class in which Yael Weiss singled me out indicates that there may have been others who knew more about me than I realized, but they chose not to act on this information.[4]

The Midrasha director's consent to my research forced my presence on both teachers and students. Since a large portion of the observations could be carried out without personal contact with them, it was easy for me to assume I was invisible. I sought to apply the transparency of the Midrasha doors to my body, and the fact that most students ignored my existence helped me in that. These power relations were disturbed by Dr. Weiss's remark, and they collapsed entirely in my relations with one of the teachers whose class I wished to observe. Then the doors became opaque, and the power relations in the research field started to become clear. The following incident exemplifies this change.

The Story of a Failure

Many anthropologists include a story of personal failure within the fabric of their reports, depicting incidents of being ignored by subjects, basic misconception characterizing their conduct at the site, an inability to rid themselves of presumptions that blocked their field of vision, and so on. One of the most famous failure stories is the one Clifford Geertz uses to open his well-known essay "Deep Play: Notes on the Balinese Cockfight,"[5] where he shares with his readers the harsh feelings that characterized the initial stages of his research. The Geertzes arrived in Bali in 1958, "malarial and diffident." The inhabitants of the island chose to ignore them. "As we wandered around, uncertain, wistful, eager to please, people seemed to look right through us with a gaze focused several yards behind us on some more actual stone or tree." The white anthropologist, who had invested substantial effort, connections, and money to get to where he was, discovered that the locals were not interested in having contact with him. The story reached its peak when the couple witnessed a cockfight—an entertainment forbidden by a new law. When the police arrived, the audience fled, and during the commotion a small garden gate opened and the Geertzes were taken in by a local who had fled with them and who was now offering them sanctuary. That gateway became a metaphor for acceptance, a true "entry" into the field. The failure story unfolds into its corrective: From there, the text evolves with academic ease, relying on the open gate and enjoying the sights revealed in the backyard of the native host.

Such stories, especially when opening a monograph, function as a kind of reading contract through which writers constitute their voice of authority, that of those who at first failed to understand, suffered, were humiliated and rejected, but ultimately, all's well that ends well, the ice melted and they got in. From there, from the inside, they urge the reader to believe them. Such stories present researchers as weak, foolish, ethnocentric, miserable, and otherwise unpleasant, diminishing their authority vis-à-vis their subjects and the reality they wish to explore and understand.

Researchers' recognition of their relative weakness, their confession of powerlessness, and their repentance for the sin of blindness are aimed at reducing their strength, which is gradually regained with the writing of their text. During the transition from their position as researchers to that of writers, a rereading of power relations takes place. While reading the text, readers are invited to recall the power relations that existed in the field. However, beyond the illusions of positioning and power embodied in the stories of failure and correction—and after the called-for critique has already been voiced—these stories seem to conceal an additional benefit. The following section, one link in a chain of failure/correction stories, offers a snapshot of the array of power relations in this specific field, but it also seems more generally suggestive.

Written on 8 December 1994: With a somewhat bent back, and reduced in stature, I entered the classroom. My things were lying in the back row: a straw bag that had been my companion at the Midrasha for two years now, a big notebook, two pens, and a winter coat hanging on the back of the chair. I gathered all this baggage with quiet movements, trying not to disturb the teacher, who continued the lesson as usual. I could feel the stares of the teacher and some of the students when I left without saying a word. Just before I closed the door I heard her say, "Come to see me after class." A few minutes before, when she finished taking attendance, I was still sitting there quite peacefully. Then she turned to me and asked my name. From her hesitant words I gathered she did not want me sitting in her class, and that I would have to go to Rabbi Cohen, the director, for an explanation.

In the rabbi's office the two secretaries smiled at me, and Rabbi Kraus, the assistant director, looked up from the photocopy machine and said: "She sent you out, didn't she? I tried to catch you before class to tell you about our conversation, but I couldn't find you. She is just afraid you would misuse what she has to say. If you're here to learn, she has no intention of preventing you, but she is afraid of research. Once she talked on the radio; they twisted her words, and she was offended. She takes her work very seriously. You should talk to Rabbi Cohen."

Taking a step out of my body, I could see the banality inherent in the rejection of the anthropologist: the refusal, the absolute recognition of foreignness. I could also see all the theories about "strong subjects" taking on flesh and blood before me. Here was a woman who was not committed to my motives, to the academy, to science, but rather, as she said, to Torah. From the distance of that perspective I could also laugh at the entire chain of events. I had not even wanted to sit in on her lesson, but my cousin had urged me to, claiming that "you cannot complete research on the Midrasha without going to Rivka Sternberg's lectures." Now, in light of her refusal, and after one quite boring lesson, I found myself anxious to carry on.

I looked at Rabbi Kraus with a smile and said: "I have no doubt I made every possible mistake, exactly what I teach my students to avoid. I didn't talk to her before class, I didn't talk to the rabbi. I was not sure if I was interested in this class. I just went in for a trial lesson, thinking I'd talk to her later. I totally understand her. She is right. You and I would have done the same thing."

Rochi, who sat by the computer, turned her chair. Her blue beret went well with the eyes that were now gazing at me: "I think you should make an effort to explain things to her. It would be worthwhile for you to attend her lessons. She is really something. The rabbi will talk to her. Perhaps she should read your book too, and see how you write and how the things people tell you come out. Anyway, I'll let him know you're here."

"Actually, she did ask to read it," Rabbi Kraus added, still amused. Since I said I could not wait around until her class was over, he recommended I write her a short letter.

Meanwhile, Rabbi Cohen's door opened and he invited me in. Facing him sat a young woman, who remained seated there throughout our conversation. As usual, Rabbi Cohen was sitting on a swivel-tilt office chair behind a large desk. The wall behind him was filled with pictures. I remained standing, since I wanted to give him a short report, sensing I was disturbing his meeting.

"You messed things up for me, eh?" he queried, turning to me with a smile. "I didn't even know you were continuing your studies this year, and that you intended to attend her class. I was really surprised."

"Surprise," I told him, "is the name of the game today. Each of us had his own surprise."

We kept talking, and I iterated my promise to send him the full written text of my study when it was finished, as well as of any article I might publish. The first article I wrote was about his lesson.

"It's in English, and it's long," I warned him.

"I'll manage," he replied.

I turned back, leaving my letter to Mrs. Rivka Sternberg with Rochi, and drove home in the pouring rain.

Written two weeks later: I missed her first three lessons. I sat through an entire one and was kicked out of another. Then there was the Hanukkah vacation, and today the rabbi will let me know what he and Rivka Sternberg agreed on. Ten minutes before class I met her in his room, a short lady, around sixty, dressed in a black skirt and a soft-colored sweater. Her head was covered with a light pink kerchief, revealing a bit of white hair at the front. Its long fringes flowed down her back. Her eyes seemed unclear behind the glasses, but her general gaze was soft.

"Okay," said the rabbi. "I spoke with Rivka, and she understands your intentions. I don't think you need me anymore; you can settle things between you."

We left the rabbi's office, and Rivka led me to her office on the first floor. It was an impersonal room shared by several lecturers. She opened her cupboard and placed some things inside, taking out a booklet of sources she had prepared for the lesson, and which had already been handed out to the rest of the students.

"You have to understand, this is a complex matter. I am now revising a book that has already been published in a third edition after the first two ran out. I won't have time to do what I would like to do, because there is a pressing demand. I build up my lessons methodically. In the introductory course I lay the foundations; we define concepts which later become our work tools. This division of introductory and advanced courses is not arbitrary, although completing the introductory course is not a prerequisite for participating in the advanced course [I had showed up for the latter]. There is deliberate and meticulous work here, and these are no simple matters."

WAIT FOR ME AFTER CLASS BY
THE PRINCIPAL'S OFFICE — THE LESSON

"I dreamed I was back in high school and hadn't done my homework," sings the popular Israeli soul-rock singer, Ehud Banai,[6] about the free adult's nightmare. In the above story, in broad daylight and fully awake, the teacher had thrown me out of class and sent me to the principal's office, asking me to wait for her there.

I had trampled over power arrays, social boundaries, and the academic literacy hierarchy out of a feeling that in any event no one noticed me and that I was an invisible researcher who saw without being seen. I had used the principal's general consent for my presence in a sweeping manner, causing the gates whose existence I did not recognize to slam shut in my face. The uneasiness, anxiety, and discomfort accompanying the teacher's act clashed with the laughter and amusement at the administrative office, while I, to my embarrassment, oscillated between them.

The story speaks for itself. My attendance in the course "Jewish Law and Morality" had not been coordinated with the teacher (a fact which was no less true of all the other courses I took). Yet Rivka Sternberg had already heard about the researcher hanging around the Midrasha and had no intention of accepting my presence just because the director had given his permission. Her past experience, her relatively advanced age, the sensitive matters discussed in her lessons (the status of women in Judaism), and her own status within her community all produced disquiet, alarm, and refusal.

Such a case makes you wonder about all the others who did agree, or did not publicly disagree; conducting research in class is not a trivial matter. The Israeli Ministry of Education, for instance, justifiably sets up many obstacles to such research. The Midrasha director often told me he had nothing to hide, he did not want his name withheld, nor was he afraid of what I might write, thus displaying ample self-confidence that surprised me each time anew. Nonetheless, as noted, I promised to send him the full text for review before it was printed. Rivka Sternberg did not possess that confidence, and she sent me back to him. Yet even she, as part of a strong/weak community, had difficulties excluding me. My exclusion would have implied the elimination of any possibility for dialogue with the academy, with the secular population, and with a Jewish woman. Waiving such dialogue is no simple matter for a religious Zionist woman, all the more so for a woman like Rivka Sternberg, who holds Zionism and Israeli society especially dear.

Beyond the power relations, then, one can discern the important elements that structure these relations, the foundation stones of the community under study: (a) desire for dialogue with the secular population, particularly if they come to study Torah, but mixed with a fear that things will be taken out of context, treated disrespectfully, taking advantage of those who seek dialogue, who regard themselves as innocent and good-hearted;[7] (b) attribution of significance to academic discourse and to modernism— research, openness, accepting criticism on the one hand, and demanding respect for its curricular priorities and scholastic-research enterprise on the other; (c) participation in the public field (an institution that belongs to the university) limits detachment, exclusion, and sectarian seclusion. All these had left Rivka Sternberg's relationship with me hanging in mid-air.

I knew there were things she said in class for my ears only. From time to time she would call me over for a conversation after class to explain some of the issues raised in the lesson in a better or different way. At the end of the year she gave me her book and I gave her mine, and for a split second we faced each other as equals. Two mature women in an ocean of students; two teachers, both researchers preoccupied with issues of Judaism and gender. But in fact, she knew I might take her words in undesirable directions and represent her against her will before a secular audience—an audience unfamiliar with her, but one whose significance she recognized. I knew she was right.

This failure story thus has no corrective story to follow it. Perhaps it is a metaphor for the state of anthropological fieldwork, and more so, for relations between religious and secular Zionists in Israel.

RENOVATION INSTEAD OF REPAIR—THE SUBJECTS' PLACE

In the mid-1980s, power relations between researchers and subjects in anthropological fieldwork were marked as the key problem of the discipline. This set of relations was titled "the representational crisis"—an acknowledgment of the political and moral difficulty inherent in depicting the lives of others and representing them for the writer's community. To remain in this state of crisis was to refrain from anthropological work and to avoid, across the board, any depiction, analysis, and evaluation of other peoples' lives.

Yet anthropology as a discipline was too big and too institutionalized back then to fade away, and the crisis was hardly unique to this single discipline. As with the rest of the sciences and arts that had undergone the postmodern crisis, a new chapter opened in the history of anthropology, one characterized by three principal directions: (a) research and discussion regarding the crisis itself—a kind of disciplinary "self-scrutiny" and reflection; (b) critical reading of existing anthropological production in light of the conclusions of this self-scrutiny; and (c) a hunt for new and creative ways to produce ethnography capable of bypassing or moderating the problems of representation: production of polyphonic research echoing the voices of different speakers and not only that of the writer, and seeking new genres of writing that would allow for layers of meaning absent in traditional scientific writing—for example, emotions, anxieties, moral and political discussion, and ambiguity.[8] Most empirical studies since the mid-eighties have, to varying degrees, incorporated all these directions simultaneously.

In this work, discussion of the crisis itself does not carry substantial weight, for it seems that this direction has already been exhausted. Most efforts were guided in the third direction. Some of these efforts were deliberate, such as restating the researcher's position described in an earlier section, or reporting how the theoretical text to be presented in the second part of the chapter was produced. Other parts were less controlled, and they stemmed from the unique situation of conducting research "at home"—a condition where the researcher and her subjects move in different yet overlapping and tangent circles and are exposed to one another. Subjects conduct a continual dialogue with their representation by the researcher throughout all stages of work. Their place within the research field is not derived solely from the researcher's actions. The following anecdote may illustrate this exchange.

The departmental seminar I gave at Bar-Ilan University near the end of December 1996 was, for me, the first official launching of the research material back to the subjects. The main audience was naturally comprised of my colleagues in the Department of Sociology and Anthropology and advanced students, but the very location, and the fact that the audience was not unfamiliar with the social reality I was about to discuss—as well as the fact that the director and assistant director of the Midrasha were present in the lecture hall—rendered this encounter a unique dialogue.

During the time that has passed since the completion of my field work, I have presented certain portions of the material, usually to secular academic audiences. The heartening fact that our daily and academic lives are not sterile gave me a brief opportunity to examine the subjects' reactions prior to the Bar-Ilan discussion. During a lecture given in Philadelphia (in English) to an audience comprised mainly of American Jews, my gaze was fixed on a colleague from Bar-Ilan and his wife who were sitting in the lecture hall. The opening lines of my lecture read: "Bar-Ilan University could have been just another of Israel's six universities (and the only religious one), if it were not for the fact that in November 1995 it became the institution attended by Yigal Amir, the assassin of Prime Minister Yitzhak Rabin." Later on, in an aside that was not included in my written text, I ironically added a sentence which implied that the general responsibility for the murder lay with the religious Zionist public and hinted at the role of Bar-Ilan University in educating an undemocratic and radical generation. At the conclusion of the lecture I was approached by my Bar-Ilan colleague. Before he had a chance to open his mouth I said: "I know my remark wasn't quite necessary. I apologize." My position as a representative of an event which I observed as a secular researcher gave me the power to say things about him and his wife ex cathedra. Professionally, I believed in what I had said, but on a personal level, I found it difficult to face him as someone who worked down the hall from me at the research institute, knowing his moderate political views.

Two teachers from the Midrasha whose courses I took, and whom I mention in this book, participated in two other meetings in Jerusalem, where I appeared. I felt they had come there to follow up on me and to see what I had to say about them, but I respected them for doing what they had to do. These encounters had a totally different feel and atmosphere than others from which these figures were absent. The current sociopolitical situation of anthropological research "at home" creates new situations never confronted in real time by classic anthropology.

The ever-present possibility that there would be religious people in my audience of listeners, readers or students guaranteed repeated instances of criticism (either direct or indirect) by the subjects of my work. The fact that I knew that the things I said reverberated within the community I studied, and that the community was to a certain extent aware of my research and its implications, became part of the work itself. This was the case when the director of the Midrasha cynically noted that he hoped he would not come out like "that *Rebbetzen*" in my previous study.[9] The fact of being under scrutiny and subject to representation bothered him to some extent, and he reminded me and himself that there are many ways to represent him textually—some desirable, others less so.

The moment Dr. Yael Weiss exposed my identity to the student body was also an act of marking and positioning. My status was defined as that of a researcher external to the community yet subject to its critique. Dr. Weiss may read my book, listen to me talk about her community in an open lecture, and choose whether and how to respond. Such cases are evidence of the subjects' awareness of their position and of their attempt to intervene in their representation. These ongoing interventions place the research within a critical framework constructed by its subjects.

The department seminar at Bar-Ilan was the high point of the dialogue. Before the lecture I spoke with the rabbi-director, confessing my apprehension. He was surprised and offered to absent himself: "If it is hard for you, or inappropriate, I can leave." "No, no," I replied. "There's no escaping this. If I can't say these things in your presence, it means I have no right to say them at all."

During the discussion that ensued at the end of the lecture, the rabbi and his assistant asked no questions, nor did they try to correct, undermine, criticize, or offer any alternative interpretation. From my place on the podium I respected their decision to remain silent. Any statement they would have made in this arena, which is to a certain extent theirs but to a greater extent my academic home, would have given their words a ring of self-justification. Instead, we agreed that we would meet shortly thereafter to discuss my findings at length. Thus, two weeks later, in the afternoon, I returned to the rabbi's pleasant office at the Midrasha.

Research at Day's End

14 January 1997: A short while before the designated time I peeked into his office. The rabbi was eating, and I did not want to disturb him. "Should I come back in a few minutes?" I suggested. "No, no," he said. "I'm finished. Come in."

This time, I said to myself, you have got to remember the pictures in his room. You always forget to take note of them. Ethnic Jewish posters, some of them from exhibitions at the Diaspora Museum, proverbs done in embroidery (the work of students?), and a few photographs—the Makhpelah Cave and the Temple Mount were somewhat smaller than the rest, leaning on a shelf on the wall behind him. "Are we friends?" he took me by surprise.

"Friends?" I was startled. "Um, I don't know. What do you mean? I don't think we're friends. I mean, I don't tell my kids we're friends either, but what do you mean by friends?" "I mean, can I tell you what I think without offending you? Can I tell you what I really think?" "Oh," I was relieved. "We're friends that way. I came here to listen."

So he spoke. First he expressed his disappointment with, not to say contempt for, the social sciences. "What can I tell you? Is this the way to conduct a research project? You attend a few classes and come out with conclusions. It's like the journalistic reportage that everyone falls for, except for those who know what it's all about. A man sits in a tent in Africa and then tells the world all kinds of things about the tribe that lives there, and he hasn't got a clue what the people really think and feel. You know, a week after your lecture there was another lecture by someone who talked about female rabbinical pleaders. A person who says '*Ha-Kabah*' [the abbreviation for The Holy One Blessed Be He], I mean that is how he says it, not '*Ha-Kadosh Baruch Hu*' [the full expression] is a person who has never heard religious people talk. Now, can I believe in his conclusions? That's one thing. Then, you are a radical feminist, and in any case you'll see what you want to see. You can't be objective. In your eyes we are on the verge of a feminist revolution within Judaism, and in your eyes our students are critical and so on and so forth. This isn't objective."

I was prepared for this kind of criticism. I was familiar with it from my previous studies: from charges that my acquaintance with 300 Gur Hassidic families did not allow me to draw conclusions about women in the *haredi* community; that a nonreligious woman would never understand a religious person; and that anthropology is the reflection of its makers. But the lesson I learned from my previous studies provided me with a reply.

"Okay. I don't want to get into a discussion about the validity of social research now, or the ability to study something which you are not. I want to ask you something else, the most important question: Do you find my description and conclusions faulty? Was I really wrong? Did I miss the point altogether?"

The rabbi leaned back in his swivel chair, smoothed his beard, and said: "As for the conclusions, I stand behind every word." But my sense of victory was not long-lived, for he then launched into a detailed discussion of the tenor and intensity of my conclusions: the unreliability of the Matchmaker, a student whose contrapuntal whispers I had overheard in one class;[10] my misapprehension of the halachic changes I predicted would result from the gender revolution; the intellectual conservatism which, in the rabbi's opinion, characterizes most of the students (and which he fights in his lessons); and a long list of additional mistakes.

"You know what," he suddenly suggested, "why don't I call a student—a rabbi's wife who is in the rabbinical pleaders program and is a very educated woman and sort of an active feminist. She conducts all kinds of women's classes. Let's hear what she thinks. I'm sure even she doesn't think that through their studies the women wish to bring about halachic changes."

While he went to get her I thought back to a similar situation I had found myself in when he had invited me to attend a lesson at the new *beit midrash*, where select women engage in Torah studies twenty hours a week. We initiated a conversation with two women studying in *havruta*. During the conversation I asked one of them whether she would like to have a woman teaching halacha. "Sure," she replied, "It would be really interesting to see how a woman teaches as opposed to a rabbi with a yeshiva background." "What's the difference?" asked the stunned rabbi. "We study a body of text, regardless of the gender of the body who teaches or learns it." During the short walk back to his office he could not stop pondering why she found this matter of a woman teacher so important, nor could he stop mulling it over in a conversation we had a week later. "It still amazes me she finds it important," he said. "It still amazes me that you don't see why she finds it important," I replied. The let's-get-the-girl-and-ask-her-opinion trick had been successful once, I thought, let's see what happens this time.

When Sara entered the room she looked somewhat frightened. She thought she had been called in because of some other matter that had stirred up her class. "No, no," said the rabbi, "it has nothing to do with that. I called you in to hear your opinion about something." After presenting her with the issue, and before she had a chance to reply, the assistant director entered the office and joined the conversation.

Sara was wearing a blue skirt and a light blue sweater; a small hat covered her short hair, which still showed in front. Her small and delicate face was flushed, and behind the thin wire-framed glasses her blue eyes wandered among the three of us, trying to figure out what she had gotten herself into. "If you are asking me whether our salvation will come from the female rabbinical pleaders, as that guy said in his lecture," she replied, "then unfortunately the answer is no. I see how the more we advance in our studies, the more the women identify with the male position, as if they have discovered that they can understand the material and find their way about it, so now they want to be like men. But if you're asking me whether through women's study of Torah I would like to see a halachic change, or whether I think it will indeed occur, then the answer is yes. Certainly. It's a matter of time. You have to be very very feministically educated and oriented for this to happen, and in the States it is already happening. There are women who follow the halacha to the letter, and through the halacha and their studies seek new ways."

"I am asking," said the assistant director, "whether through your acquaintance with the *Shulchan Aruch* you intend to find an opening that has been disregarded by the men, or whether you also wish to change the *Shulchan Aruch* itself. That's what I'd like to know."

The question of boundaries and objectives became pressing at this moment. Sara listened as if this were not the first time she found herself involved in such a conversation: "Both. I mean, both find whatever is possible in the existing material and change it. I hope to have enough power; I'm not sure how and when. You mustn't mark your targets. From my experience it doesn't work. It scares everyone, and it is dangerous. You have to advance according to your ability."

The rabbi and his assistant were clearly dumbfounded. "How far can it go?" they asked. "You see," she turned to me, "they are scared, they are simply scared." "Furthermore," the rabbi added, "I'd like to know where the sore spots are, where does it hurt?"

I found myself explaining to him where it hurts—a ridiculous situation where the controversial issue does not concern me directly, but I spoke nevertheless. In Sara's name? In the name of the women I studied? In the name of Jewish women? In the name of women in general? "It hurts when you cannot participate in something which is in your heart and soul; when you are being excluded from religious practice, from public prayer, from being called up to read from the Torah, from study, from halachic discussion, and from determining the rules for religious life. It hurts because you don't want special treatment, you just want to have more responsibility for your life, more involvement and participation. That's what hurts, when your body, your ostensible sexuality, is an obstacle."

Sara looked at me, perhaps surprised by this outburst of emotion from a nonreligious woman. For a moment she and I united on our gender axis against the two of them.

"Besides," I added, "you are asking men's questions: 'How far? Where will it lead?' All these questions are not relevant to these women. At the moment, all they want is to open a wider door for themselves, and you should know it is a lost cause, for they've already won, big." "Who won?" the assistant director who was sitting on the sofa at the side of the room inquired. "We did," replied Sara, "We women. It's only a matter of time."

During the next few minutes, until the end of this meeting—when the rabbi went to teach and Sara went to her class— the atmosphere became less tense. I felt as though we were all thinking quietly, uttering insignificant words to continue an already-concluded conversation. Outside the Midrasha, while I waited with the assistant director for his wife to pick him up, the tension evaporated. I looked at his wife driving toward us; I knew she was a professional with a prestigious occupation, and I was somewhat embarrassed at making her part of a conversation she had not participated in, part of a social transformation her opinion of which I did not know.

Returning research material to subjects is one of the most salient features of contemporary anthropology. Subjects can listen, read, and respond to what is said about them. It is no longer a study written in Western languages about a Third World society that has no access to its academic representations. Power relations are far from being resolved, but at least there are negotiations as to their intensity.

The rabbi began his response to my research material by demeaning my profession, by undermining the research abilities of the anthropological discipline and stressing its incapacity to "understand." He compared my ethnography to a "journalistic report," the kind that is dismissed by anyone who is familiar with the subject being reported. He negated the possibility that a person could understand people who belong to another group. In referring to a white man who goes to an African tribe, he used the classical anthropological stereotype, placing me as the total "stranger" and himself as part of a remote and exotic society. He did not hesitate to designate himself a tribesman, nor did he demand for himself any other place within our common home. In his own home, on the other hand, he felt self-assured, intimately familiar with and abreast of what is transpiring there. Yet the rabbi did not apply to himself the restriction he imposed on me ("a person cannot understand people who are different from himself") when interpreting the state of women. According to him, as a nonreligious woman I cannot understand religious people, while he as a man can understand women. The gender division that placed Sara and me on the same side of the fence, and him and his assistant on the other side, attests to how complex the situation is. No doubt my understanding of religious people is limited, but this limitation, it appears, also applies to his ability to understand women, even if they are religious.

IT HURTS BUT NOT AS MUCH — ADDITIONAL WAYS TO PRODUCE ETHNOGRAPHY

In my mind's eye I saw the book about the Midrasha written from two different perspectives. I wanted to add a parallel point of view of a Midrasha student to the external point of view of the researcher. Polyphonic writing has become one of the recommended cures for the paralysis caused by the representational crisis. It produces texts that embed diverse voices, a dialogue that breaks the monolithic voice of the writer,[11] or a conjunction of the researcher and one or more of the subjects.

During the interviewing phase I decided to take on a Midrasha student in the hope that our collaboration would render more than just assistance in gathering material. I picked out Ora almost immediately. We had studied together in the aggadah class, and Ora's way of thinking and her questions had caught my attention. At the end of the school year I approached her with the offer to work with me and conduct some of the interviews. Ora wanted to hear more, and we set up a meeting away from the field of research, in my office at the Hebrew University in Jerusalem, Ora's place of residence. I described to her my work up to that point, offering her a range of possibilities for collaboration, ranging from a restricted, defined task to coauthorship. Ora looked at me with big brown eyes and—blushed. Again, I thought to myself, what a coincidence. Hannah, the woman who had facilitated my earlier study in a Hassidic neighborhood, also used to blush.

"We'll see," she said. "I have to see if I'm at all capable of doing that; if I understand at all what you are expecting of me, if I can write."

At her request, at our next meeting I interviewed Ora just as I had interviewed other students, so she could experience it first-hand. Ora took
home the tape recording of the interview and called me a week later and
said: "It's ok, I can start with the interviews, but these notes you want, with
my feelings and thoughts during and after the interview, I'm not totally clear
on that yet."

In the end, Ora conducted half of the interviews for this study. For each
one, she also provided a small note in her own handwriting, in which she
laconically described her thoughts. My nonexistent experience in fieldwork
collaboration (which is very different than coauthorship with colleagues)
and Ora's refusal to commit herself to reflexive, critical writing about the
interviews made it difficult to execute a joint project. The dream of recip-
rocal work collapsed, leaving only the good interviews she provided and
an important friend in the field who was also a critical reader of the final
research product.

There is no doubt that Ora's interviews were totally different from mine.
While I tended to locate the "exceptional" students, those who asked questions, challenged teachers, dressed in a striking way, and sought an attentive
listener, Ora approached the calmer and more stable group. She tended to
select interviewees from her own circle of friends with whom she shared a
similar biography of literacy (educational institutions, social frameworks,
and so on).[12] The notes she attached to the interviews, describing her feelings, indicated that she heard her interviewees as variations on her own
voice. Often, she noted, they continued to talk beyond what was required.
During these times they would switch roles, and Ora would describe to the
interviewee her literacy history and study preferences. Their common private and communal lives gave these conversations the mutuality that was
lacking in the interviews I conducted.

In the course of the study it became clear that the essential difference
between Ora's middle-of-the-road interviewees and those at the margins is
not large, and the fact that each of us preferred to talk with a different type
of student, from a different position, enriched and reinforced the findings.
Moreover, during our meetings throughout the year in which the interviews
were conducted, I learned many things from her. I listened to the questions
she asked, noted the points she lingered over, and took advantage of her
knowledge to enhance my own. Ora, the daughter of a teacher and a rabbi
involved in girls' and women's education, was to a large extent another
informant, instead of becoming another researcher. Her collaboration with
me reinforced the legitimization of the research in the eyes of its subjects,
perhaps even shifting the power relations in my favor. However, her ability

to intervene in the research while it was being conducted, to point out hidden directions and serve as another voice, enlightened and clarified for me boundaries I could not cross and insights I could never reach.

This reading of the home map marks the different positions of the researcher and her subjects, and the power relations between them. It shows that at times the fields in which subjects and researcher move overlap; they are open, to a certain extent, allowing her to enter their domain and them to enter hers.

The fundamental components of the researched home were gender and profession. I was a woman researcher studying women, part of an academic world to which they also belonged. But at this stage I would like to argue that the structure of this research home, the possibility of moving within it, and the fact that it did not collapse despite the blows it suffered, were largely attributable to the fact that all those who went through it were Israeli Jews. Undoubtedly, being a woman facilitated my mobility within the Midrasha, just as my status as an academic researcher made the women there treat me seriously. Yet my national affiliation veiled both my gender and my profession. The motivating force behind the need to conduct a dialogue stemmed from the feeling that this was a dialogue within the home, between members of the same family, about vital issues. Although I came to the Midrasha in order to become acquainted with this junction where knowledge, religion, and women intersect, and while I spent my time at this crossroads, it was my national identity that impelled the rabbi to consent to my presence, and which motivated me to listen to voices that went beyond issues of literacy and feminism. A subtext of my research is thus a discussion of the nature of the Jewish national home, in which both they and I live and function. Since the book as a whole is devoted to feminist and literacy-oriented issues, I wish to use the last part of this chapter to clarify the national home question. I will explore this issue indirectly, while shifting from observation to writing; my observation at home and my attempts to write about those observations away from home provide a unique perspective.

Peace at Home—Writing at a Distance, Close in Time

> To theorize, one leaves home.
> (Clifford, 1989, p. 89)

I began writing this book at the Center for Judaic Studies of the University of Pennsylvania, in Philadelphia. It was the first time in my professional life that I had taken a sabbatical, and some of my expectations for this leave certainly touched upon the issue of being away from home. In the summer of 1995, at the end of three years of field work, I took my field notes, the transcribed interviews, and other documents I had accumulated. I arranged them neatly in the spacious room allotted to me at the research institute, turned on the Hebrew-adapted computer that had been provided for me, and waited for a miracle to happen.

On 7 September 1995, my first full working day at the research institute, I wrote on the yellow paper of my scratch book: "Today is Thursday, and I am writing the table of contents for the book. It is like a contract between me and myself, between me and what I observed and recorded—regarding the future existence of this book, which already exists in every way except the actual."

All that remained to be done was the realization: the task of shifting it to another state of aggregation, the writing. The journey, leaving home, moving to a different climate, to a different set of products on the supermarket shelves—all these were supposed, so I had been told, to facilitate writing. There are places where, according to people, "you write better," "you get a lot done." I almost went to such a place. I was supposed to spend a whole year at Yarnton Manor, Oxford. "Nothing," a colleague told me, "there's absolutely nothing there; only silence. Getting to the clamor of the main street in Oxford requires a twenty-minute drive, not to mention getting to London." I saw myself closed in there. For some reason, whenever I thought of the place I could smell horses. Alone in my room with a computer, facing a monotonously gray window. Noisy pubs with British humor were missing from this vision for some reason. My son would not like England, and I would not be able to write a word.

The transition from one place to another, detachment, replacement, *flâneurism,* and the wandering gaze—all these have become the working lexicon of contemporary social researchers. British culture researcher Janet Wolff criticizes this lexicon, though it is clear to her why these concepts have become so popular in the post-colonial world.[13] They are concepts that seek to undermine the existence of real places, that have a fixed, ordered, and understood essence of their own. Instead of this essence, only the observer, the subjects of his gaze, and the power relations between them emerge. These relations provide the world with meaning. Likewise, Wolff understands the easiness and enjoyment concealed in this lexicon of the "wandering gaze," which belongs to no-place, which is uncommitted, not subordinated in any way to a frame story. As a feminist, she challenges the assertion that all of us are nomads in this world. Many people in the world do not move around voluntarily. They look for a place to work; they escape poverty, unemployment and war; they are deported from one territory to another. The "wandering gaze," with its inherent relativity, disregards these oscillations. Injustice is constant rather than relative, argues Wolff, and James Clifford's theories about mobility/travel do not deal with the conditions of injustice.

Travel remains part of the constitution of strong masculinity. Women are still perceived as the stable point—as those who sit at home and wait while men wander, *flâneur*. *Flâneur* for the sake of *flâneur*, wandering for the sake of thinking, writing, and understanding—this is an act of the powerful. Women, for the most part, still lack the power to pursue such *flâneurism*.

Wolff learns of the limits of the female body's *flâneur* from the story of the Welsh painter, Gwen John, who went to Paris to work with Rodin. Wolff endeavors to trace the confines of her wanderings in Paris and find out whether this big, anonymous metropolis was truly an open place for women at the beginning of the twentieth-century, and whether it was possible for a woman to roam the streets aimlessly: not to shop, not because her little children wished to play in the park, but rather *flâneur* for the sake of *flâneur*. The bottom line is that Gwen John sat in her atelier, dreaming of the streets of Paris. Wolff does not reject the claim that women can only gain by moving around, from one framework to another. She takes *flâneurism* or travel as an option, but only one specific option.

I recall the first pages of Wolff's book. I read them in the little garden next to the research center. On days when it was possible to go outside for a lunch break, I would take something to read, get a Philly cheese steak sandwich from the food cart, sit on a bench, eat, read, and finish off by smoking a pipe. The garden is named after the Daughters of the American Revolution, those white-skinned, blue-blooded women who wandered about these very streets on the eve of the American Revolution, helping to drive out the British. They planted the rose bed at the center of the garden, fulfilling Jefferson's dream of American cities with extensive parks for the enjoyment of the common man. At times I would laugh at myself for bringing the Midrasha girls with me from such a distance here into the D. A .R. park. Racheli, Efrat, Tali, Nava, and Ayelet spoke to me in the shade of the squirrel-populated chestnut and maple trees. For children in squirrel-less Israel, squirrels signify foreign climes, the cold, northern countries where nuts grow on trees, countries that have Christmas. I was so excited when I first saw a squirrel, years ago, even though I was disappointed to see they were much smaller than I had imagined. In childhood postcards I remembered them occupying the entire page, only pretending to be vegetarians. At the D. A. R. park I saw them eating a dead bird and pestering the visitors. Mice with fluffy tails.

The fact that I detached myself from my place and traveled far away, that I took my son with me, and in my suitcase I carried my material from the Midrasha research field related in my mind to Janet Wolff's arguments. Leaving one context and entering another, displacement and replacement, matched her quote from Clifford's book—namely, that in order to theorize one has to leave home. Obviously, the voices of the young women from Bar-Ilan sounded different from a distance. During the first months everything seemed possible: going away, packing a deconstructed reality into bags, and putting it back on paper in a more organized, decoded, controlled way.

In Philadelphia things looked different. The city spaces were open for me to wander in. It was no problem for me to go out to the street and get caught up in the holiday spirit, and to admire the gentile pageant that overwhelmed the city's aesthetics. It was so easy to go see Santa Claus make an appearance in a department store in an old fire engine, where he made his traditional ascent to the fourth floor where "Mrs. Claus," who had already begun her Christmas shopping, was standing. I went there alone; my son Shaul did not want to join me. I stood next to mothers and strollers and enjoyed myself. I could go down to the gym, almost every day, run on the treadmill, lift weights. I could watch the morning news, flipping through the world's misfortunes in seconds while lingering on the weather, on how to choose a Christmas tree, or on the process of baking a zucchini casserole. You can enjoy this displacement and replacement, refrain from remembering, open up to a liberating otherness.

But just when I thought I had accomplished it, the news came from home. It was cruel and made me realize at once that you cannot leave home, certainly not when you are writing about it. The oppressive link to home did not stem in this case from the fact that I am a woman, but rather from the fact that I am an Israeli Jew.

"I have very bad news," Shaul, my son, told us when he opened the door as far as the door chain permitted (in America you don't open the door to anyone). "Very very bad news. Rabin was shot. He is in the hospital in serious condition. Someone shot him at a rally. It was a Jew. They caught him."

My mother, Yona, who was in the city for a visit, breathed a sigh of relief. "Lucky it was a Jew, and besides they will save him. They'll save him for sure." "But they said he was in critical condition," insisted Shaul. "They'll save him, I'm telling you," Yona said, taking off her coat and sweater, rubbing her hands together to bring back the warmth that had been drained in the bitter cold outside.

Our small TV stood on a plastic stool we got at Woolworth's during our first few days in Philadelphia. We had gone on a spree of bargain-hunting then, searching for products doomed to be discarded at the end of our five-month stay. There was something delightful about going into the tacky 99¢ stores that our area was full of. We would pile a limited number of necessary items in the shopping cart, taking pleasure in buying them ugly, trashy, but practical. Later on, necessity became habit, and Shaul and I became regular customers in these stores, two whites in a black crowd.

When we first arrived, Yael and Bob gave us a TV, the one that brought us the live broadcasts from Israel. They brought it down from the attic, insisting that no one ever watched it. Amid the spokesmen, the reporters, the politicians, and the commentators, we could see mainly young people, crying, lighting candles, shocked. Kids for whom the sight of burning buses and a peace rally all blended together into a single image of loss; into an ocean of burning candles, faces buried in friends' shoulders, tears shed on camera; in Lebanon, in Jerusalem, and in the square. They were singing "*Uf Gozal*" (Fly, Fledgling), as they do at the end of junior high and high school; they sang it because it was the saddest song they knew, and it made them cry. They sang "*Shir LaShalom*" (Song for Peace), because that was the song Rabin had sung just before he was shot. I watched them from a distance, from across the ocean. I heard them mediated by CNN broadcasters. The next day I heard, for the first time, the *kaddish* prayer simultaneously translated into English. I just hoped that Rabin's son, Yuval, who had been in my high school class, would not mispronounce the Aramaic.

Where were you the day Rabin was assassinated? In the wrong place. The phone calls flew around the Philly Israeli community, each one adding a new scrap of information received from Israel. "My brother was at the rally." "My sister-in-law says. . . ." "My son couldn't stop crying over the phone." Zohar called me from Malibu, California. His Hebrew was so strange by now, after so many years out of Israel, living in California with Danna, a Swedish Texan, raising their kids. Zohar called to talk about it.

"We always thought it couldn't happen to us. Apparently we're becoming more and more normal."

Who is he talking about, I think to myself, who are his "us"? Do you ever get rid of it? I let him speak to my mother—Yona or, as he used to call her when he was a kid, "Aunt Yona," though we were not related. Neighbors, two families living across the street from each other. In many ways you could say we grew up together, ate from the same plates, often slept on the same wide beds when our parents went to the movies. He and his two younger brothers, my big brother and I. We called his parents Aunt Zvia and Uncle Yefet, because when we were young you didn't call adults by their first names.

Yona and Zvia were counterparts. They came to Israel as kids in 1933, one from Poland, the other from Yemen, and life turned them into sisters. They fought blackening floor tiles, stains on the white laundry, and the prices at the grocery store. Together they went to the Carmel market every Wednesday, and, just before embarking on the journey home, they would place their shopping bags in the corner of a restaurant in the Yemenite Quarter and eat fava beans. At times they would visit Zvia's family in one of the small back streets, at other times they would rush to the bus so they could get back home before the kids returned from school.

Yona hung up the phone after speaking with Zohar in Malibu and sighed. "That's the way it is," she said. "The world sucks, if you'll excuse my language. He is in Malibu, your brother is in Miami, you and your kid are here, and the rest of the world is in Jerusalem."

Written on 11 December 1995: "Now I don't know what to write," I told Shaul on our way to the WaWa—the grocery store—on Walnut Street. "Everything I wanted to say, every single thing has changed. Nothing will ever be the same, you see. For ten days I have been pacing around the computer, reading a lot, writing a diary, but I cannot go back to the Midrasha material. The papers burn in my hands. In a few days it is my turn to give my talk about it at the institute, and I have no idea where I am."

Shaul, who involuntarily became my partner, looked at me. I think he would have preferred that I not have any problems; it's better to have a problem-free mom. "I think," he said, "you should write what you meant to write in the first place. Rather than change it, you should write what you meant to write."

Before we opened the large glass door to get into the small twenty-four-hour supermarket, Shaul looked at the homeless man at his usual post at the exit, hoping for coins from departing customers. He turned back toward me and said, "What did you mean to write, anyway?"

I didn't tell him that I had wanted to write about what I had seen at the Midrasha at Bar-Ilan University, to give voice to voices not heard in my society, that of the secular Israeli left. Up until the assassination I had to be loquacious to enable my listeners to visualize Bar-Ilan because they knew little about it. Now it was notorious. Everyone knew about the *kolel* where assassin Yigal Amir had studied and the Midrasha, where his accomplice, Margalit Har-Shefi, had been enrolled. Cameras, journalists, and commissions of inquiry were combing the benches and the lawns for the atoms, the seeds planted in the field where the "weed" had grown. I read in the *New York Times* about an all-girl celebration in Beit-El upon Margalit Har-Shefi's release from jail. The reporter wandered around Bar-Ilan, searching; he reported about extremist lecturers, weekend trips to Hebron, erotic nationalist weekends.

How would I possibly write about the interview with Efrat now, an interview which took place during the Oslo talks; the hope she had for peace, though "The Land of Israel is important to me," as she put it? I would sound like a patronizing anthropologist. What would it add to the already completed chapter about the course on aggadah, which devoted several classes to the contrast between Rabbi Akiva, who supported rebellion against Rome, and Rabbi Yohanan Ben Zakai, who a generation earlier had surrendered Jewish sovereignty to the Romans in order to save the study of the Torah? Could the rabbi-teacher's words now be interpreted as I had interpreted them before the assassination? He had, after all, characterized Rabin as a leader devoid of morality and political responsibility. Would it be possible to say now that in his conversations with me in his room he had expressed a yearning to find a way back into the Israeli collective from which he and his community had been excluded?

I turned to the interviews. The transcribed literacy biographies. It was easier for me. The biographies offer a heterogeneous spectrum along similar lines. I managed to find my way back to them without being too angry, without going crazy. I heard them talking to me. I recalled the places we sat: in the shade of a tree, inside the synagogue, in a young couple's rented apartment in Ramat Gan.

Shaul's advice about sticking to my initial intentions no longer seemed impossible. It had now become one move in my home work, the first of three.

FIRST MOVE: CHALLENGING THE "HERE"

My range of movement from "here" to "there" was defined by similarities and sustained by differences. My attendance at the Midrasha occurred
within my national, biographical, ethnic, class, and gender home. Yet at the
same time it also involved border-crossing in terms of age, religion, political
outlook, education, and literacy. Such a journey is always a movement back
and forth in time and space: mornings at the Midrasha, afternoons at home;
there with my views from here, here with what I heard and saw there. There
I see, observe, listen; here I write. Such movement at once produces and
deconstructs "here" and "there." On the one hand, it constructed as "real,"
each time anew, the groups between which the researcher alternates, helping to create a boundary between them. On the other hand, in the course
of movement, it becomes clear that the boundary is elusive, and that the
groups are not as essential as one would have assumed before traveling in
and out of them. The movement itself reveals the seams around each group,
both their strong and their weak spots. It confirms, for example, that Bar-
Ilan is indeed a religious academic institution with religious Zionist ideologies, but it is also an institution where nonreligious Jews and non-Jews teach
and study. The Midrasha is a site designed exclusively for religious women;
nonetheless, a nonreligious researcher, older than the other students, is at
liberty to be there, to study, and to investigate. Being with them exposes her
ties to "there," raising questions about her "here." Thus these two seemingly
distinct sites mingle and blend into each other.

   The classical anthropological imperative demands that its practitioners
spend as much time as needed in the field to understand the social reality
under scrutiny "through the subjects' eyes," to look through these eyes en
route to analysis, interpretation, and critique. This demand requires one
to cross the boundary, to go to the other place and try to stay there for as
long as necessary, until the site as seen "through the subjects' eyes" becomes
clear. The requirement of crossing the border, the obligation to be there but
not to get confused and turn into those "others" has always been somewhat
mystical; it is always hard to explain, teach, pass on to the next generation
of researchers.

   While this demanded "understanding of the other," it never really made
room for him "among us." During my stay at the Midrasha, I thought I
was beginning to read the peace process that was transpiring at the time
"through the subjects' eyes." The classes, my occasional conversations, and
my interviews made it clear to me that the community I was studying felt

besieged. Its ideological world, the dream of a Greater Israel, was collapsing. Its members were isolated by the Intifada and the peace process. They became a community at the center of things, but outside—they were branded as enemies of peace, mad, Arab killers, a handful of people eating up government money, people who needed reserve soldiers to protect them, people who had dragged the entire nation into a forlorn struggle the public had conceded long ago. As the following chapters will show, the religious public is unable to stand outside the Israeli collective, since such a position immanently contradicts the ideology of religious Zionism, which sanctifies all the people of Israel (secular and religious alike). It was thus clear to me that the new position assigned to the community I was studying was simply unfeasible from their point of view.

With regard to my research, I thought I had discovered the intricacy of the reality "through the subjects' eyes." All along the way I had found the Midrasha women thinking about the peace process, doubting that it would succeed, but also hoping that it would work. These were small, hesitant voices, but I heard them clearly. In the first phase of the work I tried to make them resonate more loudly, following a long anthropological tradition where the researcher amplifies voices that are opposed to the common stereotypes of the society to whom she belongs. I wanted to say the unsaid, give voice to the unheard. Politically, I thought a mistake had been made. I realized that the secular left had stereotyped the religious Zionist public, making it out to be more monolithic and more vehemently opposed to accommodation with the Palestinians than it actually was. The portrayal of this group as absolute and dangerous others was overwrought and counterproductive. I thought room ought to be made for them on the inside; that placing them outside the pale was cruel and arrogant, politically unfair and incorrect in principle. It was clear to me that there had been an attempt to isolate this group so as to depict the "home" as peace-pursuing, homogenous, sane, and enlightened. The Labor-Meretz government had attempted to delineate a new boundary separating "good" peace lovers (Jews and Palestinians) from "bad" enemies of peace (Jews and Palestinians). This distinction, which was totally novel in the history of Israeli governments, necessarily ostracized groups and individuals that did not fit in.

I wanted to conclude my act of border-crossing at home, at a place which was perceived back then (1994–95) as the center of the Israeli collective, one which recognizes the PLO and wishes to end the occupation. Crossing the border was, to use Lavie and Swedenburg's terminology, an attempt to hold a mirror up to the face of that very collective so that it would realize that its face was caked with makeup, makeup applied to cover up its wrinkles and scars, to create the smooth complexion of a "New Middle East."

I wanted to agitate the position of the strong within the home—to turn anthropology into "a thriving site of resistance and criticism"—but Prime Minister Yitzhak Rabin's assassination changed everything.

SECOND MOVE: ONLY HERE

Rabin's assassination, on 4 November 1995, left me shocked and hurting as a human being and as an Israeli citizen, and helpless as an anthropologist. I felt cheated, stupid—as though I had deceived myself. In time, these feelings turned into anger, loathing, disappointment with the border-crossing act. I wanted to take a stand consciously, tactically, politically, and ideologically beyond the border and proclaim my disinclination to "understand them," my disinterest in knowing how things look from "there."

I had had enough of the artificial anthropological twilight zone I had created. My steps inside it faltered. I wanted to go "home," lock my door, my heart, rid myself of any empathy for what happens "there," and of my criticism of what happens "here."[14] The rules of the cultural-democratic game had been broken. Instead of holding a mirror up to the face of the strong person, they had shot and killed him. Their homework became the liquidation of the prime minister. The question of whether this is what Lavie and Swedenburg really meant paralyzed me and did not let me go on. In America, away from home and from the field of research yet totally immersed in their material, I heard voices that surprised me. Gradually, after the initial shock had sunk in, a discourse of "peace at home," of reconciliation and attempting to understand reality through the "others'" eyes surfaced. These voices had a macabre sound for me: Part of the Israeli public was embarking on the anthropological journey I had wished to defend prior to the assassination, a journey I was now alienated from.

Soon the emergence of the "peace at home" discourse became a theoretical question for me. I had to let some time pass. I had to go back and pay a first bitter visit to the Midrasha two months after the assassination. The third and final home work move took place on the first anniversary of Yitzhak Rabin's murder. This move endeavors to explain the "peace at home" discourse as devotion to the Israeli home as a national home, one for Jews alone. The border-crossing it suggests is internal, aimed at shoring up the national home, and it is uncritical.

THIRD MOVE: THE COLLAPSED HOUSE IS RESURRECTED; OR, RABIN'S MURDER AS MURDER FOR FAMILY HONOR

*We must re-think the assumption that a traditional
morality and social cohesiveness are essentially positive.*

Ilsa Glaser and Wahiba Abu-Ras, 1994, p. 273.[15]

Parallel to the initial stages of the peace process, changes occurred in the image of the "national home" in Israel. The division between Jews and Arabs, between the Jewish nation in Israel and the Palestinians in Israel and in the occupied territories, was no longer self-evident. It seemed that some Jews preferred some Palestinians as allies in the peace process, and from this point onward they were not committed to the Jewish collective as a whole, or to those Jews who were not interested in peace. During the ascendance of the Labor-Meretz government, one might have gotten the impression, though it was not explicitly declared, that this new (Arab-Jewish) coalition was willing to institutionalize the shattering of the national taboo (Jews against Arabs) for the sake of peace.[16] Yitzhak Rabin and some of his followers developed a practice of exclusion, disregard, and contempt for a specific part of the Jewish public, in contrast to attentiveness, rapprochement, and intimacy with another part—Jewish and Palestinian.[17]

Religious Zionism cannot endure such a situation. Its exclusion from the collective, in parallel with talk of Israel as a country of all its citizens, is an impossible situation for this group. At such a moment, its acquiescence in democracy as a necessary evil to be borne until the coming of the Messiah becomes untenable. Not because this is the nature of modern Judaism, but rather because modern Judaism in Israel has chosen to sanctify the Jewish collective in its land, to glorify the army and state institutions, and to make them harbingers of the coming of the Messiah.[18]

Religious Judaism, by its very nature, cannot be estranged from its country and government, since this is equivalent to being alienated from the holy. Since the "national home" is sacred, some member of the family had to put it right; return the old division of Arabs versus Jews; restabilize the (national) traditional morality; and reestablish social cohesiveness. It is no wonder that this family member came from the religious Zionist community, which regards itself as responsible for the morality of the national family. Prime Minister Yitzhak Rabin's assassination was, thus, a murder for the sake of family honor.

The analogy between Rabin's assassination and murder for family honor does not assume that the two are identical. The metaphor elaborated below seeks to reveal a part of the ideological-political infrastructure that led to the murder and directed the mourning for the victim.

In Israel, murder for family honor is a term usually reserved for Arabs.[19] Glaser and Abu-Ras have attempted to decipher such a murder. They reconstruct the chain of events leading to the murder of a certain woman from an Arab village in central Israel, focusing on the discourse surrounding it. With detective-like caution the two show how gossip can gradually turn into a discourse of murder. Women play an important role in substantiating this discourse, through which a woman metamorphoses from being light-headed to being perverted, and then to being a targeted victim. When the discourse describes the woman's act as the crossing of a point of no return, the writing is already on the wall, and the murder becomes inevitable. Glaser and Abu-Ras maintain that only a vulnerable girl in a vulnerable family can be easily marked as a target. In prestigious families the process is more complicated.

It may be that Yitzhak Rabin trusted to his strong position, to his affiliation with the Labor establishment in Israel, to his biography that ran from a legendary agricultural boarding school through the Palmach to the army. No other prime minister before him had so purely embodied the essence of Zionist-Israeli nationalism in his personal biography. The Right knew that it had to give him credit for this, accepting him as the minister of defense who used harsh measures to suppress the Palestinian uprising. The Left knew how to use this credit to get back into power after fifteen years in the political wilderness.

But—returning to our analogy—the girl went bad. As defense minister she had told her men to break the Arabs' arms and legs; as prime minister she was suddenly talking about peace and love. When Yitzhak Rabin stood on the lawn of the White House and shook hands with Yassir Arafat, he fatally compromised his position as the guardian of national morality. The prime minister had cohabited with the forbidden, violated the codes of morality and chastity, and dishonored the national family.

The shame of that handshake could have been dealt with in many different ways and directions; a discourse of murder is only one of them. Glaser and Abu-Ras show that the murder discourse is protected by an even stronger hegemonic discourse. Israeli courts, for instance, tend to "show consideration" toward those who kill Arab women for the sake of family honor, rationalizing it as respect for "Arab culture." This way, the two argue, the Israeli establishment gains twofold. First, it joins Arab patriarchy, showing forbearance toward it and appearing as an enlightened ruler; here the murder discourse within the traditional moral discourse of the Arab society is supported by the patronizing morality of the courts. Second, it reinforces the image of Arab society as primitive, one that murders its daughters. Here the murder discourse is aided by the willingness of the court to preserve social cohesiveness: Jews versus Arabs—one law for them and another for us.

The cultivation of a murder discourse around Yitzhak Rabin also required wider support. This support was found in the national discourse, which is rooted in all venues of Israeli existence. The whisper had to become a loud cry—"Rabin is a traitor"—and indeed this cry was soon heard The photograph of the girl caught in the act was distributed at right-wing demonstrations, and not only by its radical margins. She was depicted in a kaffiyeh, cross-dressed as an Arab, holding hands with her man, disgracing the family. She was doomed.

The family tends to send its most suitable member to commit the murder: the one whose imprisonment will not obstruct the life continuum nor rend the family fabric. He doesn't have to be told what to do; he knows what is expected of him. The son/brother/father embarks on the mission. Then the family mourns. Really mourns. For she was our daughter, our own flesh and blood. She could have brought honor to the family, but she strayed.

The mourning discourse about Rabin's death was similar to the mourning discourse of the murdered woman's family. It was entirely mobilized for the correction of the national family, as the slogans illustrated: "Peace Begins at Home," "Reconciliation Is the Order of the Day," "Israeli Unity."[20] The Arabs disappeared from the picture altogether. It was our business, strictly between ourselves; a Jew killed a Jew. Someone made sure her lover would not show up for the funeral, so as not to upset the family. Everyone else came to Jerusalem for Rabin's funeral, but Arafat was given to understand that he would be unwelcome.

Lavie and Swedenburg talk about a mobilized anthropology that engages in magnifying the face of society: An enlargement exposes every single wrinkle and destroys the serenity of the strong home. It seems that Rabin's assassination was the ultimate magnification—a murder for the honor of Jewish nationalism in Israel that expresses the inability of Zionism in general and of religious Zionism in particular to recognize the artificiality of this nationalism. cynically and paradoxically, the murder that expressed the ultimate exclusion of religious Zionism from the peace process, and from the new collective it had created, linked it back to the collective.

It seems that the cultural lesson that followed this enlargement and subsequent destruction was different from the one sought by Lavie and Swedenburg. Instead of undermining the foundations of the national home and exposing alliances that had been contracted within it, the public discourse in post-assassination Israel sought to bring the family back together, reinforce the home's foundations, draw extremes nearer, and make peace within Israel.

It appears that the greater portion of Israeli society finds it difficult to make the passage into the "post-Zionist" era. The national component remains of prime importance, even if there is a dispute over its nature and appearance. The anger, frustration, and sadness that have been internalized find their way out in unprocessed form. Only recently have there been the initial signs of their translation into a political movement. It may be that it will take a certain amount of time for the Israeli public to recognize the artificiality of the national fabric, at which point it will not fear its deconstruction. Only then the enlargement that Lavie and Swedenburg speak of may appear, a bit late, having been entrapped within family solidarity.

My research work at the Midrasha sought to be "home work," a study aimed at the heart of what was taken for granted: the politics, literacy, and gender of religious Zionist society. The intention was to present the religious Zionist "other" otherwise, but it is not easy to turn home work into "a thriving site of criticism and resistance" when you live in it and it is burning. At best it may help one see a little better through the smoke.

I now turn to the primary voices, to the young women who study at the Midrasha.

II

NEXT PESACH — BIOGRAPHIES OF
STUDENTS AND THEIR ANALYSIS

3

~

BIOGRAPHIES OF TORAH LEARNERS

"I HAVE NO PROBLEM TALKING with you, I just want you to know that I'm not exactly a typical girl here." Ora and I got many responses like that when we approached students at the Midrasha and asked to interview them. There were almost no refusals, no one was apprehensive, and the impression was that most of the subjects were pleased to have the opportunity to assist my research by thinking out loud about their literacy pasts. The interviews were conducted in various locations, most of them around the Midrasha and the Bar-Ilan campus, a few in the subjects' homes. The fact that each of the interviewed women marked herself as being, on the one hand, willing to talk and, on the other, unrepresentative is intriguing.

In a study of people who left the *haredi* world, Sarit Barzilai Ben-Yakar found that most of her interview subjects made a point of mentioning how similar they still were to many who had remained "there."[1] In this case, these few people who had left the ultra-orthodox framework, who had rebelled against it, who had changed their lives, had a need to declare that they were not exceptional. Even though they were few in number, they wanted to say, they, and the stories of their lives, represented many others who could not talk.

I observed the reverse of this phenomenon. The young women in my study have remained in the religious Zionist framework and have taken its high road. Yet they made a point of emphasizing their uniqueness. They stressed that they had an exceptional, and critical, point of view. Each of the interview subjects described her learning past, her family, her relation to religious society, and her expectations of the future as private and singular. Despite the intimate relations each one of them has with many other learning women (and assuming that they speak freely among themselves), many of these women view themselves as being particularly questioning and different, as women who do not toe the line.

That these young women, while conforming to rigid and uniform social codes, insist on constructing an individual experience, is one more trait of modern Jewish religious society. Apparently, it allows each individual to constitute a private identity of her own and keeps private criticism from turning into sweeping public critique. Changes occur all the time, adding up to a dynamic existence. Yet the general atmosphere does not affirm these changes publicly and ideologically. It is a delicate dance, and these interviews describe its choreography. It is a personal and unique movement, and only by placing it beside others can it be shown to be more than individual. Part III of this book documents the public manifestations of these women's private criticism of their society. This chapter focuses on the personal level. It opens with the literacy biographies of six of the interview subjects and then presents cross sections taken from the rest of the interviews that address specific themes the women raised. In this way, each woman's unique and personal voice is reproduced, and each of these many similar voices resonates with the others.

The monologues presented below came as answers to a single question that was presented to all the subjects: "Tell me your literacy biography. What is your learning history from elementary school and onward, with an emphasis on the experience you have had in Jewish religious studies?"

THAT ONE WITH THE HAT ON HER KERCHIEF

I thoroughly surveyed the patches of shade that the trees traced on the grass and chose a spot to sit with Efrat. This was my first interview at the Midrasha itself rather than at the home of the interview subject, and I had thought it would be simpler. I arrived twenty minutes early, having planned to take a look at the course schedule for the following year. Efrat was sitting on the bench at the entrance to the Midrasha office reading Ma'ariv, a daily newspaper.

"We both came early, I see," she said in a strong and confident voice, looking straight at me and folding up her newspaper.

"Yes," I responded, wondering if she meant that was good or bad. "Should we sit out here on the grass?"

"No," she pronounced. "It's hot outside. Let's look for a classroom with an air conditioner."

I followed her, giving up both the pastoralness of the lawn and management of the interview. I saw her trying the handles of many doors. All were locked because of the summer vacation. The only door that responded to Efrat's touch bore a small sign that stated "Synagogue."

"Here?" I asked with astonishment. "You want us to do the interview here?"

"Why not? It's empty, it's air conditioned, and it won't bother anyone."

We chose a central spot and turned two benches to face each other, at an angle to the ark. The synagogue was equipped in the same style as the entire Midrasha: simple furniture of natural wood, with clean, square, modern lines. A magenta curtain hung in front of the ark.

While preparing the tape recorder I reflected on the uniqueness of this synagogue, which I had not even noticed during the year I had so far spent at the Midrasha. According to Jewish law, public prayer is incumbent on men, not women, and the synagogue has always been a male preserve. Public rituals—leading the service, reading from the Torah—can be performed only by men. Women sit behind a curtain or divider, in back, to the side, or in a balcony above the men, as a way of marking that they are guests, not full-fledged participants, in the public prayer service. Yet here was a synagogue just for women. Who opened the ark? Who read from the Torah? I told Efrat about myself and the research, about my previous work, and her place in my new project. I felt no need to pretend, to speak cautiously, to conceal or stress anything particular.

"You couldn't find yourself a more appropriate subject than me for this matter. These subjects you're addressing interest me, or actually it would be more accurate to say that they really burn inside me. I'm involved with it, I think about it, I live it."

I turned on the tape recorder and told Efrat that the private identifying details of her biography would be changed and kept confidential.

"I don't care at all, I'm not afraid for them to hear what I have to say." The spindles of the tape recorder, that anthropological icon of elicitation and evocation, began to turn. I wanted to listen, and Efrat wanted to speak.

It soon became clear that Efrat was deeply preoccupied with issues of women's literacy and power. She was eloquent, avoided clichés, and, though she spoke unambiguously, she seemed to be thinking as she spoke. As she told her story, she crossed and uncrossed her legs, her wine-colored skirt crumpling between her knees. She wore flat black shoes and an embroidered blue shirt, while the blue kerchief that covered her hair left a few curls exposed at the forehead. A claret-colored hat decorated with colored stones rested on the kerchief. Efrat's acute brown eyes glittered. In my notes from Yael Weiss's course, I had labeled her as "the settler with the hat on the kerchief" or as "the *rebbetzin.*"

During the course of our conversation the door opened several times and young women entered to pray. Some glanced at us in surprise, others asked if they were disturbing us, and a few simply addressed themselves to their prayer books without paying us any attention. The first time this happened, I felt very uncomfortable, and I asked the woman who had come to pray if we were bothering her. "I, when I pray, I don't hear anything. It's absolutely fine. Just go on." She took one of the prayer books that were lying in a pile on the front tables and began her devotions. So, as I spoke with Efrat, I saw, behind her back, in a direct line, a blond girl in a denim skirt, moving and swaying in the predictable sequence. Six or seven minutes later, she kissed the book, kissed the mezuzah, and left.

At the end of my conversation with Efrat I wound up the microphone wires, took the cassette out, and looked around at the walls of the synagogue, still having trouble believing that Efrat had chosen this particular place for us to talk. Walking behind Efrat I made myself a little wager. If I had really gotten to know her, if I had succeeded in understanding her, she would not kiss the mezuzah. Efrat opened the door with a strong hand, did not stretch her hand up to the doorjamb, did not bring it back to her mouth with the same unthinking, automatic gesture that most of the women had used. She left the door open for me. Got her.

The conversation with Efrat traced the clearest possible portrait of "the new women in religious Zionism"—a kind of ideal type existing in a haze of time and context, with its subtleties, subtypes, and many counter-types as well. But it seems to me that I can distill from her words a classic, ideal archetype that stands out against the background of what others said, and of the observations as a whole. This ideal, by its very definition, need not answer to empirical reality, but it can teach a great deal about the empirical. Some of the other interviews included these same central messages and even brought them to the forefront in a clearer and more revealing way, but Efrat's discourse stands out precisely because of the complexity with which she imbued it. From her outward appearance and behavior to the finest and innermost chords of her way of life, the narrative woven around her contains major insights on the place of literacy in the lives of the women under study. From my initial stereotypical label, through her understanding of the canon offered to women in her society, to her struggles and the personal paths she chose for herself on, and alongside, the high roads of modern orthodoxy, the figure of this new woman gradually became clear.

"IT IS CLEAR TO THE SAGES, IN MY OPINION, THAT WHEN A WOMAN STUDIES HER MIND OPENS UP"

"In elementary school I studied in a regular state-religious school, boys and girls together, but sitting separately. In seventh grade all the boys disappeared. They simply went to yeshiva high schools and I went to an *ulpanit*. I didn't even consider going to an *ulpana*. I actually wanted to go to a regular high school, but my parents pressured me and said that high school wasn't good enough. I'm the eldest, so, you know, all the normal pressures. I didn't like the *ulpanit* at all and didn't get along with them. The rabbi says this and the rabbi says that and you have to do what the rabbi says. They don't educate there for independent thinking, and that was never right for me. I was known as a rebel, a rebel of the positive type—that is, they liked me and I fit in well socially and academically, but I always made problems of the sort 'who said so and why?' I didn't make a fuss about insisting on going to the army, but I did insist on doing two years of National Service. They said one year and close to home, and I said two years and in a development town. I corresponded with one of the teachers for two years. She was really something."

Was the entire faculty of the ulpanit *composed of women?*

"The main teachers were, but there were rabbis who taught halacha and law and so on."

And women teaching Jewish law or Gemara?

"What are you talking about? They don't touch Talmud. Mishna yes, but they call it oral law. They would never bring a book of Gemara to class. It's simply something that doesn't exist. I didn't see it. . . . Actually, I saw a page [of Gemara] in the youth movement, but not the book. I never found myself sitting with the book, only with a photocopy. It always interested me. I thought it was a magical world that I would get to sometime. The girls made out that it didn't matter to them: Just like *ulpanit* girls, they

didn't look up to see what it was all about. There were two of us who
always talked with each other and that was it. They point you in a certain
direction. Now I'm doing a seminar paper on religious indoctrination in
the *ulpanot*, because of my approach. I argue that it comes out that reality
requires religious indoctrination, because if you don't teach insularity then
you lose something from a religious point of view. But this insularity they
teach us creates new types in our society, those who segregate themselves
in settlements or religious neighborhoods. It educates me to look only at
myself, I at myself, and those who are similar to me. In the *ulpanot* it is much
worse than in an *ulpanit*, because there you are with those girls twenty-four
hours a day, and of course they make sure that the counselor is one of the
outstanding older students that the rabbi liked. I see it today when I train
youth counselors: 'The rabbi said, the rabbi said.' It's the same difference
who the rabbi is, it doesn't matter. Every girl knows that she will have two
halachic authorities in her life, her husband and the rabbi. He, her husband,
will be a Torah scholar, graduate of a yeshiva, and he will have a full and
overflowing spiritual world, and he can tell her what to do, and of course
there will be a rabbi, either her rabbi or his rabbi. But they don't educate a
girl. They don't see any value in educating a girl to think—that is, to know
how to open a book, to decide for herself, out of faith, that she can also
determine the law. It is clear that my husband, who studied for six years
in a yeshiva, knows more than me. It is clear that I can consult with him.
But why shouldn't I sit down and study? Where is my responsibility? My
personal responsibility? That is not just in little matters of halacha, it is
in important things, like where to live, where to do National Service, who
to marry, whether to cover your hair. It's education. That's the line: 'the
rabbi said.'"

You never ran into a learned woman educator who could serve as a model?

"No. My teacher exemplified this obedience in an amazing way, three
years from tenth to twelfth grades. It was really chilling—such uniformity.
I was very attached to her. She is a very honest woman. If she believed in
something, she went all the way with it. But look, they get what they want.
Those girls will wear long sleeves, and they will look as they should, and for
them that's success. A girl like that will marry a yeshiva student and she'll
have lots of children. No career or anything like that, because that's not what
they educate for. Actually there are some channels they do direct girls to.
It's strange—law, for example, is okay. The *ulpanot* like to brag about the
number of their graduates who went into law. Still, the direction is to stay at
home and educate the children, that is the woman's job. I agree with this—if

you learn to combine it in the appropriate way with your own aspirations and your self-fulfillment."

What did you do with your curiosity, Efrat? Where did you take it?

Efrat smiled, relaxed her body, and recounted a long story about her acquaintance with the neighbors' son. Friends from preschool, they went to the youth movement together, first as members and then as counselors. At a certain stage, Efrat related, when he returned from the yeshiva high school in Kfar Ha-Ro'eh, she began to feel that a huge and growing chasm of Jewish knowledge separated them.

"There had never been a gap between me and the boys. I grew up just like them. Okay, they studied another page of Gemara. But it's not that he devoted himself to study. Suddenly, after our graduation exams, I felt that he was disappearing—Jewish thought and philosophy, Rabbi Kook, the Maharal, the *Kuzari* on a high level.[2] He would come home with knowledge from here to who knows where, and I was just a nothing, and that really bothered me horribly. And then the questions began: Wait a minute, isn't there a framework in which I can study? Why can he integrate his [military] service with study and I can't? These things really bothered me. Not that there was anger in it, but there was a huge amount of frustration, frustration on the level of why am I a girl. You should understand, in our society to be a girl means: do National Service, go to college, get married, and go to work. The Torah world attracted me and still attracts me. Torah study is qualitative. As a religious person, it has huge value for me—the whole matter of understanding what you do, this exposure to the world of understanding and identification. One could see how he was developing. He is in principle a thinking man, even though he studied a lot of Gemara, but on Shabbat I would be stuck in Or Akiva, and when I came home we would study together. Suddenly I saw all those books. He bought a huge amount of books: Aristotle and Plato—everyone who came was astonished—and of course the main thing was books on Judaism. To this day our house continues to fill up with books [Efrat is now married to this young man]. That's how I learned to open a book to pursue the question. After all, when a girl has to give a lesson at some event, what will she do? She'll open the Bible, the Torah, the commentators, she'll see what Rashi says, what Maimonides says, and that's it—that's what she received, those are her tools. Not midrashim, either. I at least did not receive the tools to open the midrashic literature, not how a midrash looks, not where I can find one, or what to do with it when I find it, nothing. Today many more girls study, and there are all these new midrashot—it looks really funny that girls shouldn't study. I solved that problem through my husband. I really exploited him, and he is so aware of this problem today that it has become a central issue in his life. He wants to teach girls, to open a place. A high school or I don't know what, where they will study differently. He says about me that I am the equal of a lot of the guys from his yeshiva in terms of knowledge."

Do women study differently, in your opinion—is there something in that?

"Look, sometimes we laugh about that, because, you know, they say that women don't have to study because they know it naturally. But the truth is that sometimes you are studying something and say, 'ah, it must be this way.' I could give you the answer right off; sometimes I feel the answer. Or because of some sort of sense I begin to go in a certain direction, but I have a long way to go until the answer; it doesn't come naturally. It doesn't bother me that girls study separately. I, for example, wanted to go to Midreshet Bruria. It was new then. But my parents were against it, and with great pain—real pain—I gave in. People said that it was a passing craze that would go away, who needs it, a girl should get married and have children and not sit for a year alone and study. But girls I knew went and it was a real high, they were really enthusiastic. The best girls end up there, and whoever was there was admired by the others, and I compromised on studying at the Midrasha. At Bruria they sit in *havruta,* not a lot of girls around one book, devote themselves day and night to study. It's something different, a different quality. They take something from the beginning to the end, not like here—they're always jumping, always a little from here and a little from there, they put the material together, edit it, don't go in order. Everything [here] is controlled."

Is there no limit to what a woman can or should study?

"No. None. You can't let there be. At least as far as I'm concerned there's nothing like that. I don't want to change frameworks. Yes, I can understand that a woman's role is to focus more on the education of the children, and the husband is perhaps out of the house more, and that is important to me to a certain extent. But, yes, I will want to develop my career and do things outside the house and put that together with the education of the children. A boy studies because he is commanded to study, and it doesn't matter how much. My husband, for example, helps at home, but in the end the responsibility falls on the woman. There will always be frameworks for the boys, and the boys are the rabbis, and the girls can only be a rabbi's wife—that's the way it is, even if it can change. I personally don't want to, but if there's a woman—and there may very well be women like that today—for whom it is important to sit and study all day, then let her do it.

A woman who wants and can be a rabbi, not because of some feminist and political hoopla but because someone really wants it, then why not?"

What are the rabbis scared of? Why are they not advancing orthodox women into prominent religious roles?

"I don't think they are afraid of what tradition once thought of as 'trivializing the Torah'—that women will simply dabble and chatter—but the opposite. Women today are career-oriented. And the fear is not only on the halachic matter. It is clear to the sages, in my opinion, that when a woman studies her mind opens up, she is more aware of herself, wants more and demands more, and maybe they are scared of that—what will happen to the children at home?"

Do you really think that's what they're afraid of? Of damage to the traditional division of labor at home? After all, that's happening anyway, and not specifically in the context of study.

"With me it's connected, because it comes out of my husband's appreciation of me, I think that a husband whose wife doesn't study, he appreciates her accordingly. It is a kind of message. Here I am studying just like you, or at least as much as I can, and I also want to sit with the girls in the evening in *havruta* and study—and I did that last year, with all the work and all the mess—so please, the laundry can wait. Maybe I've got a wonderful husband who sometimes does the laundry, but it seems to me that there is mutual appreciation here. Both of us are independent entities, both of us have a desire to get the most out of ourselves, each one in their own field and in what interests them. And as for the rabbis, there definitely is a challenge to the social order here. But today they can't do a lot about it. What can they do? Forbid it? They need to forbid everything, no university or anything. And Rabbi Cohen [the director of the Midrasha], if you ask him why it is permissible to teach women Gemara nowadays, he will tell you: 'Are you trying to be funny? A woman who studies physics shouldn't study Gemara?' That's his answer. Maybe they should have thought of all that in advance, but now it's a lost cause for them."

And how do you see the connection between your studies and your political views?

"It doesn't pull toward any necessary connection. There's history, there's home, there's education. I'm not, for example, very drawn to politics. The Land of Israel is important to me, and I'm right-wing in my opinions, but not very much. I'm pretty centrist in the right-wing direction, a kind of classic National Religious Party person. In my set of values the Jewish people is much more important to me. And now with the agreements and all that

[the conversation took place around the time of the first Oslo accords], it
scares me, what will happen. Settlements will be dismantled. It will be hard
for me if they give back parts of the Land of Israel. But on the other hand,
I'm happy with peace, and if I were in Rabin's place now I would do exactly
the same thing. It seems logical to me, despite what I already told you about
the anxiety and fear and the tie to the Land of Israel."

*You know, when I saw you in Yael Weiss's class and I heard you talk, I would
write down what you say under the heading "the settler." Do you realize that
when you walk around Tel Aviv everyone thinks that you live in the territories?*

"That's obvious. What can I do about it? It even makes me laugh. Because
when we got married we didn't even think about going to live in the territories. It was clear to us that we would live in a development town, just like
what in fact happened. On the matter of the image, it's hard for me—for
example, with the head covering. I haven't resolved that for myself yet. I have
a hard time with the stereotypes they put on the public that I am a part of,
and I also have a hard time with the stereotypes that my public creates. So I
do the best I can. I study communications in Tel Aviv at a private school with
all the North Tel Avivians [north Tel Aviv is stereotypically secular, left-wing,
and upper-middle-class]. And, true, it took those guys two years to understand that even though I'm religious I'm normal, but they understood, and
that's a bonus. We go to the movies a lot—there's almost no good movie I
haven't seen. I read literature and listen to good music.

"I don't do those things because it's fun and afterward go study in order
to make amends or keep myself together. As a religious woman it's the
combination, it's the complexity. It is to take something to the very end but
not be fanatic."

*In other words, you don't study in order to protect yourself against secular-
ization, against the world outside?*

"If you are asking me if I need to study more and be more religious
because I do many things today that my mother never did, and am I part of
a more secular society? Yes, in practice that is what happens, but that's not
the reason. I don't do it because being more extreme will protect me inside,
no. I don't accept that connection of being more religious in order not to
take a fall, in order to be protected against the world in which I live. I see the
connection in the pure truth. In other words, whoever goes after the pure
truth and for whom it is important to do what he thinks is right, he becomes
a complex person. He simply becomes a complex person. And I see a lack of
complexity in my parents' generation, in their traditional perceptions. And
that's funny, because they maybe see a lack of complexity in my religious

extremism. But I think that complexity lies in succeeding in being religious all the way. It's not that I'm modern because its convenient for me or because I like it, or because it's fun to study at the university and go to good movies (which is what the *haredim* will probably tell you). But rather because I think it is right to go to a good movie and to listen to good music and to live among secular people in a development town, to study and to teach at an integrated school. For me, complexity is succeeding in being a religious woman all the way while not being a fanatic, that is what being modern is to me — combining it all, everything that I believe in. For that I have to study. In my study I find the guidelines for what I do in the afternoon."

So in fact you are bringing modernism to the most classic and demanding limits it contains. For you to be a modern woman is to live according to ideals and to fight for them and to seek to realize them in a democratic spirit.

"Definitely. And I have more appreciation of a secular person who follows his ideas than I do for all sorts of equivocators in my own society who really do what is convenient for them and not what they believe in. Everyone needs to search out for himself a holistic way of life from the beginning to the end. That includes all areas of life. Every little thing becomes part of the larger goal, and that is very difficult, and because of that I study — study is part of that. You should understand: My husband studies because he is commanded to and I study because I need it, because it's important for me, because I want it, because it moves me forward."

Efrat's ideological demands for a holism of values is not new in religious discourse, nor is her repugnance for equivocators of various types or for those who live a lie. Her notable innovation is her objection to the all-too-common functional explanation about the place of study in a woman's life.

Study cannot be used as a means of survival in religious society in its modern context. It is not a utilitarian activity; it is not the remedy that will keep a woman of restricted religious literacy from turning into a secularly educated worldly woman.[3] Increasing religious study and practice is not, according to Efrat, an act of survival. The project of scholarship is not an ex post facto action intended to reestablish an old male/female order. Women have not been given a dispensation to study so that they may be saved from secularism, nor has study been granted as an intellectual panacea for souls that cannot make do with just an emotional and moral education. Study, as it emerges from what Efrat says, is at the heart of her modernistic project as a religious woman. It is the thing itself. This assigns the classical modern ideal — the life of the enlightened individual, who lives in accordance with her ideas—an importance greater than the goal of remaining in one or another religious cubbyhole. Such an ordering of priorities, and the ideal images derived from it for women and men, delineates a society (the religious Zionist community) that sanctifies the modernist ethos. The implications of this are especially fascinating because of the postmodernist context within which they take place, and because of the common Israeli view that religion is antimodern and chauvinistic.

In Tel Aviv and Jerusalem Everything Is Really All Right

MICHAL. A TEL AVIV LAW STUDENT

Michal lived with her parents and sisters behind Dizengoff Center, the large downtown Tel Aviv shopping mall, on one of a cluster of out-of-the-way streets that remain quiet against all odds. Her childhood and adolescence passed by across from a small park, among a population that is mostly secular. These homes, from the moment you enter them—even after passing through a standard stairwell with an intercom system and a weary philodendron—have an internal aesthetic of their own. The large bookshelves full of Jewish tomes and the Shabbat table standing next to it are visible as soon as the door opens, testifying that the people who live there are different from the people across the hallway. The fact that these items were located in the large living room that also contained the family television set did not make them fundamentally different in their significance from the same items that I invariably encountered in the crowded and adamantly tv-less homes of the *haredi* neighborhood where I did my earlier research. There was that familiar couple, the bookshelves and the table, enveloped in homey aromas. The table was there for the noisy meals of a large family with children and grandchildren, and the books were there for endless study.

Michal's mother opened the door dressed in a green housecoat, from under which legs in loose cotton pants and tennis shoes peeked. Her head was bare. Two of her younger daughters, one about fifteen and the second about ten, came out into the hallway to see who the visitor was. Both were dressed in long, full denim skirts, and they also wore white tennis shoes. Michal appeared in a different corridor: "I didn't think you were coming. You said you would call a day in advance. You're lucky you found me at home."

Michal was wearing a black sweater, loose cotton pants, and warm winter slippers. Her curly hair was gathered up casually in back, and she had a pen in her hand. I suddenly recalled those winter nights of my own high school days, when I would delve into my books and papers in a tiny room that had been partitioned off from another room, convinced that at that hour there was nothing in the world other than my floppy slippers, my long hair wrapped around my head, and my father's big sweater.

We sat on the gray sofa in the living room, facing the television, which was turned down and displayed pictures of mud and soldiers in Lebanon. The younger girls watched us for a while longer from the kitchen. Michal's mother passed by from time to time, and her father walked through when he came home. I explained my research project to Michal, her place within it, the Midrasha's sanction of my work, and some of the findings that I had already collected. I switched on the tape recorder and we began to talk. About a half hour later her mother and father joined us and asked to hear a little more about the research. Then they wanted to watch the news. When I had satisfied their curiosity a bit, we went into Michal's room. From this point to the end of the conversation, my high school memories were quite at home in this setting that so closely matched my own: the narrow bed, class pictures, overloaded shelves, and a small electric space heater.

Michal speaks: "I'm a Tel Avivian from birth, I was born and grew up here. I went to a coed state-religious elementary school, but with the boys and girls in separate classes. Afterward I went to an *ulpanit.* A year of National Service and then straight into the Bar-Ilan law school. As a pupil, I was very diligent. My studies were always the center of my life. Today maybe they're not the center of my life, but still. Of course there were always other things, but I was always aspiring for a 100, to the point that even a 99 got me upset. You know, I was the industrious type; that's in my character. I'm the third of five, and that's the way it is with all of us. Our parents never had to motivate any of us to study, to say 'that's enough television,' to threaten. Apparently it's in the genes—a kind of high-achiever kind of thing, self-motivation.

"If you're interested particularly in Jewish studies, then about elementary school there's nothing to say, because then we didn't think too much. We studied Torah, and that was taken for granted, and in high school we actually studied the same subjects. Thinking back, despite the fact that even when I was in school I felt it—and it bothered me—there was a kind of uniformity, homogeneity when it came to teachers and materials. After all, Judaism, as much as it seems uniform, is very much nonuniform. It's very heterogeneous, and there are stricter and less strict, more Zionist and less, a sea of variations and forms and opinions. They gave us one line. The school was supposed to be in the spirit of the Mizrachi [the original religious Zionist movement]—the knitted *kipa* and all that goes with it—but the teachers were not always like that themselves. Most of them were 'black' [*haredi*], not the Mea She'arim type, but, you know, rabbis. The principal, true, was from Merkaz,[4] but in his opinions I really don't think so; he also got more extreme over time. The type of studies was very homogeneous. Actually, when it came to teaching Judaism we wouldn't see a knitted *kipa* in the class. With the approach of the High Holidays they would bring us lecturers, all of them rabbis, 'black.' I don't remember if I listened to what they said at all. The way they looked was so foreign to me, all black, and I, like most of the girls, didn't come from a house like that. The problem is that in Tel Aviv there aren't a lot of options. The municipal high school, Tzeitlin, is too open and not selective, and I didn't want to go to *ulpana*. That's why I enjoy the Bar-Ilan Midrasha so much. When I see someone who's a rabbi and has a knitted *kipa*, everything fits together. Our main teacher taught us Torah and Bible, a rabbi taught Mishna. We didn't, of course, study Gemara. We actually studied Mishna from the inside,[5] from the source, with commentaries. We also learned Jewish philosophy, and here so much depends on who you study with, and again it was a *haredi* rabbi, so you can picture it for yourself what that was like. In a very general way I liked school. What I'm telling you now is, like, looking back. Except for once when our main classroom teacher was *haredi*—and then we really rebelled—we did not ask for much. You know how high school girls are. Today I run after lectures and search out Jewish studies with a magnifying glass, but back then we would sit in the lectures and make faces at each other, fall asleep and dream. We didn't listen. That's the way it is.

"In Bnei Akiva it was a little different. There we found ourselves a boy to teach us Gemara, an older boy, a former counselor. In that there was, of course, something of the forbidden fruit—like just because in school they did not let us study Gemara, so just for that reason we wanted to know what it was. It was very important for us to study Gemara. That was in tenth grade, about, and I have to say that the forbidden fruit tasted very good. We studied once a week, according to subjects, according to the calendar—say, before Tisha B'Av we studied legends about the destruction of the Temple. We didn't sit with Gemara books. The instructor would photocopy the relevant page, and I didn't learn how to study Gemara—that is, we became acquainted with the Gemara, but we did not learn how to study, how it was done. I felt then that it was terribly important for me to go to that class. Even though there are people who think it's bad or inappropriate, I knew that I was not doing a bad thing. That one way was Torah and the other way too. It's not that they actually forbade us to study Gemara; they didn't say don't open it, there simply wasn't a lesson like that in the curriculum; there was no period for that. When the teacher would tell us in our discussion period to choose a subject to talk about, we would from time to time bring up the subject: 'Why don't they teach us Gemara?' But to the same extent we would ask to talk about boy-girl relations and such things. And we would always get excuses, and I always remember that I was not convinced, that it was very clear to everyone that they were avoiding the issue.

"At home, even though my father is a lawyer, there is always an atmosphere of study—you see the books. He himself goes to study every evening. On Shabbat, true, we don't talk about Gemara, but about the weekly Torah portion, but we always talk about Torah and study. I didn't feel bad around this table, even though my brother of course knew more, but it was clear to me that someone who studies at yeshiva from morning to night will know more, and that did not frustrate me.

"I went to National Service without even thinking about the army. (Maybe today, now that I'm more mature, it looks different to me, but then there was no question.) There—and this will interest you—I taught Judaism to secular children. That was in Haifa, and the children would come to us. They forced them; it wasn't their choice. Every day a different class from a different school. We didn't know them, we didn't even try to learn their names. Once I tallied up that some 100,000 pupils passed through my hands. There I encountered enormous ignorance on the part of the children and on the part of the teachers, including teachers of the Bible. I also ran into a powerful 'anti' attitude. Sometimes they would tell us after a session, 'Okay, it wasn't as horrible as we thought.' I could understand because they were forced to come. We tried not to be coercive and not to sound like preachers, but that's problematic. I learned a lot of things from that experience, but not Judaism. There I gave and didn't receive. I felt the lack of study that year; I simply like to study.

"After that I didn't think of going to a midrasha—to Bruria, for example. First, it wasn't very famous. I didn't even know about the existence of some places like Midreshet Ha-Rova and Midreshet Ha-Kibbutzim. People thought any girl who went to study Judaism for a year was crazy. Even now, with all my love for Jewish studies, I don't know if I would go for an entire year to study Judaism from morning to evening. I was very unsure about what would come next, and in the end I decided on the law. Despite my father, and even though my brother and sister studied law, I didn't take that for granted—maybe even because of that I didn't want to be 'just one more.' Today I enjoy it. I'm not one of those who don't think about anything else, but it's interesting.

"The decision to study at the Midrasha despite the double demands came because I understood that the Jewish studies on campus, in the framework of the 'basic Jewish studies,' were not on a high level. In addition, even though I'm not an *ulpana* girl,[6] and I'm open and all that, it is still fun. At Bar-Ilan there is some sort of secular atmosphere. I study with a lot of secular students, and it's nice from time to time to return to a place that reminds you where you came from. I also meet with friends; we have set days we get together on. The cafeteria is very nice, warm, there's music, it's pleasant there. It is definitely a home. When there's nothing to do and there's time between classes, you go there and you always meet a friend. As for the courses, in general they're on a high level. I'm not disappointed in the big picture. Yes, it's more class hours, and I have friends who study economics, computers, psychology; they've got big course loads and they don't come. There are those who figure that in the general foundation courses they will get higher grades and that will raise their average toward their master's degree, but I don't want to think like that. I come because I want to and because I'm interested.

"I chose the classes by the teachers. I fought for a whole year to get into Rabbi Yadid's class, and I'm very happy I did that. I like studying the Bible, philosophy less. I like to follow a text, not to hang in the air. I enjoy hard questions and explications, and I'm not fond of talk about 'the divine good.' The truth is that I didn't run after Gemara—maybe because I didn't want the teacher who was teaching it. Maybe because of the difficulty. After all, it's something different;, it's a different language, beyond the Aramaic. When you start studying it in fifth grade, like the boys do, then its like learning a language: It's understood, organized, and you pick it up. When you jump on it in the middle, it's difficult; it's not easy. In law school we study Jewish law, get the Gemara indirectly, and then it's already our language, not in the yeshiva way, not in the form of actual learning. I took more courses in the Midrasha than I was required to, and I'm already close to the end. There's no doubt in my mind that I most enjoy Rabbi Yadid. The fact is that I come to class with my eyes burning from fatigue, and I sit there and don't even feel that the time is passing, I listen to every word. He's a real person, a redhead with the character of a redhead, gets excited and shouts and whispers and makes a show of it. You can't sleep in one of his lessons. And beyond that, it's interesting. He teaches in a way I didn't study in high school. In high school we went from one section to another, then Rashi, Nachmanides, Eben Ezra, problem and resolution, and on and on. He takes a subject and goes all over with it. He's not chronological. He suggests unacceptable ideas, bases them on midrashim, not on the regular commentators. He's simply a great man. His class is a one-man show. The girls don't play a role, but that's not such a horrible thing. What is true is that he brings in a lot of political opinions by the back door, sends his regards to Shulamit Aloni [an outspoken left-wing secular Israeli politician] and her friends.

"The class on aggadah caused me a 'positive crisis.' Rabbi Cohen is an open man, very very liberal. I mean that in different ways. For example, we had a lesson on God's intervention in our personal lives. He said things that in the *ulpanit* we would not have dared to think. A rabbi stands in front of you and cites sources, and I saw girls whose faith was simply shaken. I, for my part, had a ball. I enjoyed every minute. Finally someone was letting me hear and decide. I felt that there are different views. You asked me if I felt that they were teaching me as a woman, and if the same teachers would teach differently in a yeshiva. So here Rabbi Cohen simply does it intentionally—that's the way it seems to me, at least. He knows, after all, where we've come from—from a nursery hothouse—and he wants to shake us up, for everyone to get out of their shells. Maybe you should do the same thing with boys, even though I never studied in a yeshiva. My impression is that the knitted *kipot* yeshivot—I don't want to talk about something I don't know—but it may well be that they need to be shaken up there, too. I'm sure he would trust them more. He doesn't, so it seems to me, expect much from us, and sometimes that has offended me. Not personally, but as part of the class and as one of the girls; he didn't expect that we would grasp his meaning. I can't say that he thought that we'd say stupid things, but sometimes there was an impression like that, that everything that the girls might say was unimportant, and then he would say what he had to say, and that's the correct answer. So maybe I won't take another course with him, because despite that good shaking up, it hurt me. Especially if that was a priori, that is, an assumption, and not because of a specific class, something inherent and basic, that girls will say stupid things.

"Another course that really touched on this matter of women—I understand you're also taking it—is Rivka Sternberg's course. Now here I distinguish between her as a person and the course. As a person I admired her, her smile spoke to me. I saw right away that this was a real person from whom

you could learn, no matter what she said, and, in a way, I became attached
to her—because I'm not one of those who goes up to the teachers after the
lecture. In terms of what she taught it wasn't anything new for me. That
is, I don't want to brag or anything, but she didn't tell me much I didn't
know already. As for what you say about her attempt to show that there isn't
discrimination against women in the Torah. I know that there's no problem
with women putting on tefillin, for example, but I remember that she also
always said that a girl who wants to so much, go ahead, put them on, but
in general it comes from a sense of inferiority. I can say that the message
I received from her was 'you're equal in essence, you aren't less equal, but
what can you do, you've got other duties and a different personality structure,' and 'the king's daughter's honor is inside.' So in practice, with all her
openness—and she's a very open woman—it is actually on the exterior.
Inside, she's not very different from others among us.

"Only for me study is a need, I could study Koran, everything, the more
the better, but when you believe in something you need knowledge about
what you believe in. And if I live in the light of my faith, it's kind of half-
baked not to know. So I think that I will always try to study, never stop.
I don't always remember all the details; I don't have a good memory. For
example, I listen to Motti Elon's lecture on the Bible and sometimes I say to
myself 'what did he talk about last week?' But the main thing is the spirit of
what he says, a kind of motto that repeats itself, things that come between
the words, a kind of invisible education, so it's important to me who I study
with, not only what I learn. It's not that I'm not critical. I don't shout or
anything, but I listen with a kind of internal critical attitude, I don't let
myself go like a 'lamb to the slaughter.' It's clear to me from my studies that
you can be lenient in a lot of things. If there were, say, a Sanhedrin, then a
matter like wearing modest pants—which on the face of it there is no reason
not to wear them—would be accepted. Something like that would make me
very happy. In parallel, my mother didn't cover her hair, but my sister and
sister-in-law do, and I think I'll cover my hair too. I still don't know how
and with what kind of stuff, but my inclination is to think in that direction.
It in any case marks you and symbolizes something, something that sets
you apart—I don't know. In many things I'm like you and like anyone else
on the street in Tel Aviv. I read novels, only good things. I read slowly and
put a lot of time and thought into it so I want to read good things only. I
go to good movies, and if I miss going to a movie with someone, I get very
mad at myself. Now I'm reading Grossman's *The Yellow Wind* [a book about
the Palestinians; Grossman is a well-known young left-wing Israeli writer]

in order to 'know the enemy'—not! I don't want to close myself off. We're right-wing at home, but it's not a subject for the Shabbat table. We're not among those who want to go live in the territories, we don't fight and we're not among those who take it personally."

RAYA. STUDYING BIOLOGY, FROM JERUSALEM.
RAYA WAS INTERVIEWED BY ORA

"We're seven children at home, and I'm the second. My mother went to school at Horev in Jerusalem, and so did all of us [Horev is a school attended largely by children from the stricter, more conservative end of the religious Zionist public; there are separate schools for boys and girls]. My older brother, me after him, and then the ones after me. One of my brothers just recently transferred out, and I'm very happy that he got out of there. Today, looking back, I see things I didn't see then, or that didn't bother me, because I was a run-of-the-mill pupil. But there is that attitude, that insularity. The teachers only know how to deal with the quiet, attentive student who behaves well. But 'educate the child in his own way' doesn't go over so well. To accept someone who maybe has the talent to study, but can't sit forty-five minutes in one place—to let him wander around, get some air, not that. So now my brother is in another place, and he's thriving, really happy.

"To get back to me, I studied there from first grade through the end of high school. The Jewish studies began to develop around eighth or ninth grade. In general I don't read a lot, but what I read is mostly sacred books, books of ideas, Jewish philosophy, and it began then. For example, Rabbi Salomon's book *With a Jewish Eye* or Rabbi Druckman on the weekly Torah portion, which goes beyond the portion. In our *havruta* lessons at Horev we studied ethical books like *Mesillat Yesharim* [The Path of the Righteous] and *Orhot Tzadikim* [The Ways of the Just], things like that. The *havruta* lessons began as required classes, with leading questions and summations, and developed into informal lessons, where we had to choose what and how to study, and submit a paper at the end. Most of the girls turned it into free time, a time to take care of things; they showed their faces, chattered, sat and talked, and passed the time. As far as I can remember, my *havruta* held up the longest; for those forty minutes we sat and disputed and tried to understand the point. In the end we also got dragged along by the current, and we stopped. I personally really enjoyed it, because it was a period in which on the one hand they forced us to study, but on the other hand I sat down to study what I wanted to. Sometimes it's hard for a person to find herself an hour to study even if she wants very much to do so, so when they gave it, it was an opportunity, and when you come right down to it, I liked it.

"In retrospect, they gave in too easily, because I heard, for example, that in Kfar Pines they really studied in *havruta*. If they don't bring that in and get us used to it, it won't happen, because there's always something more available and more urgent. You ask whether it is because we are girls. I don't know. But perhaps you mean that they accustom them [the boys] to it, and that really is important. They are used to it, they know how to study alone, that's important. On the other hand some of them maybe have bad memories that they were forced to do it and we weren't. Sometimes it's precisely that that causes girls to sit and open a book—because they don't remember that overbearing, imposing someone who assigned them a time to study. That, after all, is what the sages said: that we have it more, and therefore you don't have to force us to study, and they are commanded to do so.

"All in all I agree that girls sometimes lose their real role. Because to sit at home with the children, and even the physical care, is no less important than sitting and studying Torah. But even so, in any case a mother does need to find time to study Torah. God forbid, it shouldn't come at the expense of child care, because I do think that that is her main job, but in order to be 'a cup from which water is spilled,' and as part of her being an educator, she needs to study in order to be filled up, so that she won't reach a point of emptiness. Today in any case you see a woman who goes and studies secular studies for years, puts herself in it until she even gets a Ph.D., so it's inconceivable that the Torah be neglected. Again not because she is commanded (that's the boys) and definitely in order to educate her children and to know halacha—what to do in such a case and another case—but also philosophy and principles, everything that develops a person. There are those who are privileged and reach a high level. Look at Rivka Sternberg, for example; it doesn't seem to me that that comes at the expense of her family. As much as it is her job—and, I repeat, a woman is obligated to her children and their education—if she needs to sit for a year and study Torah, if she needs to go out in order to give to her home and to herself, then I'm in favor of that. I don't think that women should sit at home, and that all of them have to be housewives. According to their characters, work and study, sacred studies, everything.

"At home with us there was always a kind of friction, with the sacred studies, of course, on Shabbat. Today there's more—because we were little— now my brothers and sisters have something to say. Once it was important to balance the discussion, so that it wouldn't come out just my father and mother and the older ones talking; not that anything big comes up but still, here a discussion, there a clarification. You could say that I had a very significant experience as a learner and a teacher in National Service. I was in a chapter of Bnei Akiva in a development town in the north, and I put everything I had into it. Hours of preparation—because when you give a lesson on Rabbi Kook, you have to know what you are saying. The whole encounter with secular children and immigrant children gave me a great deal; you can imagine for yourself that at Horev there weren't opportunities like that. So I was sorry I left after one year. I really wanted to continue, but my parents were against it. I didn't continue only out of respect for my parents, you know; they're in a rush for studies and. . . .

"I worked in El-Ami [one of the organizations that coordinates National Service]. We would go into the classes, and the kids would be waiting for us. They would see us and run to us: 'Are you coming to us today? No? Oh, why not?' Not that it turns the world around, but some of the children became attached to it; they are still children after all—I don't want to say innocent, because they're not. They would ask questions that we didn't know whether to laugh or cry at. Such ignorance. Once we asked them who Jacob's wife was, and we saw that they didn't really know the names of the patriarchs and matriarchs. So we went back to Abraham and Sarah, Isaac and Rebecca, and then Jacob and Rachel. And we said, and who else was his wife? So they began to guess. We told them it starts with an L, and they tried Limor and Lilach and Liat, and in the end we got to Leah. They put the accent on the first syllable instead of the second and began to sing a popular song called 'Leah.' At the time, the situation is funny, but afterward you get sad. So when you see that a little something has gotten in, it's hard to leave. There was a girl in the Bnei Akiva chapter that we really had an effect on. She suddenly saw what a religious boy is, what a religious girl is. She would come to synagogue and say that she wanted to marry a religious man. And when you have something like that it's hard to leave. Sometimes I go visit there—I notify her in advance. She meets me, and we talk and go to synagogue, but there's no ongoing connection.

"When I had to decide where to study, I was debating between Orot College [a postsecondary school for religious women] and Bar Ilan. I knew that I wanted to study biology, and I wanted a high level. Not that, God forbid, I look down on girls who study at Orot, but what can you do? At the university the level is higher. I had a teacher who had a master's degree in biology—a woman who lived it, not one who just knew a little beyond high school exam level. Again, according to the theory I told you before, a person who is a cup that spills over has to be filled up. So it's important for me to study biology to the end. I chose Bar Ilan and not the Hebrew University, even though it is easier for me in Jerusalem, because it's a religious university. With all that it's not just for religious people, there is a certain kind of religious atmosphere. The very fact that you walk around here and you see a large percentage of religious people, that affects the atmosphere on campus—the fact that there's a *kolel* and a midrasha here, it works. So I also came to the Midrasha. I did a lot of research before I registered for courses. I asked girls who they were pleased with, who they recommended, and all in all I'm satisfied with what I take. I have a schedule with two full days at the Midrasha. It's fun to break up the biology with two days of sacred studies. Maybe next year I'll actually include at least one hour of sacred studies each day. When I come here I feel the same level of concentration; it's not different. Even biology—when we learn beautiful and fascinating things I am amazed by the beauty of creation, and sometimes I say, 'Hey, what has God made here?' And the people around me laugh.

When I come to the Midrasha, I am amazed, too; sometimes it really twists my soul around, makes me think all day. Of course, Rabbi Yadid's class. He speaks about our matriarchs and their character—actually he talks about Sarah and Rebecca—and beyond what he reveals to us about our forefathers, he teaches in a way, with a depth that I never studied before. I leave the class and say to myself, 'Wow, you can learn so much from them,' and I continue to take it onward and onward, to try to understand it in depth. Everyone talks about his ability to convey things, and right, everything he taught was good. But he doesn't float around in distant worlds. He's here and he's with us. You can learn a lot about us from that.

"The class on the halachot of the Land of Israel is also important (although everything is a letdown after Rabbi Yadid, because I'm a fan of his). When it comes down to it part of the struggle is to know and to understand what our place here is. If you study the commandments about living in the Land of Israel, and what the boundaries of the land are and the importance of the land in the halacha, then it's much more with you. After all, Rashi says that when Jacob came to the land and Esau was there, Esau was very much a local. He had wives from the land and flocks and everything, but when Jacob came it is written that Esau 'went into another country away from his brother Jacob.' He, Esau, who was here in the land, understood that he had to get up and go because Jacob conveyed to him his understanding that his place was here, and that's it. So it's important, because it's relevant. I also enjoy the course in prayer. It gives me the ability to think and direct my prayer—you understand the meaning of the words, prayer turns into something else."

BETWEEN HAIFA AND BROOKLYN

THE STORIES OF SHIRLI AND ADINA

It was clear to me that I had to talk to the two women whose voices were so prominent in Rivka Sternberg's classes. They challenged her attempt to present a coherent view, questioned the logic of her arguments, resisted her pedagogy, and voiced their doubts about the messages that were derived from all these things together. One of them did this in a cutting Sabra accent, the other in a strong American accent. One had curly, wild hair under the hat that marked her as married, and wore disheveled clothes and battered sandals; the other wore makeup, had carefully styled hair, and dressed fashionably—fashionably to the point of being on the outer limits of what was acceptable in the religious Zionist milieu. Shirli, the native Israeli, would enter the class in high gear with a huge backpack on her shoulders, choose a chair in the row closest to the door, throw her appointment book on the desk, pull out her notebook, and leaf through it forward and backward as if it were a topographical map that helped her get oriented in her surroundings. Adina would enter the class as if she were a model parading down a ramp in a fashion show, aware of her elegance and of the glances of the other women. She also always sat close to the door, in the last row, surrounded by two or three friends who arrived before her and who chatted with her before the class began. Each of these two women challenged the teacher in a different way. They were sensitive to different elements in the lessons and, in general, were not sparked by the same subjects. Likewise, the teacher's reactions were differential. She viewed Shirli's criticism as coming from home, as a challenge that had sprouted in the best-tended flower beds of the religious Zionist school system. She knew Shirli's husband—he was a student of her husband's—and was apparently assuaged by the fact that this woman was married. Despite the unique positions she expressed, she remained within the framework. This was not her reaction to Adina. Adina got her angry and shook her out of her composure. Sternberg generally responded to the problems Adina raised by firing the problem back at the questioner, claiming that the question itself was a product of Adina's cultural origins.[7]

Here is a condensed version of the interviews I conducted with the two of them on the same patch of lawn next to the Midrasha, on the same day. Both of them gladly responded to my request and warned me (each on her own and in a different way) that what she said did not represent the mainstream. I told them an anthropologist has no sources more important than people who do not represent the mainstream.

SHIRLI FROM HAIFA: BETWEEN THE DISCO AND THE GEMARA

During the course of my interviews, I learned that Haifa is a "different place." This emerges also from the work of Shlomit Orian, who wrote ethnography from within the *haredi* Beit Ya'akov school in Haifa.[8] When I read the first editions of her work I encountered pupils with names like Yael, Anat, and Michal. I told her then that she should do a better job of choosing aliases for her *haredi* girls—the ones she had given them were hardly current in that community. Shlomit responded that these were her subjects' real names. In Haifa, it turns out, *haredi* girls are given names that, while still coming from the Bible, are seldom given to their peers in the Tel Aviv area.

Five of my thirty interviewees were from Haifa, and while each was an individual, they as a group stood out as "religious girls with a difference." Their homes were less conservative, they had grown up in mixed religious/nonreligious neighborhoods, most had not attended *ulpanot*, and, reading themselves retrospectively, they defined themselves as not having been "serious" about religion.

Shirli speaks: "I grew up in Haifa on Mt. Carmel, and I went to a regular state-religious school there, and afterward to the municipal religious high school. It's a girl's school, and we didn't learn all that much there. You know, we would skip the oral law class. I wasn't so interested in Jewish studies. I didn't work hard at my studies at all. I only liked phys ed. I did gymnastics for eight years—practice, competitions, training—that's what interested me. So that by the end of twelfth grade or so my knowledge of Judaism was really shallow; here and there I studied a page with my father, but no more than that.

"My home was liberal and open. My mother teaches Bible and history in a regular secular public school, and my father is an accountant. Sometimes, around the Shabbat table, my mother would talk about how the secular people don't know anything about Judaism. For me, it didn't interest me. I knew that there's a God, I didn't challenge that, but what was in my head was my social life—girls and boys and all that. Social life and social pressure really determined everything I did. You ask if I considered going to an *ulpana*—not at all, none of the girls went, so neither did I. It really depends what everyone else does; in the class behind us, suddenly some girls went, so they all went. In Bnei Akiva they were more religious, and that annoyed me. They would force you to go to prayers, and I would argue with the counselors: 'Why can't I just come and enjoy the activity and that's all?' You should understand that they chose the counselors according to whose skirt was the longest. I think my crisis began there.

"So in eleventh grade I joined a religious Nachal group, and that was the greatest thing in life that could have happened to me.[9] I had a boyfriend for two years; there were all those hikes where the boys help the girls down the cliffs—which doesn't happen in Bnei Akiva, because there the boys are forbidden to touch the girls. In the framework of the group we thought of attending the girls' midrasha at Kibbutz Ein Ha-Natziv and study there; we knew it existed, and in fact we were unsure whether our group should be a regular Nachal group or a Torah one. For me it was important that there be good people; it didn't matter to me how religious they were. But what I quickly came to realize was that the good and serious people were also the more religious ones. Some of those actually left our group because it wasn't religious enough for them. It was really too bad, and I was sorry, because they really were great people. It wasn't just that they were, like, more religious—not according to some scale or something—but they were more special. There was one amazing boy who studied at a yeshiva and came to us, and I said to him, 'You'll be ruined here,' because I could tell; and in fact he isn't religious today. Not that he's sorry or anything, apparently that's what he wanted from the start. So it worked out that we remained, especially wonderful girls from the group, really each one special in her own way. Today most of us are married; all cover their hair. There are even three who live in Kiryat Arba [the Jewish settlement next to Hebron, in the West Bank, with a reputation for extremism in both religion and politics], just so you understand what a distance they went. We were a close-knit group, open with each other, really a top-quality group.

"Even with all I've told you, I didn't wear pants; any girl who wore pants was looked on as loose, really a harlot, someone you should keep a distance from. When we got to the kibbutz we encountered women in pants. I was really opposed. Even when I finally started wearing pants at the kibbutz, I would still change into a skirt when I left. I was afraid of what they were always nagging us about—that we would 'go bad' in the army—and it was extremely important for me to show that that wasn't so. And then I internalized two important things: that there were girls who are stricter than I was in important observances, who knew more than me, and . . . they wore pants. I would see a girl coming out of the bathroom and saying the blessing, and I thought to myself what blessing is she reciting? Do you get it? I didn't even know there was a blessing you say when you come out of the bathroom, and she wears pants. So I really did 'go bad' at the kibbutz, but in a positive way. I understood that it's what's inside that makes the difference, that I had a long way to go in terms of study and observance, that I wanted to study more and more, that I could wear pants or dance in the kibbutz clubroom and not be a whore. At the kibbutz I understood there was nothing at all wrong with that; you dance because you are happy, and there's nothing erotic about it. And it doesn't lead to someone asking you to go outside with him afterward. You dance together because it's a group, because it's an open society that doesn't stigmatize people or rate them according to their level of 'religiosity.' That brought me to study. I wanted to learn more in order to understand that, to develop.

"Only during our last period at the kibbutz did I begin to study for real. They sent five of us girls to the new midrasha they set up for 'faith in religious Zionism.' There was a discussion there about faith in God, and they prepared us to work with religious teenagers who came to get reinforced. They taught us six stages to prove God's existence. Now, if I think about it, there wasn't much there. After all, it's impossible to prove something like that, that's nonsense, but the fact that we sat and studied and debated was a beginning. Actually I understood with a kind of internal enlightenment, which is a matter of emotion, that I don't need to prove the existence of God. If I wash my hands ritually before eating, I hold myself back, if I say a blessing over something I obligate myself to someone else above me, not because it's written, as a duty, but because it is a self-evident need.

"That was my first religious development that required a great deal more study, but it was the most important turning point in my life. I broke up with my boyfriend at around that time, and it was clear to me that I would marry someone more religious. Liberal religious, but religious, a liberal yeshiva student. Then a friend of mine told me that she knew a boy in her settlement who was right for me. He is in fact my husband now. I don't like the word 'husband,' so from now on I'll say Dani.

"At a later stage Dani told me that he had decided for himself that if the girl (that is, me) met him for the first time in pants he would go out with her, and I, before I went to the settlement—which is a horribly conservative settlement—I told myself: 'There's nothing to be done. I don't like wearing a skirt.' And I went there, to his house, with my friend, in pants.

"The first time we went out alone we went to the Bible Lands Museum in Jerusalem. He knew so much about the Bible, about research, about biblical criticism, that I was attracted to him like a magnet. That integration of knowledge and openness and personality simply made something click, loud and clear. At that time he was studying at the yeshiva of the Religious Kibbutz Movement, which to this day he sees as his yeshiva. I began to learn a lot. We studied Gemara and the weekly Torah portion every Shabbat. For an engagement present, he asked my parents for the Biblical Encyclopedia. We would study for hours; you know, for a long time; lovers have no time constraints, they can devote a lot of time to it. We would go to his yeshiva and sit together and study; there they let boys and girls study together, there's a special place for it. As a whole the Religious Kibbutz Movement offers different possibilities. Everything fit together for me: You can be an open-minded, enlightened person, one who gets along with secular people, and be religious.

"Look, when David came to God and asked: 'Who shall abide in thy tent? Who shall dwell in thy holy hill?' God didn't say 'whoever dresses most correctly' but rather 'he who loves justice, loves his fellow creatures, and makes peace with his fellow.' That's why I was so disappointed when I came here to study at the Bar-Ilan Midrasha. It's so unlike what I had gotten used to. This whole super-religious approach. Not to mention the boredom, but this limitation, this closed-mindedness, and don't think that it's any better for Dani—he's studying here in the men's *kolel* and he's suffering, too. It's not anything like what he's used to and the way he wants to study. He goes there and punches the clock in order to get his scholarship, that's it. This year I already made sure to take some better courses, but there are still enough that drive me crazy. It's really an *ulpana* with brainwashing.

Everyone here says, oh, that's Shirli the exceptional one, but I don't care, I keep on wearing pants even to the Midrasha, and wear a pony tail out-side my hat, because that's allowed. Even in Rabbi Cohen's class we proved that it's possible. He surprised me, the rabbi, because I came with mate-rial from home to show that you can let hair out, but he himself reached that conclusion—though, of course, afterward he said: 'Ask your future husbands.'

"That discrimination between women and men drives me mad. After all the only reason that women's status is low in the Torah—and it's low, don't anyone tell me otherwise—is because of the time in which it was given. Now the times are changing; that's why we have the oral law, so go on, change it. No. They prefer girls with skirts above their knees and everything tight and immodest to one with normal pants. I'll educate my children in an egalitarian way in all ways, in secular life and in religious matters. That's hard, because there aren't a lot of communities like that.

"I was once in Jerusalem at the Yedidya synagogue.[10] That was the first time I was called up to the Torah alone, I was excited that they let me dance with the Torah alone. I was excited by the modesty, because there was separation between men and women, but still, there were strange things there. Girls with *kipot* and that kind of stuff, and that seems to me to be turning the world over for no reason. What for?

"We have a lot of secular friends; we even set up a kind of mixed study group. Many of them are, like, left-wingers, and still it works. I was once more extreme right-wing. Now I'm for the Likud, but I get along with them without any problems, because the main thing among us is the matter of openness."

ADINA: "ALL MY LIFE I'VE FOUGHT AND
I'VE FOUGHT, AND IT'S COST ME PAIN"

Adina sat down on the grass with her legs folded diagonally at her side. She wore an overall-dress of delicate denim fabric, under which was a pink shirt with short sleeves. Her face was fully made up, her hair nicely trimmed and her blue eyes were warm and curious.

Adina speaks: "What can I tell you? I think that when I was still in the womb my mother was already reading me homilies by the sages. I grew up in a neighborhood near Brooklyn, a kind of Jewish enclave. I went to a Beit Ya'akov kindergarten, and the things that really got me excited were the stories. I really loved my grandfather's stories, and they interested me, but even then I really remember that if they threw halachot into the story I didn't like it. When I think about it now—that they said that whoever speaks slander will have a tongue longer than his mouth, and how I was sure that I could not get my tongue into my mouth after I said something bad—it's terrible. Why should a kindergarten teacher say such a horrible thing?

"My mother is the daughter of a rabbi from California, and my father is an ordained rabbi, even though today that's not his occupation. They sent me to the Springs Valley Yeshiva, a school for girls in which the majority were more religious than me. Half the day they taught us to read Bible verses. If we read correctly we would get a sticker; everything worked with stickers there. Or there was a teacher who handed out chocolate, and I think she was a little sick, that teacher, because she described the chocolate in a way . . . something strange, how it looks and what it tastes like and that kind of thing. At home, too, whoever knew on Shabbat the answers to questions on the weekly Torah portion would get some sort of food. Strange, isn't it? Everything was connected to food.

"We're four children at home, and my mother wanted to bring us up a little differently. She would buy us other clothes and we didn't always wear stockings, and at one point she took off her head covering there; only here, after many years, she suddenly started putting on the head covering again.

"One day my parents decided to move to Israel. My aunt, my mother's sister, already lived here on a religious kibbutz, and she seemed to know everything and decided what was good for us. We almost went to pieces from her arrangements. We almost went back to the States. They sent us to a school for disadvantaged children—it was a nightmare. They transferred me very quickly, and I managed there. I had a good teacher, a boyfriend, everything. Jewish studies weren't a big thing there. When it was necessary to decide what to do next, they didn't ask me; they decided that I should go to the Amana Ulpana in Kfar Saba, like my cousin. That she's different from me, that she has two braids and a long skirt, and she's very religious and eventually married a rabbinical judge, they didn't take that into account. What was good for her was good for me and that was that. At the time it was high-class to go there. It was private, not everyone was accepted; there was racism of a sort; now that there's more competition they're less selective. For a thirteen-year old girl to go to school until five and come home in the dark was a shock, but I liked it, the girls and the social activities. Finally there were Jewish studies with a challenge, there was Jewish philosophy. I began to take an interest and to ask questions. I was always bold, the one who asked if God exists and all that, even if all the other girls acted like their own grandmothers and tut-tutted. That would silence me, but only for a little while. The level of the studies was high and the girls were smart, really on a high level, the counselor too. I enjoyed studying there, Jewish philosophy, laws, and everything. I didn't want to study Gemara; I didn't seek that out; it didn't come up.

"When I transferred to the *ulpana* boarding school I built up anger. There was more social pressure on us; for example, on Independence Day they force you to stay there, so that you don't 'wander the streets.' But we would run away. Because of that I didn't recommend to my sister to go to an *ulpana* but to an *ulpanit* instead. Yes, there I began studying in the evenings a little, alone or in sort of *havrutot*. I didn't think then about Gemara, no one talked about it, it wasn't a subject that came up. That was more talked about in the United States, but not here. Here there were "study hours," mostly Jewish philosophy, and I liked that. I liked everything having to do with Judaism, except maybe Rashi, who was hard for me, because I began late. Socially, they always admonished me that my earrings were too large, that the slit in my skirt was too high, that my hair was too short and stood up. They always told me that everyone was looking at me, that I was an influence, and that I had to use to good purpose my influence and the example I set. What was I when it came down to it? Okay, I was a little wild, but not anything horrible. All in all I was a good girl. Then of course the principal played the well-known trick: He asked me to be a counselor for the younger girls, and that worked, of course. I didn't want the girls to suddenly see me outside school with a short skirt or anything, and I began to think about everything: swimming with mixed boys and girls, yes or no; dancing; suddenly I thought twice about everything. I wasn't prepared to give a talk on modesty, and I wouldn't agree to talk about something I didn't do. I didn't want to be part of the whole double message, because just like they talked a lot, there of all places, at one of the parties the school organized I met a girlfriend who is nothing special [religiously], and there I also met my former boyfriend.

"Now you're asking about the studies and all that. In Bnei Akiva it wasn't anything special either, nor in high school when it comes down to it. I can say that now, because I've already studied in a different way—it wasn't serious, it was sealed off, closed.

"I didn't even consider going to the army, principally from the side of femininity, I'm nauseated by mud and things like that. It was clear to me that I would go to National Service. Before that I went on a mission to the U. S., and again I had to be an example for the young girls. That whole situation where I had to be, with all my 'differentness,' a counselor, that moderated me a bit, and there I also had to learn a little more in order to teach others. There I also heard about the girls in America who studied Gemara. Suddenly that actually seemed cool to me, and it began to attract me.

"In National Service I was in Jerusalem as a coordinator of volunteer activities. I would refer yeshiva boys and religious girls who came to Israel for a year from overseas to do volunteer work. That year is very significant for them. There are those who go to extremes and become 'black.' There was, for example, a really amazing guy—the girls simply fainted over him—and he grew a beard and went to a yeshiva, simply went to the extreme. There are others who become serious, continue another year and think about

Zionism, about Israel. And there are those who—everything with them is fake; they come and get excited, put on a *kipa* and *tzitzit*, afterward take everything off and go home to college. But I saw all those aspects, and I learned to look closely. I knew who was serious, who would keep at it, and I learned something on doing acts of kindness. I was exposed to other people. All my definition of what it was to be a cool person changed—from a person who sits on the railings after school, dressed well, to something mixed, responsible. I also understood that mixing boys and girls is not necessarily bad; as they say, there can be a serious and good society that is mixed, it depends who makes it up. But for that I had to understand more and learn more, and so in Jerusalem I began to learn more. It began with Rabbi Elon and went on from there.

In Jerusalem you have that, there are classes all the time, I was close to it, I began to open books myself. I'd never in my life taken a book of Jewish thought and read it just like that. I began to feel how important it was for me to understand that I was devoting more time to the exercise room than to more meaningful things. I studied at Midreshet Nishmat, which is simply wonderful. For the first time in my life I studied in *havruta*, I studied seriously. To tell you the truth, I also felt a little suffocated, and I would sometimes go out to enjoy myself, because I'm not willing to give that up ever. But there for the first time in my life I didn't feel different and an outsider. They didn't look at me in a nasty kind of way. And Rabbanit Henkin, the principal of the midrasha, is simply unbelievable. The whole place, women of all ages, women who've just gotten religious, well-versed women, inexperienced women, *haredi* women, national religious women, everything. I studied Gemara and enjoyed it. It opened my eyes, and despite the difficulty I liked it. It was so difficult, I never made my brain work so hard in any kind of study. Jewish philosophy isn't easy either, but there's a difference. We also studied Hasidism, and that was fun. So it was also clear to me that I would study at the Midrasha at Bar-Ilan in parallel with my academic studies. But now I can say that it's not like Nishmat. I want to study more, but to study in a different way. The boys have a place to go, a place to draw from, and we don't. True, I whine that the synagogue is not ours, but I myself don't get up early on Shabbat to pray. So first I need to go to synagogue, to do the maximum that I can, so that it becomes mine—but I want to know it's possible, and at the moment it isn't. I believe that will change, because in America it is changing; here they still emphasize appearances.

"There's this kind of atmosphere here. For example, I'm taking a course on "Between Man and His Fellow-Man," because for me the main thing is the connection between religion and acts of kindness, so it's hardly surprising that I'm a coordinator on campus for a program in which students tutor children from disadvantaged neighborhoods and that I am studying social work. So in this course they miss the meaning by a mile. Wonderful looking girls in long skirts who go to pray, and I don't look down on that, but they also gossip. Gossip can destroy worlds; I know how painful gossip can be. God said, I don't remember where in the prophets, 'I don't want your sacrifices,' just look at what you do to other people. After all, it's not just to study Torah, it's also to take action. It's not only to dress in a certain way, it's far more than that—and that gets lost. I wear a short skirt, but that doesn't mean I'm not a good religious girl, and it doesn't make any difference how I look. But there's nothing to be done, people put labels on you, and I live within a community, and that community is important to me, I want to be part of it. I believe, I am searching for meaning in life, and I want to remain inside. So I personally don't feel that I'm naked or cheap when I show my knees and elbows, but they think that, and I'm already weary of it. Sometimes I think to myself, I know that that girl with the long-sleeved shirt is no better than me, but if that's what it takes, if that's what you want from me, okay, I can do it. Sometimes I decide to force myself to give in to society, because for years, all my life, all I've lived until now, I've fought and I've fought—and I can't go on. So maybe the pleasure of wearing a short skirt or of going to some place or another is not worth it. It costs me a lot of pain. It costs my parents a lot of pain, especially my father. You know that sometimes I think, if you can't beat them, join them."

IRIT'S TEARS

I am going to the Midrasha for an interview with Irit; I don't know her last name. Irit had caught my attention a long time ago. Tall skinny, looking a bit older than the rest of the girls. Dresses unusually: long, loose skirts of the bohemian type; fashionably high shoes; long, loose, curly hair. The way she moves, her physical presence, and her habits set her apart from most of the others. A week previously we had sat next to each other in a class, and she asked me what exactly I was writing down. I confessed to her that I was doing research and added: "Now you're in for it, because I'm going to ask you for an interview." Irit said she would be happy to be interviewed, except that she suspected she would make the study go off in unexpected directions. The sense of marginality she expressed no longer surprised me.

She forgot to show up for the first interview, and the second went as follows:

"I'm twenty-two now. For as long as I remember—and after all, when it comes down to it, our memories are made up also of what our parents tell us about ourselves—I was a girl who did not accept things as they are. That is, from a very young age I was curious about everything. I didn't understand, for example why other children could watch television and I couldn't.

What kind of environment did you grow up in?

"My home was a religious one. It's very hard for me to go into terms that maybe you wouldn't understand. . . ."

Try.

"Well, my house was . . . my parents were religious; I'll use outside appearance, 'knitted *kipot*.' My mother doesn't, for instance, cover her hair. When my parents met, my father wasn't religious, and my mother brought him back—that is, he came from a home where they observed some traditions, and she made him more religious and made him stronger in his observance. Now, over the years, both of them have gotten more devout, especially over the last ten years as a result of my big brother. When I was little, religion was more a function of a way of life, a social way of life. Today, when I look at that from a distance, it seems to me that it filled social functions more than it was something that you really believed in, something that you really lived."

Are your parents from Ashkenazi families?

"No, they're Sepharadi, both of them. And that's very much imprinted on the family's mentality. Even if all our extended family is secular, both on my mother's and my father's side, still . . . that is, belief in this way of life is still very strong. That is, I don't think they did not live in . . . they really did live with faith, but they didn't seek to investigate. It was so obvious to them, just obvious, and I was always the one who was searching. At some point there was a television, and today there's a VCR and there's cable. I loved to read from a very young age, and they never restricted me to one particular type of book. . . ."

And you went to a state-religious school?

"I went to a coed state-religious school in Herzliya. I grew up in Herzliya. My inclination to ask and to search faded at some point, about midway through elementary school, and then reawakened at some point in high school. At home they accepted that inclination, because there's a great deal of openness of thought. Also, they never forced things on us as children; that is, they always accepted me with all may strangeness, from a young age."

Tell me about your siblings—what order were you born in?
"I've got a big brother, me, and a little sister. That is, my brother is twenty-five, I'm twenty-two, and. . . ."
And is he a very important figure?
"He's a very dominant figure at home. He always studied and always tried to learn more. One day when he was six years old he came home and told my mother—actually he never even told her, he simply began to grow sidelocks [sidelocks are typically found among the *haredim* and not in the religious-Zionist community]. Today, to make sure no one mistakes him for *haredi*, he's an infantry captain. He always knew what he wanted. In high school it was already clear that he was getting more religious, then he went into a religious pre-military program. Over the years he's continued to become more devout. What is nice is that he integrates things; he sees his army position as a calling, quite simply a religious calling, a mission. On top of that he studies. On Shabbat, when he's at home, he gets together with a friend and studies. That is, from his point of view—in conversations between us—he says, 'today I can tell you: I don't live a religious lifestyle—that is, as far as, maybe insofar as my social definition 'yes,' but with regard to my own definition, I don't live a religious lifestyle.' In talks between us he always talks about being open, being a thinking person, asking questions and going to people and trying to learn from them and to dispute with them. To grapple with everything that bothers me through study. He is definitely a figure who affects the whole way of life at home; he is a very dominant figure, very strong, who is very much appreciated at home, and what he says is taken very seriously. In high school I was already more in the secular direction, but he helped me.

"I went to a coed religious high school in the city. There they don't offer any stimulation to study; they absolve themselves of that by twice a year sending you to some sort of seminar. I think that's not so great, because that's the age at which questions arise. And when it comes down to it, we get set in our ways. That is, three or four years down the line most likely, you know, that's it. I'll be set and less dynamic and less open to changes, and what remains is a sense of ickiness that a psychologist will solve for me, no one else. And . . . that's it, it's a very critical stage."
In high school did you feel that you wanted to know more or that you wanted to know differently?
"In high school I had a rebellious thing. At one point, at the end of eleventh grade and the beginning of twelfth grade, that was replaced by a desire to study and know and investigate things. Then I really began going to lectures and to search for things, to begin to study alone. . . ."

What about Bnei Akiva?

"I was in Bnei Akiva, and I was a counselor, too. In fact at the end of high school I went to a place called Ofra; I went to Midreshet Shuva there. Why are you nodding? Have you heard about that place? You know more than it looks like you know. Anyway, I really enjoyed it. I studied there for a month and a half or two months. I really enjoyed it. It gave me things I had been looking for for a long time. Answered all kinds of questions. I went around with a feeling of real euphoria. The direction there fit me so well, because it was work on the Hasidic emotional level.

"Because, you know, they tell you that when you begin to get religious you need to do this and that and the other thing; that really turned me off and got me angry, because there was something insincere in that. I don't reject that; it could be that it's appropriate for other people, but for me it didn't work. That is, I had to get excited and feel that I was doing the real thing. That's all. So I went and studied there for a month and a half and it really affected me, and then I was supposed to enlist in the army. I was supposed to go into the ROTC program, but in the end I canceled that and decided I was going to National Service—that is, out of a belief that that was the right thing and the best alternative framework for a religious girl, that is, from my point of view, that is, for me, for what I am, because I felt that I needed to shore up my foundations.

"The first year I served in the town of Shlomi. Throughout the year I went to lectures. I studied by myself every day. What interested me were values and morals. Also laws, but more on the theoretical level."

What was it you were actually searching for in your study? You are describing a very turbulent period. . . .

"I was looking for meaning. I was looking for . . . I was looking for justifications for my way of life, and then . . . it was a very fruitful year of study. . . ."

Did you make any attempts to search out the answers in other places, or did you look there only?

"No, only there. That is, I looked in my back yard. Then the second year I served as a counselor for girls in trouble. That's round-the-clock work, no question about it. It's in a settlement in the territories, a primal place, very pioneering, and the counselor is really everything. So it's not like being a counselor at a boarding school where you've got half a day free. I had no privacy, and that was a very difficult period—especially after Shlomi, where I had had a lot of time to myself—and I put a lot of stress on the matter of my personal development. I was cut off, I didn't study. Simply, it was hard.

Then came the stage when I had to decide where I was going to go to study, what I was going to do with myself. It was very clear to me that I wanted to continue immediately to study; that is, I didn't think of any possibility of time off or anything like that. I had a lot of doubts. A framework like a university scared me, and I was very frightened that I would find myself, the way I know myself, nonreligious within a short period of time.

"So I checked out all kinds of places, and I got to the Girls' College in Bayit Ve-Gan, if you've heard of that. And . . . that is, I was looking, it was very important that it not just be a place to study to get a profession, but that beyond that there would be Jewish studies. For me that was essential fuel. The college is really a teachers' college. In retrospect, I compromised. In order to receive that Jewish fuel I chose to learn educational counseling, which was not my dream, even though the classes were fairly interesting in the end. There was a very interesting dynamic, but at that point the crisis began. . . ."

You're talking about the year at the college?

"Yes, last year, because those Jewish studies I had been looking forward to so much were a real horror. It was terrible. I saw how I was being drained of what was still left in me. It's mostly rabbis that teach there. I don't know, the studies there were very much on the level of law, what can I say about it. . . ." [At this point some of the tears that had already filled her eyes began to fall. The tears continued for the rest of the interview.] "I can't get into that at all. I had thoughts, whether this whole way of study, whether there was really anything in it—that is, whether it wasn't really. . . . What can I tell you? That was not it."

And did living in Jerusalem help a bit?

"Look, you've got possibilities. As it happens I lived in the dormitories there which were a world-class horror. That is, I don't know how I survived there. Because I was there with two good friends, so I survived somehow. But look, the framework there was of a very total institution, just like Goffman says (I just had a sociology test this week); they really get into your life and it really really bothered me. . . ."

And were you always different? Were you always labeled 'different'?

"Always. There, too. In fact I think I sought out those friends and I went to that college in order to finally be a normal person, you understand; at one point I even did it consciously. And that was, I felt I was being strangled intellectually. There are good girls there, good people, and I like people who are good, but they're girls for whom from a young age everything was very clear, what the framework of their life was—that is, it was clear to them that they would study this and that, they'd do National Service or not, would go to a college and study this and that, within the range of the options. I won't say limited, because that's judgmental, but in the range of the options they had, which they accept just fine, and everything is clear to them. And they'll marry a boy from such and such a yeshiva. That's the way it is. It's clear as day and, in parentheses, somewhere inside I envy the simplicity, with everything so clear. But in fact, it drove me crazy because they have a very specific way of thinking—that is, not open-minded at all, everything just as it is supposed to be. It wasn't right for me. I felt that I wasn't developing."

These agonies and heartaches and tears of yours, do they come out of some desire to be like those girls, except that you can't be?

"I don't know, I haven't investigated that very much; that is, I haven't investigated that in depth yet. It would seem that if I'm crying it's a sign that the subject is a charged one for me, but it could also be from all sorts of other reasons. Then. . . ."

You decided to transfer to Bar-Ilan?

"It wasn't just to decide to transfer to Bar-Ilan, it was to decide to abandon a way of life, that is . . . it was to begin . . . differently. Suddenly the [Jewish] studies didn't attract me, and since the studies no longer attracted me, then, practically, I had no fuel to get me going for the little things of everyday life you have to do. So I simply stopped; that is, slowly, bit by bit, I began to decline. What kept me going was that I hoped I would be accepted into psychology. I applied to Bar-Ilan because I thought my chances would be better here, but had there been a chance in Haifa or in Honolulu, I would have gone there."

And now that you're already studying psychology, why did you come to the Midrasha?

"I had a need for it. I didn't want to give up on it yet. I tried to go on, so I took the Midrasha program. But I don't think I'll continue, because it doesn't give me anything. It's like going back to the enthusiastic seminars from twelfth grade. Horrible, there's no intellectual level. Maybe in Rabbi Yadid's class there is. Listen, I've got classes that I don't know how I signed up for them. I go just so there'll be a check by my name, and I hate every minute of it. I hate the class and its hypocrisy. There are all sorts of things that . . . that's it, that when it comes right down to it, it would have been appropriate for me at a different stage in my life, not today. This whole approach really gets to me, with them trying to bring actual ostensible evidence: Like, one teacher said that she read in the newspaper that they discovered that a woman who keeps *nida* [the laws of ritual purity that apply to women] never gets cervical cancer; really, even when I was religious this kind of study didn't click with me. It's so shallow, so not—I don't know, look, I don't put it down, because if it's right for certain people—that is, I don't say whether they're above me or below me, so I don't have anything to say. Everyone has a different way of connecting, and that's legitimate. It's just not right for me, you understand, so if, for example, someone asks me how this teacher's or that teacher's course was, I won't blacklist it."

Next year you'll take regular classes?

"Next year I'll take classes in Jewish studies, I'll search out courses that really interest me. Most likely I'll take something on Hasidism, something on . . . things, that is, that I'm really attracted to.

One of the things that fascinates me in research is to investigate the connection between knowledge and the appetite for study or the need to pursue Jewish religious studies and the ability to continue to live as a religious Jewish woman in a world that is so complex. You told me here about a persistent attempt to find meaning for your life in Jewish religious studies, an ongoing effort that has brought disappointment. I would like to understand whether from your point of view this is really disappointment, if this means giving up on the search for meaning at one site and transferring the search to other sites.

"First of all, in my opinion, I didn't search to the end, and in my opinion, I could have continued searching, but somewhere I gave up simply for reasons of convenience. Convenience, it's comfortable for me, good for me, at a very simple level, and I tell you that directly. There are places inside me that are still telling me that this is the real way, in many areas. But for me personally it is difficult to connect. I don't know, maybe at another stage in my life I'll succeed. I don't know. That is, a lot of things can happen."

When you say, in my personal life I live a secular life, what do you mean?

"Everything. In all areas. Really, in any area you care to take, completely, even in the way I dress, also as far as. . . . I come here as I am supposed to come because I respect the place."

By here do you mean Bar-Ilan, or only the Midrasha?

"No, the Midrasha."

In terms of friends, your social life. . . .

"These days I have nonreligious friends as well; I had a nonreligious boyfriend until not long ago. That is, you see, I also have close friends from my religious world, I'm not willing to give them up."

[Irit went on to talk about her psychology studies and about her plans for the future. We spoke about her ethnic origins and the attitude of religious Zionist society to Oriental Jews. Then she began to talk again about her family and about the change that had come over her life.]

"My sister, for example, the little one, she sees religious life as something else, as a social function; it's comfortable for her. She has a nice boyfriend. I suppose they will get married a few years from now. I believe that they live a religious life because it is comfortable for them. Because they have lived in religious society all their lives. To switch, I can tell you from personal and painful experience, to get up and switch to a different social group is hard, it's not easy. In terms of social codes, in terms of a whole lot of things that you need to learn and you need to decide. You don't have a general framework of values, and you have to set the limits yourself.

"It's best if the situation doesn't set the limits for you but for you to set the limits yourself. That's very very important; that is, more and more I'm convinced of that. It's not easy because it's complicated. That's it.

"I don't know, again, listen, I don't rule out the possibility that I'll find myself religious a few years from now. It could be that it's a matter of a phase in life. It could be that it's part of a process that I'll get through. But I simply at this moment feel myself very extreme; that is, if I switch, then it will be to the other extreme. I have some trouble with in-between situations."

Are your good friends, the religious ones, aware of the process you're going through?

"Yes, very much so. I wouldn't have put up with all the criticism, then and now, without them. It is important for me to involve them in every stage, because otherwise we would become disconnected, we would lose each other. And for me that's not worth it.

"It was also very important for me to get support from them. I can say without bragging that whoever is a friend of mine has to be very open, accepting, and sensitive. So as hard as it may be for them to accept it and hard for them to accept the transition, they were with me and helped me at many junctures. And today I'm on the line—that is, on the borderline between the two worlds, in the passageway. Now I'm moving into a rented apartment, so I'm detaching myself really from my home, and that's another stage. Another stage after I found myself regular work—I for myself."

ANTHROPOLOGY WITHOUT TEARS

None of the other young women we interviewed cried.[11] They doubted, fell silent, asked, laughed, confirmed or rejected what we said, but not one of them broke into tears. When it came down to it, what did they have to cry about? It's not as if the questions we asked were reasons to cry. The request we made that they lay out their literacy biographies before us was located, ostensibly, beyond their personal sphere, close to the institutional areas of the schools, the youth movements, the books and worksheets, far from the intimate and closer to the intellectual parts of their lives. When I asked about "home," I asked to know what had taken place there in terms of the attitude toward a girl as a "knower." When I spoke about relations, I was not taking an interest in tangles of emotions or psychological complexities. I took it for granted that all that existed, but what I sought to learn was their impact on these women's literacy. Many of the interview subjects were emotional, getting excited or despondent at times; all kinds of thoughts welled up within them. It seems to me that such reactions are only to be expected when a woman surveys her past. The need and the desire to be empathic, the psychological effort involved in doing interviews—which was new to me—brought forth a type of behavior that contained an entire range of both spontaneous and premeditated responses. Each interview was different, unlike its predecessor, but the encounter with Irit was unique—Irit cried.

This may sound romantic, but it was actually the June heat that drove me after the interview to sit at a small table at the Tel Aviv marina and try to understand why she had cried. This is what I jotted down for myself on the restaurant's paper place mat:

Irit's tears are a symbol of all the other tears that were absent from the interviews. The place these tears came from is the place I am aiming at. The attempt to understand these tears in the context of her life, as it was presented to me, is my project. Where does Irit's sense of failure come from? What was she searching for in her studies that was supposed to save her from her fall? What does it mean to be "different" for so many years, within great love and appreciation of the society from which you are different? What is the price of such a search? Of the struggle to remain inside, of the insistence on getting on the canonical religious track? What chance of success is there through study? Why was the experiential dimension of the studies so important for Irit? Why does she still grasp that as a possibility for remaining?

I can see before me the paper tissues I pulled out of my straw basket and offered to her one after another, the slender hand bringing them straight to her nose and eyes. Her chin trembles slightly, but her speech flows freely, accompanied by the reflexivity of a psychology student. Piles of wet tissue build up on the grass at her crossed feet, hidden under a long dress. She plays with the corners of the tissue and the tears continue to trickle slowly from her eyes. Behind me, women, apparently friends of hers, pass by, and a few of them call out to her, throw out a meaningless "what's new," and she wrings out a smile of "everything's fine," or blurts out, in a strained voice, "I photocopied the article." I do not turn my head to look, continue to concentrate on her face, on her redone nose, her brown eyes, her long, curly hair, her slim body. They came quickly, Irit's tears, not in response to a particular question, not because she had arrived at some sensitive period in her life. They came from the fact that we were sitting on the Midrasha lawn, from the very fact of the story she had begun to relate and whose end she knew, from herself listening to herself, and from the place from which I listened to her. At the end of the conversation we rose and smoothed out the creases in our dresses, which had stuck to our bodies. When we turned to go, she said to me:

"That was very important to me. You know how to listen and be empathic. It was a very important conversation for me. I really want to thank you, and I hope you got something out of it."

I got more than I could take. At the edge of the large sheet of paper I wrote myself a sort of conclusion. Irit's tears are the boundary of study's ability to save. They point to the inability to accept an answer from the mind when the heart has already decided otherwise. They also point to the impossibility of feeling in the heart what the mind has already rejected.

Daniel Boyarin tells a similar story.[12] His personal biography wends from a secular Jewish childhood in New Jersey, to religious Zionism in Israel, to left-wing, anti-Zionist, and feminist orthodoxy in Berkeley. His academic work is portrayed as an oeuvre searching among the pages of the Talmud for a place for his complex identity.

Looking back, Boyarin claims, he indeed found comfort and happiness in those pages. The interpretation, analysis, and critique he conducted while engaging in a feminist reading of the Talmud created for him (and, through his work, for others) a place of his own in orthodoxy. But in retrospect, and in pain, Boyarin acknowledges that there are obstacles that study cannot remove, and that his desire to live his identity with internal honesty removes him from the orthodox Jewish community.

Irit's life story can be cross-sectioned into the same subjects drawn out of the other interviews. There can be no doubt that it provides information on the place of the home, the school, the youth movement, and the society of women in the literacy field. One can mark in her narrative the evolutionary line that repeats itself in most of the stories, the points of crisis and

the beginning of the change. But Irit's story is more appropriate than any
of the other interviews for marking the boundaries of the power of literacy
in and of itself, the inability to use study as a social tool for remaining in
a society, the imbalance created when only study (even with its emotional
aspects) is taken into account, in hope that life will follow knowledge. Irit
took to the limit the tenuous dialogue that most of the women pointed to.
There can be no doubt that study is a central element in the existentialism
of these women. Each of the interview subjects redefined its indispensable
power, the vitality they derived from it, the impossibility of living in this
era without it. However, each of them also described the negotiation conducted between the facets of study and daily life, largely the performance of
religious precepts, and faith as well. This dialogue, which ranges from study
in its different aspects to all areas of life, is the axis of religious existence for
these women. Without this negotiation the package falls apart.

One of the insights that comes out of this is that one may continue to
study without observing a religion's precepts, but it is much harder to do
the opposite. Irit can study and wants to continue to study even after she
has ceased to practice the daily observances of her religion. The struggle she
engaged in all her life in order to be a "good girl," the tasks she set herself
when she passed over military service in favor of National Service and when
she went to the Women's College, when she chose friends who were stable
in their religious observance and insisted on studying at the Midrasha, are
clear signs of her reluctance to give up easily. Irit described the double life
in which she was perceived as "different" at the same time that she walked
the central path. As such she very much recalls Adina's life story; in her
externalities and opinions, Adina was a "different girl" even though her
biography included all the requisite stations: *ulpana*, youth group leader,
and National Service. Adina turned to study and to changing women's status
in religion in order to survive, but she has internalized the requirements
made of her in her daily life. Irit turned in a direction that is uncommon
in this society, because of the disassociation between study and its context,
because of the impossible role she expected study to play. This turn of hers
represents, then, the limit of the literacy power for a modern woman in a
religious society.

4

SIX COLORS — MANY VOICES

THERE WERE FIVE COLORS IN the set of pens I received from the research institute in Philadelphia where I worked on the interviews. I add the silvery shade of a lead pencil in order to have six distinct colors. These six signifiers were meant to distinguish between the different themes that came up during the interviews with the Midrasha women. This should not be taken to mean that the ethnographic material had demands of its own, requiring precisely six colors for precisely six thematic axes. Clearly, no classification is given, automatic, or self-generating.

Thematic reading, the search for subject axes in the transcripts of interviews, is much like scanning anthropological field journals in search of repeating patterns of behavior. The most significant difference between the two genres is quantity. My interviews provided me with many—a total of forty—parallel and different stories, all built around one leading question.

Anthropologists conduct interviews of all types: open and structured, initiated and fortuitous, voluntary and imposed. They weave the interviews into their writing in a variety of ways, and in doing so they position the speakers and the listeners, and establish the validity of what they say and the impression their words make. In the classical method, the words of the interviewees are subsumed within the information gathered by the anthropologist and presented as part of the anthropologist's knowledge about the subjects. The words of the interviewees are taken to be facts in the form of testimony from local spokesmen. Some of these informants receive biographical presence within the text and become real characters, while others are left out. In recent years, however, there has been increasing awareness of issues of power and representation between researcher and subject. This has led to an increasing tendency to retain the spokespersons' own voices—to preserve a complete narrative, and give readers coherent testimonies that are not sliced up and packaged according to the anthropologist's interests. This does not mean that the problems of power and representation have been solved or that there is now some sort of balance between the voices that was previously missing. What it does mean is that there is a conscious and tenacious effort to minimize an inevitable problem. The primary way this is done is by saturating the text with multiple oral sources, one after the other. This sabotages any inclination to let only one voice be heard, and it invites reflexive writing.[1]

My attempt to preserve the voices of the interview subjects is manifested in two ways in this chapter. First I present the full text of some of the interviews, thus allowing the reader to hear the unfiltered voices of the speakers. The reader is already acquainted, from the previous chapter, with a number of the speakers, and with the time, place, and context they chose to describe. In general, they tell their stories along a chronological line, in response to the question "Please tell me your literacy biography." Thereafter I will present selections from other interviews organized by theme—the themes being the issues raised by a large number of the women. That these issues were articulated by many of the women indicates their pervasiveness in the lives of the interview subjects, yet they were expressed in many different ways.

In my reading of the transcripts of the interviews I found six issues that form thematic axes in the literacy biographies these young women were asked to describe:

1. The chronological-historical axis, which follows the series of educational institutions in which the women were educated.
2. The social-civil-national axis, along which lie the speakers' attitudes toward their position in Israeli society.
3. The gender axis, which revolves around their status within the religious Zionist community as girls, adolescents, and women.
4. The axis of study as a value in and of itself.
5. The axis of study as practice.
6. The reflexive axis, which brings together thoughts, reflections, and criticism of the other five axes.

In presenting the material, I have followed two axes: the chronological-historical axis and a literacy axis. The other axes listed above are woven into these two, so as not to lose sight of the whole.

So Then: The Chronological-Historical Axis

"My name is Moria. I come from Jerusalem. I studied at Horev through twelfth grade. I did National Service for two years in Kiryat Shmonah, and now I'm studying psychology and Jewish history."

"Okay, I was born in Haifa, and I grew up there. I went to a religious high school for girls. I didn't think of going to an *ulpana* because of the approach at home. I did a year's National Service in a hospital in Petach Tikva, and now I'm studying computers and biology."

"I grew up in Dimona and studied at the local religious high school, which is coed. I did a year's National Service and came here to study English and oral law."

"My name is Naomi. I was born in the United States, and I immigrated to Israel at the age of six. I studied at the Noam girl's school in Jerusalem and afterward at Horev. I served for a year in a hospital in National Service, and afterward I combined studies and National Service at Midreshet Nishmat for another year. I'm studying Bible and mathematics."

"I was born in Lebanon, and I immigrated to Israel in 1976. I ended up in Netanya and wasn't in very religious surroundings. The high school was coed, and most of my friends weren't religious. Afterward I did National Service in an old-age home, and now I'm here. That's the basic framework before we go into details."

"I'll tell you a little about my background. I was born in Ramat Gan and studied in a regular state-religious school and afterward at an *ulpanit* in Tel Aviv. I served in a development town in the center of the country, and afterward I came here to study economics and education."

These lines are taken from the first sentences that the women spoke after the tape recorder spindles began to turn. Since they were asked about their biographies as learners, they rattled off the chain of educational institutions they had attended, one after another, mentioning, without exception, their National Service as an inseparable link in that chain. Most likely they did this because National Service parallels military service, which is one of the stages in the adolescence of most young Israeli Jews — part of the classic sequence of elementary school, high school, army, and university. National

Service is doubly relevant to these women's literacy because in many cases it included study and teaching. The variations in this sequence came at three points—high school versus *ulpana*, one year of National Service versus two, and Bar-Ilan versus another postsecondary institution. These junctures of decision are important loci for understanding the fine differences between the women. They themselves point to these as significant distinguishing factors in their biographies, positioning themselves and others within the religious Zionist community.

HIGH SCHOOL VERSUS *ULPANA*

"I never even thought of going to an *ulpana*. I wanted a regular coed high school, but my parents forced me to go to an *ulpanit*, which is at least not a boarding school. That's how it began. I'm the oldest daughter. They pressured me, wanted me to show the right direction at home."

"I went to the municipal high school, Zeitlin, in Tel Aviv. I didn't want a boarding school, and there weren't many options. I can't say that there was a high level of religious observance there or anything—there wasn't—but it didn't bother me so much at the time."

"From first grade through the end of high school—Horev, you know, that was clear. My mother went there, and her sisters went there, and we went there. My brothers also. There wasn't even any discussion, even then we were already living in a settlement and I had to commute to Jerusalem."

"I studied at a coed religious high school in our town. I didn't consider going to an *ulpana* even though there were girls who went, because they thought the level in our school was not so great. I thought to myself, they bring in young people from outside to us in order to raise the religious and social level, and the good kids from the town run away elsewhere? I decided that I was staying. And it was good."

"I went to a coed religious high school in Holon. The teachers there just wanted us to pass the graduation examinations. Stuff like belief and all that wasn't exactly a top priority for them, and for me, the truth is, at that age I didn't miss it."

"I went to a religious high school in Haifa because I wasn't accepted by an *ulpana*. I don't know, there was a whole group from Neve Sha'anan [a Haifa neighborhood] that they didn't accept."

"Okay. At the age of twelve, when it was necessary to decide what to do next, they didn't ask me. They decided that I should go to the Amana Ulpana in Kfar Saba, like my cousin."

"I went to *ulpana* because that was the best choice. The boys left for yeshivot. The high school wasn't so great. In the class before me they didn't go, and in my class almost everyone went to the *ulpana*. Even though for me it was nearby, in the family (because my sister went there) I had apprehensions. I didn't want to leave, and right at that time they were talking a lot about the *ulpanit*, which isn't a boarding school, but I went and I'm not sorry. It's not that I don't have any criticism, but it was an exceptional period."

The history of girls' *ulpanot* and their social significance will not be surveyed and discussed in this chapter.[2] Nevertheless, it is important to make clear how women place their memory of high school within their literacy continuum, and how they locate the decision between high school and *ulpana* in their history as religious students. This matter will be presented at length on the literacy axis. But two things should be noted here: High school is generally perceived as a period in which there is still no great and sincere interest in Jewish religious studies, and the decision about what institution to attend during this period is determined by a broad range of factors.

The decision to attend an intensive educational institution such as an *ulpana* is an ideological one, but it is not merely ideological. There are homes in which it is considered unacceptable a priori for women to go to a boarding school, and others in which the girl herself fears being away from home. There are girls who cited "fashions and social trends," in which their decision to attend a particular school was dictated by what other girls did. In many cases going to an *ulpana* was the only way of avoiding what was considered a mediocre public school. *Ulpanot* are not open to all comers, and this selectivity produces student bodies with a fairly homogeneous level of religious observance, academic ability, economic status, and generally also of ethnic origin. In general, an *ulpana* in a woman's biography is a mark of strict religious observance. It indicates a conservative family and guarantees that the woman received an uncompromising Zionist-nationalist education. However, as can be learned from the interview subjects, and as will also be shown below, the stereotypical trait of the "*ulpanist*" is the lack of a critical faculty.

ONE YEAR OF NATIONAL SERVICE VERSUS TWO

When Ora and I first read through the transcripts of the interviews she and I had conducted, I noticed that she had made a point of asking each woman how long she had spent in National Service. Ora also, at times, asked whether her interlocutor had made a choice between National Service and enlistment in the army. The answers she received showed that this was indeed a central and distinguishing feature of their lives. I had known that many girls serve only a year in National Service while others served two years, equating their term of service with that of the military service required of nonreligious women. But I had not been aware that the decision to serve two years was a statement of principle. I began to explore this point as well.

"I served for two years in National Service in a midrasha in Kastina. It was clear to me that I would do two years."

"To this day I regret it. I wanted to do a second year, and my parents opposed it. It was hard for me, but I did it out of respect for my parents. I don't think there has to be some sacred value of doing a second year, nor a value of not doing a second year. You have to judge it according to the circumstances, and for me it wasn't right [to do only one year]. Things I saw didn't have and still have no continuation, and they are even going backward. I worked hard. I began to see something, and . . . it was over."

"I knew that I wanted a development town, I knew only for a year, and that's the way it was. Afterward I debated whether to go to Midreshet Bruria for a year. I didn't go, but the truth is I'm not sure why; it's not really clear to me why. Perhaps because there is a kind of view that it's for girls who don't know what they're going to do in life—sort of another year that doesn't put you face to face with life's decisions. Like I said I really wanted to go for a year to study Gemara, but my parents didn't want me to. When it comes down to it you've got to plan out your life in an efficient way and not waste time, especially if you're planning to have a family in the future. Another thing that was connected to that debate was that if you look at the girls who study there, they get into a kind of . . . they're kind of strange. There's a kind of flight from reality, you know—a kind of loss of contact with reality. As if they're in a kind of permanent group dynamic. They're strange. Not that I have anything against strange people, but it was scary."

"I didn't even think of going to the army. Beyond that, at the *ulpana* they were very much against it and spoke to us about it."

"The truth is that I didn't debate between the army and National Service. Maybe today, now that I'm older, I would decide differently, but then it was clear—National Service, for one year."

"It was clear to me that I would go into the army, and that I wanted to be with a religious crowd. So we set up the religious Nachal group and that was it."

"I wanted to do a second year, but I couldn't be in that hospital any more, I was simply drained. Then it turned out that I could work with newly religious women from the United States who came to study at Nishmat. So it worked out that I was able to do a second year of National Service and also study and be at Nishmat, which is an experience from a different world."

Only one of the forty women I interviewed had enlisted in the army. The message given by the high schools in the cities and in most of the *ulpanot* seems to be that girls should not go to the army, and should instead do one or two years of National Service. The abbreviation of the service period to one year shows the inclination to push the girls to abbreviate their adolescent and single woman period. This same tendency was evident when some of the women debated whether to spend a year studying at a midrasha before going to college. Such a year is seen to be one of marking time, a movement alongside the legitimate cycle (although not outside it or against it), suspending for a time a series of important life decisions and putting off opportunities for marriage. A few women remarked that participating in Torah study was a kind of dream. The words they used were "I really wanted to," "an experience from another world," or, as Adina said, "a year of a journey to yourself and to your culture." Nevertheless, at the time the interviews were held, the women learners still suffered from an image of being "strange."[3] Part of this is connected to stepping out of the de rigeur sequence leading to marriage and children—by the age of twenty-five at the latest. Another part of this image is tied up with the connection between gender and Torah study, which will be addressed further on.

Not one of the interviewed women mentioned the "big trip" that is so much part of the biography of other young Israelis: a lengthy backpacking trip, generally to out-of-the-way areas such as the Far East. (However, some of the boys in the religious Zionist community, young married couples, and a small minority of women do observe this precept.) Nor did any of them talk about some other kind of break between National Service and their studies—indeed, quite the contrary. Their chronological stories were sewn up with strong, close stitches that created a predictable, almost mandatory fabric that left very little space for doubts. The way in which the speakers read their paths in retrospect combined their gender affiliation and their national duty. A second year of National Service could, in their opinion, have led to better achievements in the fields of immigrant absorption, education, and love of Israel, a more profound acquaintance with religion and Jewish tradition, and so on. But a second year would have put off the beginning of their postsecondary studies, and would have delayed marriage and the establishment of a family. The speakers expressed regret, sometimes even anger, at not having been given the opportunity to do what they had been educated to do, what they had done with love and devotion, because at this juncture their gender affiliation and their respect for their parents were decisive and took precedence over their social-national duties and their personal desires.

BAR-ILAN UNIVERSITY VERSUS ANOTHER POSTSECONDARY INSTITUTION

"A framework like a university scared me, and I was afraid that, since I know myself, before long I would be hanging out only with nonreligious people. So I chose Midreshet Bayit Ve-Gan. But it was horrible, really horrible."

"The truth is that I also thought about religious college. I wasn't sure, but in the end I understood that the matter of a degree is no less important, and I came to Bar-Ilan. The truth is that I thought the atmosphere would be more secular than it is. I like to come here."

"I thought to myself, if a university, then only Bar-Ilan. I wanted a religious university and a religious atmosphere and a midrasha for Jewish studies. A little spirituality among all my real world subjects. At the religious college in Jerusalem, for example, they require you to take twenty hours of religious studies a week, and here I choose—my schedule is my free choice, and I like that."

"I came to Bar-Ilan because of the Women's Midrasha. Otherwise I would have gone to the Hebrew University to study psychology, because that would have been more convenient. I've been disappointed by the Midrasha, but in any case the atmosphere is religious here. It's a little too superficial, but still you feel at home."

"It was important for me to come to study at a place that was set up from the start to be a religious university, and where in practice religious and nonreligious people study together. Almost all types of religious people and almost all types of nonreligious people. The real goal is for the Jewish people to get to know you and for you to get to know the Jewish people, and this is the place that gives you the religious support. So I didn't think of going to the Hebrew University, where there isn't any Torah atmosphere. The very fact that most of the instructors here are religious, that there is the Midrasha that exposes you to all kinds of religiosity and opinions, that you study together with nonreligious students, all that made it the obvious choice."

The decision whether to study at Bar-Ilan University or at some other postsecondary institution is based on a broad range of factors. Still, it is clear that those who decided to study at Bar-Ilan made decisions in favor of an academic rather than a manifestly religious institution. To a certain extent the decision was to prefer an institution that is "less religious" in both its structure and its essence. Bar-Ilan offers almost the entire range of disciplines and is committed to the Western academic code. It accepts non-religious and non-Jewish students, and lectures are given to mixed classes of men and women by both male and female faculty members. On the opposite side, the choice of Bar-Ilan over another university was a kind of balancing act that mitigated this preference for an academic institution over a more traditional Jewish framework. The reasons the women gave for choosing Bar-Ilan range from an ideology that depicted Bar-Ilan as a site of intercultural encounter for the Jewish people as a whole, to a sense of privacy—a pleasant sense of feeling at home. The establishment of the women's Midrasha and the higher yeshiva for men within the campus, and their integration into the curriculum on a religious and gender basis, were additional incentives for those in doubt.

It can be said, then, that the women I spoke with moved along a fairly predictable chronological educational path that allowed them to feel themselves a part of the group of religious women who study at Bar-Ilan in general and at the Midrasha in particular. At this point, however, they launched into a process of fine but critical distinctions among themselves. The women noted these differences at the very first stages of their biographical narrative. Each one returned to and emphasized, throughout her interview, the elements that made her unique, at each juncture of her life and with varying intensity.

The three junctures so far identified—the choice of a secondary school, the length of National Service, and university studies—touch on the link between the speaker and public institutions. The selections above reveal that another institution, "the home," is the mediator of this link.[4] It is therefore necessary to consider the place of the home as a concept and idea among the speakers, to see how they perceive the homes from which they have come and the future homes they imagine for themselves. This latter "home" is the endpoint of the chronological axis on which they have moved before the interview, the extrapolation of their paths.

FROM HOME TO HOME

"In my house we debate about everything: current events, society, Torah. Everything comes up at the Shabbat table. Everyone prepares something for Shabbat and says it, and that already requires the others to respond, and then the discussion begins. The thing is that we think together and begin at a young age. At first I had nothing to lean on. My parents always directed me to aspire to have something to lean on, to formulate an opinion and to know what I actually think.

"At home they were strict about clothes, about separation of girls and boys, but in the youth movement it was different, and I had to justify myself to the group about why I went in to pray the afternoon prayers and didn't stay outside to chat. In the future I would like my home to be like my parent's home in terms of the Shabbat table where we talk about everything. But there are things that are linked to their character that of course won't be in my home. In any case the differences won't be matters of principle."

"My parents came out of a *haredi* framework in Jerusalem into a more Zionist framework, but they sent us to *haredi* schools, and that didn't fit. I didn't like Beit Ya'akov, and in the end I transferred to Horev. When I came home with my questions, my parents didn't really know what to do. They actually allowed me to ask everything, but my sisters thought that questions about the existence of God were real heresy.

"In my house, God willing, not only will I not interfere with asking questions, but—and this will be the difference between me and my parents—I will prod the children to ask questions. I hope that I will be able to do that: that I won't be a mother who gives answers to questions but rather one who asks the questions and only gives the tools for answering, supplies them with books, sends them to seminars (if that's in their character). Definitely, I hope that I have a family that will discuss and elucidate a lot of questions."

"Look, I didn't come from an Ashkenazi home, and for us the definition of what it is to be religious was different. That my mother didn't cover her hair didn't determine it. I only hope that I can achieve what my mother did. It's my dream to be a mother like she is, and she didn't receive any tools for that. If I'm religious today, even though I had one foot outside, a lot of it is thanks to her. When I get married, I'll cover my hair. By the way, my mother covers her hair now, too."

"Our house was religious but open. My mother, for example, doesn't cover her hair, and my oldest sister doesn't either. My second sister does cover her hair. I've been through a lot, and I've come a long way. I knew that I wanted to marry a boy who was more strictly observant than my father, but also open. Today my home is not like my parents' home. We study more, and in some things we are stricter. But everything I have comes from them, and I would not have taken this path without what they taught me — to think, to be open, and not to accept anything as given."

"My parents are from the United States, and my home is a religious Zionist one. I always thought I would marry someone nice, religious, who had gone to college. But after I got to know other families, I wanted a home of learners. A husband who is a religious scholar, for whom that's his way of life, and a wife who studies also. Today I've already seen homes different from the one I grew up in, different from the way most of my friends grew up, and it's another world — it's another kind of family. When I look around me, I see people who don't know what side to lean toward, either extremists or almost nonreligious, especially in the religious Zionist movement. I want a clear and not extremist direction."

"Look, in Haifa it's a bit different. My parents are religious but open-minded. My mother doesn't cover her hair, and they swim mixed with men and women together, and all that. My sister, who is married, doesn't cover her hair and wears pants at home. In the future I actually see myself covering my hair, but I would want a husband who knows how to accept things. Sometimes on hikes I wear pants, and sometimes my shirts have short sleeves. I want a religious and observant and intellectual person. It is important to me that he study and have a *havruta*, but it is a matter of principle for me that he work and not study at a *kolel*."

"At home there was an open-minded atmosphere. My father worked, and he had a *havruta* once a week. But for me, from about the middle of the *ulpana* — when I would go to elective classes in the evening and study — it was clear to me that I wanted to marry a yeshiva student. It's not that I have anything against home, or that I think that everyone who studies at a university is not right. That's what I wanted, and thanks to God I found what I was looking for."

In presenting their biographical stories, the women conducted a reading of their lives from back to front. This reading reveals a certain amount of re-flexivity; it is contemplative, develops in the process of talking, and includes criticism. The criticism is directed largely against the schools they studied in, the people responsible for the National Service program, and the youth movement, but also against their homes and parents. This criticism could become quite intense and reach the level of real anger. In general, such a climax would be followed by the speaker taking hold of herself, taking a certain distance, and assuming a measure of modesty. The speakers tried to find sincerity in the other party—the good will, the lack of evil intent. They did not retreat from their criticism, but there could be a sudden fear of violating the religious strictures against slander, against pride, and against disrespect for parents. Many times criticism of parents and the home was followed by a declaration of great appreciation for them and what they were able to do in their time and place. Very few of the women expressed sweeping criticism of their homes; their criticism addressed specific decisions made about their lives, or about the general character of the home. The process of the retreat from or minimization of the criticism was for all intents and purposes an effort to place the home within its historical and geographical context, in order to enable them to turn away from the home in their own time and place. The culture of open criticism, which can include alienation or an expression of negative emotions toward parents and the home (expected in Western culture, which has internalized the psychoanalytic discourse) cannot be found here—at least not in explicit form. This point is important beyond the difference between legitimate types of discourse in different cultural contexts. Its sociological meaning is its view of a generation of young women who are carrying out a fundamental change and who are sweeping along their parents' generation.

Their generation is not reproducing the way their parents lived; it is not conservative or apathetic—quite the opposite. *In all significant areas of life in the national religious community, these women are acting differently than their mothers did.* The burden of this revolutionary change is being placed on the sacred framework of the family. The students' criticism of the homes they grew up in does not impel them to distance themselves from "the home" as a problematic site, or from the institution of the family as a conservative framework. Instead, they place all their hopes for innovation and transformation in their adult homes.

The selections from the interviews quoted above point to a tendency to imagine a "more religious" home, a place in which more religious precepts are observed and more laws followed. Such homes are ideal models, imagined frameworks dreamed of by young women who have not yet married or by those who married not long ago. These frameworks of "home"[5] or family are complex sites that include within them the significant facets of the lives of these women. Ideology, religious practice, employment, gender perceptions, and the division of labor between husband and wife all collapse into this framework.[6] All the women's private emotional and romantic expectations, as well as their social and national affiliations, are directed to this site. Even if there is some similarity between this and other systems of expectations outside the religious Zionist community, the weight and totality of these expectations, which are surrounded by an aura of sanctity, characterize the community under study.

Squeezing and filtering the images of the future family leaves the following essence: "In the future I will be *more religious;* my future family will be *more knowledgeable and stricter* than my present family. To achieve this I want *my husband to study* always, in one way or another. I, too, will always continue *to study,* because one cannot live otherwise. *My home will not be like my parents' home,* even though they made me what I am."

The realization of the ideal of the future family, which holds the key to the realization of so many other important expectations, leads to study. The man studies and the woman studies. It would seem that it is clear to all the speakers that they cannot reach this destination without entering into a new experience of study. This study broadens the field of participation in Jewish existence and can thus turn it into a more literate and more religious society.

The teaching of Torah to women as a matter of principle and study as a matter of practice define the next axis I have used to organize the narratives of the interview subjects — the literacy axis.

THE LITERACY AXIS AS AN AXIS OF LIFE

The possibility of realizing the utopian "home" depicted above feeds into study — study that is participation. The connection between personal, family, and social aspirations is perceived as being dependent on Torah.

The Jewish study undertaken by these women thus becomes a tool, an applied science, but at the same time it is also existential and a way of life in and of itself. These young women described study as obvious and inevitable at primal and functional levels, but study is also something more complex, as will be explored below.

"I want it to be clear that I am not studying Torah as part of my academic expectations at the university. I have to study Torah, I simply have to. In order to believe in something I have to know things about that something, and, even more, I have to agree. Every human being with at least a mediocre level of intelligence wants to know that what he is doing in life are things he agrees with, agrees with in accordance with his understanding. So it comes out that you have to study."

"Look, a good part of my time I spend with nonreligious people, and it is hard for me, each time all over again, to enter into this closed-off world of ours, but I understand that there is something bigger than me. I haven't yet managed to find it, so I have to study, I have to do something positive with my life. I know, after all, what it is to have a good time. I know the quality of the enjoyment I feel after going out, and what I feel after I've understood something in my study—when something opens up to me in a class or, alternatively, when I do some sort of voluntary act, it's another kind of enjoyment. It stays with me, it accumulates, it doesn't pass."

"Torah study is quality study. As a religious person it has huge value for me. The whole matter of understanding what you do, the exposure to the world of understanding and identification. Do you understand?"
"I study because I need it, because it's important, because I want to, because it advances me."
"I was of the mind that if I believed in what I was doing, and if I believed in the general direction, then the laws and the little daily things and the ickiness and the yucky strictness would come to me naturally, that I would flow with it. . . . So I went and studied. . . . Unfortunately, it didn't help, and today I'm for all practical purposes outside."

"When I got to know a religious friend who was open, who didn't stigmatize, who didn't spend all day making diagnoses, that gave me a desire to study. I wanted to develop myself, to know more. I studied slowly. I began Gemara, little by little."
"Look, now, after my studies at Nishmat, when I know what it is to study Torah, to open Gemara, only now do I comprehend how profound it is. How vital it is and how important it is. It changed my whole way of looking at the world—my expectations from a wedding, my role in life, everything. Everything comes from study."
"I don't come to the Midrasha in order to have a clean conscience. I feel a thirst to study. I don't want to be pompous and talk about thirst for God's word, but I feel a kind of feeling that I need it for myself, that it's a real lack.

I go to the library, and I read and read, and every Shabbat I sit down with books. A day like that with books is a year of Midrasha for me."

"The reward for Torah study for boys is higher because they are commanded to study. We don't need to be subject to divine bookkeeping. We need to delve into Torah as women, so that our generation will be a generation of Torah, a generation of faith that can educate the Jewish people to Torah and the commandments."

These voices depict the literacy sphere as an axis of life, a multifaceted source of vitality that enables them to be what they are, to imagine their future, and to change themselves. Study is perceived as both the primary requirement and the last refuge of being a religious woman at the end of the twentieth century. Irit, whom we heard in the previous chapter, sought out Torah study in order to find a general principle that would help her to face the little duties that repelled her—and she failed; today she is no longer religious. Shirli turned to study in order to anchor the new and liberal religiosity that she developed for herself during her military service. Michal decided to load herself down with more studies because she likes it and because it seems to her illogical to do something without knowing it. Ayelet set herself a broad and ambitious mission that combined means and end. For us to have a Torah generation, we must study Torah, she said.

The rational claims of the type "a person needs to know what he is doing" sound so simple. Sometimes it seems that by and large the discourse explaining these young women's increasing involvement in religious studies is a rational, pragmatic, and functional discourse. In other words, the greater part of the description of the reason for studies is in line with secular rhetoric—it is logical and utilitarian. The expectation that there will be spiritual, historical, or theoretical arguments is again revealed as the assumption of a listener who is outside the culture of the speakers. These are phrased—within the "regular" speech that deals with religion and faith, the observance of precepts, and national affiliation—as if they were an accounting problem. As they continue to speak, a complexity is revealed that does not present the above logic as false but rather as very much incomplete. Study indeed has a role to play, yet this conclusion, like all functional conclusions, is partial and circular.

It would seem that the most efficient way of understanding the meaning of study lies in the narratives and among them. Crossing the literacy axis with the biographical axis indicates a turning point in the history of each of the speakers, a moment in which their attitude toward Jewish religious studies changed. Exploring this point indicates more interesting reasons for the growing interest in Torah study.

THE TURNING POINT: "I SUDDENLY UNDERSTOOD WHAT IT IS TO STUDY"

Without exception, all the women interviewed described a literacy continuum in which they had been familiar with Jewish religious studies of a certain type—until they encountered Jewish religious studies of another type. At times this first acquaintance was disappointing; sometimes it was characterized by apathy with regard to sacred studies; and in a very few cases the women's literacy memories registered an encounter that was intriguing, exciting, and stimulating. Whatever the case, each of them pointed clearly to a specific event when she experienced a different encounter with "the Torah." Not a single one of the speakers experienced that moment of change and revelation within the formal system. There were no such moments in school or at home. The important encounter took place in satellite frameworks, such as youth movements, school seminars, voluntary study groups, National Service, or studies at the new midrashot. A small number of the interview subjects located the literacy change as part of a new relationship with a boyfriend or husband, conflating the romanticism of studying Torah with their partner and a desire to close the knowledge gap.

The following quotes begin with experiences in extra-curricular frameworks during the girl's school years and in their youth movements, through National Service and study in the new midrashot, and culminate with the picture of a young couple sitting shoulder to shoulder, bent over the large pages of the Talmud.

"I remember a notebook, one of those thin ones they used to have. A twelve-page notebook. That notebook was my oral law notebook in eleventh grade. A year later I erased the '11' and replaced it with a '12' because there was still a lot of space left in that thin notebook. Now maybe you can understand how they taught us oral law in high school. The first time I understood that you could study in another way was in a seminar we had during summer vacation. Four very intensive days. We studied from morning until evening with a lunch break; we were a group of about twenty girls, and we didn't want to go to sleep. I remember a sense of wholeness, a real sense of wholeness. When I came back from that seminar I understood that was the general direction, and that I would not compromise on it."

"The *ulpana* in Kfar Pines had, in the evening, optional extra study classes in Gemara, prayer, Rabbi Kook, and all sorts of things. I began there, because up until then I hadn't taken any great interest, and when I began to take an interest I had nowhere to turn. We would sit, a few of us girls, and study. Then, when I was so young, that gave me something—in the sense that I knew that was my direction, that was what I wanted to study. It built within me the view that I wanted a home with Torah, and a husband who sat and studied."

"The *havruta* lessons [at Horev High School] . . . developed into informal lessons where we had to choose what and how to study. . . . Most of the girls turned it into free time . . . , they . . . chattered, sat and talked, and passed the time. As far as I can remember, my *havruta* held up the longest. . . . I personally really enjoyed it."

"Who took any interest then in sacred studies? We would tell the teachers that in order to annoy them, to get them angry. Why no Gemara, why no Gemara? But really we didn't care that much. Until between eleventh and twelfth grades I went to a seminar that for me was a very important event. The subject was 'from exile to redemption,' but the content was not what was important. Instead it was the discovery, the sense that you'd found it—that you're where you wanted to be, in a place where they study Torah seriously, where there's a sense that it's real, you know, that this is where it all comes from. Maybe it had something to do with the doubts I had previously, because my view wasn't 'see it and sanctify it,' but there I understood that you can be a good Jew, whole in your outlook, in my own way, too, and for me that was a discovery."

"[I]n lectures [on Judaism at school] we would . . . fall asleep and daydream. We didn't listen. That's the way it is. In Bnei Akiva it was a little different. There we found ourselves a boy to teach us Gemara, an older boy, a former counselor. In that there was, of course, something of the forbidden fruit. . . . I have to say that the forbidden fruit tasted very good."

"In National Service I had to teach, and for that I had to study. The truth is that I was in despair. Here I had finished high school and now there was more school. But the way they taught us at the training seminar, that experience of real study, dialogue, the independent study, and also the teachers there—then I understood what it was to study."

"In my second year of National Service I worked at Nishmat, and there I understood what it was to study Torah. The way they did it, the method, the serious observance and the heart came together into something enormous.

There I understood a lot of things about myself and about what I want for myself."

"The first time we went out alone we went to the Bible Lands Museum in Jerusalem. He knew so much about the Bible, about research, about biblical criticism, that I was attracted to him like a magnet. . . . We would study for hours; you know, for a long time; lovers have no time constraints, they can devote a lot of time to it."

The book *Women's Ways of Knowing* depicts several scenes taken from the literacy memory of its interview subjects.[7] They each speak about a learning experience etched in their memories. For some of them this experience became a source of strength in other study tasks, and for others it was an alienating and insulting memory that repelled them from study. Either way, the speakers place the teacher at the center of the experience. The teachers are presented as mediators between "knowledge" and the student. On the one hand, they are able to alienate and repress the learner, to make her see herself as stupid, without any chance of "knowing"; on the other, they can integrate knowledge and student, an act that brings with it empowerment.

The difference between an experience that distances and one that attracts can be extracted from the broad collection of examples presented in the book and contains two elements. One is based on the gender affiliation of student and teacher; the second is based on ways of teaching and learning. In practice, the authors of the book seek to join these two elements together and portray the difference between "good" and "bad" teaching as resulting from the encounter between gender and knowledge. This connection robs knowledge of its status as objective, universal, and true, and turns the knowers from objects into gendered subjects who possess race, class, and biographies.

Criticism of *Women's Ways of Knowing* focused largely on its substantive claims about the way in which women transmit and receive knowledge, on the overwhelming weight attributed to gender over other social categories in learning processes and the creation of knowledge. There can be no doubt that the fact that the speakers in the book are women is a central factor in decoding the learning experience they report. In the present study, the fact that the speakers are women is of even greater importance. Their entire pasts as learners were conditioned by their gender affiliation. This past included curricula designed for them, the way the knowledge was conveyed to them, and many other elements that have appeared in this work. My claim, however, is that gender affiliation should be decoded in its communal-cultural context—common perhaps to all, but a phenomenon whose countenance changes from community to community.

It seems that the key to explaining the change reported by the speakers in this study is the change in the extent of *participation*—that is, the transition from comprehending sacred studies as policing and restricting to a view of them as allowing more activity within the community of observers/believers. In the religious community of observers/believers the separation between knowledge in context and knowledge detached from context is problematic. Knowledge always involves doing something, observing precepts, and faith. Doing things is part of the daily, ongoing cultural context and cannot, in any case, be detached or without relevance. Lave and Wenger claim that "'decontextualized learning activity' is a contradiction in terms" (1991, p. 6).[8] The transition from context-dependent knowledge to abstract knowledge is a back-and-forth process. Formal knowledge of the world, Lave and Wenger maintain, involves broadening participation and activity in this world. This participation (all of which is embedded in being, and therefore contextual) facilitates the claim of possession of independent knowledge. Such knowledge is thus tied to action—in a hierarchy of doers and of power relations.

The memories we recorded above describe a historical moment in which these women's attitudes toward study changed. In rereading their accounts, we discerned elements of gender encountering knowledge, learners facing teachers, alienation ranged against connection. It seems, however, that the scenes contained within these descriptions offer more than these dichotomies. They can illuminate an additional corner of the link between knowledge, power, and social context in the direction that Lave and Wenger indicate. Not a single speaker cited a specific teacher as the cause of the change within her. None took the trouble to note what material they were studying when the change happened, or, if they did so, they dismissed its substantive importance. The voices did not say that the change involved breaking through the narrow bounds of their literacy. Most of the speakers had encountered, over the course of their literacy history, a broad selection of texts, and different types of teaching, decoding, analysis, and orientation. They had been exposed to different educational genres and had heard many voices. Their schools, together with youth movements, seminars, National Service, and their homes created a fairly heterogeneous literacy mosaic.

Nevertheless, even though they noted the different voices they had heard, most were able to unify, in an indiscriminate way, the general character of the voices they had encountered before the change they underwent. All these voices were presented as a single unit, in contrast with subsequent study. Up to a given point, and hand in hand with their chronological age, adolescence, and so on, sacred studies were perceived as part of an educational system, used to justify laws and regulations after the fact. The speakers testified that they had not taken any special interest in these studies both because of the way they were presented and because of their obvious connection to the processes of justifying the religious way of life. Up to a certain stage in their lives this way was not perceived as problematic, and it was hard for them to understand why it was necessary to try so hard to justify it. From the moment that their future path as religious women, and the laws and practices involved in this path, began to interest them, they discovered that their sacred studies did not involve such dilemmas but were instead transparent tools of policing, a pedagogy labeled, by both the women and the teachers at the Midrasha, "*ulpanist* education."[9]

Whether or not they actually studied in an *ulpana*, "*ulpanist* education," as a concept and a symbol, sums up what sacred studies were for the women up to a certain point. The studies were meant to dress up an isolating, limiting, or partial experience in the guise of religious truth. Even without getting into the material in depth, the young girls were able, apparently, to sense that their religious studies were clouding their field of vision and hiding the full extent of Jewish life. As girls, and as religious girls, they simply turned their backs on these studies—they acted up, talked in class, made provocative remarks, did not really study, and did not internalize. The material passed by them as it was supposed to. They went over it and were tested on it, but the place of the texts as a central corpus of knowledge in their lives as religious people was absent. At a specific point in the history of each one of them a new encounter was created between the world of knowledge and their individual existence, and at this point it turned out that the world of Jewish knowledge could be an energetic source of enablement and empowerment that would enhance the space of their participation in Jewish practice.

The learning woman does not locate the turning point in the material or in the bond created between her and the material. What changes is her perception of her ability to participate. In other words, the attitude toward study changes only when it is decoded and experienced as an opening for broadening her participation in Jewish life, instead of, as before, as something that justifies restrictions on her participation. Study, Lave and Wenger argue, exists only as the ability to participate.

The structure of the story of the "moment of change" recurs among the majority of the interview subjects. It begins with a description of how sacred studies lacked relevance. Sacred studies are described as not being study at all. The best articulation of this came from Miri, who noted that everything she had learned in two years of high school oral law classes fit into a twelve-page notebook, with room to spare. Others emphasized their unwillingness to accept their genuine lack of interest in Jewish studies up until the other experience. The words they chose to describe that experience are a string of superlatives: the experience was true, a source, perfection, a discovery, a direction. When these terms are connected to the place and time of the event, they produce romantic images of the term "study" — sleepless nights; an intimate group that studies together, debates, and grows closer; youth movement kids seated around a charismatic counselor; a girl studying and dreaming about her future spouse, or two lovers studying together. The special age at which the change took place, and the way in which it was experienced, do not detract from the real potential revealed to the studying women. Underneath the superlatives and romance they seem to have discovered a realm of possibilities that caused them to depict their religious futures as tied to the practice of study. Tali said, "I understood what there is for me there, and I haven't stopped since." Yael said, "This is my direction and I will not compromise it." Naomi said, "I understood many things about myself and about what I wanted for myself." And Shlomit expressed it in this way: "I understood that I could be a good Jew and coherent in my thinking in my own way, and for me that was a revelation."

Obviously, then, they discovered something that made what came next more fluid, possible in a variety of ways or in a specific way. Most importantly, a site of action and participation was opened. A kind of cycle of study was created that enabled participating action, which in turn led to further study. This cycle, which may well be a male Jewish convention, is a new thrill for women, one that encompasses their entire experience, in its social, national, gender, and religious facets.

The connection between participation and study is made in a later work by Lave.[10] In the introduction to a book she coedited on the wide-ranging practical aptitudes of apprenticeship, she told of a preliminary meeting conducted by the writers in order to discuss the book's general contour. The subjects proposed touched primarily on the social and learning context. The prominence of social context surprised no one, she related, but everyone was surprised that study had garnered so much attention, when the research issue at hand was in fact practice.

It would seem that the sequence of intellectual interests is reversed here. The authors in Lave's book were interested in the training of apprentices and their active participation and found themselves addressing study. This ethnography began with the act of study—from the studying women and the search for the motives for their study—and found itself explaining study in terms of participation and practice.

The transition from study to participation can be learned about from the way in which the speakers described their way to knowing. The following sections describe and analyze the struggle for the dream of learning.

THE STRUGGLE FOR THE DREAM

"I EXPECTED THAT THE MIDRASHA WOULD GIVE ME ENTRY TO DEEPER STUDIES"

Identification of Jewish study as an indispensable form of practice pushed many of the speakers to choose Bar-Ilan University. There, they supposed, they would be able to create a meaningful link between academic and Jewish studies, a link between what interested them professionally and/or intellectually with study that would allow a broadening of their participation in the community of observers/believers. The Midrasha became a home on campus, as I described it at the beginning of this book, a place where women come to pass the time between classes, whether or not they are enrolled in the Midrasha program.

The warm language the speakers used to describe the Midrasha as a "site" changed entirely when they discussed it as a place that should be satisfying their expectations of their studies. In that guise they judged it by the quality of the teaching, the teaching ability and charisma of the faculty, as well as its curriculum, pedagogy, and ideology. The criticism heard in the interviews demonstrates the great importance the speakers ascribe to their studies there and the inherent difficulties in realizing their expectations.

The speakers came to the Midrasha by almost absolutely free choice. The amount of the scholarship they receive is not high, and to get it they must put in a greater amount of time than would be demanded of them if they fulfilled their Jewish studies distribution requirement outside the Midrasha framework. They were interested in making an intellectual and emotional effort in order to advance along the path they had chosen for themselves. After years of non-empowering experience, and after turning their backs on sacred studies or checking its limits in a demonstrative way, they felt that the time had come to study seriously.

"I came to the Midrasha and was very, very disappointed. The classes, everything was like that it's obvious that there's Torah, it's obvious that there's God, everything is clear already. A horrible brainwashing. I hated it. During all of last year I would say 'yes' and leave. I was really turned off by that method of teaching—so orthodox, so religious. After I had studied with my husband in such a fun way, with such openness, I couldn't take it.

"This year I went to Rabbi Cohen and told him 'Either I can go to whatever class I want or I won't come any more.' So, that's it, all my courses are marked as being for 'graduates'—as if after they give them a brainwashing for a few years they can study interesting stuff. This year my classes really are better. There are those that I still suffer in—that are really like *ulpana*, retrogressive—but in general it's much better."

"The fact that the basic [university] courses in Judaism are together with nonreligious people is not bad, but you need to take that fact into account and express yourself in a different way, because there are people who aren't religious. Here I feel at home, the girls are from the same background as I am, on the same wavelength. I come here from biology, and it's an escape for me. Two hours a day of another place. I looked forward to these studies and in general I'm pleased, some more and some less, that's the way things are, but for me it's new and different and fulfilling."

"I expected the Midrasha to provide me with an opening to deeper study, and that didn't happen. I'm very, very disappointed with the Midrasha. During the first year I kept my mouth shut, but in the second year I went in to Rabbi Cohen and told him: 'I don't know what I'm doing here. I don't enjoy it, and I don't have anything to learn. I feel that the teachers are just boring me and leading me on. I'm studying like it was in high school and that's not what I'm after.' He took it very hard and seriously, and it seems to me that the program for the graduates is the result of pressure from me and from other girls."

"Here, as far as I'm concerned, it's back to the high school seminars. It's not on a high level. I hate every moment of it here. If this is all that the Midrasha is about, I'm sorry I didn't go to the Hebrew University, I would have saved myself the commute."

"Look, you can talk about this course or that course—there will always be differences. In general I really enjoy the studies at the Midrasha. If you manage to make yourself a good schedule, there's a good chance of enjoying it. There are some really excellent teachers here, and I was introduced to a new approach here—to thinking that I hadn't known before."

"Two things have to happen for me to come out of a class with a 'wow.' Either the things said there have to sound intelligent to me, or I have to be enthusiastic about the person, the teacher. Of course, both of them can happen. But most of the courses are banal. The ideas repeat themselves; they don't assail new issues; there is nothing new. I think that the main thing in Judaism is innovation. There's no exhilaration, there's no excitement. In my opinion, it does more harm than good. I expected the studies to be more serious, or maybe I didn't know what to expect from Jewish religious studies in the university. It could be that my expectations were wrong."

Discontent with the Midrasha was common to almost all the students. Even those who were generally pleased with their studies did not talk about the Midrasha in an overwhelmingly positive way. Still, those who were dissatisfied nevertheless reported having had some very good classes, and they stressed the importance they attached to the Midrasha framework. The administrators and faculty of the Midrasha, as well as the Bar-Ilan administration, are aware of this discontent and have taken various steps to improve the situation and provide more challenging programs, as reported in part I.

It is easy to say that women's high expectations of the Midrasha, and the importance of religious study for the community of believers/observers, made it almost inevitable that the project would find itself foundering before it was launched. Instead of the life preserver they sought, the women found courses that dragged them back into unpleasant experiences from the past. Yet their disappointment, born of their seriousness and their expectation of change, requires a more detailed explanation, particularly of its nature. We need to understand *what* it is these young women want to study, *how* they want to study it, and *for what purpose*. Acquaintance with these three primary elements of what, how, and why can make this "study"—and its gender, social, national and religious context—more intelligible.

WHAT TO STUDY: "I'M MORE DRAWN
TO PHILOSOPHY, ETHICS, AND BIBLE"

Many of the women who study at the Midrasha had their first encounter with the Gemara there. After voicing in the interviews their desire, even longing, to study what had deliberately not been taught to them, one might expect that each of them would try to include a class in Gemara in their schedules. The way in which they can study Gemara has changed over the years of the Midrasha's existence—from a situation in which there were almost no classes that addressed Talmudic material as a subject in and of itself, through classes in Jewish law that divided the Talmud according to specific subjects, to the establishment of the *beit midrash* program, in which about sixty women study Gemara *al ha-seder*.[11]

The encounter with Talmudic material is not simple, and, as will emerge from what the women have to say below about "how to study," it is clear to them that this is a language they do not know. The Midrasha offers them a specific and heterogeneous encounter with religious studies, according to the patriarchal canon—that is, the study of Gemara. Some of them have studied and are studying Gemara in other places, some of them are studying it in the Midrasha. But many women do not take Talmud at all. The voices describing "what I actually want and like to study" raise several central questions regarding the link between gender, content, and study.

"It's really strange, because I am drawn just the same to Gemara and Jewish philosophy. I'm now taking three courses in philosophy and two in Gemara, and I think that the aptitudes and my best work for the moment are in Gemara. It's the kind of thing that if you get what it's about, if you have enough intelligence, and if you can follow the logic of the argument (and those skills you can, of course, improve and develop), then you succeed."

"I don't know, I'm one of those that all those areas of philosophy don't much interest me— the opposite. I'm drawn to Gemara, which is more real, and it's something I never studied. I ran into it at the Midrasha for the first time. It's interesting, and I enjoy it."

"I always had a powerful love for the Bible, to the point, as I told you, that I went to the Bible Quiz. Whenever I had time I would sit and study; it's part of me and an asset for my whole life. Today, too, Bible is first, but since then I've learned to approach other things as well, and I try not to neglect them."

"The first semester that I was here, of course, I took a course in Gemara. You know, all these years I so much wanted that, and here I really saw the Gemara for the first time and . . . I didn't really like it much. I mean, the Gemara didn't attract me. All the preoccupation with small details made me lose my patience. I couldn't see what was so great about it. It turns out that I'm more into philosophy."

"When I studied Gemara for the first time it opened my eyes, but it was hard. I got a headache. Philosophy is also hard, but not like that. I still like philosophy better; it's more relevant to me, close to me, it says something to me."

"If I had begun at the age of five or six like my brothers then maybe, maybe I would like it, but today it doesn't speak to me, I admit it. I tried it, and I didn't succeed. The Gemara classes I took here seemed exasperating."

"I don't know, maybe something in me is plugged up already, but I like the principle, the generality, the thought; all the preoccupation with 'this way and that way' don't seem so simple to me. I once had a class in Gemara when I was in National Service, and that was very interesting—maybe because we studied on our own. Here it's nothing special."

The two initial voices in this collection speak of a positive experience with Gemara study. Yael, who has a penchant for "real" and precise study, enjoys Gemara. After many years in which her study of Judaism was subject to a specific type of thinking and interpretation, a new world appeared to her, a different way of experiencing sacred studies. She testified that she did not like "philosophy"—a term that in Hebrew carries a connotation that goes beyond the discipline of philosophy and expresses her discomfort with hair-splitting and disputation. For Yael the study of Gemara is an intellectual and religious possibility that was kept from her because of her gender. Jewish studies were for her, until now, doublespeak, a not very interesting experience—certainly not one that brought her closer to these studies, but this changed when she was able to study Gemara.

Zehava expressed equal interest in two fields. In fact, she was surprised at herself and at being torn between her love for Gemara and her love for philosophy. For some reason, they seemed to her to be diametrically opposed. When she evaluated the situation out loud in the presence of the interviewer, she found that for the present she was developing more aptitude and having more success with Gemara study. Before what most likely was the astonished

face of Ora (who interviewed her), she went on to say that she could improve
the abilities that lead to her success—in other words, all was not lost.

Zehava's need to explain her success derived from the feelings of difficulty, failure and lack of interest in Gemara that were ultimately expressed
by most of the other speakers. A collation of the substantive preferences
of the interview subjects indicates that they remain within the accepted
boundaries: Bible, ethics, and Jewish philosophy. The women generally did
not reject the new materials, but they rather positively cited the subjects
they liked. They pinpointed their interests as a product of their personalities rather than as something inherent in the material itself. Tali said of the
Bible, "it's part of me." Nava testified that she was drawn to the study of
philosophy, as did Adina: "I like it, it's relevant to me." Michal remarked
that Gemara did not speak to her, and Shlomit thought "maybe something
in me is plugged up." They sought to leave the discussion in the private
realm rather than attribute general significance to their preferences. Efrat,
who tended to express herself in a more critical way—as well as Michal and
Shlomit to a certain extent—indicated unease with the material itself and
described Gemara study as exasperating, preoccupied with details, and "not
so great."

Reading these selections reminded me of the excitement I felt before the
first class I was going to take in Talmud at the Midrasha, before the *havruta*
study session that took place in the library every Tuesday prior to the class
itself. I recalled the bitter taste of the experience and the way in which I tried
to explain it to myself. I also assumed that it had something to do with me,
with my literacy past, with the tools at my disposal, and with the intellectual
preferences imprinted on me. Still, I understood, just as the women I spoke
to understood, that the matter also depends on the way the lesson is given
by the teacher.

Beyond this, the selections clearly highlight the question of the connection between fields of knowledge and gender, between the desire, ability,
and preference for becoming acquainted with a world of knowledge and
literacy discourse on the one hand and gender affiliation on the other. This
question, which stands at the center of *Women's Ways of Knowing*, has been
dealt with at length in feminist philosophy, psychology, and pedagogy.[12]

This study does not attempt to solve the riddle of what women can or
prefer to study. The power of anthropological study is in description, reportage, and analysis of a specific reality. It may be possible to return to this
riddle in retrospect, but for now we must broaden the canvas and hear how
the women would like to study.

THE TEACHERS: "IT'S NOT WHAT, IT'S WHO AND HOW"

"It's absolutely clear to me that the determining factor is who the teacher is. After three years in the Midrasha, after having sat and chosen interesting subjects, I understood it. It's not what, it's who and how."

That is what Miri said on the verge of completing her studies at the Midrasha. When I asked her if she had had good female teachers, she said: "Look, I studied with one woman, so it doesn't say much. I'm sure that I have things to learn from women. But I don't know, because I just think that a woman has a tendency to teach like a schoolteacher, and I'm not comfortable with that—a kind of person who forces herself on the students. I didn't like that in high school, and I have no intention of getting used to it now. The rabbis don't give you that feeling; they don't put you back into that category of teacher and pupil."

In a few words, Miri effectively portrayed the vicious circle in which women find themselves as teachers and students. The Midrasha's teaching staff, at the time Miri studied there, included three women, only one of whom had a Ph.D. (in philosophy). The Midrasha had no women who had trained themselves to teach Jewish studies in para-academic institutions—in the seminaries of the Conservative movement or in the new midrashot. Women without academic degrees taught at the Midrasha because of their social/ religious/moral position—for example, Rivka Sternberg, or Rabbanit Esther Lior, who taught in the summer session. These instructors had extensive experience as educators and teachers of girls and women that had required them to pursue intensive study on their own. Female instructors with academic degrees taught on the basis of their professional qualifications, but the intellectual discourse they offered lay to the side of, rather than within, the rabbinic discourse.

The result was, then, that the teachers' status was divided between, on the one hand, esteem and prestige based on an academic degree that is not part of the traditional hierarchy (she is a Ph.D., but not a rabbi), and on the other, the intra-communal respect accorded to a *rabbanit*. Yet this latter respect is mixed with suspicion (she is a *rabbanit*—she wants to get me to behave properly, not teach me).

The learners' desire to be exposed to new and different knowledge coincided, to a certain extent, with their desire to be taught in a different way. They wanted to work in a new way and become acquainted with types of teachers they had not known during their elementary and secondary school educations. The Midrasha did not bring them into contact with learned women who deconstructed the boundary between gender and study of Gemara. It recreated the male teacher's link to the Gemara and the female teacher's link to education in the sense of teaching proper behavior and morals (except in the case of the women with academic degrees, who abstained from both these types of teaching).

In such a situation, female students sought in the rabbi-teacher an inspiring personality, enthusiasm, and profound knowledge. They expected him to open doors to worlds of knowledge they had not known previously. Moreover, they expected him to treat them as intelligent adults. (In addition, a kind of intimate and romantic situation is created between a single male teacher and his young, female students, most of whom are not yet married.)

The presence of men in the women's Midrasha was noted in part I. The form of teaching, it should be recalled — the rocking of the body, the "disputation chant,"[13] the mixture of Hebrew and Talmudic Aramaic, and so on — are, in the society under study, manifestly male signifiers. When a rabbi presents a line of argument to his female students using the disputation chant, he is displaying a male act to them. He is doing what male learners do — and what the women do not know how to do. The use of male practice in the teaching of women reminds them that they still "do not know like the men," but it also allows them to brush up against the world they desire. There is a religious-erotic fusion here that is expressed in the classroom by the embarrassed smiles of the women.

One teacher, among the entire Midrasha faculty, won almost unanimous accolades and admiration from the women — Rabbi A. Yadid.

"The class that is really almost fresh air for my soul is Rabbi Yadid's. After one of his classes I come out with things I need to think about. Any subject he teaches will be like that. It's him, his charisma, it's his ability to get to the depth of things. Along with that, it's not that you are floating in a higher world, as sublime and profound as it is. It's here with us, it's real and relevant. After him anything else is a letdown, because I'm simply an admirer of his."

"Most of the classes are substandard for me, brainwashing — except for Rabbi Yadid."

"He's simply an exceptional personality, a kind of living, lively figure. He speaks with a lot of enthusiasm, doesn't just stand there and lecture. The fact is that it's the first time that I've studied Bible in that way. It amazes

me: his ability to lead you through the breadth of the subjects, to sweep you
along. For example, in the last class we spoke about Elijah and how he went
to comfort Yehiel, who built Jericho. It was very much relevant to current
events. He spoke about Jericho, about "Jericho first" [the ceding of Jericho
to the Palestinians as the first step in the Oslo accords]. Now, it's not that he
stood there and lectured to us about his political opinions, but rather that
he tied things together and that was interesting. It could be that someone
who doesn't agree with his political opinions would not think that, but the
class was amazing."

"Rabbi Yadid is very interesting. He has that exceptional ability of a
teacher to take you with him, but to let you think. He put me in contact
with sources that had been hidden from me, with commentators I had not
known. I relate to the course as a 'luck' course—lucky that I signed up
for it."

"When I came to the Midrasha I had in my pocket the names of teachers
that I had to take. Rabbi Yadid, of course. I fought for a year in order to
take his class, and I'm happy I succeeded. Aside from the fact that I like
Bible and enjoy being anchored to a text instead of talking about the 'divine
good' and things like that, he's simply a phenomenon. I come over from law
school collapsing, tired, fatigued, go into his class, and before I know it two
hours have gone by."

This wholesale enthusiasm for Rabbi Yadid depicts an ideal type of
teacher and class that the women were searching for when they came to the
Midrasha. Yet I also heard, on occasion, reservations about him, or claims
that he was appropriate only for certain groups. In one of the interviews
someone told me: "Have you heard about Rabbi Yadid? No? You should!
Actually, I don't know what you can say about him, you know? I'm really
interested in knowing what you'd think of him."

I did not attend his classes, and I did not go to hear the lessons of other
rabbis whose names were cited in interviews—including one who was mentioned because of his political opinions, or Rabbi Golan, who was one of
the first teachers of Talmud for women. Many of the women mentioned
Dr. Admiel Kosman as a person whose teaching was extraordinary. His field
was the connection between art and religion, and he allowed the women to
experience, express, and be exposed to a new combination of knowledge,
emotion, and thought.[14]

The enthusiasm about Rabbi Yadid's teaching or Admiel Kosman's class
leaves us within "feminine material"—within an emotional learning-

religious experience conducted by a charismatic man. This enthusiasm does not point to a change that has taken place in women's expectations of their teachers but rather to a demand for a higher level of learning. The change is more clearly noticeable when the discussion focuses not on the teacher, but on the text.

HOW TO STUDY: "THERE FOR THE FIRST TIME WE STUDIED FROM THE INSIDE, IN AN ORGANIZED WAY"

"This year I finally entered the Beit Midrash, and there, when I think about it, we worked very thoroughly; I look back and I see a road. We went down a road. It was hard, but it was worth it. For the first time the way they taught and the material we studied jived."

The most obvious unease of the women regarding the way the Jewish corpus was presented to them has to do with their lack of familiarity. The important thing here is not lack of familiarity with the material in terms of knowing it, but in terms of being oriented within the text.

The women learners had in their pasts encountered parts of books (with photocopied or mimeographed texts), and had read collections and readers whose direction was never made clear to them. They jumped from subject to subject, following the weekly Torah readings, the seasons of the year, or the life cycle. They never got the feeling that they had covered a given piece of ground, that now (unlike before) they knew something thoroughly. This fragmentation may perhaps be explained as part of traditional Jewish study, which is not linear but jumps from text to text and is not disciplined in the Western sense. Yet for the women this kind of study produced a sense of relative weakness and lack of control.

There can be no doubt that the teaching these girls were exposed to produced a preliminary acquaintance with a selection of sources and writers. The girls emerged well-versed in the Bible and certain commentators; they had solid knowledge of Jewish history and the first glimmers of knowledge of Jewish philosophy. The women I sat with in classes demonstrated an excellent ability to read Hebrew texts from different periods, knew how to express themselves properly in good Hebrew, and could follow genre transitions given to them in their lessons.

However, these women live alongside a male educational system that enjoys great prestige. The men know other things—and know them in a different way. These facts constitute a standard by which the women measure their own knowledge. Efrat said of the gap in knowledge between herself

and her boyfriend/husband: "Suddenly, after our graduation exams, I felt
that he was disappearing—Jewish thought and philosophy, Rav Kook, the
Maharal, the *Kuzari* on a high level. He would come home with knowledge
from here to who knows where, and I was just a nothing, and that really
bothered me horribly. And then the questions began. . . . I at least did not
receive the tools to open the midrashic literature, not how a midrash looks,
not where I can find one, or what to do with it when I find it, nothing. . . ."

The sense of loss in many cases grows out of the fact that they did not
study "from the inside"—from the text itself, as Ayelet said, comparing her
studies at the Midrasha to studying at Midreshet Shuva: "There for the first
time, as a girl, I studied things and not about things. I read the Maharal and
not about the Maharal. You understand—I don't know how to explain it.
There you study the things from within and not from the outside. Dr. Weiss,
who teaches Rabbi Kook or Maimonides here, teaches that way. She makes
sure that we read Maimonides himself, always the source and in a certain
order. That's the only way you feel that you know something."

Studying from the text itself is not sufficient. Women know that the
traditional Jewish form of study is denied them, since they have not studied
in a *beit midrash* or in *havruta*, as Zehava said when she described the
experience of study in Midreshet Nishmat in Jerusalem: "Everything there is
different, the whole shape of it. You study there *al ha-seder* and in *havrutot*.
Every class has time for *havruta* study, including Bible, Jewish philosophy,
law, Gemara, and Hasidism. In each of those subjects there is about an hour
and a half of *havruta* study and then an hour and a half in the classroom—a
direct lesson, true, but with discussion. The secret is in the *havruta*, studying
together with someone. To be within a sea of books, to go from one to the
next, and to know how to read them—that's the secret, and in the Midrasha
they haven't discovered that yet. They're starting now."

The in-depth study that is the basis of education for boys includes horizontal movement—the student goes from one text to another searching
out cross-references as parallels. Gemara study thus familiarizes the male
student with the entire range of halachic, aggadic, and rabbinical texts and
provides him with the tools to decode them as well.

By contrast, the horizontal movements girls encounter are thematic
rather than intertextual. Women often have no idea of the sources of the
texts they are studying. When they read an aggadah or midrash, they are
generally not told what work it has been taken from. Often teachers give
them a photocopied page that does not even cite the source. Even if the
source is cited, they do not know what the Gemara was discussing one line

SIX COLORS — MANY VOICES

previously or one line thereafter, nor do they know the subject of the debate that led the sages to cite the aggadah that has been plucked out of context for them. They have no idea why several aggadot appear on the same photo-copied page one after the other, what connects them, who connected them, and why. During the lesson, the teacher connects the aggadot or other texts and, as we will see in part III, presents these connections as data. The women must follow the terrain marked by the teacher because they have no com-pass of their own. They thus walk a world that is managed comprehensively by texts and their interpretation, with little bits snipped out of context and placed in their pockets.

Many hoped their current studies would purposefully rearrange and en-rich those bits of knowledge. They wanted their new study to begin after the old order of knowledge had been upset. They gave high marks to rabbis who shocked them, who shattered conventions, who swept out from under them the little they had. The aggadah class given by the Midrasha's director (see chapter 6) stands out as an experience of this type. Many remarked that they had been offended (personally and ideologically) by the way in which the rabbi shattered their line of thinking. He did not listen to their argu-ments, portrayed them as little girls (calling them precisely that), mocked the "*ulpanist*" education they had received, dismissed the priggishness they displayed, and made fun of their political positions and their reading of his-tory. Nevertheless, most of them recognized the great value of the shaking up they had gotten there. They distinguished between his method and the result, condemning the former and valuing the latter.

As Michal said: "[H]is class on aggadah caused me a 'positive crisis.' Rabbi Cohen is an open man, very very liberal. . . . He said things that in the *ulpanit* we would not have dared to think. A rabbi stands in front of you and cites sources, and I saw girls whose faith was simply shaken. I, for my part, had a ball. I enjoyed every minute."

The experience of discovery and innovation in study involves challeng-ing previous knowledge. This is no big news. Critical studies of education and pedagogy have pointed out the differing conditions for a shake-up that empowers and brings a learner closer and one that distances and alienates her.[15] Michal's words show that she knew (as did many others who spoke in a similar way) how to differentiate between the negative and positive parts of the act of challenging previous knowledge. Michal took from Rabbi Co-hen's class the news that there are indeed different opinions and that there is not a single "correct" view. The different opinions are part of a broad spec-trum that can include views that, in the old knowledge order, were heretical.

Others mentioned that after taking his class they had learned to criticize the sages fearlessly and openly. He liberated them from the uncritical reading of the sources that results from awe and ignorance. Rabbi Cohen revealed to them a part of the Jewish knowledge industry: the relations between the personalities involved in it and its ideological power structure. In order to benefit from these resources—to be acquainted with them, master them, internalize them, and turn them into personal assets—Rabbi Cohen's pupils had to undergo a kind of "hazing ceremony." This condition alienated some of the students from the assets themselves. The demand that the learner expunge her literacy past, shed her moral positions, and disparage previous interpretations was more than they could bear. Not all succeeded in separating the method and the goal, and these women lost out twice. Their previous knowledge was erased, and in its place were bitterness, exasperation, and disbelief in their literacy power.

For young women in the religious world engaged in constituting their Jewish/national/female identity, this is a heavy price. There were those who fought the rabbi and refused to expunge their previous knowledge; the students did not lose much, but neither did they benefit. They rejected the power of criticism and the empowerment offered them because they could not make the distinction that Michal made. Avishag testified to this: "I know that he is trying to teach a method, but everything is connected to everything else. If he blocks every idea I present, it is hard for me to learn his method from him. If I read an aggadah after the course, the only benefit I get out of his teaching is that I tell myself—wait a minute, this is a first reading, now what can I ask here, what are the problems? But I don't know if I can cope with it and answer myself, because he didn't enable me to learn a method."

It is no wonder, then, that in citing their desired "way of learning," they seek methodical, complete, fundamental, and comprehensive knowledge. Yet they do not ignore the implications of the method of instruction and the personalities involved in it. They seek to learn "from the inside," from within the books themselves, not from photocopies, collections, and so on. They prefer studying the text itself to studying about the text. They have high praise for study in *havruta*, in small groups, in the company of their husbands or boyfriends, or even alone. In practice, they try to minimize the amount of mediation between them and the sources and/or to control the quality of that mediation. There can be no doubt that they have come to see that the mediators that connected them with Jewish religious studies in the past often did more harm than good. They have looked around them and seen that another kind of encounter can take place, and that there is no reason for women not to have one. Still, within this demand for change one often hears the defense of knowledge in its "other flavor"—the "not exactly male" one. Many women said that they prefer general, sweeping, and ideological knowledge: something that says something, that remains with them, that they can connect with, that they can get excited about, rather than dry, hair-splitting, scientific, intellectual knowledge.

Some of the Midrasha students were majoring or minoring in a field of Jewish studies at the university—Jewish history, Jewish philosophy, or oral law. They expected the studies in these departments to be complex—scientific/religious or even scientific and "feminine"—that is, serious but also relevant to them. Sometimes (generally at the request of Ora, who was studying oral law at the university), they made comparisons between the instruction in the university departments and at the Midrasha.

"I expected that the studies there [in the university department] would be more serious, but they weren't. There was actually great scholarly precision, but it didn't interest me. The method of Bible study, for example, all the grammar in the verses, the search for ancient sources, that doesn't attract me. In oral law it wasn't the approach, it was the level of instruction—it was just a very low level, one big crib course. I've had bad courses here at the Midrasha, but I've had really superior Bible courses. Why? Because they take it further. Details and scholarship are all very well, but what about the meaning? Where does it lead me? At the Midrasha they related to that."

The criticism that demands a different type of study recreates the familiar dichotomy between experiential, emotional study and "cold," intellectual study. It may well indicate chains of additional divisions into dichotomies such as feminine/masuline, Jewish learning/academic learning, and ideological/objective. Some of this criticism indicates that women have no desire to subsume experiential study under intellectual study, whether that intellectual study is scholarly or traditional Talmudic disputation. It seems to me, however, that this is not the main force behind the criticism. That force connects again to the field of participation and action in a community of practitioners/believers, and it is revealed when one collates the voices describing the "why"—voices that seek to explain why and for what purpose women must study.

This chapter, based on the voices of the women, opened by following the literacy axis as biography. Afterward it returned and appeared as an "axis of life": a spine of meaning, a division of time and space that allows an understanding of the past, a decoding of the present, and a setting out of the future. The literacy sphere, in its practical aspects, cut through the voices of the women for a third time with the goal of understanding study as practice. Now these axes can be tied together, in relation to gender and nationality. The level on which all of them meet (having been there all the time) is the level of meaning: "Why? What will I get out of it?"

Formulating meaning in terms of benefit derives from the internal language of the religious women, which always connects the two.

WHY STUDY? "I KNOW MORE THINGS ABOUT MY LIFE:
WHAT NOT TO DO, BUT ALSO WHAT ELSE IT IS POSSIBLE TO DO"

"When you suddenly understand what the meaning is, then prayer turns into something different."

"You ask whether my study builds me up. Of course it does, in many areas. Spirituality, knowledge, intelligence, even the area of self-confidence. It also has advantages in my connection with my husband; we have many more subjects for conversation than if I didn't study. I can bring him things I know and teach him. It's not the case that the knowledge is his and all I've got is common sense. I feel that together we have a kind of joy of creativity and joy of study during which we contribute to one another."

"It's connected to the ability to ask questions. The teachers themselves show you the obligation to ask. Sometimes the question borders on heresy, but you give it a try: the fear, the searching, and if you have luck, the exhilaration of discovery. You listen, study, and you have something—a basis when you go to study and ask and inquire. You suddenly understand that every problem has different solutions and that you have to decide. After all, everything comes together in the end. Everything flows to the sea, but you can choose the river for yourself."

"Look, you can say what did I really learn in such and such a class. I learned, for example, that on Shabbat it is forbidden to read the want ads in the newspaper. Big deal. But if you look at it another way, you see that study gives me more ability. I know more things about my life—what not to do, but also what else it is possible to do, things I don't do today, for example. So study like that touches on me. Beginning with the study of the *Kuzari*— which seems to be in the sky, but it speaks to me and about my life—and down to laws that seem petty, but they make up my daily routine."

"I examine myself: What I came out with, what was here. Do I have tools or don't I? Will I be able to study such material myself or not? I learned a work method here or I simply marked time. Those are the things I check. Aside from the matter of study, you know, I check also if it fits in with my life, what I gain here in a practical sense, what I can do with this knowledge, how it ties in with actions. It can be a very advanced class, but if I came out of it with a question or an idea or a decision to do something, that's a lot."

It would be hard to avoid comparing these voices to the distinction I made in my last research project between the "substantial" and the "practical."[16] This represents the binary division between knowledge that is relevant and applicable, and knowledge that touches on the life of the knower only in a limited way. This distinction is not necessarily identical to the binary distinction between concrete and abstract knowledge—that is, there is no necessary connection between the "substantial" and the abstract or between the "practical" and the concrete. The only criterion for assigning knowledge to one of these two poles is the extent of its relevance to the life of the knower. This criterion was an appropriate one in the lives of the Gur Hasidic women, just as it is valid in the current case. And perhaps, as Jean Lave argues, this is the most significant standard for decoding any learning process.

There can be no doubt that the women speaking here say, bluntly and clearly, that they expect study to give them something. They do not talk about study for its own sake. They have a wealth of explanations for the immediate and long-term benefits this study produces. In this sense they are close to the discourse on *haredi* education for women, which shaped its sense of meaningful education for women around the immediate practicality of the study for women. Nevertheless, I want to demonstrate that the women at the Midrasha give this discourse a different cast and rearrange its boundaries. It would seem that the striving for the practical that has been injected into their education from the youngest age receives a significance that goes beyond the observance of religious precepts—and perhaps even reverses its logic.

Haredi women's education seeks to allow education because of "historical circumstance," yet it also sees to it that this education will recreate *haredi* women who resemble their mothers. Studies of *haredi* society have shown that this is a paradoxical goal, and that learning women develop a reflective position that allows them to think of themselves as also being outside the ruling ideological discourse. This possibility is not translated into a revolution or into rebellion, and it is not even expressed in many changes. But the *haredi* woman's position as a woman who "knows" or "knows more" distances her from the generations of her mother and grandmother.

The practice of bringing knowledge down to the level of practicality still governs the teaching and learning discourse for *haredi* women. It is not always clear whether it has penetrated and become a matter of personal preference, whether it is a linguistic convention, or whether it is a public ritual that indicates respect for hegemonic rules of the game. *Haredi* women continue to take pride in their practical approach and judge the quality of their learning experiences by "what it gave me," by whether "I got stronger," and so on.

In many cases, young women from the Zionist-religious camp are like *haredi* women. They preserve something of the ambience that links female-ness to practicality. The desire to do something for its own sake is balanced by a consciousness that they should exude efficiency and diligence. They continue to speak of themselves as secondary knowers, because he, the man, is commanded to study, and they are not.

Nevertheless, many of them have already given up the romantic image of mother and housekeeper (this is discussed in more detail in chapter 5), of the woman who knows only what she needs to know in order to raise her children and manage a kosher Jewish home. For others, this image serves as a cover or preliminary stage before the transition into another discourse about the woman who knows for herself—a discourse that takes in, around the axis of Jewish identity, both national and gender identity. In this way study turns into a move aimed at redefining the areas of activity and participation of the speakers as Jews, Israelis, and women.

THE PERCEPTION OF THE CHANGE:
NEXT PESACH I WILL BE A DIFFERENT WOMAN

How could it be that I'd know next Pesach exactly
what I knew about the holiday last Pesach?
Miri K.

Why did Miri decide to give this answer to my question "So why do you study?" How did she arrive at such a fresh definition of religious study? After all, the reason for observing the Pesach holiday does not in any way depend on what a person knows about the holiday or on the gap between what she knew last year as opposed to what she knows this year. Miri knew this, of course, but she was speaking about herself—a woman approaching thirty, about to complete an M.A. in Talmud at the university, who also studied at the Midrasha. Miri, as one of the women, and Pesach, as an allegory, combine into a clear portrait of an educated woman who must carry out an entire range of difficult and annoying actions because she is religious. Before performing those actions—and there is no doubt that Miri will perform them—she seeks to see herself as someone who, between emptying out her drawers for Pesach cleaning last year and covering her kitchen counter with aluminum foil to make it kosher for Pesach this year, has read something about the holiday—how could she not?

Miri's intention is to depict the time that has passed between her previous and her current Pesach cleaning as a period of development. Her holiday preparations, and her meticulous observances of the holiday's precepts, have not changed—their performance is their substance. But Miri is dynamic. Things have happened to her during the year, and she observes the precepts from a broader base. Apparently, the only way a woman like Miri can see herself doing exactly the same thing all over again is to do it differently.

What makes it possible to do the same thing differently, to change is, according to Miri, study.

Miri was the oldest of the interview subjects in this study and also the one with the most formal education. In her full interview she spoke about her feminine identity, about her social views, and other matters, but the sentence quoted above pinpoints the reason she studies. It is located at the religious site and confines the religious experience to the performance of religious observances. Miri's ability to make this restriction is illuminating. It focuses the major part of being a modern religious woman (and to the same extent a modern religious man) in the present. According to her, "everything remains as it was except for me."

The other women interviewed needed much lengthier and more convoluted statements to describe their trajectories of change. As they spoke, they brought in the social, national, and gender facets of the modern religious woman. Here is a compilation of their words, composed of several voices. It contains the entire spectrum of reasons the speakers cited in explaining the meaning of study.

"There is no equality between man and woman, and there shouldn't be. But I think that because the woman is the major element in the home and she is the educator, it is extremely important that she study and know. And then come all the feminist stigmas that people have about women who study Torah, and they think that such women must be feminists. If you have to decide which of the two will study Torah, because someone has to do without, then it's clear that he studies, because he's commanded to. But I think that it's very important for a woman not to give up study; with all her other duties, she simply needs to study. It is clear that he should be a scholar, because the image of the father sets the tone at home, but that is very difficult, because she acts, she does things in reality, and she must know.

"The whole charade that the husband studies, that it's a demanding vocation that takes all his time and therefore she must defer to him—that's just not correct. Torah scholars are the most considerate, their time is the most flexible, they are the ones who care the most about their wives' growth. I know that from the reality of me and my husband. I see all around us couples who decide to do all sorts of moonlighting to improve their economic situation—okay, I can accept that, but you should recognize that the motive is economic. We decided to make economic sacrifices so that both of us would have more time to study.

"It was clear to me that when I got married I would not go to live in a settlement, even though I'm right-wing, and I'm in favor of holding onto the territories. Why? Because if we all did that there would be at most 200,000 people there, and the rest of Israel would be populated by nonreligious people. That's a horrible breach. Everyone is getting more extreme and pulling the reins in their own direction. Secular people don't know anything about religious people. We have to build bridges, and bridges are not merely having conversations and meetings. It means living together, really living together, because when you live together it's very difficult, it's a very difficult spiritual battle.

"But ever since I began to work on myself so that I can communicate with every Jewish person, it is no longer the case that I get along well with population x and not with population y. I can get along with everyone—new immigrants, city people, development town people, everyone. If you really love the entire Jewish people, then you find the point that connects you with everyone—secular, religious, haredi, everyone—really everyone."

When the women I interviewed speak of themselves, they are always speaking of themselves as religious women. There is never "simply me." The short path Miri made between study and herself as a religious person leads, for the others, through their husbands, children, and Israeli society.

The composite speaker accepts the conservative social reality: "There is no equality, and there shouldn't be. He is commanded to study, I'm not. The major part of the burden of the home falls on me, and I accept that." But another reaction always comes immediately thereafter. The additional statement does not contradict the first one but expands it, leans on it in order to stretch it. It's a kind of "yes, but"—I also need to know because I perform observances, because I can learn, because I'm permitted to.

The Torah scholars for whom the woman is supposed to give up her studies appear as men who value their wives' growth. Constraints imposed by life and family are presented as economic matters that can be managed in such a way as to allow both husband and wife to study. In her relations with her husband and her children the woman appears in her traditional image. She accepts this role, but in the same breath she broadens it. This is not an attempt to challenge the role of mother and wife, but rather to develop it to the point where it includes the image of the modern woman who is meant to fill that role.

The mirrors in which people seek themselves simultaneously reflect many other faces. In searching for her image as a learner, the speaker examines herself facing her husband and facing her children because of the religious and halachic definitions that obligate her. As a product of Zionist religious education, she examines herself facing society, facing the Jewish people. Here study appears as a possibility for realizing Zionism and love of the Jewish people. Critical readers will no doubt sense a certain sentimentality when they reach the last part of the above quotation—"If you really love the entire Jewish people." A momentary suspension of skepticism and criticism makes it possible to appreciate how long and demanding the journey is that this young woman must make in order to reach herself. Only after she has done right by her husband and her (usually future) children, and after she has shown that her study benefits the entire Jewish people, can she talk about herself.

The twists and turns of this journey are presented in the next part of this book from an additional point of view. Instead of the private voices of the women in these interviews, the following chapters are based on ethnography of what takes place in the classrooms of the Midrasha—dialogues of Torah study and the constitution of identity performed in the public arena by teachers, students, and texts.

III

DIALOGUES ON TORAH STUDY AND THE CONSTITUTION OF IDENTITY

THE DIALOGUES[1] PRESENTED IN THIS part of the book were taken from classes at the Midrasha. Each of the classes ran the length of the academic year and thus comprised approximately forty-two hours of class time. The field journals I kept during the classes contain a great deal of material, including transcripts—as precise as possible—of the dialogues between teacher and students, conversations among the students before and after classes, and conversations among the students that took place during class in my immediate vicinity, where I could listen in on them. As I was making this transcription, I also recorded thoughts and comments about what was taking place. To select a part of this whole is to make a deliberate choice. Each class contained so many threads and lines of thought that they could easily have been spliced into different combinations of conversations. Nevertheless, it seems to me that there was a certain atmosphere that pervaded all the classes and that this consolidated into a characteristic frame of mind. A central structure of discourse thus emerged around the texts chosen for the labor of interpretation shared by teacher and students.

With some reduction and generalization, each of the classes can be organized around a central subject that both explicitly and implicitly directed the dialogue there. Thus the ethnography has been arranged around these subjects. By its very nature, however, ethnography reproduces polyphony, including the confusion and tension around the dominant voices. Extending this approach, it can be said that the three dialogues presented here mark the boundaries of the identities of the research subjects. They connect the points that define these women as modern Jewish believers and observers, Israeli citizens and patriots, civil and national beings, and current or future wives and mothers. The discourse on the constitution of the identities of these young women takes place within and around these boundaries. It draws on the private history of each of them, their public experience in their community, their images of "others," and their visions of the future. More than anything else, in this context, the discourse on the constitution of identity organizes itself around the study of "Torah"—that is, around Jewish sacred studies. Contemplation, questing, disquiet, or, alternatively, the journey in search of the "truth" have traditionally taken place around Judaism's canonical texts.

The assemblage of women on the journey here described is not at all traditional; indeed, it marks a revolutionary precedent in Jewish history. The literacy journey of these women and their attempts to constitute an identity around the study of a text and its interpretations is fascinating. It is a journey of great opportunity and great danger because it has never been tried before, and it is being fashioned as it occurs. The dialogues below depict the balance between opportunity and risk as understood by individuals and groups, and they show the new image being woven around the young religious woman during the course of the journey itself.

This part of the book is divided into three chapters. The first begins with the most common site for discussing the identities of women: their role as mothers. The following chapter presents dialogues dealing with democratic citizenship and national identity. The last chapter in this section focuses on questions of faith, the place of the Torah in relation to science, and the position of woman as believer in the modern or postmodern age. It should be noted again that the classes did not address these issues in a focused and exclusive way—it was after the fact, after my rereading of the ethnography, that these topics can be seen as having been at the center.

5

⁓

BETWEEN JOY AND ENSLAVEMENT—
CONSTRUCTING THE NEW MOTHER

*From the end of the sixteenth century to the middle of the eighteenth century
most men—among them the most respected of their age—united in a single
refrain to discourage women from following this path [of education]. From
Montaigne to Rousseau, Molière and Fénelon, women were beseeched
to return to their natural role as housekeeper and mother. Knowledge, they
said, spoils a woman by distracting her from her most sacred duties.*

Badinter, 1985, p. 83

THIS CHAPTER DEALS IN A direct and very intensive way with gender. Of all the classes described in this part of the book, the ones described
here deal in the most direct and reflective way with the learners as women. It
is here that they speak about their futures as believing women who live under the canopy of the halacha. Their journey is long and convoluted. Sometimes it wears a simple, conservative, unquestioning guise, and at other
times it takes on sophisticated, critical, and subversive forms. This is a journey from themselves to themselves via classic and modern texts, all of them
Jewish and religious. During the journey the young women are meant to examine and cleave to their status. Their status becomes problematic as they
confront the texts, the teachers, and their lives. As in every pedagogical process, and thus in every pedagogical-religious process, educators try to offer
solutions to problems that arise, and these solutions cast new light on the
boundaries of the woman's identity as a participant in a society of believers/
observers.

The chapter is based on ethnography taken from three different classes.
The first is an intensive four-week summer course given by Rabbanit Esther
Lior. The second is a year-long course on halacha and ethics, conducted
by Mrs. Rivka Sternberg. The third is a course on aggadah (the narrative,
nonlegal portions of the Talmud and other rabbinic literature, consisting of
homilies and parables told by the sages), taught by Rabbi Yitzhak Cohen,
the director of the Midrasha.

The discourse presented here seeks to encompass women's identities as citizens, workers, believers, and observers of religious precepts, and to bring them into their small but large role of mother. How banal, how predictable, yet how surprising. On this reflective journey the women stride, with considerable courage, through the busiest intersections in the life of a modern religious woman—intersections where religious law, tradition, and mores run square into the axioms of modernity. The issues include religious study for women, the status of women's testimony in rabbinical courts, women's ritual impurity, and women's participation in public prayer. The journey is directed, however, toward a single station that is known from the start, yet regenerated—motherhood.

These complicated acrobatics, including new exercises (modern scientific knowledge, feminist scholarship, new halachot), as well as consideration of women's literacy and their experience in a multicultural society, ends with them falling onto the safety net of motherhood. They leap from the trapeze in order to see themselves from the outside, to conceptualize and discover more about themselves. As they soar skyward they find power, innovations, a variety of possibilities, and no little opprobrium. But the orthodox/patriarchal gravitational force predetermines the end. In the face of sweeping changes in the status and literacy of women, incessant efforts are being made to again mark motherhood as an anchor.

The fact that the fabric of the women's lives as presented in the Midrasha can be folded up and fit into their wombs is not characteristic only of a woman's midrasha, of religious Zionist education, or of Jewish life. Limiting discussion of women to their motherhood—or focusing on this alone—is one of the most vexatious issues in feminist thinking. The role of the mother is the link between the public social realm and the woman's body. This link has thus become the densest region in the map of explanations for the differences between the sexes.

In an article describing the development of the attitude toward motherhood in feminist theory, José Bruner laid out a path that began with the effort to detach the link. Simone de Beauvoir, who discarded the role of the mother, saw this as the only way women could join the world of men and maintain their rights. A more complex attitude later developed that tried to expand the dimensions of the link, to invite men in and, in parallel, to let some women out. But in fact one might say that most feminist discourse about motherhood is torn between two extremes. At one end of the spectrum is an essentialist discourse that accepts motherhood as a uniquely female experience which serves as a private enclosure for personal, emotional, social, and political empowerment. At the other end, constructivist discourse rejects this essentialism and sees motherhood as a social role and cultural product unconnected to gender. Despite Bruner's attempt to demonstrate a chronological progression in this discourse and a definite direction of development, it would seem that at any given time both these position are at the base of the discussions, even as, over time, the discussions become more complex and sophisticated, and utilize new terminology. De Beauvoir's radical approach, for example, calling for an end to motherhood, echoes today through biotechnology, in vitro fertilization, and payments to surrogate mothers. The essentialist motherhood of the 1980s is expressed today in the form of female writing or speech, under the influence of French feminism.[1]

Current studies of motherhood thus tend to break away from the dispute between these positions. They make an empirical and theoretical effort to find other terms to describe motherhood, terms that are neither gender-loaded nor genderless. Many scholars present the phenomenology of motherhood via detailed descriptions of mothering practices in social and cultural contexts that allow a great deal of variation in the role of "mother." These details bring with them different perceptions of motherhood, focused on the woman-mother as a subject and not on her children, family or the social framework she belongs to.[2] Another facet of recent discourse on motherhood views it as strategy, examining the possibility and value of using the role of mother as a basis for demanding civil rights. There are cultural and political contexts in which it is worthwhile for women to use their roles as mothers in order to demand what they deserve as citizens. This is "feminism for hard times," in which a discourse on women's rights develops on the universal basis of the phenomenon of motherhood.[3] Such a discourse resonates in the following selection, through which it is possible to pass from the general context of the issue of motherhood in feminist theory to the specific Jewish and Israeli context.

> Rav said to R. Hiya: How do women gain [the next world]? By bringing
> their sons to the synagogue [to study], and by sending their husbands
> to the homes of rabbis [to study, sometimes for long periods], and by
> waiting patiently for them until they return from the rabbis' houses.
> Babylonian Talmud, Berachot 17a

This path, which links Jewish women to the public that gains a place in the next world, passes through their role as mothers and wives of men who study. This is one of several paths that link Jewish women to the public. The uniqueness of this one is that it does not address women's rights in this world but instead sets out their duties. It circumvents the issue of their exclusion from study (which brings the reward of the next world) by giving them responsibility for men who study. It promises an abstract future equality on the basis of a concrete inequality in the ongoing present. This path, with its twists and turns throughout Jewish history, marks, today too, the most significant area for understanding gender relations in orthodox society. Many other issues are ranged around it, including sexuality, the body, emotion, and intellect—all of which take on new meaning at this junction of religious study.

Today, more than ever before, that junction is a busy one. This is because religious study has always been the salient marker of the Jewish male, and the innovation of sacred studies for women has thus shaken the entire system of gender relations. Obviously, there is no simple causal sequence here, but rather a complex development affected by the places and times in which orthodox Judaism exists. Among the range of sites at which one may decipher the system of gender relations in orthodox Jewish society, the site that ties gender to religious study seems the most fascinating. It can shed light on other sites as well. The attempt to understand why discourse on femininity in the Midrasha centers around the role of mother will be addressed at this site.

The tension between fertility, birth, and child care on the one hand, and the practice of religious study on the other, emerges as central in a large range of studies on Judaism and sexuality.[4] It seems that most of the discussions about women in the Bible, in the literature of the sages, and in subsequent religious texts revolve around the dichotomy between mind and womb. At the expulsion from Eden, women's punishment was to bring forth children, whereas man's mission was work. The transition from this mission to the constitution of the Jewish male's identity around the act of religious study came later, in the Second Temple period. At that time ideal types were established for both sexes.

Daniel Boyarin returns to that time in his attempt to read the gender order of the Talmud.[5] Boyarin begins by adopting Foucault's approach, which argues that gender categories are a phenomenon unique to Western culture. Historically, each culture has constructed a characteristic system of gender. Greek and Roman cultures, for example, were based on class relations, and this led to the construction of sexual relations between the master, the boy, the wife, and the prostitute. Hellenistic masculinity is based on an extroverted and aggressive phallus. People possessing such a phallus are permitted to penetrate those who lack one, whether the latter are men or women. Such a concept of masculinity is not possible in Judaism, because in Judaism the sexes possess integrity by the nature of their creation; mixture is forbidden. The cultural encounter between Hellenistic and Jewish gender systems was fateful, since it accelerated an alternative process of constructing Jewish masculinity. The Torah, the family, and the male *havruta* comprised an alternative to the extroverted phallus, but it was a fragile alternative. Any challenge to it—whether it be women studying, single-parent families, homosexuality, or unmarried men and women—is a direct threat to the formation of a more complex man (which in his later writings Boyarin calls the "sissy"). The delicate balance requires that the woman be the absolute "other"—she does not study Torah, and she gives birth to children. Yet this woman also has the "male" possibility of making her presence felt in the home and outside it because of the empty space left by the non-macho Jewish male.

The aggression of the Jewish male, according to Boyarin, lies in his study, his language, and in the halacha that grows out of both of them. This belligerence receives violent expression in the Bible and seems like a more heterogeneous area of conflict in the rabbinic literature. Either way, fencing in the woman's identity around motherhood and keeping her away from study are the best insurance for the continuation of the constitution of the Jewish male as a religious scholar. (Moreover, using Boyarin's approach, one can argue that a woman who studies religious texts does far more than challenge the link between ownership of knowledge and social power—she upsets the gender order.

When a man exchanges his male *havruta* for a mixed-gender one or for his wife/girlfriend (which happens sometimes in the modern orthodox community), he gives up homoerotic relations—the intimacy possible within a group of learning men. Such a man switches the feminine object of desire—the Torah—for a real object—a woman. In doing so he endangers his non-macho identity. A man who studies with another man may have a more complex gender identity than a man who studies with a woman.

The dialogues presented below come from a different perspective than Boyarin's. Instead of the group of men occupied with the constitution of their identity in the Second Temple period and the scholars who continues their work, we hear the voices of women studying in the summer of 1994 and in the following academic year.

MOTHERHOOD IS HAPPINESS

At the end of the summer, a room at the Midrasha fills with women. The sheet describing the special program quotes the Song of Songs: *Ani le-dodi ve-dodi li*—"I am my beloved's and my beloved is mine." The initial letters of the Hebrew verse spell out the name of the Hebrew month, Elul, the month preceding the Days of Awe, Rosh Ha-Shana and Yom Kippur. The class is part of the Midrasha's special Elul program.

Four days a week, six hours a day, for four weeks. Whoever can handle the schedule need not pay; the classes are funded by a contribution from a philanthropic family and exempt the student from three year-long courses at the Midrasha. When I entered the room that morning at 8:45 there were only a few women there. I sat in the right-hand corner, in a row perpendicular to most of the seats, which gave me a view of the entire class. The slight chill left over from the night was reinforced by large but quiet air conditioners. Little by little the room filled up. A few of the faces were familiar from my own student years at Bar-Ilan; others looked younger. I learned afterward that some of them were in National Service and had come to earn credits or "just to listen." There were ecstatic encounters, embraces, calls from one side of the room to the other.

"I can't go on. I'm in shock. Every minute somebody else. It's been a long time since I met so many friends."

"You? You don't know how amazed I am! I can't believe who I'm meeting here." (She turns to someone who has just entered.) "You're a liar, you said you wouldn't come—to what do we owe the honor?"

Next to me two seated girls are talking.

"For me this is a great place. There's good merchandise here, a huge number of girls."

"What do you mean?"

"Oh, you don't know? I do a little matchmaking. I've had a few successes, and this is such a good place."

Just before the class began there were about seventy women in the room, most of them young, unmarried, their heads bare. Ten had their hair covered, among them three older women (forty and over).

At nine o'clock, Rabbi Yitzhak Kraus strode in. He was about thirty-five years old and had recently been appointed deputy director of the Midrasha. He introduced the woman beside him.

"I don't know when the first of you set out this morning, but Rabbanit Lior left home very early in order to get here from Kiryat Arba, and that is

how she asked that I introduce her to you—the *rabbanit* from Kiryat Arba"
[Kiryat Arba is a Jewish settlement adjacent to Hebron].

Dressed in pastel colors, with a narrow skirt, a white shirt with sleeves down
to the elbows, the *rabbanit* from Kiryat Arba wore a black kerchief on her
head, over which was a small straw hat. After handing out photocopied
sheets of source texts, she took her place behind the lectern. The first selection was the passage quoted above from the Babylonian Talmud tractate
Berachot, page 17, side a. The *rabbanit* began her lesson.

"How do women gain the next world? I looked for sources that emphasize
the special value and power that women have, and I decided that we should
devote our four meetings to the merit and distinction of the women of the
generation of Egypt—especially to Miriam—and also to the merit women
gain from religious study. I want us to know ourselves. Aside from being
Jewish people, we are primarily women. As the poet Rachel said: 'Only of
myself I know to tell.' I also seek to know myself and the Creator. And
that with the power that I have, not what someone else has, and without
comparing a man to a woman. Each woman is someone unique, but the
unique facet that we have here is the fact that we are all women. Let us study
that facet, and if we come to know it and internalize it and use it to serve
the Creator, we will find a great deal of strength to cope with problems.
We are in a difficult situation, perhaps confused, perhaps on the verge of a
breakthrough. Let us take strength from the Bible, from the Israelite women
in Egypt, in order to find a way to cope and to work. As for the facet of
religious study—here I feel at home in our own public. We know that
the Jewish people have nothing but the Torah. If something is wrong and
things go badly around us it is because our Torah is weak. What can we
do to strengthen the Torah, especially, and egotistically, what can I as a
woman do?"

Student: "Two things bother me. First, whoever is sure he can contribute
something and does so doesn't look for justification in the Torah for his
ability to make the contribution. Second, not all women are the same, even
if that is what is common to all of us."

The *rabbanit:* "Thank you for the question, and for asking. I don't know
if I can answer you, but I want all of you to ask questions. Right now I am
asking why the question 'How do women gain the next world?' is asked in
the Gemara."

The student sitting by the matchmaker in a low voice: "Why? Because
men wrote it."

Another student, out loud: "Why doesn't the Gemara ask 'How do men gain the next world?'"

Another student: "Because the woman's at home and you don't see what she does."

The matchmaker, softly: "Given the number of children she has, it's pretty clear what she does there."

The *rabbanit:* "A good question, and I hope that with God's help after these classes you'll understand a little more and you won't have any trace of a sense of being inferior or exploited, because I don't find in the sources any reason to feel inferior."

Another student: "The very fact that we preoccupy ourselves with it at every opportunity, time after time, shows that we have a problem."

The student next to me, quietly: "It's inferiority disguised as ideology. Instead of teaching us to be equal, they perpetuate our inferiority."

The *rabbanit:* "In the meantime, the Gemara asks the question, and for me that's enough. Let's see what the Gemara says—and it should be clear that I don't intend to teach Gemara here. I don't know Gemara, and you'll forgive me for my Aramaic because I don't understand Aramaic."

The *rabbanit* reads the text fluently and translates it without any difficulty.

"Women merit [the world to come], according to this gemara in Berachot, for three things: for taking their sons to synagogue [to study], for causing their husbands to study Mishna with the rabbis, and for waiting for their husbands until they return from the homes of rabbis [sometimes for many years]."

The *rabbanit* adds, immediately after her translation: "I interpret this with regard to the reality we live in today. I have no intention of talking about years of devotion, but rather about a day—about hours in which wives don't ask their husbands to do one thing or another, to help them here or there, but allow them to study. In our generation they entice and tempt us with other things—with equality in study—but the woman who brings up her children joyfully, sends them to study, and allows her husband to study is complete; she is a woman of substance."

Student: "And a woman without children, without a husband, she doesn't have substance?"

The *rabbanit:* "Why talk about a pathological situation? About the abnormal?"

The same student: "Why isn't it normal? There are situations like that. And what about a single woman—she has no substance?"

The *rabbanit:* "Then she's on the way to. . . . She hasn't yet fulfilled herself."

The same student: "What do you mean? At the stage she is at, she's a person, isn't she? If she doesn't give birth, then she's nothing?"

The matchmaker, in an undertone: "You can fulfill yourself very well without a clutch of children. My sister, every year, pop! she whelps a kid. Pregnant from the first night after the wedding. From the first day she's allowed to sleep with her husband, pop! another one."

The friend she has been talking to giggles and says "Stop it!," but she goes on. "It's true, you know. I mean what I say—she whelps."

Older student: "Giving birth is something all women share, something they have, and if they don't give birth they miss something. They haven't fulfilled themselves."

The *rabbanit:* "On the way here I gave a nonreligious soldier a ride, and we talked, you know, about his plans, and thank God he's got plenty. But a wedding and children he still doesn't see on the horizon. So I know that with the nonreligious the home and children are not such a great challenge."

Student: "Why do people always talk about the nonreligious as if they are some other kind of people? I'm very much involved with nonreligious society through my work, and they all want a home and children, just like we do. People are always saying 'the nonreligious, the nonreligious.'"

Older student: "What about their divorce figures?"

The matchmaker to her neighbor: "And what about our unhappy couples?"

The *rabbanit:* "Girls, why talk first about the exceptional? Let's talk about the normal. After all, when it comes right down to it, the majority of women are married with children. Let's see what Rabbi Kook says about it."

The *rabbanit* reads from a photocopied page of sources she has brought with her. The quotation from Rabbi Kook appears without a bibliographical citation to indicate which of his works it was taken from.

"Rabbi Kook explains the great promise God made to women in that he promised them in accord with nature—that is, he gave them duties compatible with their human nature, while men were given a purpose that requires them to fight their human nature. Women naturally assist men to learn [to do the unnatural].

"You already understand what Rabbi Kook wanted to tell us. The combination of our character and our purpose is more natural, more harmonious, easier. My natural purpose is identical with my spiritual purpose. I can reach God's throne with internal integrity, so I do not need tefillin and 613 mitzvot. I naturally love my children and husband, and help them study Torah."

Student: "So why don't men want to be like women? Why is it the opposite? If it were that way everyone would want to be in our place. And here, in the blessing 'that he did not make me a woman' they even give thanks that they were not made women. They're glad."

The matchmaker, in an undertone: "How much can people talk about that? Someone wrote a mistaken prayer—they just didn't think enough—and it stuck, it just stuck, and now they're splitting hairs over it. That he did not make me, that he made me, enough already! To split hairs over a mistake."

A young married student: "Excuse me! Men are also created to love their children and their wives naturally. That naturalness applies equally to women and to men. To love their homes."

The *rabbanit:* "Yes, but for you it's your job, and for him it's not. So for you it's easy, and for him it's hard. At work you think about your children all the time, and he doesn't."

The married student: "So for whom is it hard? For me or for him? Besides, let me tell you that when I come here I don't think about anything: not about the children I left at home and not about the work I left there. Nothing. I come here to learn, to think, to enjoy myself. Children are when I'm at home. Not here and not at work."

The *rabbanit:* "We're talking here about a situation of primal, immediate, natural feeling that mothers, or grandmothers, have. When I see my grandchildren—I'd be embarrassed to let you hear the way I go crazy over them. That's something that women have, and you can't dispute it. The midrash we'll read today about Miriam and the midwives shows us what great spiritual powers lie in this motherly love. It is love that includes self-sacrifice. Allow me one word about politics and then I'll get away from it immediately. In these times we will not be able to carry on the struggle for this land and this nation if we don't know here [pointing to her heart] what we actually are. The values have to be clear, otherwise where can we take the spiritual strength from? And I'm defending the nation here, because I am really full of anger, frustration, sorrow, I don't know what, because the situation is terrible. But these people don't know what they are; they don't understand. Zionism has taken them to this point and their batteries have worn out. Where will they find spiritual strength? Only from someone for whom values and spirit are clear. And since we can't do anything practical right now (and I'm sorry if that sounds like despair) we have to strengthen our values so that when the critical day comes we'll have something to support

us, and our support as women is the power and happiness of motherhood."
This produced an uproar in the class—the students talked among themselves, and there was a real commotion. The *rabbanit* let them talk and did not try to shout over them or impose silence. My two neighbors continued their conversation.

The matchmaker's friend: "So, what do you think? Isn't she a little extreme for you?"

The matchmaker: "Her? If you'd lived for two years in Kiryat Arba, your mind would have closed, too."

The next dialogue comes from Rivka Sternberg's course on halacha and ethics. This course, given on both introductory and advanced levels, was directed at the female student as a woman, wife, and mother. It did not address these identities indirectly, as part of a discussion of other issues. Everyone at the Midrasha knew that under the rubric "halacha and ethics" there was a pedagogical event that discussed the contemporary woman living under the canopy of the halacha. This class, at that time nearly ten years old, had grown from a one-year into a two-year course in response to student demand. The students had wanted to further develop issues that had not been included or that had only been touched on in a general way during the first year.

As I have already mentioned, I did not at first intend to take this class, but many of the women I interviewed, and in particular my cousin who was enrolled at the Midrasha, urged me to do so on the grounds that "you can't possibly write a book about the Midrasha without being in Rivka Sternberg's class."

The instructor prepared a booklet of readings for the course, through which the class progressed during the year.[6] The booklet covered a large number of subjects, among them human nature and the sex drive; equality and diversity among human beings; observances incumbent on women and observances women are excused from; the family; the marriage ceremony and marriage; ritual impurity and purity; and forbidden sexual practices.

Yet this entire broad fabric of subjects touching on femaleness was organized, explained, and discussed solely in relation to the women's roles as wives and mothers. These burning issues, with their implications for the women's gender, were articulated entirely around these roles. This was the case for all the issues that preoccupy religious women of this community in this age: their participation in religious rituals, their ability to give testimony in rabbinical courts, religious study, career, civil-political activity, and life in a multicultural setting. Those tendencies emerge clearly in the following dialogue, composed of selections from three class sessions.

Motherhood Is Slavery

In a full classroom of about fifty students, Mrs. Rivka Sternberg continued to discuss issues raised in the previous class session, reiterating her guiding precept: "I go back to the principle that we noted in the last session, and which will accompany us throughout the year, which is [she writes on the blackboard]: *Understanding the status of woman begins with understanding the status of the human being: moral equality—personal difference.*

"I will not address the difference between men and women. The feminist literature does that exhaustively, and the rabbinic literature provides us with a large number of texts on the character and essence of women that I have no intention of dealing with. As far as I am concerned, the only difference between the sexes is pregnancy and birth. A man and a woman have intimate relations and only she becomes pregnant and gives birth, and whether that is good or bad is open for discussion. I do not intend to argue that women and men are equal in every way as the feminists have done—a position they are now retreating from, because this matter of pregnancy and birth cannot be denied.

"Our discussion of the law that states that women are exempt from the performance of time-dependent mitzvot must take place in this context. Various societies around the world have relegated women to the kitchen, to the children, with a kind of contempt that makes this occupation an inferior one. These roles are, after all, routine, unending. Washing dishes and floors are jobs that have to be repeated over and over. Children get things dirty, cry at night, take control of our lives, upset our schedules.

Allow me to point out that a woman's jobs are not at fixed times, and everyone who raises children knows that the job does not go according to the clock. When a child cries you can't leave him crying. There have been many mornings that I've thanked God that he exempted me from putting on tefillin. He understands me, while modern society many times does not understand me, is not considerate of me. True, today we have solutions—day care centers, play groups, and so on—and I'm in favor of those solutions, but they don't invalidate the principle of pregnancy and birth, and the halacha is determined according to principle. From here on out we will be educated to exercise good judgment, to formulate a set of priorities, so that we can, as women, do more."

Shirli: "So maybe the halacha has to be changed to say that a person who is caring for children is exempt from time-dependent mitzvot, not necessarily just women. For instance, I see my brother-in-law standing outside the synagogue with the children while his wife prays. The law just has to be changed, because you said that a man who is performing a mitzvah is exempt from another mitzvah, and here he's responsible for the life of the children.

Sternberg: "More than that, Shirli: You didn't mention girls before they are parents, or older women and so on. What does the halacha say about that?"

Shirli: "Exactly. It simply has to be changed. When you are not involved in raising children you are obligated, and whoever is occupied with raising children, whether it's the man or the woman, is exempt."

Sternberg: "I see that men are taking on more and more jobs in the home, and that's good, I'm in favor; but he can't nurse and it all begins there. Not all of you know, for example, that a woman can perform kiddush for her husband on Friday night, but I would nevertheless recommend that the father continue in that role, because research has proven that the more the father functions within the family, family life improves. But it's important that you know that you can."

Shirli: "I want to second what you said. When there's a group of girls they always look for a boy to make kiddush for them, and it's so ridiculous, because they can, too, but they still look for a boy. They should do it themselves."

Sternberg: "The father's role in the family is very important, for the other side of the exemption from the positive time-dependent mitzvot is the positive mitzvot that are not time-dependent, and with those women have the same obligation as men, with three exceptions: 'be fruitful and multiply,' Torah study, and the redemption of the first-born."

Osnat: "What do you mean women are exempt from 'be fruitful and multiply?' A woman isn't required to have children?"

Sternberg: "That's a subject that requires organized study, and there is a dispute about it, since it says 'and God said to them: Be fruitful and multiply and replenish the earth and subdue it'—using the plural, but the ruling is that it's his mitzvah. That's the plain law but there's a debate about it."

Yael: "Okay, that's because you can't command a person to do something that often results in death."

Sternberg: "That's also disputed, but perhaps it's worth emphasizing that there's no point in commanding her to do something that she wants to do anyway. You have to command him, the man, and to that is attached the commandment to provide for the children's needs, to care for them, to teach them. There's no need to command her, for her it's self-realization. Jean-Jacques Rousseau told the French nobility to raise their children themselves, but he sent his own five children out of the home. This already brings us into a moral discussion of imposing a commandment on another only if you observe it yourself. Perhaps that is why women are not commanded to be fruitful and multiply."

Efrat: "Maybe there are women who don't want children, or who want to do other things, or who maybe can—and that's their business—manage with all the mitzvot and with their children. By exempting them from the time-dependent mitzvot, which are important, and especially from study and from Gemara—when all our lives are based on that, on study and prayer, and it belongs to everyone and affects everyone—that's what brings about inequity."

Sternberg: "Look, Efrat, you are raising the matter of study, and that's a subject unto itself that we will talk about—and really on its own could be the subject of a course or several courses—but anyone who tells you that it's possible to manage with everything isn't telling the truth. Raising children is slavery. You can see it as a harsh fate or as a meaningful destiny. You have to look at the Torah's principles. The attitude toward you is in principle one of equality, and personally as a woman there is a difference, just as there is a difference between a lay person and a priest. In the Jewish method the value of mankind is equal due to the presence of God's image in both sexes. Even if there were a pattern of a father outside and a mother at home, there would be no division of prestige here, outside being good and the home inferior. Raising children is not considered a lesser matter, that's unambiguous; it is a role of superiority. I'm not saying that that solves the problems and answers the questions. After all, people say: 'It's wonderful that you've raised children, but what about you? You haven't realized your own potential.' If I'm a nurse or a teacher who does it for others that's okay and creative, but if I do it for my own children it's not? It is a great thing to raise children; after all, to raise a girl is to raise yourself, Efrat."

MOTHERHOOD AS WORK OR
MOTHERHOOD AS AN IDENTITY

*When mothering is construed as work rather than "identity" or
fixed biological or legal relationship, people can be seen to engage in
mothering with differing expense of time at various periods in their lives
and in various and often changing sexual and social circumstances.*
Ruddick, 1994, p. 35

As with all ethnographic material, the above selections invite a large number of readings and a variety of analyses. It is especially tempting, however, to track the diversity of linguistic levels of discourse, perhaps because of the form of the story, perhaps because of the large number of linguistic layers that appear in it, and perhaps because of the salient voices. The sharp transitions from the pedagogical language of religious instruction to colloquial language, the sliding into modern examples from the ancient Talmudic context, and similar phenomena, are very characteristic of orthodox and *haredi* discourse.[7] Still, the ethnographic analysis below is focused more on content and less on form.

Close reading of Sternberg's and Lior's lessons reveals completely different representations of the concept of motherhood. Rabbanit Lior presented motherhood as an identity, whereas Rivka Sternberg constructed it as work or, more precisely, slavery.

Rabbanit Lior's opening words alluded to familiar subjects. The mention of the generation of Israelite women in Egypt[8] and the right of women to study Torah were subjects that came up again and again each time a Midrasha teacher spoke to an audience of women. The teachers merely made a quick reference to the general field of discussion and proceeded to the personal-feminine level.

"Aside from being Jewish people, we are primarily women."

These opening words would fit well into any feminist meeting in which women come to study themselves for themselves, on the basis of their common gender, without comparing themselves to men. Leaving the private "I" and connecting this "I" to the words of the Hebrew poet Rachel—"Only of myself I know to tell"—the *rabbinit* moved her monologue away from the religious-sectarian context and opened it into a modern Israeli-Zionist one. Locating femininity as an area of power—which can be internalized in this case for the purpose of worshiping the Creator on the one hand and coping with the political situation on the other—is a common activity in essentialist feminist discourse.

Surprisingly, Rabbanit Lior's students did not allow her to remain at the spot she wished to mark as a base. They refused to be locked into their gender, to unproblematically accept their "female difference." At this point they began to needle, contradict, and challenge her—to read out loud, whisper, laugh, and be disruptive. These activities apparently caused Lior to cut short her feminist introduction and go more quickly than she had originally intended into the main part of her presentation.

In this first of four classes there was a clear link between femaleness and motherhood, and between motherhood and study, knowledge, and power. Motherhood, so she told her audience, is natural for women, and

giving birth is an experience they all share. This is their purpose in this
world, and it is their merit for the next world. To be a mother is to be
yourself, and therefore it is a task of endless happiness. Motherhood is the
source of moral judgment and national strength, which the national religious community is in need of, especially in the political context in which
she was speaking—the period following the conclusion of the Oslo accords. Motherhood is an *identity* that embraces everything. It accompanies the woman-mother wherever she goes and is present in every other
facet of her identity. This is gender-conditioned motherhood, carried out
by women only.

Rivka Sternberg offered her audience an entirely different representation
of motherhood: It is restricted to the woman's body and is represented as
a simple biological fact that one can be happy or upset about. "A man and
a woman have intimate relations and only she becomes pregnant and gives
birth, and whether that is good or bad is open for discussion. . . . [T]his
matter of pregnancy and birth cannot be denied." According to Sternberg,
motherhood is an unending series of routines that have no intrinsic worth.
Such activities as cleaning, preparing food, and doing laundry—which lack
intrinsic value—receive meaning when they bring about the growth of another person. Sternberg did not offer her students pleasure, joy, or happiness. She spoke about sleepless nights, hectic days, and children who take
over one's life. The object of the work, the child, turns into a subject around
which motherhood is constituted, while the subject, the mother, becomes
an enslaved object. The halacha takes account of the woman's situation and
excuses her from positive time-dependent mitzvot so that she will have time
for her work. In this way, according to Sternberg's methodical thought,
the halacha places child rearing alongside other important precepts. The
reprieve women have received from prayer, for example, does not derive
from denigration of women but rather from consideration of them and
their work.

Yet this is not work in Ruddick's terms, because the work cannot be transferred. Although the central focus of the discussions was ostensibly about
halacha, the teachers asserted that the Torah is constructed on principles
and recognizes women as motherhood workers. Whether motherhood was
presented as work or as identity, the teachers found no room in their con-
ceptions for people who do not give birth. No real broadening of femaleness
beyond motherhood was accomplished. Such motherhood, by its very nature, cannot arouse discomfort or frustration. According to Rabbanit Lior,

motherhood is all happiness and joy, and cannot ever bring with it feelings of inequity and resentment.

A woman who is not a mother is represented as "pathological," and no general conclusions can be deduced from her case. According to Sternberg, frustration is misplaced, because frustration indicates that life according to the natural order is not fulfilling, and that would mean that the Torah may have erred. Since the principles of the Torah are correct a priori and eternally, careful study is required to find the logical axis linking the woman's (ostensibly frustrating) situation to the principle. It will then turn out that she has no reason to feel inferior. In the classes described above it emerges, for example, that child rearing is equated with other important precepts that provide an exemption from positive time-dependent mitzvot. It seems, however, that the most significant connection these teachers make to motherhood returns to the classic site of study—and, more specifically, to religious study. There each of them traces, in her own way, the boundaries of women's participation in the community of believers/observers. Rabbanit Lior chose, via the title of her course and the quote from Berachot, to redefine the role of the woman-mother as a person who enables the study of the "others," the men—the husband and sons.

The woman's Torah is the Torah she makes possible for her men. So, as the feminist scholar of education Valerie Walkerdine states (she writes specifically about the female teacher), the woman must enable male pedagogy. The woman-teacher must embody the violent logic of this pedagogy and turn it into a symbol of the regime, of the law. She must resolve, through her traits as a woman, patriarchal restrictions.[9] For Rabbanit Lior the limitation is the role of study, given to men, but which they have trouble fulfilling because of their stormy dispositions. For Sternberg it is the difficulty of being a father that a woman must help him with. In the first case, the woman will gain merit for the next world if she urges her men to study Torah. In the second case the woman will gain a placid and happy family if she restricts her roles to child care and does not "steal" the role of the "knower," the kiddush-maker, from her husband the father. Either way, the woman should not break through the boundaries of the role of care giver for men-children. She must not ask for herself what the halacha does not deny her. She must not undo the mind-womb dichotomy. The price, Walkerdine argues, is paid by the woman-teacher, just as it is paid by the woman-mother. She is passive in the face of her children's activity. She works for their entertainment. She serves the omnipotent child whose needs she must supply at all times. In this

way men are removed from the role of motherhood as work, and the labor
is to be done by women alone by force of their identity (Lior) or biology
(Sternberg).

These representations of motherhood were directed at the audience of learners who had come to the Midrasha in order to increase their knowledge
through sacred studies. A small portion of them were already married and
mothers, others observed the families they grew up in or the families of
those close to them. They knew that the labor of motherhood is performed
by both men and women, and that complex combinations can be made
between biological givens, the work of the family, and sacred studies. These
young women were seeking to broaden their circles of participation in the
community as believers/observers and as citizens. They came to the university in order to study academic subjects that would assist them in shaping for
themselves a career as working women, and they added to that many hours
of study at the Midrasha in order to gain more knowledge of sacred studies.
Most of them had engaged in more sacred studies than their mothers and
observed more religious precepts than their mothers did, yet their teachers were offering them "motherhood" circa the time of their grandmothers. These women were not looking to leave the orthodox community—on
the contrary, they were seeking a way into the depth and breadth of that
community.

At the Bar-Ilan Midrasha, in the educational framework of the community establishment, they found themselves in a paradoxical situation. They
had to revise their gender ideology in order to become a more real part of the
community that produced this ideology. They did not act outside the community but rather within it; they did not want to leave it but rather to enter it
more deeply. Even though women in that community had a status much like
that of nonreligious women in civil society, the possibilities of criticizing, of
being alienated, of creating alternative communities, and other such options
were limited, because the women accepted the canopy of the halacha and the
rule of the rabbis. The social and religious reality in which the women found
themselves taught them that they could do what the teachers refused to confirm. They interrupted, asked questions, inquired, did not let the teacher off
the hook, made fun of her, or offered examples from daily life—all in order
to express the discontinuity between their lives and the representations offered them from the lectern. These representations, which turned a blind eye
to what was actually happening in the lives of the students, caused them to
doubt the teachers, the texts, the sages who wrote the texts, and the motives
that led them to write what they wrote. In the teacher evaluation question-

naires on Lior's class (which I was allowed to glance at) I found a great deal of criticism. Among other things, one student wrote: "We've already heard this nonsense in *ulpana,* we came here to hear something different."

THE GREEK CHORUS—
THE REACTIONS OF THE STUDENTS

Maybe it was ethnographer's luck that led "the matchmaker" to sit in the chair next to me. Chance could have left me with a different record of the class, one lacking her acerbic commentary. The interviews I conducted taught me that the criticism voiced in private conversations did not, in general, find its way into the public realm and the public class session.[10] These interviews allow me to assume that even though the matchmaker's outspokenness was unique, her comments do not represent an exceptional position. Likewise, sitting in another corner of the room, next to other women, might have exposed me to a different form of criticism that I did not hear. In any case, the public discomfort expressed in the two lessons was sufficient to inform me that neither of the motherhood pedagogies of the two teachers found an attentive ear. Rabbanit Lior, who could not abide the comments and questions, asked at the beginning of her second class that no more questions be asked (this after, in the first class, praising the first questioner and telling the students to ask a lot of questions). Instead, she asked that all questions be submitted to her in writing at the end of each session.

The first objection was raised by a married student (wearing a hat), who immediately refused to be a party to the discourse contract concocted by the *rabbanit.* "There are two things that bother me here: First, whoever is sure that he can contribute something and does so doesn't look for justification in the Torah for his ability to make the contribution. Second, not all women are the same, even if that is what is common to all of us."

This woman's refusal to seek her value in the texts could have come out of her previous experience as a student in the religious Zionist system. Women were required to lag behind the (male) public and hang onto fragments of verses and midrashim that refer vaguely to them as also being human beings. This woman refused to be classified as part of the half of mankind that must search the religious texts for proof they are human. Women are not a uniform group as far as she was concerned, and she had no intention of going on a quest for her moral status. Both the classification and the expectation that she justify herself were in fact an a priori declaration that she was of lesser value. Whoever believes in herself and observes the precepts of Judaism needs no justification, she maintained.

The rapid link the *rabbanit* made between mother and woman led immediately to further objections by a large number of students, married and single, younger and older. The women did not accept the statement that only a mother is a full woman, that women think about their children always and in every situation, that men are not wired to love their children, and that non-religious Jews do not value their families and children as religious Jews do.

"Excuse me!" said one pregnant student as she adjusted her legs to sit more comfortably. "Men are also created to love their children and their wives naturally. That naturalness applies equally to women and to men. To love their homes."

The *rabbanit*, who was surprised by the sweeping attack, went deeper into the matter of naturalness: "Yes, but for you it's your job, and for him it's not. So for you it's easy, and for him it's hard. At work you think about your children all the time, and he doesn't."

The student did not yield. Instead she deconstructed the screen of naturalness, striving for the construction of the role of the mother. As a woman who was in the role of a learning women in the midst of pregnancy, she replied: "So for whom is it hard? For me or for him? Besides, let me tell you that when I come here I don't think about anything: not about the children I left at home and not about the work I left there. Nothing. I come here to learn, to think, to enjoy myself. Children are for when I'm at home. Not here and not at work." Her body declared that motherhood was not genderless, but her voice stated that this fact can be organized in different ways.

Similar messages pervaded the running commentary provided by the matchmaker. She, who viewed the Midrasha as a "great place" with "good merchandise," knew that there are men and there are women, and that in the modern religious community marriage, family, and children are a central axis. As part of this industry, she had no interest in hearing romantic stories that sugar-coat a complex part of life.

Why does the Gemara ask "How do women gain the next world?" "Because men wrote it," her friend answered, energetically knitting a *kipa* as she spoke. The *rabbanit's* words made the matchmaker suspicious, and she left no sentence without a response, deconstructing the entire edifice the teacher wanted to erect. The sages became male chauvinists, her sister a whelping woman, and Kiryat Arba a town of narrow-minded extremists. Still, she continued to assist the production of brides, who would, most likely, have many children. She like her friend knitted *kipot* for men and came to listen to a lecture (for which she received no credit) from a *rabbanit* from Kiryat Arba. Her criticism of the community from within is what is interesting here.

Her ability and desire to continue to be part of the whole that she criticized was the most important element in her subversive activity. It was subversive because she, like her peers, demanded to participate from a fuller and more relevant position. Their participation would change the whole, because the broadening of the circle of observers and actors is in itself a social change.

Sternberg's class did not elicit the aggressiveness of the sessions with Rabbanit Lior, nor did I hear the same kind of anger and cynicism. But the students protested no less. Rivka Sternberg was an important and well-loved figure at the Midrasha. Her teaching project consistently conformed to the slogan "equal value—personal difference." Her working hypothesis was that all human beings are in principle of equal a priori value and that the difference between them is individual. She did not address the fact that women (or any other category of people who are differentially treated by the halacha—such as slaves, priests, and the mentally deficient) are a separate social sector or public. She found the differences on the personal level. There is one rule for everyone, which is then adjusted in accordance with the requirements of different individuals. Using this principle, she cut through the entire range of burning problems in the lives of modern religious woman, and from its perspective she approached the issues of women's testimony before rabbinical courts, women and sacred studies, women's ritual purity and impurity, and other issues that disturbed the students.

The ethnographic segment taken from her classes presents a very small part of her work, but it accurately represents the character of her pedagogy. Sternberg opened up the students' learning and thinking horizons, invited them to question, and demonstrated to them how it is possible to find many more paths than are commonly trod through the Bible and halacha. But once the expansion began and the horizon broadened, she folded up her social scholarship project and restricted it to the areas of pregnancy, birth, and child care. Her refusal to read the writing that she herself wrote on the wall was a locus of discomfort in her classes. Sociology, the lives of the students, and the new link created between the students and the sources made a brief appearance and then vanished under excuses that had nothing to do with the texts. At this point Sternberg found it necessary to refer to "scientific studies" that show, for example, that it is best to encourage the husband to continue to play his traditional roles in the family. Or she cited

Jean-Jacques Rousseau, who spoke one way but acted in quite another way with his own family. Yet her audience did not give in.

Shirli told about her brother-in-law who watches his children outside the synagogue while his wife prays. She went on to express her anger at girls who look for a man to make kiddush for them when they could do it themselves. Shirli demanded a halachic change that would exempt from positive time-dependent observances whichever parent is caring for the children, no matter what the gender. Efrat had no need for rabbinical judgment of her situation and demanded that she be allowed to manage on her own.

For her part, Sternberg did not deny these realities, in which men participate in the work of motherhood and women choose how to divide their time. She even provided a wealth of halachic facts that depicted a boundary that is more distant than that known to most of her audience, and she encouraged them to think: "From here on out we will be educated to exercise good judgment, to formulate a set of priorities, so that we can, as women, do more." But she refused to take that further and confirm Shirli's claim that a halachic change is necessary. Instead she retreated into conservative positions that presented the range of possibilities as lying within the woman's body. She undermined the modern notion of "self-fulfillment." The woman's self blurs into the object of her work—the child. The way for a woman to find satisfaction can be exhaustively defined as her task of raising another person: "It is a great thing to raise children; after all, to raise a girl is to raise yourself," she answered Efrat.

Between motherhood as identity and motherhood as work, the reality the students actually experienced was eliminated, and the future they depicted for themselves was taken away. Their demand for participation in the community of learners-observers and as citizens was restricted to the site of motherhood.

THINKING MOTHERS THINK ABOUT MOTHERHOOD

Sarah Ruddick, who developed the idea of "maternal thinking" and presented it in her book (1989), constructed a complex theory that lays out how viewing the practice of motherhood as work can develop into a sociopolitical perspective. In a subsequent article, and in light of the stormy discussion her theory produced, she concentrated on pregnancy as a critical time preceding the work of motherhood. Among other things, she said: "I was moved to speak about mothering partly because of a feminist desire to challenge the dominant culture ideology of mothers as naturally loving and necessarily female. But feminist thinking was of limited use in forging a representation of mothers as thinkers."[11] It will be recalled that this inadequacy in presenting child-caring women as thinking beings also preoccupies Valerie Walkerdine. She observed that caring women (in her case, teachers) were expected to minimize their thought and free up as much room as possible for the development of the thinking child. These two theories, taken together, create a way to demolish the view that mothers do not think—that women who want to think must, in fact, only care.

The young women at the Bar-Ilan Midrasha confronted a similar viewpoint. They insisted on broadening the levels of their thinking. They sought to know more and to know differently than their mothers did. They packed the midrashot for Jewish studies, and from that vantage point they sought to push out the limits and challenge the restrictions imposed on believing and observant Jewish women in the areas of knowledge and practice. Within the Midrasha they encountered teachers, male and female, who were, in fact, partners in the project of broadening their knowledge. Yet when these teachers dealt directly with the students' identities as women they did so while denying the process they were part of: the attempt to silence the voices now being heard as well as those that may be heard in the future.

The texts presented to the women located their identities in the mind-womb dichotomy and implied that the two possibilities are mutually exclusive. Sometimes this was depicted as an inevitable and natural choice (Lior), sometimes as a simple biological fact (Sternberg). Either way, the position of literate women, who know and observe, was not raised as a real alternative. The position of women as mothers who are also knowers was presented as undesirable or impossible. This representation was rejected by the students, who refused to choose between mind and womb—even though, as part of the religious Zionist community, they accept a priori that their job is to be wives and mothers.

It may well be that representing their female identity as learning, knowing, and observant women would strengthen their bond to motherhood and develop an essentialist discourse celebrating the experience and uniqueness of motherhood. But the one-sidedness of the representation on offer induced discomfort, alienation, and criticism. The "discourse of entitlement" presented by Lior, in which women receive merit through their husbands and sons, may perhaps fit the concept of maternity presented at the beginning of this chapter. This kind of discourse, described as "feminism for hard times," is perceived by women today as a thing whose time has passed. Their rights as citizens derive from an extra-religious source that has received full recognition within their community. These rights are fully exploited by the community, which has become political and requires as many partisans as possible in its campaign for Greater Israel. Religious women's right to pursue secular studies has long been established, and they make use of it to train themselves for professions.

Now they seek to do the most difficult thing of all: to demand their rights at home, at the location where knowledge is linked to the construction of gender around the site that Boyarin has designated as the most fragile of all—that of sacred studies. If this is indeed the last outpost of Jewish manhood, there is no wonder it is so difficult to break in. The women's demands to study sacred texts just as men do and to broaden their participation in religious practice of precepts and rituals—and even to participate in the decision-making process—are convulsing the system.

This study focuses on a modern religious community at a moment in time where the women have scored a success in their efforts—in cooperation with the men and the religious establishment. The quality of this cooperation and the barriers that are erected in the course of this revolutionary process turn transparent elements into opaque ones. What was previously taken for granted becomes problematic, underscoring the boundary of gender discourse in orthodox Jewish society. Trying to enter the grove of academe, the Jewish woman runs into her body and her gender, and these interfere with her efforts to get through the gate. Beyond the gate lies the Jewish man, who constitutes his fragile identity as a learner and as a spiritual person in an arena empty of women; he faces a female object of desire—the Torah—together with his male colleagues. The approaching (and in many ways already present) woman can change the process by which she constitutes her identity, but this will also require a change in his identity. Study in mixed company, or with a partner of the opposite sex, could develop identities that are more similar. Yet, to continue Boyarin's line of thinking, this may also sabotage the complexity of the Jewish male, especially his non-macho aspects. In the meantime, the educational front applies itself to fencing in adult female identity around the role of motherhood, relying on existing halachot and abstaining from producing a new halachic discourse. Simultaneously, it obscures the sweeping new reality in which men, like women, also engage in child care and motherhood.

The experience of these women in a local context and in a given time frame offers an insight that may contribute to feminist thought at the junction of motherhood. It is not necessary for women to shed their identity as mothers in order for motherhood to be seen as work that is transferable to a man. At the very least it is not a necessary condition for changing the status of women, as Ruddick argues, and it is certainly not appropriate for all women in the world. Ruddick maintains that only when motherhood ceases to be perceived as a natural biological identity based in law and becomes a type of work will women be able to break out of the rigidity of their identities—and men be able to participate in the work of motherhood. The women in this study would seem to embody another possibility, one in which the female mother identity need not be discarded in order to demand and realize a change. Such motherhood is part of the history they draw from and accept. They feel themselves part of a chain of Jewish mothers that can be both loved and criticized. The young women at the Midrasha seek to transcend the dichotomy of identity or work, mind or womb. They demand expansion and sharing—an expansion of their identity beyond the role of mother so that it can include the woman as worker, believer, learner, and participant; and a parceling out of the work of motherhood so that many others, who are not necessarily childbearing mothers, can participate in it.

The social reality revealed at the Midrasha would seem to point to a way out of one of the burning dilemmas in feminist discourse. The young women there do not hesitate between essentialist (natural) motherhood and constructed social motherhood. Instead of being either one or the other, they demand to be both.[12] Their uniqueness as religious women lies in their investment of purpose and sanctity in their identities as mothers, but from their position as literate women at the end of the second millennium they know that this identity is not uniform—that there is room in it for additional facets. They have already made some of these facets part of their identity-in-formation, and they are conducting a resolute battle for the remaining ones.

COSMIC MOTHERHOOD AND INSTRUMENTAL MOTHERHOOD: SUING THE FETUS AND STEALING SEMEN—SUBLIME REASONS TO BECOME PREGNANT AND FOR MOTHERHOOD IN GENERAL

Toward the end of the last trimester of the 1993–94 academic year, in the framework of a class in aggadah, Rabbi Cohen, who taught the course, chose several rabbinical stories whose protagonists are women. For two sessions out of twenty-eight, the class addressed the gender issue directly.

In comparison with the class on halacha and ethics or the sessions conducted by Rabbanit Lior, the teacher here did not choose texts that address current dilemmas facing the community of women believers/observers (such as the issues of Torah study, testimony, and ritual impurity). These stories centered on a heroine. The rabbi interpreted them in accordance with a firm thesis about the connection between the Jewish religion, Jewish nationhood, and women's craving to become pregnant.

The selections presented below are a fascinating example of specific representations of the view of motherhood held by the religious-Zionist establishment—the kind of motherhood in which it seeks to enclose its women.

HANNAH AND THE MATRIARCHY OF THE HOUSE OF DAVID

"'Now Hannah spoke in her heart' [I Samuel 1:13]—Rabbi Elazar said in the name of Rabbi Yosi Ben Zimra: about the preoccupations of her heart. She said before him [God]: Sovereign of the World, [In] all that you have created in a woman you have created nothing for no purpose, eyes to see, ears to hear, a nose to smell, a mouth to speak, hands to do work with, feet to walk on, breasts to nurse with. These breasts you have placed on my heart, what are they for, not to nurse with? Give me a son and I will nurse with them." (Babylonian Talmud, Berachot 31b)

The rabbi presented the students with four selections about Hannah, the mother of the prophet Samuel, and led a discussion focused on Hannah's barrenness. In these dense passages Hannah appears as a demanding, aggressive, and strong-minded woman who demands of God that he give her a son.

The rabbi: "Why did the Talmud decide to change the biblical character of the beseeching Hannah into a strong woman? You might even almost call her a feminist. The interpretation the sages give to sections of the Bible is arcane, complex, goes far from the simple meaning of the text, and it is obvious that a huge amount of effort was expended here. For what? What do they want of the Bible? What do the sages want from Hannah? Why do they go to the trouble of changing her character?

Yael: "Maybe to show that all means are legitimate to get a son?"

The rabbi: "All means are legitimate? If you had a neighbor who hung out with men [one of the stories depicts Hannah doing this] in order to get a son, I'm sure you wouldn't speak to her, right?"

Yael: "Obviously."

Efrat: "Maybe to show how determined she was—that she wasn't necessarily a wretched woman?"

The rabbi: "Could be, but what is the principle here? Well, don't you all see what this whole complication is about? Look, she first asks in the regular way, out of hunger, out of her basic need for a son, and only afterward, when she is not answered, does she ask from another position—not out of her own hunger and needs. She argues that if she does not become a mother, there will be something imperfect in nature, that the whole system of reproduction will be damaged. She finds nothing amiss in her own behavior. She doesn't think she deserves to be barren, so she blames the manufacturer."

Yael: "That's a pretty serious charge, to blame the damage on God."

The rabbi: "Generally women petition about themselves and for themselves, whereas Hannah is interpreted here by the sages as petitioning for God's own honor—as someone who is actually demanding of God that he fulfill her role because he will then be doing his job properly. It's her evolutionary purpose. If that doesn't happen, there is something wrong with God's creation, since her organs, including her breasts, are part of creation. She asks for cosmic rectification. So, as you can see, this Hannah is not nice. She is forceful and demanding, and she is explained in the end by the sages as sacrificing herself for God's honor. It was clear to her from the start, as the Bible shows, that she would hand over her baby; she calls him Samuel because she has borrowed him from God. And in fact, when she finishes nursing him, she brings him to Eli."

Hanita: "I still don't understand. What are you actually saying about Hannah—or actually, what does it say about barrenness in general as a phenomenon?"

The rabbi: "Look, maybe there is a kind of secret here: that a woman who succeeds in understanding that her purpose in life is to fulfill the divine purpose, to help God actualize his creation, will not be barren. She can't be barren. But that would have to be a woman whose level is that of Hannah."

In the next session the class read an aggadah that appears in the Babylonian Talmud, Sanhedrin 107a, which speaks about a trial that King David underwent. David complained to God that he was not counted among the patriarchs, and he was answered that they successfully faced trials. When he asked that he also be tested, he was warned that his test would be one of prohibited sexual relations. The selected text forced the rabbi to speak about the male sex drive, male appetites, women as objects of desire, and unfaithfulness, but he seemed to be directing his words at still another area: suggesting that the story of Hannah demanding to be made pregnant offers a starting point toward a new destination.

The rabbi: "Nachmanides argues that the test is given for the good of the person being tested and allows him to actualize the traits that are potential with him. Maimonides, by contrast, argues that the test is meant to teach those who watch the person being tried about the power of the individual. It is logical that a trial would test the strengths of a person in an area in which he is active. So why was David not given a trial in the area of governance, but rather in the area of forbidden sexual relations?"

Tobi: "Because that is a king's weakness: multiplying women, multiplying horses. Kings fail in that."

Miri: "If he cannot be faithful in his own house, he will not be faithful to his people. There is a comparison here between his kingship in his home and his kingship in general."

The rabbi: "Yes, but that's not the major principle of kingship. That's an explanation, but a strained one."

Yael: "Actually, he proved himself well in every task of kingship—in war, in honor, in charisma. Why did he fail in precisely this area?"

Hanita: "Perhaps because his entire line suffered from this thing. [Hanita, a married woman, blushes and lowers her eyes.] Maybe here he was given an opportunity to make up for that."

The rabbi: "Shall I explain what you said?"

Hanita (blushing even more and smiling): "Yes, please."

The rabbi: "David's descent is somewhat dubious. There's Judah and Tamar, Lot and his daughters. There's Ruth, too, whom we read about with such great enthusiasm. I told you last week that if we were to find out that one of the girls in the Midrasha acted as Ruth did, we would expel her. She didn't exactly act in a modest way. In our society today we would not accept it, and in those days it was certainly not accepted. I ask you: Why are the foundations of the monarchy built around a not exactly respectable family—and even the Messiah is supposed to come from this family?!"

Drora: "Maybe to show that it is precisely a miserable, humiliated family that will bring the redemption. That magnifies the power of the Messiah, or shows that a corrupt mind can repent."

Shoshi: "Maybe the entire line of the Messiah is damaged because then Satan will not look there, so Satan won't have anything to say."

The rabbi (in a dismissive tone): "Satan? Who's Satan? Where does he live?"

Shoshi (who is one of the few women in the class of Oriental origin and who answers quietly): "I meant God's attribute of judgment."

The rabbi: "In each of these three stories the protagonists are women—Lot's daughters, Tamar, and Ruth. They had special traits with internal contradictions: loyalty and boldness, devotion and temptation. Tamar, out of complete loyalty to her husband's family, did what she did with Judah and paid a very high price for it. Lot's daughters wanted their father to have descendants, and they performed a most horrible deed. After all, everyone understands that they did not do it out of physical desire. Ruth, who did not bring descendants to her husband in the conventional way, took an unacceptable route. So that in David's line both elements exist—loving-kindness and heroism. The people who bear these elements and pass them from generation to generation are the women. They want the Messiah to have both these elements, genetically. In this, the kingship of David is different from every other dynasty. David is the man of passion—the artist, the poet, the lover—but also a man of blood and war."

Miri: "Excuse me, but why this way? Why do these women have to go through all that? Why through corruption and incest? Why through tripping up Judah and Lot?"

The rabbi: "There is no other way. David wanted to run away from it, from facing the test, and he did not succeed. As is written: 'Man has a small organ. If he satisfies it, it is hungry, and if he starves it, it is satiated' [from the same aggadah]. Both elements were mixed in him. Are you asking why this particular failing? Maybe because David brought repentance to the world."

MODELS OF A MOTHERHOOD THAT ARE NOT TAKEN FOR GRANTED

When Hannah sought a son for herself in the usual way, she was not answered. Her entreaties and bitterness as expressed in the Bible turn in the aggadah into anger and demands. Only from this position, when she imputed to God that his creation was imperfect—inasmuch as her body, which was meant to hold fetuses, was empty—was she answered. She was answered only when she distanced herself from motherhood as something to be taken for granted—where a woman gives birth to a child for herself and her family—when she depicted her pregnancy as an actualization of the order of God's creation. Her promise in advance to bring her parenting to an end at the time she stopped nursing, and to return to God what she had

borrowed from him, showed her determination to be a "different mother."
As such, she could not be barren.

The rabbi led the class from matter-of-fact motherhood, private female
and family motherhood, into motherhood in principle. He went on to argue
that it may well be that a woman who sees motherhood only at its matter-
of-fact level is liable to be barren, and vice-versa. Hannah's opinionated way
of handling this, as described in the aggadah, is described by the rabbi as
almost making her into a feminist—different from the weeping, bitter, and
angry Hannah whom Eli the priest mistakenly thinks is drunk. In doing
this, the rabbi offered the women an ideal model of motherhood that is not
linked to the body in a necessary way but which exists in the body as a part
of creation. A woman who is not a mother is not incomplete—rather God
is incomplete. Still, he "saved" Hannah from her feminist image, from being
interpreted as an impudent woman who demands rights for herself or as a
lawless woman who threatens to hide herself among men in order to achieve
the child she longs for.[13] Hannah's position, the tools she used, and her way
of acting worked for her, but they did not offer the women in the class an
accessible option for themselves. They were left with the distant ideal image
of cosmic motherhood—meant only for women of Hannah's degree—and
with a threat of real barrenness for anyone who seeks to give birth only for
herself and her family.

The distancing of motherhood from the private woman received another dimension in the next lesson, when the class read the story about
David being tempted with forbidden sexual relations. The king received
his share of criticism, but this did not get the most attention, and he was
even being given a positive cast by the end of the session. In the meantime
the heroines were presented—Lot's daughters, Tamar, and Ruth—as additional examples of motherhood of the not-to-be-taken-for-granted type.
These women's cravings for pregnancy were not directed at satisfying themselves or rectifying cosmic evolution. These women proved they were able to
get pregnant no matter what: sleeping with their father, their father-in-law, a
stranger, and through drinking and drunkenness, disguising themselves, or
seduction. Thus they demonstrated that they too bore complex and high-
quality genes. They did not submit to their fates, they shaped them; they
did not accept their empty wombs, they filled them up. These women, the
rabbi said through the aggadah, are worthy of being part of the royal line.
Since they are women, they are assigned to bear this genetic potential from
generation to generation, to take risks for it, to outwit and humiliate, to put
down and be put down, and so on—until the birth of the Messiah.

The rabbi's choice to address motherhood, of all the subjects marked as "female," is fully comprehensible, and it was discussed at the beginning of the
chapter. But the fact that he chose these particular stories and interpreted
them in this way requires a bit more thought. The rabbi proposed to his
young students (a small portion — about one-seventh — of whom were already mothers, and the rest of whom intended to be mothers) two models growing out of the aggadah around female protagonists. As a man, as a
rabbi, and as the holder of a high position at the Midrasha, he found the
time to discuss one of the central elements of female life with them. His
interpretation did not grow out of the experience of parenting or of motherhood, nor out of the laws governing women's status as mothers, and not
out of the standard national patriarchal preaching of "the mothers of the nation."[14] In fact the rabbi distanced the women from the axis of motherhood
as work or as an identity, from romantic essentialist motherhood and from
inevitable motherhood. No pregnancy here results from "thy desire shall be
to thy husband, and he shall rule over thee." Women determine events. They
demand a fetus or steal semen — they are active. This motherhood, which
is not organic and private, is depicted as a cold, calculating, genetic move,
building up an elitist matriarchy.

Ostensibly, there is empowerment of women here; the model presented
to them did not bind them against their will to motherhood. Miri, who
did not feel comfortable with the model, identified victims, both men and
women: There were those who lowered themselves and cheated — and those
whose seed was taken through trickery. The rabbi gathered all his
work into a single point: King David. This line of women imbued him with
contradictory but desirable traits, traits the Jewish people required in a king,
and the result is what makes the difference on the public level. The repentance that David brought to the world is consolation on the private level.
The models remained distant, inaccessible, and irrelevant. The immediate
lesson from these stories was not the kind of empowerment that might be
inherent in them but rather the warning not to act as Ruth did — because a
girl who acts like her gets expelled from the Midrasha.

6

~

BETWEEN YAVNE AND JERUSALEM—
NATIONALITY AND CITIZENSHIP:
AN AGGADAH CLASS

IN JANUARY 1994 THE FACULTY at Israel's public universities had
been on strike for two weeks. Bar-Ilan University's lawns were empty, except
for those around the Kolel and the Midrasha, which are located opposite
each other on the northeastern corner of the campus. These two institutions were holding classes normally. There are no strikes when it comes to
sacred studies. The Midrasha newsletter I held proclaimed in huge letters:
"Attention! Midrasha classes are being held during the university strike."
The Midrasha's students, most of whom were also students at the shut-
down university, had come specially for sacred studies. Few were absent.
Some came from nearby and others from farther away: Jerusalem, Petach
Tikva, Netanya, or Rechovot, as well as from neighboring Ramat Gan and
from Tel Aviv. Others came from settlements in the territories—the West
Bank and the Golan Heights.

I watched them from my vantage point in the third row, on the side, as
they entered the classroom. They bore huge backpacks that seemed to be
permanently stuck to their spines in a style that seemed half a symbol of
Israeli pioneering and half American fashion. These synthetic-fiber knap-
sacks with all the best accessories held everything the women needed to get
through the week. They were Shabbat-to-Shabbat portmanteaus accommo-
dating notebooks, appointment books, long dresses, spare socks, and prayer
books. The backpacks also provided a display space, serving as billboards
for countless political stickers. Alongside the name of the manufacturer, the

backpacks proclaimed "The people are with the Golan," "Thou shalt not be disloyal," "Hebron now and forever," and "Yesha [the Hebrew acronym for Judea, Samaria—the West Bank—and Gaza] is here." When their bearers lunged into the swivel seats connected to the long tables and took out their necessities, these items—the notebooks, pencil holders, and appointment books—also bore witness to their political views. Then they would look around to see who had arrived and what was new. A long, comprehensive, and far-seeing gaze. Then another look closer up to see who was sitting nearby.

Yael was sitting in the row in front of me, next to Rachel, as always. Yael's long Indian skirt, loose curly hair, and political backpack had little in common with Rachel's external appearance. Rachel sported a fashionable hat that revealed some of her hair and a pair of glasses with a delicate gold frame. Her preference was for narrow skirts, ending below her knees, and soft shirts. On her feet were white Keds with short, floppy white socks sagging over them.[1] What connected these two? What was the source of the delight in this weekly encounter between Rachel and the protest girl from the territories who spent her vacations in Jewish summer camps in Ukraine, who tutored a disadvantaged child, and who studied chemistry? Rachel had been married for about a year, was studying psychology and education, lived in nearby Givat Shmuel, and worked in an investment firm. Had they been roommates in *ulpana?* Had they been counselors of parallel groups in Bnei Akiva? Maybe there was some sort of family connection? Or maybe they had worked together in National Service? Were there, I thought to myself, real differences between them that were exemplified by the different dress codes they abided by? Did those dress codes go hand in hand with their positions on politics, religion, and feminism? I tried to solve such riddles during the long interviews I conducted with the women, when I had an opportunity to test my preconceptions based on their external appearance. I was often pleased to find that I had been wrong. There are no automatic links between the length of a woman's skirt and the way she thinks.

Rabbi Cohen, the teacher of the class on aggadah and the director of the Midrasha, arrived almost on time. His class was very popular and had drawn about sixty students. During the course of the year he built his lessons around six central subjects. Each was addressed through the reading of aggadot—homilies and stories written by the rabbis of the Talmudic period—and other texts he found appropriate. The texts were photocopied and distributed to the students. The course began with the creation of the world and continued with the struggle between Cain and Abel. When the binary categories of spirit and matter, righteous and evil, reward and punishment, good and bad had been established, the rabbi went on to King Hezekiah, whom he presented as an archetype of a thinking righteous man, and Isaiah, whom he presented as an archetype of an emotional righteous man. The lessons I have documented here (in edited and abridged form) came after this. The year ended with a discussion of the link between gender and nationalism, although not under that heading, of course. The clear foundation of the classes was, as I have noted, binary, and in addition to those mentioned above there were further dichotomies: the Jewish people and the gentiles, passivity and activism, preservation and innovation, instinct and mind. The tension in the selection presented here is between Jerusalem, the spiritual capital centered on the Temple, and Yavneh, the small town where the Jewish religious leader Rabban Yohanan Ben-Zakkai set up a center of study and the seat of the Sanhedrin after the destruction of the Second Temple by the Romans in the year 70.

Before the rabbi began his lesson, and before he went to his desk in the center of the room, he strode past the seats straight toward me. "You remember our understanding from the beginning, don't you? As we said, you've come here to study and nothing else."

My two neighbors smiled in discomfiture, and a familiar feeling coursed through me. Fear of the lie, conditional acceptance, the fear of losing material. At the same time I tried to reassure myself that I already had something in hand, that it was now too late for him to renege on his decision; I could still get away with my spoils. Yet I wanted things to be otherwise. I wanted to continue to interview more students. I aspired to that impossible position in which the investigator is welcome and accepted.

"Of course I remember, you don't know how well. I actually was thinking about coming to talk to you about that, because it wasn't that, that wasn't exactly our agreement. You know I said I would study and study—that is, I would study sacred texts, but also, a little, about how the girls here study and all that."

"I just don't want to come out like that Gur Hasidic *rebbetzin* in your last book."[2]

The class was about to begin and the room was full. The girls were looking at us, which was pretty embarrassing. We exchanged a few more words. I gave him regards from a student of mine who was a neighbor of his, and he began his lesson.

"You must remember what we read in the last class, from the tractate Berachot 28b. There we met Rabban Yohanan Ben-Zakkai on his deathbed, bidding his beloved students a tearful farewell. We tried to understand from the written text what he was afraid of. An utter saint like him, what fear could he have of the judgment of heaven? After we read selections from the Bible and from other places in the Gemara, I want to mention a section of the Gemara that you are all certainly familiar with. It is the section in which Rabbi Akiva criticizes Rabbi Yohanan Ben-Zakkai and explicates the verse: "turns wise men backwards and makes their knowledge foolish" [Isaiah 44:25]. That, of course, is about his having, during the Great Revolt against the Romans, preferred Yavneh and its sages to Jerusalem. You must also certainly be acquainted with the book by Yehoshafat Harkabi [a political scientist and former Israeli intelligence officer who had published a book condemning the religious and military leadership of the Jewish revolt against the Romans of 131–135 A. D.] that presents Rabbi Akiva as a fanatic nationalist who incorrectly read the military and political map and brought catastrophe on the Jewish people by supporting the Bar-Kochba revolt. And I ask you, dear girls, what? Rabbi Akiva hadn't read Harkabi's book? What, he didn't study for the test? Ah, that's funny. Okay, so he didn't read the book, but do you think that he didn't know then what Harkabi understands today? I presume that he knew what the Romans' strength was—after all, he could see their might with his own eyes. He understood what risks were being taken here, and in any case, what brings Rabbi Akiva to choose the nationalist sovereign side and to criticize Rabbi Yohanan Ben-Zakkai, seventy years after the event, for having chosen the Torah and not national sovereignty?

"So girls, what do you think?"

The young women in Rabbi Cohen's class knew from the start that he would call them "girls." They knew that he would ask their opinion and accept only his own. They knew that he would disparage the answers of those who dared to speak, and that he would demand a reply from women who had chosen to remain silent. Nevertheless they chose, year after year, to fill his course, because the word was that he was interesting, that he said things others did not dare to say, and that he "opened up your mind." At the beginning of the year Rabbi Cohen thought it necessary to tell his students that he knew he was perceived as a teacher who caused offense, and he apologized in advance, because that was not what he intended. Still, after each question there would be a short silence that only a few brave women dared break.

Efrat: "Rabbi Akiva symbolizes the Israeli Jew, the one who will not com-promise his honor, who will not surrender—like the Jews who fought in the Warsaw ghetto and did not go like lambs to the slaughter. Rabban Yohanan Ben-Zakkai symbolizes the Jew of the Exile who calculates everything: There are children here, there are women, let's surrender and obtain what we can. In the Holocaust there were people like that, too, and we know where that calculation led them."

Yael: "In our times there are also people who try by force and there are those who go on the spiritual-Torah side. Rabbi Akiva simply wanted to show that the Jews had power. That lets the people know that there is a chance and that miracles can happen, and that you do what you have to do without compromises."

Rachel: "Yohanan Ben-Zakkai was willing to give up the trappings of sovereignty in favor of wisdom and knowledge and the Torah. Rabbi Akiva simply didn't believe that it was possible to live only under the crown of the Torah without the crown of the kingship and the priesthood. Those are simply two different opinions, two worldviews. It's not that one is right and one is wrong."

Efrat: "It is simply amazing, if you think about it in the context of our times."

The rabbi: "The truth is that I don't really want to speak about it in the context of our times, but since you've already touched on that: On the eve of the declaration of independence in 1948 there was a big discussion about whether to issue the declaration or not. Ben-Gurion decided to declare, against the opinion of many, who were afraid of the reaction of the Arabs. Do we know whether the decision was a correct one? We don't know, be-cause not enough time has gone by. I only want to talk for a moment about the doubt, about the mind of a leader who has to go to the grave with that doubt. That is why Rabban Yohanan Ben-Zakkai cries before his students; he is still not sure whether he acted properly. Here, Menachem Begin pun-ished himself while he was still alive. He put himself under house arrest be-cause he understood in retrospect that his decision to launch the Lebanon War had been a mistake. That's a matter of the moral greatness of a leader. I don't want to go on with the analogy to today, only to say to you that as great a leader as Yohanan Ben-Zakkai lived with doubt, and that shows us what level he was on and what depth he had, because today it seems to me that our leaders don't agonize over anything."

Shlomit: "Maybe that's tactical. Maybe they agonize but radiate confi-dence on the outside."

The rabbi: "I really hope you are right. I have a feeling that our leaders today are not of the same moral stature. But let's go back to the matter at hand. Who, in retrospect, was right—Rabbi Akiva or Rabbi Yohanan Ben-Zakkai? Today we have the historical distance to judge them."

Even though they knew that history had shown Rabbi Akiva wrong, and that the Bar Kochba revolt had led to the exile of the Jewish people, and even though they knew that the Jewish people had survived in exile thanks to the Torah and despite the lack of national sovereignty, the women had a hard time criticizing Rabbi Akiva. I felt their silence in my chest; the rabbi's anticipation was enveloping me as well. The sudden collapse of the myth of Rabbi Akiva, the hero of the Land of Israel, was not an easy matter even for people educated in secular Zionism. While in the school I had attended Rabbi Akiva had been glorified primarily for his patriotism and his support of the use of force, we were also well acquainted with the legends of his great longing to become literate and his maxim "love thy neighbor as thyself." The women around me no doubt added to this the religious dimension, and together it was difficult to violate the silence.

The rabbi: "Hey, girls, you don't want to say bad things about Rabbi Akiva? You don't want to say that he made a mistake? You're allowed to, you know. What, in *ulpana* they don't say that rabbis made mistakes? After all, on the face of it, Rabbi Yohanan Ben-Zakkai was right."

Leah: "Maybe, but it might be that Rabbi Akiva's way would have taken less time—the Exile, I mean."

The rabbi: "Hey, you've forgotten an important historical fact. Rabbi Akiva was already coping with Christianity, which offered a universal religion detached from national identity. The concept of the chosen people was being threatened. Every man could join the new religion no matter what his nationality, and that is what Rabbi Akiva was afraid of. In his eyes, Rabbi Yohanan Ben-Zakkai's offer of spirituality that did not depend on nationalism endangered Jewish uniqueness. And that is still on offer today. If you cross the bridge over the highway here, next to Bar-Ilan, into Bnei Brak, you will hear the same opinions. Yes, today. Spiritual Judaism that does not depend on nationalism. Even if Rabbi Akiva failed militarily he did not fail historically. Why? Because he injected the aspiration for national existence, the desire for national revival, into Jewish discourse. There have to be opposing forces of thrust and braking in the nation. That is how criticism grows, that is how development happens. Like the tension between the Hasidim and the Lithuanians—in the final analysis it helps. I don't want to think what would have happened to the Jewish people if both those forces had not existed within it—spirituality and nationalism."

The class went silent, and the rabbi observed his students. They were used to his long pauses and to his short speeches. They were used to having him lead them, at the end of two or three class sessions during which they had read a variety of seemingly unconnected texts, to the destination he had chosen. But now it seemed that other things were interesting him.

Efrat: "Rabbi, I know, you've already said that you don't like to talk about relevant things, but with everything that is happening, and the situation now, it is very difficult not to extrapolate to today."

The rabbi: "To extrapolate to today? What, do you want me to talk politics?"

Efrat smiled expectantly.

The rabbi smiled back and said: "Oh, all right. Close all the windows. Tamar, stop writing, and. . . ."

All eyes turned to me, and I heard laughter. Not everyone knew who Tamar was, and they followed the gazes. Someone said: "She must have one of those dictation tape recorders."

The rabbi: "Look, in my opinion everything that is currently happening is actually an expression of a profound and ideological war of cultures that is now taking place in Israeli society, with the debate over the territories being only its outer shell. I am in favor of putting the cards on the table. We need to find out what kind of Jewish state we really want here. There are several models: Rabbi Shach's model, Shulamit Aloni's model, ours, Rabin's, all kinds. A decision has to be made. I'm not afraid of a struggle, but it doesn't have to be a struggle with guns. It is a profound struggle, and it should be carried out. I don't want a country in which all kinds of perversions are suddenly considered legitimate by some woman or other in the Knesset, a country in which we give up the heart of Judaism."[3]

Orly: "Rabbi, maybe the time is not ripe for decisions. It's like us not having a constitution, because it's impossible. If a decision is made there will be two nations here, there will be a split."

The rabbi: "I prefer a split. I want to underscore that. Without a split, without an ideological cultural war, there will be no rebirth, the Messiah will not come. If someone thinks that big yellow signs will bring the Messiah,[4] fine, but anyone who looks into the sages sees that they understood it in a more complex way. Sometimes we are afraid of struggle—let it pass, it won't happen as a natural and normal development of people returning to religion, for example. We won't be able to achieve change if we do not knock this society down. And that can't be done in slow stages; only after we destroy the society will we be able to build a new society. I know that I sound like a Bolshevik, like Lenin on some balcony, but that's the way it is. Not necessarily by force, but there has to be a war."

Orly: "But a cultural war is always accompanied by a physical war. And we're talking here about Israel imposing itself on other nations, not only at home. After all, they won't want it of their own free will, right?"

The rabbi: "For the moment, we rule in accordance with the school of Hillel, because we live in a good world, and we must rule in favor of peace, consideration, and understanding. But in the future, when we live in a world of truth, we will rule in accordance with the school of Shammai. The school of Hillel says we should always say that 'the bride is beautiful and modest' [even if that is not true]. But the school of Shammai says we should describe the bride as she really is."

Ravital: "So much the worse for us, the brides."

The rabbi: "That's not a problem, because in any case it will be a world of truth."

The laughter that broke out in the classroom let loose some of the tension that had been created in the dialogue. The class dispersed and returned, a little calmer, a week later. But the question that had reverberated in the room in the previous session continued to trouble the women. Had the hour of truth arrived? How could one know when to go from a ruling of peace and consideration to a belligerent one?

The rabbi: "I know that I confused you a bit, but I wanted to address matters that are important to us."

Ora: "What wasn't clear to me is how we know when we go from one time to the other, from one era to another. When do we know that the time has come? Because one sector thinks it has heard the voices and that something has to be done, and another sector thinks it has heard other voices and that we have to do something else. And there are those who don't want to hear, and there are those who don't care. So what do you propose practically?"

The rabbi: "Now you must understand why the sages did not want that time to be in their own era. But seriously, there can be a change by evolution and by revolution."

"But rabbi," a student in the back of the class interrupted him, "all revolutions have been processes. The industrial revolution, the Enlightenment, Christianity—everything was a process. It didn't happen all at once. It can't happen any other way. Besides, what will happen if we make a clean cut and you don't agree with the decision that is made. If you aren't pleased with the outcome of the war, what then?"

The rabbi: "If the state is not a Jewish state, *al yehi helki ima*—I will not be a part of it."

The class fell silent, and it seemed to me that the rabbi himself was caught off guard by his own vehemence. He went on—to the subject of destruction and redemption, the Temple, and the chosen people—but the noisy dialogue that had characterized the previous group of sessions did not return.

At the end of the class I walked with the rabbi to his room, next to the Midrasha office. Several students also wanted to speak with him, but he put them off for a few moments. With the door to his office open, we sat facing each other across his large desk. I gazed at the pictures hanging behind his back, at the vase that always contained fresh flowers. The rabbi offered me dates from a plate at the edge of the desk, prized *majbul* dates grown by religious Zionist farmers in the Beit She'an Valley.

"The truth is," I told him, "I am pretty shocked by what you said."

I tried my hand at an alternative interpretation of the legend of Yohanan Ben-Zakkai. I tried to deepen the moral and pragmatic doubt that had come up in the classroom about the efficacy of cultural and national coercion. I spoke about the inescapable necessity, even desirability, of separating religion and the state. It seemed to me that he was listening to me with utter seriousness, and I went on to compare Yitzhak Rabin to Yohanan Ben-Zakkai.

The rabbi: "I simply don't think that Rabin today has the same moral fiber that Rabbi Yohanan Ben-Zakkai had, even if they made similar decisions. I'm not sure that he doesn't sleep at night, that he has the same measure of greatness of the soul."

"I'm not sure, either," I answered, after he had referred to Rabin by several derogatory names. "He doesn't seem to me to be a great spiritual leader, and he doesn't need to be. He is carrying out a great move that, it turns out, only he could lead. I don't believe in his sensitivity or in his morality, I believe in the path he is taking. He's the prime minister who was elected, and that is what is relevant."

The rabbi: "Maybe we have to give it a chance, maybe we have to try it. I don't know. It doesn't seem right to me, but maybe. Why don't you raise your hand in class and say that? It's very important that you let these things be heard."

By chance I did not make it to the next class, but in subsequent ones I did not talk either.

BORDER CROSSING AND PARTICIPATION
IN THE ZIONIST COLLECTIVE

My unraveling and reassembly of the dialogue quoted above is based on two
different approaches in the analysis of literacy. Both are presented in detail
in part IV of this book. Here these approaches will be placed side by side
in a practical test of the act of ethnographic reading. The act of unraveling
ethnography is guided by Giroux's theory, which proposes a pedagogy of
"border crossing" as the literacy of the postmodern era. The gathering up
of the deconstructed ethnography is based on the motif of "participation"
as developed by Lave and Wenger.

"The importance of the debate on literacy, difference, and schooling
raises important questions about the fragile nature of democracy itself." [5]

The pedagogy of border crossing takes as a primary duty the presentation
of multiple literacies in the class. It seeks to make many literacies present
in the classroom, to offer learners systems of thinking based on a variety
of value scales, different social histories, and the wealth of personal, class,
and gender experiences that shape human knowledge. This pedagogy is an
alternative to education for social unity—education that is beholden to a
uniform curriculum that derives solely from certain specific worldviews.
The recognition that every educational process involves a struggle for power
and position in society, the knowledge that even the ability to read depends
on a student's social position, requires the school to deal with social boundaries. Dealing with social boundaries underlines their existence, and from
this the pedagogy of border crossing has two objectives. The first is to allow learners to identify the boundaries, to cross them, and to experience
the transition—to become acquainted with those on the other side of the
fence and to choose which side they want to be on. The second objective
is to recognize the difference or otherness within the borders as a real and
qualitative phenomenon. In this way, Giroux argues, the pedagogy of border crossing aids in the creation of a democratic society, in which differ-
ence/otherness is learned and confirmed, instead of being presented as an
essential phenomenon and dismissed from the agenda because it threatens
the nation's unity.

Giroux dealt, of course, with groups rebelling against centers of power
in the United States. His interest was in ways of empowering these groups,
and he proposed, like other investigators of society at the beginning of the
1990s, the politics of difference.[6] For Giroux, the site of this political activity is the school. The school must turn from a stronghold that replicates

ideologies of the powerful to a place in which literacy hierarchies are deconstructed. In this way pedagogy brings a double benefit: recognition of differ-
ence/otherness, and criticism of a center that feigns uniformity and unity.

The religious Zionist group cannot be placed under Giroux's rubric of
the powerless. Still, its position in the literacy hierarchy is not clear. If we
look at it from the outside, it is self-contained. Its difference is recognized
by national law, which mandates the existence of a state-run religious school
system and which recognizes the *ulpanot*, yeshiva high schools, and *hesder*
yeshivot. From one perspective, it appears that Israeli society—because
of its apprehension about the discourse of the melting pot, and despite
its concern for national unity—has actually achieved Giroux's "messianic
vision." There are separate educational paths for secular, national-religious,
and *haredi* Jews, and also one for Arabs. Or it can be seen another way:
Apprehension about the ability to achieve the melting pot led the state to put
the "others" in ghettos, evicting them from center stage to ensure that they
would not interfere with the official state-sponsored educational system.
Yet from the moment relative independence was given to these different
educational systems, there was no way of preventing the growth of different
languages, and these, in contradiction of Giroux's vision, were not aimed
at sanctioning difference and maintaining democracy. It seems that these
languages serve, more than anything else, as a refuge from democracy and
from the real need to experience it.[7]

A close examination of religious Zionist literacy of a specific type (education for young women at the Bar-Ilan Midrasha) indicates that it is indeed
continually involved in scrutinizing alternative literacies, in social, gender,
and ideological border-crossing exercises. To conduct observations as a participant in the Midrasha during the years of the Labor-Meretz government
was to view a group under siege. The national situation placed the community at the margins of social and political events, facing in the opposite direction. Those events cast doubts on the group's ideology and on the practical
consequences of that ideology. A fascinating situation was created here, one
of marginality for a community that had for a fairly long period enjoyed a
position at center stage. The relative centralization of this group (compared
with other groups), its practical commitment to the implementation of its
national ideology, and its relation of this to religion all turned the religious
Zionist community into a unique cohort in the context of flexible border-
crossing.

Clearly every process of teaching or preaching makes use of alternative literacies. These are often raised only in order to strike them from the

agenda, as a way of examining all the options on the road to the "truth." According to Giroux, we should inquire into the goal of this examination of alternative literacies, as well as its depth and the force of self-criticism and criticism of the alternative discourse. The central criterion for evaluating the border-crossing exercise is democracy, which marks the outer borders of the areas within which the crossings are made. Therefore, it is necessary to break down the ethnography into the different types of literacies that appear in it. Such a reading deconstructs the text into its components and reveals the dynamic of border-crossing within the class.

ACADEMIC LITERACY/TORAH LITERACY

One part of the series of class sessions described above took place during the Israeli faculty strike of the winter of 1994. Bar-Ilan University participated in the strike, and the students supported it. During the strike there was a public discussion of the role of the universities in the country's cultural life, and the status of university faculty members as educators, researchers, and intellectuals. The future of Israeli higher education was examined in light of the challenges that society would face in the coming millennium, and apparently its positive role in forming that future was not a matter of doubt.

While Bar-Ilan's academic faculty struck, classes proceeded normally at the women's Midrasha and at the men's higher yeshiva. Teachers in the campus's academic departments did not teach (including those who taught sacred subjects such as Bible, Talmud, and so on), but they continued to teach at the Midrasha. In doing so, they sought to confirm the difference between the secular literacy of the university and the holy Jewish literacy of the Midrasha. University study was presented as an activity that could be bargained over—merchandise that required proper commercial conditions. Religious knowledge appeared to be a goal in and of itself, an act that cannot be reevaluated or reexamined. The fact that the academic departments and the Midrasha are all under university governance—and the fact that more than once students acknowledged that the level of studies in the academic departments of Bible and oral law was higher than that in the Midrasha—only served to emphasize the dissonance of the linkage between academic and religious literacy. The declaration on the Midrasha newsletter that there was no strike at the Midrasha was meant to mark boundaries and create a literacy hierarchy, instead of presuming, ostensibly, to join the literacies together. The fact of the establishment of the Midrasha and the higher yeshiva on the campus was part of this marking process, which placed religious literacy above academic literacy. The former is a sacred obligation and the latter is merely an option.

Marking a clear boundary between the university and the Midrasha contains a certain criticism of academic education and its presumed place in the dominant secular discourse. But this boundary was depicted as artificial, especially when it came to fence in those who had internalized the dominant discourse, and who had decided to enroll at a university and devote themselves to secular literacy rather than concentrating on religious studies. The position of the rabbi instructor in these literacy fields was a complex one. He was teaching in the university's department of Talmud and also directing the Midrasha. He moved between the academic discourse of sacred studies on campus and the discourse he formulated in the Midrasha. His consent to the presence of an anthropologist in his class indicated, among other things, recognition of the research imperative. Nevertheless, he sought to influence the way he would be represented in the research. The rabbi had read my previous study, and his comment at the beginning of the encounter revealed his anxiety about the way he would be depicted in my next work. In requesting that he not be portrayed like that "Gur Hassidic *rebbitzen*,"[8] he was doing two things. First, he was signaling me that it was obvious to him that the way he would appear in the study was not a "scientific matter" out of my control—that he and I could shape it. Furthermore, he was distinguishing himself from the "*rebbitzen*": He is a man, a rabbi, and a religious Zionist rabbi.

TALMUD LITERACY

Religious study means Talmud study. The Jewish male hierarchy of literacies has always placed the Talmud at the top of the scale, even though variations of one sort or another have occurred in various communal and historical contexts.[9] The women at the Midrasha did not study Talmud *al ha-seder* at the time this study was conducted.[10] The class taught by the Midrasha director was one in aggadah, the Talmud's "soft" material—the literary and narrative portions of the Talmudic text that do not deal with legal rulings or establish normative behavior. The rabbi would distribute photocopied pages of texts to the students. Generally he noted the source of the material on the page, but there were times he forgot to do so, and when this happened, the women did not ask about it. The collection of aggadot that he presented was not organized in any particular way: according to the Talmudic sage who had told them, by period, or by subject matter. The sheets were the teacher's private collection, which served him in the construction of his thesis. Reading from photocopied pages is a common practice in teaching girls and women, who are not expected to inquire into the source. The skill of looking up cross-references and related texts, the possibility of placing the text in its context, familiarity with the structure of the page and the tractate are generally not imparted to women.

In one lesson the rabbi "confessed" that he often photocopied the ag-gadot from *Sefer Ha-Aggada,* a modern compilation of aggadic material first put together by the secular Zionist poet Chaim Nachman Bialik in 1908 and then reissued in expanded form in 1930 by Bialik and his collaborator, Y. Ch. Rabanitzky. Bialik and Rabanitzky abridged their selections and presented them out of context, and their express purpose was to make the aggadic and midrashic literature available and accessible to the nonreligious Jew. While the book is acknowledged as a modern classic, it is of limited use as an aca-demic, scholarly reference. It is not considered, especially in religious circles, to be a work from which a religious scholar can conduct a systematic study of rabbinic literature. Rabbi Cohen said, however, that "In general I am not disappointed [by Bialik], and he's only caused me problems once or twice."

This is how the aggadic and midrashic material makes its way to religious Zionist women—not directly from the large pages of the Talmud, but in-stead from sheets of paper from the photocopy machine in the Midrasha office and via Bialik and Rabanitzky's Zionist literacy project. The book that sought to provide a link between the Talmudic literacy of the Diaspora and the Hebrew-reading Zionist generation belongs to everyone. It can be found in both nonreligious and religious Zionist homes, and selections from it are studied in the state nonreligious school system. Ironically, however, today it is probably much more widely read in religious homes; in secular fami-lies it remains on the shelf—something one's parents read but that is sel-dom opened by the younger generation. Bialik, who as a young Jew fled his yeshiva, bared his head, and became an icon of secular Zionism, has entered the Midrasha with his *Sefer Ha-Aggada.*

WOMEN'S LITERACY

The rabbi knew that the young women with whom he was conducting his dialogue had come to him after proceeding along a carefully laid out path through institutions appropriate for Jewish women. He presupposed that they had a wealth of knowledge and a good memory that would enable them to anchor his references in the appropriate places. Alongside this, he minimized their literacy, belittled it, and marked it as "literacy for little

girls," "*ulpana* literacy." "Hey, girls," he needled them, "you don't want to
say that he made a mistake? You're allowed to, you know. What, in *ulpana*
they don't say that rabbis made mistakes?"

Rabbi Cohen portrayed *ulpana* literacy as sanctimonious, uncritical—
curtailing the value of the women facing the text and its authors, and giving them absolute moral values. He challenged this literacy, presenting the
women's previous scholarship as limited and proposing that they "move up
a grade." But this offer contained no real encouragement for women learners
to assume a critical stance themselves. Instead it provided them with a kind
of dispensation to stand beside the masters who knew how to examine texts
critically. Women's literacy was cheapened. The ticket to enter the male literacy world was held out to them and then snatched away before they could
grasp it.[11]

HISTORY

Historical scholarship, in its various branches, and its textual output have always represented a parallel literacy to that of the canonical Jewish texts. Jewish historiography began only in the period of the Jewish Enlightenment.[12]
The rabbi had no hesitation about referring to Yehoshafat Harkabi's historical study, and he even assumed that all the students were familiar with it
or at least aware of its main conclusions. His presentation of our childhood
hero, Bar-Kochba, as a nationalist radical who brought destruction and exile on the Jewish people was a bitter one in its time, and not necessarily
just for nationalist-religious Zionism. Transforming him from a redeemer
of the national honor into a leader who had put the physical existence of
the nation at risk was opposed to the ethos constructed by both the secular
and religious state school systems.[13] The rabbi did not question Harkabi's
scholarly findings nor did he seek to expel historical literacy from the curriculum, as is often done in *haredi* discourse. He did, however, transfer the
center of gravity of the historical interpretation from the set of physical con-
siderations (the military strength of the opposing forces and the chances
of victory in battle) to an alternative, ethical system, as will become clear
below. In this way he proposed to the members of his audience that they
cross a critical literacy boundary from accepted scholarly conventions into
a different literacy system.

HOLOCAUST LITERACY

Religious discourse about the Holocaust is unending. The great question
about God's role in the fate of his people during World War II is perhaps

the most difficult question of all for believing Jews. The national-religious discourse has adopted the Zionist interpretation of the Holocaust, stretching it to its limits. The link between the Holocaust of European Jewry and the rebirth of the State of Israel lies at the basis of the national discourse and reinforces the messianic ethos.[14]

When Efrat immediately drew a comparison between the Holocaust and the case under discussion in the lesson, I was shocked. Israelis have generally tended to reserve the Holocaust argument for the last moment and to use it with great caution. Efrat's casualness and her ability to offer the Holocaust as an analogy for the Bar-Kochba Revolt without anyone objecting testified to the existence of an entirely different Holocaust literacy in the Midrasha. It may well be that the great rebellion that led to the end of Jewish independence in Israel and which marked the beginning of the Exile shines in Efrat's memory with the same vitality and immediacy that the memory of the Holocaust does. It may be that these two events stand beside each other on a linear continuum of the fate of the Jewish people, eliding time and place. More evident than anything else was the binary division at the base of Efrat's contention, one between passivity and activism. It was apparently on the basis of this division that Efrat compared the two events. Some Jews, as she understood it, were pragmatists who "calculated" the pros and cons and surrendered to the outside gentile force in order to save (so they thought) their skins. This was the behavior of Yohanan Ben-Zakkai and of some of the Jews in Europe. In both cases, Efrat argued, "we know where that calculation led them." There are Jews who don't tally pros and cons, and they get a moment of national glory before their deaths. Efrat did not want to speak about the inevitability of those deaths, but about the moment of glory that was applicable to the reality that could be seen from the Midrasha's windows. The division between passive and active Jews was also applied for the purpose of separating (passive) *haredi* Judaism from (active) religious Zionism. This division became, in Efrat's eyes, especially problematic.[15] It separated the Labor-Meretz government—which, according to this logic, was engaging in a practical accounting of the situation that led to concessions—from the political opposition of the time. The dichotomous literacy of passivity-activism stands firm until someone casts doubt on it. Since no one does, it remains stable and natural, and it can be used ahistorically to classify the Holocaust, the Great Revolt, religious groups in Israel, and government actions.

Into this activist atmosphere, on which religious Zionism has no monopoly, Yael injected the religious added value. If one demonstrates strength, she argued, God will join in. Rabbi Akiva wanted to show, she claimed, that "the Jews had power." Yael's formulation made, in an unsophisticated way, a crude connection between the human and divine realms. This transition, which was not problematic for her, from women's strength to God's miracles, was based on this same naive and childish "*ulpana* literacy." But in fact it was a transfiguration of the most common literacy in religious Zionism, which includes an ongoing tension at its philosophical base between national activism and expectation of the Messiah.[16] This transfiguration turned Rabbi Akiva into a religious Zionist, one who did not wait for miracles to happen but took action in order to bring them about.

PLURALIST LITERACY

Rachel added another level to the discourse, this time a pluralist one. "Those are simply two different opinions, two worldviews. It's not that one is right and one is wrong," she said. The existence of two opinions, contradicting each other philosophically and practically, is not foreign to Judaism. Rachel, like her fellow students, is familiar with the tradition of interpretation, with debate, and with the different schools that exist side by side within religious discourse. With the aid of secular and especially academic discourse, she tried to formulate a compromise that called for not judging either, and for recognizing their unique value and the fact that they were two different worldviews. It seems, however, that she did not mean to confirm relativism or phenomenology, nor the inability to determine who is right. The context in which she spoke gave her words a shade of moral modesty in the sense of "*we* do not have the right to judge them." This is a restructuring of the modest *ulpana* literacy, which is not without opinions and clothed in a pluralist justification. If this is indeed the correct interpretation of her comments, she supported not a tolerant viewpoint but the opposite. She was avoiding the task set her by the rabbi (to choose, to decide), obscuring the range of possibilities that exist in the Jewish repertoire, and evading once again the fact that all interpretation is choice.

THE LITERACY OF MORALITY

As the lesson progressed, more and more levels of discourse structured the dialogue between the teacher and his students. But within this jumble of literacies the rabbi/instructor honed in on his target, the answer to the question he had posed at the beginning of this series of class sessions: "Why did Rabban Yohanan Ben-Zakkai cry on his deathbed?" From a given point onward (at the end of the rhetorical questions and the students' attempts at an answer), the rabbi challenged the foundation on which the students' comments had been based up to that point and sought to construct the entire discourse on an alternative foundation.

This was no longer history, facts, and national ideologies. In an impressive pedagogical act he diverted the discourse into the literacy of morals. David Ben-Gurion and Menachem Begin, at opposite poles of Zionist politics, found themselves side by side on the moral scale—Ben-Gurion, who could not sleep on the eve of the establishment of the state, and Begin, who cut himself off from the world because of the escalation and outcome of the Lebanon War. The political acts over which these leaders agonized were ones the rabbi accepted; it is reasonable to assume that he rejoiced in the establishment of the state, and it is reasonable to assume that at the time he had supported the Lebanon War. In the rabbi's narrative, Ben-Gurion did not agonize over having established a country that was as secular as he could make it, and Begin did not regret giving the Sinai Peninsula back to Egypt. This perspective effaced the fundamental nature of political action and judged it on terms other than its own. Indeed, the moral depth of the man who carries out the action emerged as the most important thing. Was the man unperturbed, confident, and without doubts, or did he, on the eve of his action (or thereafter) torture himself with doubts and have sleepless nights? This diversion ended discussion of the practical political action and subsumed it under an examination of the politician's personality. It was easy to focus the diversion on the figures of Ben-Gurion and Begin. Both of them were symbols of national leadership and of devotion to the country as a whole. Each had the stature of the ruler and espoused down-to-earth populism. Begin and Ben-Gurion had profound bonds to traditional Jewish texts, and each in his own way displayed great interest in Jewish history and tradition. By contrast, Rabin was presented to the class as a person whose moral standing was in doubt, whose character traits were evinced only in his recent political actions. His military career as an officer in the War of Independence and as chief of staff during the Six Day War, so admired by the religious Zionist public, was obliterated.

Thus this literacy of morality is neither free of ideology nor disconnected from political action. The transition that the rabbi made from historical political literacy to moral literacy allowed him to return to his own positions. The answer to the riddle he posed to his students was offered to them toward the end of the session. After sending the students back and forth between different levels of discourse, after they had crossed the bridge between

Bar-Ilan and Bnei Brak and back, the rabbi explained why Rabbi Akiva had in fact been right in giving preference to nationalism—Jerusalem—over the Torah—Yavneh. Rabbi Akiva, he told them, had faced a new phenomenon that Yohanan Ben-Zakkai had not had to confront: Christianity. The possibility of joining a religion that was without national affiliation, that challenged the ethos of the chosen people and the unbreakable bond between nation and religion, was what had tipped the balance for Rabbi Akiva. The Christian threat, assimilation, the elimination of the connection between the people of the Torah and its land were what led him to join the rebels against imperial Rome.

So, after offering his class numerous passages between the different literacies of the *haredim*, of the secular left, and of the Rabin government, he concluded the border-crossing exercise at home, within the boundaries of Jewish nationhood and far from the State of Israel as the state of all its citizens.

THE BORDERS OF BORDER-CROSSING PEDAGOGY

Our identities are constitutive of the literacies we have at our disposal
through which we make sense of our day-to-day politics of living.
McLaren, 1992, p. 85

The different literacies that we are exposed to, McLaren says, are what mold our identities. McLaren is an anthropologist of education and a prominent ethnographer of the critical pedagogy group.[17] His work assimilates the changes that have taken place in the anthropological discipline,[18] and he prefers to analyze the possibility of "border-crossing" by the subjects of his research (generally school pupils), as well as by researchers, with the use of the concepts of identity and otherness. His approach is helpful in examining the extent to which it is actually possible to accomplish a literacy border crossing, to experience difference, to scrutinize, choose, and constitute identity.

This chapter's deconstruction of the ethnography into different literacies has already shown that the border crossing accomplished in the Midrasha is a manifestly limited one. As has already been noted, the journey between the different strata of discourse and the detour the rabbi made from one literacy to another was not directed toward the goals that Giroux refers to at the beginning of this chapter. No attempt was made to understand the others from their own place, and home literacies were not examined in light

of alternatives; indeed, the case was quite the opposite. All the levels proposed imploded into religious-Zionist literacy. Such a conclusion is almost
trivial and may well be valid for most pedagogical acts. It is therefore worth
taking a look at the limitations of border crossing. Such an examination of
difficulties, obstacles, and preconceptions can provide a more interesting
explanation of the ethnography and serve as a critical tool for the border-
crossing theory and the research act itself.

Of the wealth of literacies alluded to in the class, no small portion of them
were common to the students and to me. Our biographies were not so different from each other. My parents and their parents, my grandmothers and
their grandmothers came from similar backgrounds. We all spoke Hebrew,
were also exposed to a fairly similar daily reality, read common texts, and
accepted the need for the State of Israel. "They" and "I" were Jewish women.
However, my decision to go "there" and study "them" was based on my
awareness of our "otherness" and a certain feeling of rivalry.

   This long stay among these "similar others" was therefore accompanied
by an unceasing crossing of borders. During this period we were required
at moments to reconstitute my and their identities so that this same special
mixture of "similar others" not fall apart. The moment the rabbi was asked
"to talk politics," he turned to me and asked me to stop writing. His request
did not come out of his fear of my written words, because if that had been the
case he would not have allowed me in the Midrasha. His request was an exploitation of my presence in the class and use of a stereotype of me—an
academic, nonreligious Ashkenazi. In an instant I had been removed from
the public of studying Jewish women in order to be the stand-in for the
"others," those left-wing secular Jews who were running the country. As far
as he and the students were concerned, there was no need to investigate my
political positions. They could be taken as known. In this way I became the
"ultimate other"—the one who might well stop writing but who probably
had a tape recorder picking up the rabbi's subversive statements.

   In the same way, I was busy distinguishing myself from the rest of the
group. When I sat in the cafeteria between classes, for example, it was easy
for me to feel that I was part of the place. The cafeteria manager treated me
warmly, remembering me from a lecture we had heard together, and spoke
to me about her plans to study for her master's degree. Some of the women
gave me half-smiles, and the entire place became pleasant for me after a
while. The everyday conversation of the women helped blur the distinctions
between us. It was definitely possible to immerse myself in the hominess of

the cafeteria.[19] When we passed each other sections of the day's newspaper that were scattered over the tables, I listened to the reactions of the readers. It seemed to me that every news item I rejoiced at caused them concern, and that every statement I was repelled by aroused in them hope that the peace process might be suspended. It was on those boundaries that the "otherness" took form. As McLaren wrote, "The other therefore becomes a cultural generality that accounts for the ethnographer's difference."[20]

It is possible, of course, to hold onto such a construction of difference, because it does not threaten my fundamental assumptions. Their identity shored up mine and vice-versa. They were branded enemies of peace, dangers to democracy, people who did not intend to recognize Israel's cultural and national heterogeneity. They assisted the rabbi, who enlisted the male literacy of the Talmud, his reading of history, his moral approach, and his political commentary to glorify an absolute national ethos. They themselves added the literacy of the Holocaust and activist Zionism and did not challenge the rabbi's project of interpretation. In doing this, they reconfirmed my identity as the "righteous person," the "pursuer of peace," the person who combined a correct reading of the local reality with a universal approach. In such a situation, the border crossing between the different literacies presented above turned into a pointless exercise. The rabbi strove for a rupture, for a culture war that would destroy the existing society and establish on its ruins a rectified one. If the State of Israel was meant to be a state of all its citizens, including those with "all kinds of perversions," then, the rabbi said, "I will not be a part of it." Giroux's vision of a pedagogy thick with literacy, in which learners can recognize and experience the strata of others' discourse, and thus also accept the heterogeneity of their society as legitimate difference, was not about to be realized in the Midrasha. The necessary appearance of the "collective" as a concept that organized thought and action, the refusal to dismantle it into its components, and the insistence on continuing to fight for its character indicate that Giroux's border-crossing theory is a social utopia more than a theoretical structure for deciphering social reality.[21]

THE LONGING FOR PARTICIPATION

The presence of these many literacies in the class can be decoded as a desperate attempt to change or reorganize the identity of the group under study. Such an attempt could undermine the identity of the researcher and of the group she symbolized to her research subjects. Such a multiplicity seeks to bridge over the problem of the "double consciousness" that Young points to: "The point of view of the dominant culture which defines them as ugly and fearsome, and the point of view of the oppressed who experience themselves as ordinary, compassionate, and humorous."[22]

Religious Zionists as a group do not belong to the category of the oppressed in Israeli society. However, the power relationship at the time of my observation was definitely not in the group's favor. Nationally, religious Zionism was portrayed as the hard ideological core of the right wing, the part of the right that was most committed in action and in ideology. The Israeli settlers in the occupied territories, among whom religious Zionists were the most prominent, were depicted, more than ever before, as the clear enemies of peace; they were distant from the focuses of power that had once pampered them and cut off from the dominant discourse. This discourse, which derived from the sociopolitical focus of the center and the left, had never sounded more secular and universalist. The leaders of the 1992–96 government had not clearly formulated a future order in which Israel would coexist with a Palestinian state—with which it would share Jerusalem as a capital—nor did they speak of an Israel that was the state of all its citizens who would enjoy a separation of church and state. Still, it was clear in the Midrasha classroom that this was the real issue of the struggle, and that it was intimately related to the existence of a democracy.

In the winter of 1994, ten months before Yitzhak Rabin's assassination and seventeen months before the change of government, the battle lines were drawn. Though it seemed as if several escape routes had also been included, these faded over time.

Orly, Ora, and another student pressed the rabbi and caused him to make himself more and more explicit. He found himself speaking honestly about a culture war, about revolution as opposed to evolution. He was subverting the traditional doctrine of religious Zionism, which advocates "ways of pleasantness." "It won't happen as a natural and normal development of people returning to religion," he said. "We won't be able to achieve change if we do not knock this society down." He founded his tactical analysis in the words of the rabbis and gave them an almost causal connection with the coming of the Messiah.

These were uncompromising linkages that fell on concerned ears. The rabbi's timing, his claim that the voices were now being heard and that they should not be allowed to pass unheeded created a charged atmosphere. Some members of his audience sought to undermine the uniform fabric he had woven. Orly said that just as Israel had no constitution, the religious public should not seek battle. "If a decision is made there will be two nations here," she said. Then she went on to argue that every culture war was accompanied by a physical war, and that the cultural coercion in this case included coercion of a foreign nation. Orly challenged the theoretical possibility of conducting a war that was not bloody. Another student tried to shoot down the concept of revolution. "All revolutions have been processes," she said, trying to reject revolution and save the possibility of evolutionary change. Ora swung in with the matter of timing. "When do we know that the time has come?" she demanded to know. Who could guarantee that we indeed hear the voices, since everyone claims to hear a different voice?

The dialogue created toward the end began to crystallize, and the rabbi enumerated the different possibilities for the state. The nonnationalist Jewish way of Rabbi Shach, the human rights democracy of Shulamit Aloni, and the pragmatism of Yitzhak Rabin would in the end lead to the loss of the dream of Greater Israel. A democratic decision between the different possibilities was not acceptable to him. "If the state is not a Jewish state, *al yehi helki ima*—I will not be a part of it."

But in the rabbi's office it sounded different. His willingness to forego participation in public life and withdraw from the Israeli collective began to sound impossible. Postmodern and post-Zionist Israel, in which homosexuals were acknowledged, was the line the rabbi was not willing to cross. But it turned out that he had nowhere to go. His raison d'etre as a religious Zionist was the link between the political-secular-Zionist fabric and the Jewish people—whether they are religious or not. This link separated him from the *haredi* community and made him part of the Zionist project, in which everything was a priori sacred. Any action touching on the Zionist project, whether carried out by nonreligious or religious Jews, was a sacred link in the chain leading to redemption.[23] The rabbi thus could not stand aside and let events take their course, be alienated and cut off from them. Religious Zionists have become leaders in all of Zionism's three central enterprises—settlement, immigrant absorption, and defense. They cannot at this point simply cease to participate, nor are they willing to accept a change in the goals of the Zionist enterprise. The Labor-Meretz government forced them to the wall on exactly these two points.

In his office at the Midrasha the rabbi asked to hear my opinions, to see if perhaps he could find some footholds in the left-wing discourse familiar to him. Perhaps it was my family history that led him to presume that I could not intend evil to the nation, perhaps it was our brief acquaintance that caused him to try to hear what I had to say. I certainly felt strong during those minutes in his office—like someone who saw developments taking the course I had always wished for. From this location I had no difficulty seconding the doubts the rabbi had about Yitzhak Rabin's character, but I sought to divert the discussion from the prime minister's character to the path he was taking. I tried to amplify the doubting voices of Orly, and Ora, and their classmate into an alternative interpretation of the story of Yohanan Ben-Zakkai and keep the discussion within the Midrasha, close to the Jewish texts. I wanted to echo the alternatives found within Judaism that could serve as a way back into the collective. It seemed to me that the rabbi was inclined to listen to me: "Maybe we have to give it a chance, maybe we have to try. I don't know. It doesn't seem right to me, but maybe. Why don't you raise your hand in class and say that? It's very important that you let these things be heard."

Protected in his office, and partitioned off from events outside it, the rabbi made room for some doubt and adopted the liberal position that it is worthwhile and good to hear everything. He sought to cross the border in order to participate, in order not to stand in opposition. This border-crossing constituted a threat to both my identity and his. If his desire to listen to me was a real one, there was no longer any way of knowing who he really was (who they really were), and thus it would be hard to know who I was (and who we are). Under the multiplicity of literacies present in the class and in the office lay fear, lack of faith, concern, and anger. But there was also a certain heedfulness, and that was confusing.

My initial inclination was to read that heedfulness as real attentiveness to the discourse of peace, even if it was motivated by a theological inability to remain outside the Zionist collective. This interpretation, which was guided by religious Zionism's need to participate at any price, left the act of crossing the border to me. This was because I had to understand the cultural-religious context in which functioned a group that was a political rival, a context that had nothing to do with democracy. The rabbi did not seek to listen to the discourse of peace simply because its representatives had been legally elected to fill their positions. He did not try to understand it because it was one of an infinite number of roads that one could take, other than total nationalism. In order to understand him I had to pass into a different level of historical and political insights. Perhaps this was the border-crossing that Giroux and McLaren spoke of. McLaren claims: "Ethnographers should examine the central discourse in the presence of the new critical voices coming from the margins, such as the voices of feminists, Afro-Americans, Latinos, and other voices that we have silenced until now."[24] However, McLaren goes on to argue, this critical exercise, which comes to shake up the superiority of Eurocentric determinations, cannot be maintained outside the democratic framework. This paradox of logic, in which the groups that threaten democracy participate in it and provide the main criticism of it, is not new. Neither is the need to build democracies free of European ties surprising, and to a certain extent the State of Israel is one of these hybrids.[25] Every acceptance by me of his attentiveness to my words transferred both of us to the level of participation: He and I want to talk together. The price he must pay is giving up his dream of a greater Israel, and my price is leaving the standard democratic discourse and stretching it to new borders—in order to continue to stride together, to participate and help others to participate, to include and not to prescribe.

The "participation" approach, presented in a broader way in part IV, is a requirement of the social reality it seeks to understand. It is not utopian or moralistic but rather strives to decipher knowledge-power connections as a process of participation (or proscription) in the community of observers. The religious Zionist community's steadfast desire to participate in the national arena pressed me to think that it (they) was prepared to pay the price, and I (we) was able to believe in the sincerity of its attentiveness. But matters developed quickly and in a different way. Its (their) return to the collective came from the least expected place.

The event that expressed the climax of the alienation, the vastness of the disconnection, and the exit from the Jewish-democratic collective was to became in a baleful and horrible way the rope that hitched religious Zionism to the cart once again.

THE FEAR OF THE CHOICE OF "DIVERSITY"

Without a common vision (even if it is temporary or unstable) of a democratic community we risk fostering struggles in which the "politics of diversity" will collapse into new forms of isolationism.
McLaren, 1992, p. 207

The cracks in the ethos of the Israeli melting pot have become visible fissures, and what was once a subversive discourse of diversity has become institutionalized, beginning with the political reversal of 1977. Still, it seems that the recognition of the sociocultural segmentation of Israel has been accompanied by a constant taste of failure and a threatening appearance.

The texts of the morning after election day (and not only after the elections of 1996) are loaded with descriptions and fear of the difference expressed by voting patterns. Academic research has been called on to estimate the depth of the ruptures and their affect on the stability of the "collective." Both in the public-media discourse and in the central stream of research it has been difficult to hear voices that accept diversity as a welcome reality or as a vision to aspire to. Everyone is busy with demographic computations that show when this group will overtake that group, and whether by that time there is a chance that that group will be able to control this group. The assumption is that it is a zero-sum power game, and it accepts neither the politics of diversity nor even liberal pluralism. This duality is perpetuated by the simple fact that it is not possible in the Israeli reality to construct a formal legitimate diversity under the aegis of a democratic organization. Democracy itself, so it appears, is an outcome of these culture wars, not a social working assumption.

The small test case of the Bar-Ilan Midrasha embodies the entire story. These young women are not full members of their community, and this book is devoted to a description of their struggle to broaden their participation in it. In the context of the educational act being performed on them — on their bodies, minds, and hearts — they are continually perceived as women within a religious Jewish community that has its own cultural definitions in all matters, including gender relations and the rights of each gender. Nevertheless, each one of them is perceived in her community as a full-fledged citizen, a complete participant in a political struggle — she has a voice, an opinion, power to act and influence, and, most important of all, the democratic right to vote once every four years. On the civil level, then, the young religious woman enjoys full recognition of her power and ability, and she has made full use of that recognition from the first days of the settlements in the territories to the present day.[26]

7

BETWEEN TORAH AND SCIENCE—THE LAST
MODERNISTS: A CLASS IN THE PHILOSOPHY
OF RABBI AVRAHAM YITZHAK HAKOHEN KOOK

*In all the enlightenments, and all the divine philosophies, we see only a broadening of
the inner point of the instinct of faith and the clear and natural fear of heaven, so that
in order to push the limits further off, to develop the power locked up within it, all the
types of study are needed, both the practical and the theoretical, the mental and
the emotional, and on this depends the success of the studies, when they are
well connected to the living inner point, which is natural to the soul of man.*

Rabbi Avraham Yitzhak Hakohen Kook, Orot Ha-Emunah, *p. 66*

OF THE THREE CLASSES GIVEN in the graduate program that I enrolled in during my first year at the Midrasha, I completed only one. That
was a class given by Dr. Yael Weiss on the philosophy of Rabbi Kook. Dr.
Weiss taught in the Bar-Ilan University philosophy department, at the Midrasha, and at other non-academic institutions for Jewish studies, so she
had experience teaching in both academic and nonacademic frameworks.
She has taught religious and nonreligious audiences, women and mixed
groups, Israelis and English-speakers, feminists and nonfeminists. Some of
the students in the course had taken other classes from her in the philosophy
department, in various institutes in Jerusalem, and in the Midrasha itself.

Dr. Yael Weiss was unique in that she was the only female teacher at the
Midrasha who had advanced academic credentials.[1] Her class reflected this:
It was academic in character and followed an ordered sequence of thought.
The students were not given a syllabus, but the course's structure was clear
from the anthology of selections from Rabbi Kook's writings prepared by
the teacher, as well as from the supplementary books she asked the students
to read and the list of guiding questions she left in the library so the students
could study the material in *havruta*. Because the course was conducted at the
Midrasha and not in the philosophy department, and because the students
came from a wide variety of disciplines, the class had a special context,
turning it into something "different." The dialogue reported below tries
to capture this difference, to describe and interpret it. It is not meant to

provide an account of the material being studied but rather to recreate the ambience of the class. In this, it does an injustice to the literacy Dr. Weiss sought to construct, inasmuch as it amplifies the voices of the students, their motivations, and their constant shifts from texts to personal experiences.

This unusual atmosphere shaped the class in Rabbi Kook's philosophy into a dialogue on the ability to reproduce halachic practices and a position of religiosity from the time and the place in which it occurred. It was a philosophy class that explored how it was possible to live as religious women alongside nonreligious Jews, as women who studied both Jewish religion and academic subjects, as human beings seeking cover under a canopy of frozen halacha in the midst of a seething world.

At the first session there were twenty-six women in the class. Most of them did not have their heads covered; six had their heads covered with a kerchief and/or hat, and one woman, the oldest, wore a wig. One nonreligious woman, a member of the university's administrative staff, also participated in most of the class sessions. Even though Weiss's class was part of the "graduate program," it was attended by many students who were not graduates of the Midrasha's regular program but who had received special permission from the Midrasha director. Dr. Weiss herself wore colored kerchiefs that matched her clothes; the kerchiefs were tightly tied around her head and covered all her hair.

After reading out the names of the participants and exchanging greetings or special smiles with the women she already knew, she began her lesson.

"Rabbi Kook's philosophy is fraught and relevant. In a way it is possible to say that I have had a long romance with him over the course of thirty-five years. My children have more than once asked whether we are 'Kookists' at home. When one of them was small, he asked me if Rabbi Kook was an uncle of ours, because we talked about him so much at home. But I do not characterize myself as a 'Kookist.' I have a great deal of interest, and I invest a great deal of thought, time, feeling, and study, but on the inside I am not a 'Kookist'—at least in the way the term 'Kookism' is commonly understood today.[2] Maybe because I do not see myself as seeking to reproduce the discourse of the past in the present. It could well be that in this way I carry on Rabbi Kook's thinking, since he himself did not believe that what had been said in the past, even by sages, was necessarily relevant to the present.

"I would like to address for a moment the status of Jewish philosophy in our corpus of texts from the point of view of Rabbi Kook. [She read a passage from the course book.] As you can see, he himself viewed the study of philosophy as very important, and this is not a matter of using philosophy as a tool of war. Not every philosophical book answers the need of our generation. There are indeed things that have become obsolete, or those that our generation is not concerned with—some of them perhaps because we are so materialistic. The goal of study as I understand it in his light is to turn a person into a thinker, much like in the study of Jewish law, and also into a creative person, and so one studies a large number of opinions. The past is meant to serve as material for creativity and originality; there is no point in copying from there to here.

"The study of Rabbi Kook's philosophy is not an easy matter, and we will need several background lessons in order to get started. I highly recommend that you try to wrestle with the questions I will leave for you in the library, to read the supplementary material that I have supplied beyond the collection of sources, and to study in *havruta*."

Dr. Weiss set aside the source book and drew a batch of folders, photocopies, and books out of her large briefcase. She read out loud several passages that were not included in the students' material.

"It is actually easy for me to begin our acquaintance with Rabbi Kook as a man with what Brenner, Klausner, and Agnon said about him, as you have just heard.[3] More than anything else, Rabbi Kook registers as an exceptional figure who cannot be put into any familiar category. This man, born in 1865 in Latvia, studied in the Volozhin and Ponivetz yeshivot and served as a rabbi there. He moved to Palestine and served as the rabbi of Jaffa and the Jewish farming settlements from 1904 to 1914. He then served, until his death in 1935, as the Chief (Ashkenazi) Rabbi of the Jewish community in Palestine, alongside the Chief Sephardi Rabbi. I begin with Brenner, Klausner, and Agnon, because everyone connects Rabbi Kook with the subjects of nationalism and secularization. He saw the national renewal as directly serving religious purposes. He gave his sermons in Hebrew, saw himself as the rabbi of the entire nation, and was proud to sign his name with the title of Rabbi of Jaffa and the Jewish Settlements; he thought in inclusive national terms and was open to general culture. Rabbi Kook attended the Hebrew University's opening ceremony on Mt. Scopus in 1925. The students at his yeshiva studied modern subjects that were not studied in other such places and thus meshed with their time and place. His literary style, his rhetoric, his poetry, and his writing, alongside his work on [religious issues such as] the sabbatical year [and its implications for the new Zionist agricultural settlements] and nationalism, were an integral part of religious activity.

In the future, for generations to come, his contribution will undoubtedly be his thinking, especially his epistemology, the meaning of religion, and other abstract questions. The political interest in him is an anachronism. I would sum up the unique nature of his writing in three points: One, he is a man who draws from everything and relates to everything; two, reflexivity—he speaks about himself, he exists within the text, is involved in it, and reveals his involvement; three, inter-textual tensions—the ostensible contradiction of Hasidic and Lithuanian thinking, strict observance of Jewish law versus anarchism, spiritualism versus realism.

"Rabbi Kook appears before us as a torn man who is self-aware, does not remain silent, and is not apologetic. Tensions and rifts become a platform from which he aspires to reach unity. The reason it is so easy to distort his thinking and put it to all kinds of pragmatic uses derives from the methodological difficulties of reading his philosophy. There are a wealth of writings, only half of which have been published. There is a huge inventory of subjects he addressed. His writing is deliberately holistic, and everything touches on everything else. His deliberately associative style moves and connects between levels of existence and experience and rational planes. As a result, every reading involves editing, and all editing means interpretation. If we add to this the ongoing dispute among his executors, we discover that there are several barriers between us and him, and how easy it is to enter a text at any point and act upon it."

QUESTIONS OF SELF-LOCATION

On the face of it, it is hardly surprising that Dr. Yael Weiss's first sentences touched directly on the sensitive questions of positioning. The religious Zionist context of Bar-Ilan and the nationalist home atmosphere of the Midrasha created a background in which every utterance could be presupposed. Audience and speaker seemed to be a homogeneous unit in which every opinion or thinker bore a known collection of meanings. Such a situation requires a precise labor of positioning. This is not unique to the Bar-Ilan context, but it is of special importance there. Dr. Weiss, like her students, was aware of the entire range of connotations that the name "Rabbi Kook" contains. She apparently assumed that it was clear to all of them why this particular person had been chosen to fill the Jewish philosophy slot in the graduate program. She also assumed that they knew that Rabbi Kook was often automatically lumped together with his son Zvi Yehuda,

who drew practical political conclusions from Rabbi Kook's thought and
became a leader of the Greater Israel movement. Dr. Weiss did not mention
the special position held in the religious Zionist community by Merkaz Ha-
Rav, the yeshiva Rabbi Kook founded and which his son also headed, and
by Gush Emunim; she simply used the term "Kookist."

It would seem that this ostensibly clear line of associations required Dr.
Weiss to situate herself with respect to the positions from which the students
read, and to mark them in a new way that challenged what her audience
took for granted. She opened with a complex confession that distanced her
from the "Kookists" and placed her closer to Rabbi Kook himself, and to
his philosophy. She depicted him as an intimate acquaintance, a person
who was the subject of conversation at her family dinner table. Later she
suggested that perhaps her distance from the "Kookists" actually allowed her
to understand Rabbi Kook himself better. The fact that she did not use his
philosophy in a political struggle was closer to his own view of philosophy,
she said. Philosophy's main purpose is to develop thinking, imagination,
and creativity—not to copy, as she said, "from there to here." Having made
this confession, which to my surprise did not elicit any reaction from the
students, she went on to position Rabbi Kook's philosophy. This labor of
placement itself turned into a series of door-openings, filling the classroom
with further gusts that did not create a storm.

First, it was necessary to say what place Jewish philosophy has within the
entire range of texts—or, more precisely, in comparison with Jewish law,
Bible, and history, which together with Jewish philosophy constitute the
four great branches of Jewish studies.[4] The students, as women, were already
accustomed to Jewish philosophy being marked as "their" material. Unlike
Jewish law, philosophy had long since become a regular part of studies for
girls and women. As such, its position on the scale of importance of the textual corpus has become problematic (or the opposite may be true—because
of its relatively inferior position it may be taught to women).

The literacy history of religious Zionism shows changes in the textual
hierarchies. These will not be detailed here, but it should be noted that the
prestige of Bible studies and of Jewish philosophy in this sector have at times
overshadowed that of Jewish law.[5] Weiss chose to note at the very beginning
that Rabbi Kook attached great importance to philosophy. Later she added
and claimed that this part of his teaching, particularly his epistemology,
would be lasting, while the political aspect would lose its relevance.

After positioning herself and her discipline, she began the work of
positioning the texts. Here she dealt with the multiple constructions and

aggregations of the man and his teaching. Writers and literary critics, nonreligious and religious, entered the room. Two different Polish yeshivot floated
in the air alongside the newly established Hebrew University. The post of
chief rabbi of the pre-state Jewish community in Palestine stood beside the
secular social spirit of the Zionist pioneers, the Hebrew language, and general culture. The rabbi's poetry and rhetoric were placed beside his innovations in Jewish law. Weiss gave herself over to a unique image of Rabbi
Kook that allowed the collapse of the dichotomy. After the atmosphere in
the room had thickened, she made it even thicker with the multiple time
linkages she made to evoke Rabbi Kook's uniqueness. He drew from everything and related to everything, he was present within the text and displayed
reflexivity, and his texts contained levels and strata that seemed to be in opposition to each other. It would seem that here Dr. Weiss reached a point of
exponential increase. Each of the points she set out made what she had said
previously more complex, and, as if that were not sufficient, she concluded
with psychology, depicting the rabbi as a torn man, dissatisfied with himself.

On the verge of a new literacy journey, facing a public of students that
had a special relation to, but unorganized knowledge of, Rabbi Kook, Weiss
created a complex and multifaceted atmosphere. At the climax of this in-
determinacy, and with its help, Dr. Weiss erected, in the meantime, only
one guidepost: caution. She seemed to be asking the students to sit up in
their places and pay attention, not to sink, not to settle into conventional
thinking—to be aware of the redaction carried out by of the rabbi's executors, the editors of his texts, and the political movements that have claimed
him as their own. The message was to beware of solving methodological
problems in a pragmatic way, to avoid focusing on only a single voice in
the dissonance. The students had no reaction. This, the most political statement of literacy policy made by the teacher, aroused no debate. The teacher
laid down her tools one after the other, located them in space, marked the
boundaries of her discourse, and blurred the boundaries of Rabbi Kook's
discourse, all without any intervention by the students.

In the class sessions that followed, Weiss provided a thorough and fundamental treatment of the connections between Rabbi Kook's philosophy and
Jewish mysticism (Kabbala), and then methodically set out the major points
of his epistemological ideas. The number of students dwindled steadily over
the course of the year; fifteen remained by the time the course ended. Even
fewer took the final exam. Given the rumors about its difficulty, those who
took it were particularly brave.[6] The dialogues in the class were conducted

by a fixed minority. Some of them had been Weiss's students in other courses in the past and were familiar with her way of teaching; they felt comfortable expressing their opinions. Over time, certain of the students took on established roles, and these gave a kind of predictable rhythm to the lesson. This rhythm was constructed out of unending attempts by the students to organize Rabbi Kook's philosophy into clear molds, to locate his words in a way that would rise above the disputes among his interpreters and fit into the categories of issues relevant to them. The silence that pervaded the opening lesson became, over the course of the year, a persistent voice that called for a dispersal of the fog, for a recreation of the presumptive. In many ways this is a characteristic rhythm of most learning processes, including the study of philosophy, but it was of a special character here, given that the students were young religious women.

The place of the women as readers examining the teaching before them on both the theoretical and practical levels became the class's center of gravity, with the teacher as counterweight. Dr. Weiss's course was the most fascinating of the classes I took at the Midrasha; its adherence to the academic mold made my participation easier. Despite my strong desire to ask questions and express opinions, I held myself back. I asked to pass when it was my turn to read, and I was drawn in only when a comparison was made between the binary structure of Rabbi Kook's philosophy and the work of anthropologist Claude Levi-Strauss. The ethnography presented below is made up of three edited compilations of discourse conducted around subjects that in retrospect proved to be central. They are not central because the teacher saw them as such but rather because they cast light on the major dilemmas that ran through the class, explicitly and implicitly.

RABBI KOOK: MODERNIST OR TRADITIONAL THINKER?

When the divine enlightenment is small, then the picture one draws of the divinity is also small, and since the divine contents illuminates the infinite minimization of man before him, then, there can be no measure of how man is made into a crawler and idler by fear of God that has no thought in it. And how can man arrive at a measure of divine greatness, in a way that the essential form of the soul's glory will not be blurred but rather will broaden—by broadening his power of thinking, by freeing his imagination and the flight of his thought, by knowing the world and life, by the richness of feeling in all existence which really require engaging all the wisdom of the world and all the theories of life, and all ways of the different cultures and the contents of the morality of every nation and tongue. (Rabbi Avraham Yitzhak Hakohen Kook, *Arpilei Tohar*, 46–47)

Weiss: "For Rabbi Kook there is no contradiction between inspiration and cognition. Intuitive knowledge seems superior—it is holistic and hetero-geneous—while methodical inquiry seems on the face of it to be in an infe-rior position in comparison with inspiration—but it has a very important role. There are scholars who say that Rabbi Kook's philosophy is part of modern thinking. It is difficult to know exactly what he read, but I presume that he read secondary texts—that is, not the source but rather summaries by central scholars and philosophers in the Western world. He undoubtedly mixes methods, and we will take a look at that further on. I ask whether Rabbi Kook was a modern or a traditional thinker not so that you can write something down in your notebook, to make it clear that Maimonides was x, and Agnon y, and Rabbi Kook z, but rather to lay out a path from which we can begin to study his teachings."

Yael: "The minute Rabbi Kook asks new questions he's a modernist."

Weiss: "The Maharal, for example, in the sixteenth century, asked new questions—does that make him a modernist? This game of definitions and boxes is a product of our own needs. But let's continue with it a little fur-ther."

Michal: "Maybe modern is the extent to which the environment affected him?"

Yael: "Don't forget that there are also opposite directions of influence, that there are Western thinkers who are influenced by Judaism."

Weiss: "Of course there are, but you have to check it carefully, you have to see how much."

Rachel: "Not that I know a lot, but Rabbi Kook's name is associated with mysticism, and that doesn't exactly go with modernism."

Weiss: "Why not?"

Rachel: "I don't know. In the last class we inquired into whether Rabbi Kook was a mystic, a kabbalist, or not. And now the discussion is on moder-nity, and that doesn't fit."

Na'ama: "You can also put a new question in here: Does everything a person thinks fall within the normal framework? Isn't mystical experi-ence outside the normal? Maybe you should make mystics meet the reality principle?'"

Laughter in the classroom. I looked at Na'ama and her friend from the psychology department. At the beginning of the year we had been *havruta* partners. The attempt to conduct the graduate program differently than the rest of the studies in the Midrasha was based, in part, on the creation of an independent study framework. The rabbi who taught halacha and Dr. Weiss both left discussion questions in the library to be used as guides for students who studied the texts together in preparation for the class meetings. I put a lot of hope in the *havruta*. In my imagination, my scholarly curiosity about the unprecedented literacy innovation being offered to the Midrasha women combined with my desire to recreate such study for myself. I fantasized about stormy debates, piles of open books, and friendships being woven around disputation. But the *havruta* I stuck with was a wan and awkward circle that lasted only a month. Some of the women dropped out of the program and others stopped coming to the period of independent study, but Na'ama and her friend remained, somewhat familiar faces who responded with a half-smile to my greetings in the corridors and classrooms. At the center of the other *havruta* I tailed after were two knowledgeable women, graduates of Midreshet Bruria,[7] former students of Dr. Weiss who had experience in Gemara study. We sat around them more or less silently, letting them run between the books in pursuit of the discussion questions and letting them read out loud (not too loudly, because we met, after all, in the library) in Aramaic while we held the annotated Steinsaltz edition of the Talmud that includes a Hebrew translation. In that *havruta* I was a grateful outside observer. Two months after the year began that framework also fell apart, and with it my dreams about *havruta* study.

At the end of my three years at the Midrasha, after having gone away for a sabbatical, I returned for a visit, and the Midrasha director greeted me with these words: "You've got to see something—come, I want you to see this." We left his office, and I strode after him in the direction of the library. When he opened the large wooden door for me, I saw the old picture from my imagination. Young women sat in pairs, studying around groaning tables; some of them browsed through the surrounding bookshelves or discussed some point with the teacher of the class at his book table. "This is our new *beit midrash*. We set it up under pressure from the girls. Three hundred applied to study here and we accepted only fifty."

So my *havruta* fantasy of 1993 became flesh in 1996, perhaps because fantasies were not enough for these women. But in Dr. Weiss's class that day, Na'ama and her friend Orly were for me a reminder of an attempt that had failed.

After an extended discussion of the tension between modernity and traditionalism, the teacher continued.

Weiss: "Perhaps we can join the two questions together toward our discussion of myths. The modern period has examined myth critically. Religion has tried to present itself in a rational light. More recently there has
been an attempt to 'save the myth,' to recognize its internal value. Does the
myth reflect truth or is it a sociocultural phenomenon? Does it represent
reality or create reality? Does the myth exploit a person's 'thinking nature'?
Is there a connection between the signifier and the signified—do you know
what I mean? The demythological approach deconstructs the myth and removes its primitive guise in order to draw a qualitative meaning from it that
the modern ear will be receptive to."

Rachel: "That is really a problem, because every child knows science, but
he doesn't know religious philosophy."

Weiss: "Rabbi Kook truly tried to be creative and introduce historicism,
that is science, into religion, into religious thought. In order to move along
two axes from time to time and to progress."

Rachel: "Then it really is a problem, because on the spiritual side we are
stuck. We don't have great men like Rabbi Kook, and the spiritual side is not
developing. But on the scientific side there is huge progress. Maybe we need
to prevent people from getting a scientific education in order to overcome
that gap, religion's lag. The fact is that it works in some circles."

There was a minor stir in the class, smiles, anticipation of Weiss's response.

Weiss: "In Rabbi Kook's opinion, that is not feasible and not correct. On
the one hand, if the scientists were bolder and grew up immersed in the
humanities, they would be able to make even greater breakthroughs. On
the other, he believed that we as modern people should not impede the
development of science, because it can benefit the development of religion."

Shira: "What motivates us? The desire to adjust ourselves to religion?
No. I want to understand this. That is our problem, that we need to adjust
ourselves to scientific achievements?"

Weiss: "We need scientific explanations. What primitive man accepted
simply, we need to understand in a sophisticated and exhaustive way. For
example the story of the expulsion of man from the Garden of Eden according to Rabbi Kook. In his understanding this is mythology and not a factual
story. You have to reach a moral lesson beyond the ontological matter. The
moral of the Garden of Eden is that you can damage the perfect. That is not
in the factual stories. The Torah does not intend to give us scientific facts; it
is concerned with human existentialism."

Shulamit: "Therefore you have to approach a scientific theory with a religious position, because otherwise science shapes your religious outlook."

Weiss: "Have you studied Maimonides?"

Shulamit: "I've studied, but theories still get replaced, and a religious person who adopts a theory that fails, what does he do?"

Weiss: "That's why I asked you about Maimonides. He was a little naive with regard to the power of the mind and was a great believer in rationalism. Rabbi Kook is much less naive and is more doubtful when it comes to the mind."

Rachel: "The question is whether the moral message we extract from the Torah can be fixed."

Weiss: "No! According to Rabbi Kook, religious truths develop like science. And the clash between science and religion develops religious insights and vice-versa. Science and religion necessarily nourish one another—every development on one side requires an examination of the other, which also develops, and so on and so forth, in a spiral."

Rachel: "Then there is nevertheless adjustment to science?"

Weiss smiled, her blue eyes observing Rachel. She looked like a teacher who had already seen many unsure students, who had already heard all their confused questions. Her easygoing manner never evinced boredom, smugness, weariness of the students' lack of knowledge or their difficulties, of their endless attempts to organize what she sought to unravel. I never heard her dismiss a question or belittle its importance, although she did not address every question.

Weiss: "No, Rachel, there is no adjustment to science, because there is always a gap to be closed, and it is not closed. Today science is winning—that wasn't always the case. Today you can't accept explanations of the type that were accepted thousands of years ago. There are those who say that the difference between a *haredi* and a non-*haredi* person is the difference between the person who accepts the myth in its literal meaning and the person who peels off the story to get the moral lesson. But it seems to me that the difference is between simple faith and open-eyed faith, and there are people of both types in both groups."

Efrat: "If we take that further, then maybe none of it really happened—not Abraham and not the Makhpela Cave and not Sodom and Gomorra—it's all myth. What can we do with all the interpretation of the mythology? Put it aside? All the midrashim?"

Weiss: "There is a difference between a mythological text about a talking snake and a genealogical text. The Torah contains different genres, and you know how Rabbi Kook would have answered you here? He would have said to you that we should trust to the healthy instincts of the Jewish people, who have already determined what is true and what isn't."

Efrat: "It's a little hard to trust to that."

Weiss: "What's up, Miri? I see that you aren't comfortable either. Do you agree with Efrat? After all, you've already studied this."

Miri: "Exactly. I studied it and I'm still angry."

Weiss: "So, that's good. We need to look into that."

Miri: "What angers me is that the rabbi says that the nation knows how to extract the truth. But the nation is entirely divided about the truth. What is that truth if everyone thinks differently and is sure that he knows it? The secularists, for example, will say that this is an admission that the entire Bible is a legend."

Weiss smiled again. She adjusted her glasses and asked Miri to read three selections from the source book. One of them was as follows:

> Human depictions, however they are in relation to the form of reality, also certainly have a special role in the development of man in his morality, and the rest of his sublime goals, from generation to generation according to his depictions, which are always being replaced, to adjust everything to the goal of the general good and God's lovingkindness forever. (Rabbi Avraham Yitzhak Hakohen Kook, *Eder Ha-Yakar*, p. 38)

Weiss: "As you have heard, human images are a model, a construction. They are not only a description of reality, but also a structuring of it. And if the secularists say that the Torah is a legend, then you shouldn't give the accepted response—that because these legends have helped the Jewish people so much that means they must be true. No, not at all. According to what we've read here, the answer is, if these legends have worked, that is a sign that their source is divine."

Yael: "Presenting it that way carries a lot of risk, doesn't it?"

Weiss: "There is a risk here, of course, but it seems to me not of the type you are anxious about—that everyone will do as they please. There is rather a danger of complete relativism, perhaps something that is happening in that cluster of Hasidic sects that base themselves only on one's set of beliefs."

Miri: "So maybe the entire world is an illusion?"

Weiss: "Very good. I'm waiting for that idea to seep into you, because that is a tremendous idea that carries great dangers. The idea can be found, of course, among all the Jewish thinkers of the modern age, and it pulls in the direction of the pantheism we spoke of."

Yael: "Can it lead to apostasy?"
Weiss: "We will see that, at first blow, it has a destructive force."

THE LAST MODERNISTS

In many ways, the religious Zionists are Israel's last modernists; the literacy event described above is just one of many examples of the religious Zionist public's attempts to salvage both the Torah and modernism. At a time when the *haredi* community adheres to an antimodernism—or better, amodernism—that rejects the concept that the pursuit of scientific knowledge brings progress, and when the secular public has adopted a postmodern, skeptical, and relativistic view of knowledge and ethics, the religious Zionists continue to believe in a human spirit that strives for progress through enlightenment and education, in exploiting science for spiritual ends, and in an intrinsic, absolute, and universal scale of values. They have a concept of an ideal society and believe that the state can be an instrument for achieving it. Facing both a *haredi* public that constitutes itself on values that are the antithesis of modernism[8] and a secularist elite with its challenge to modernism, the religious Zionist community feels a duty to stand up for both religion and modernism.

The dialogue heard in the classroom might sound too narrow to bear out such a statement, but in fact all the components are there. Simply by addressing Rabbi Kook's teachings, the class positions, a priori, the major part of the discussion on the fault line between tradition and modernism, and in this there is no innovation. Consider how the women sought to restructure this old debate. It seems they did not feel that embracing both the sacred and the profane implies godless modernism or a relativistic pluralism of ideas. The gap between this public's perception of itself as modern, on the one hand, and the theology they were reading, on the other, meant they were toying with apostasy in a game constructed out of their anxieties and fears. From within the complexity that Dr. Weiss structured, and after she warned against unnecessary categorization, a dialogue on power grew. The students no less methodically structured a discussion about who is stronger than whom, who is influenced by whom, what is better and who will win. Weiss addressed these learning religious women as "modern people" and made the modern experience axiomatic. The question for the women, as they encountered Rabbi Kook, thus became how it might be possible to integrate primal natural thinking and abstract thinking. But they were in fact preoccupied with other aspects of modernity: Is to be modern to ask new questions—to be influenced, to influence, to be entirely rational, to eschew mysticism (to meet the "reality principle," as Na'ama suggested)?

After Weiss discussed at length the place of myth in religion and in the life of modern believers, and after she opened many lines of discussion for her audience on the power of myth to represent and create reality, the students chose to return to power relations between science and religion. Their return to the binary structure and their flight from complexity led them, paradoxically, to acknowledge the superiority of science and to depict religion as being entirely myth. The spiral movement in which religion and science nourish, challenge, and advance each other found no takers among the women. They preferred to entrench themselves in the binary structure that assigns ranks. Rachel proposed, with a certain amount of defiance, that the religious Zionist public mitigate its familiarity with science—bring it to a complete halt, as the *haredim* have done—in order to achieve a balance between the two forces. Shira insisted on knowing whether religion's motivating force derived from its desire to chase after science. Shulamit proposed going into the field of science wearing the armor of a religious position so as not to allow the former to influence the latter.

Up to this point it sounded as if everyone agreed that "today science is winning." Science as a basis for knowing, and perhaps also as a system of standards and even morality, is in a process of growth, and its vitality threatens religion. Not a single one of the women took a skeptical view of science itself. They did not cite the current critique of scientific standards or of science's claim to objectivity. The ideal portrait of science remained in this class in the form of its modernist-classical image—the ancient enemy of religion and tradition—and it received in this religious Zionist class more respect than it could have gotten anywhere else in these turbulent times. When Dr. Weiss brought the discussion back to the matter of myth and its status as a text, offering complex readings derived from various religious camps and quoting Rabbi Kook to the effect that the nation already knew how to distinguish between an ontological truth and a moral story, the students once again entrenched themselves.

"How," asked Miri, "is it possible to trust to a nation that holds such different ideas about the truth? What is that truth? If it is possible, according to the rabbi, to describe large swathes of the Bible as mythology, what will we say to the secularists?"

Efrat was worried about the slippery slope. "What will we do with all the texts we have, in which people saw ontological value in what is presented here as mythological?" she wanted to know.

The class did not challenge the rabbi's teaching nor the teacher's interpretation. The students did not try to argue with the claim that the Garden
of Eden story is, for example, a moral allegory. They were concerned about
power relations in their existential field. Their concern turned the entire
Bible into a myth, and they lost the ability to distinguish between the different genres within it.

Weiss's answer roused additional fears. Voiding the ontological value
of a part of the Bible and anchoring it only in its divine origin did not
make the class feel better. This part of the lesson left the women with a
fear of apostasy—and their experienced teacher with the hope that this fear
would allow her to further their education and their enlightened/believing
adherence to the modernist-religious tribe.

FROM HIS SIDE AND FROM OUR SIDE: RABBI KOOK
BETWEEN THE HASIDIM AND THE MITNAGDIM

The lessons that followed were focused on Weiss's positioning of Rabbi Kook
as one in a line of allegorical commentators on the concept of *tzimtzum*, or
divine self-contraction and self-limitation. These discussions required examination of the concepts of theism and pantheism, which she contrasted as
understanding the significance of the world "from his (that is, the Creator's)
side" and "our (human beings') side." The discussion also required knowledge of the fundamental elements of the Kabbala, which deal with systems of
relations between different worlds, between the part and the whole, between
disconnection and cooperation, between the existent and the nonexistent,
between absolute truth and the reality of human life. These issues were discussed in conjunction with readings from Rabbi Kook's writings and an examination of the central lines of interpretation of the Mitnagdim and the
Hasidim. The major message was that Rabbi Kook subsumed the debates
between these two streams and to a large extent went beyond them. In a
simple and simplistic way it could have been understood that Rabbi Kook
confirmed that the reality in which we live and in which we interpret our
existence is indeed our reality. It is the light (as the Hasidim understood it),
detached from the divine, from the producer of light. But this disconnection
is a result of the limits of our powers of interpretation and comprehension.
It lies in our blindness; in fact, one may presume that divine and human realities are a single continuum (as the Mitnagdim understand it). *Tzimtzum*

does not mean that God has vacated this world but rather that he is covered or unseen.

These complex and shrouded journeys between worlds were not easy. The class was held between 2 and 4 P.M. and sometimes the students were exhausted. Yael Weiss's organized attempts to progress according to her plan frequently ran into a series of questions that sought to undermine her first principles.

Leah: "You're saying, in fact, that it is better to understand creation as an emanation, as part of the divine world, rather than as creation de novo. Because in that method there is no disconnection. That helps man in his belief, in his longing for God, in the desire not to feel alienated and distant. Okay, I understand that, but I keep wondering whether the rabbi said that for people's good. Or that that's the way it is in reality, really truly. In other words, that's the way it really is, so that people can love and worship God."

Weiss: "It is not a matter of being beneficial for me or for you—for him it is an existential truth. Once people wanted to believe in creation de novo. They were more primitive; they needed that. But not today."

Yael: "It sounds a little like halacha and not like philosophy. Something you need to update according to the generation and the era."

Hagit: "Halacha is still halacha, and it is always practical. Here you're not looking for the practical. Here you're searching for the truth."

Weiss: "There are those who argue that all halacha after Moses is not connected to truth and falsehood, only to the practical. In philosophy in any case there are attempts to understand the heart of the matter."

Yael: "In philosophy it's even less important what interpretation you make, because it's not practical. Everyone can really believe what he wants. It doesn't determine how you'll behave."

Weiss: "It seems to me that Rabbi Kook's new idea is that he shatters the self-satisfaction of religious people who are persuaded that they possess the truth. He shows that every interpretation is possible, because truth does not rest on a single point."

Rachel: "That simple desire to believe something, something that is true and absolute—is that a childish desire? Primitive? Too low, too simple? I don't know. I think about it all the time. There's something insulting about that."

Yael: "For him it works. You said it's intersubjective, but I think it's subjective. For him it's okay—but not for everyone."

Weiss: "Rabbi Kook speaks from within the status of an educated man, but he also tries to understand the generation in which he lives—the new humanity—and he will acknowledge at times that not everything works for everybody."

Yael: "But the desire to believe is a fundamental matter and is common to everyone, isn't it?"

Weiss: "Certainly. That's why the rabbi speaks of the fundamental faith that is common to all men, and the external faith that is relative to every people and every place and time. You should know, I'm warning you, that Rabbi Kook has astounding things to say about paganism and the primitive beliefs that we have lost. Let's read—Efrat!"

> All thoughts are logical, and they are connected systematically. Even those in which we see but a flicker of an idea, when we delve well after their roots we will find how they link back to the source of logic. Because that is the nature of thought. And therefore we know that no thought in the world is ever superfluous, there is nothing that does not have its place, because all come out of the source of wisdom. (Rabbi Avraham Yitzhak Hakohen Kook, *Orot Ha-Kodesh* I, 17–18)

Efrat (after reading): "I understand according to this that the Bible and the Koran and the New Testament are on the same level, have the same status. Unfortunately, that's the way I understand it."

Weiss: "No, when we read further we'll see that there is truthfulness in everything, but there is also a hierarchy of truths, and the Bible is at the top. The question is what formulation affords the most possibilities for the flowering of faith—to what extent is the morality of the explanation inclusive and comprehensive. The Jewish formulation is complete and absolute because its concept of holiness is the most inclusive. We will speak about that and will become acquainted with Rabbi Kook's proof according to his formula."

HERE WE SEEK THE TRUTH: THE DANCE OF THE BELIEVERS

Intellectual experience never remains disconnected from the students' lives. Studying philosophy as an intellectual exercise, as a broadening of the mind or the soul, is not, it turns out, possible. The students are women who believe and observe religious precepts and who are involved in a new process of study for the purpose of broadening their participation.[9] The democratization of learning, the opening of the ranks and the books, create new situations for the untrained believing public. In these situations young women are expected to dive into complex texts, to encounter new languages and types of discourse they had not previously known. These situations are thus new literacy experiences whose quality and strength need to be examined.

In the part that dealt with modernism and mythology it turned out that this new literacy experience caused these women students to prefer the familiar binary poles to the foggy areas between them. This preference recreated the tension between science and Torah, and reconfirmed their identity as modern believing women. The tension was thus not resolved; it was part of their very existence, and thus they continued to strive for the clear point that in this section of the dialogue bore the name "truth." Along the way, between them and the truth, was Rabbi Kook as an interpreter whom they sought to understand, and Dr. Weiss was meant to help them do so.

Did the rabbi say that "for people's good"? Leah asked. Or is that "the way it is in reality, really truly"? Are we progressing toward knowledge of the truth, or did Rabbi Kook make life easier for us and say things that would make our believing lives possible?

"Here [we're] searching for the truth," Hagit said, meaning that philosophy was a legitimate framework for seeking out the absolute, in comparison with halacha, which is tailored to the needs of the time and place.

The reading of the texts distanced the students from that goal, and Dr. Weiss exacerbated the situation by saying that Rabbi Kook was interested in challenging the self-satisfaction of the religious person who is sure of his truths. Here Rachel expressed distress. She took advantage of the supportive atmosphere that always pervaded the classroom in order to confess, in order to point to the simple primal need of a believing woman to know the truth. Is that "childish"? she asked. "Too primitive? Too low, too simple?" She wanted to know. Was she demanding to know? The factors that constituted her life as a girl, teenager, and young woman seemed to become inconsequential in the face of this new literacy experience. As noted previously, the entire process of deep study engenders this emotion, and the fact that students must respond to the religious code turns this feeling into genuine distress. The relevance of the material under study grants the literacy experience other responses that are simply not evoked when the challenge to what is taken for granted is not tied to the women's immediate existence.[10]

The experience of critical thinking and the reading of texts that contain phenomenological and relativist thinking upset the familiar order. In this situation, the women sought to construct an alternative order. Nevertheless, it looked as if the new order gravitated in the direction of the order that had been undone.

The attribution of logic and value to all human thinking of whatever kind—as in Rabbi Kook's writing—induced Efrat to ask whether all the monotheistic religions are identical. This forced Dr. Weiss to drop her listeners a lifeline. "No," she told them, "there is a hierarchy of truths." But this lifeline was braided with scientific standards—economy and generality. The Jewish formulation, Weiss argued in Rabbi Kook's name, provides the best formula. It does not provide the truth, but rather the most precise and general semblance of the truth that the students seek. The class's dance around "the truth" had a particularly complicated choreography. The students moved in a circle of critical thinking and relativism fed by the texts, the literacy practice, and the teacher, while attempting to reach the center, the "truth."

The unremitting attempts to return to questions of absolute truth and faith sometimes went in other directions that bothered the women: issues such as nonreligious Jews and apostasy, as well as the ability to argue with the halacha, to renew and break the conventional framework.

TRUTH AND HALACHA: WHAT WOULD RABBI KOOK HAVE SAID ABOUT NAOMI'S PANTS?

The women were overtly delighted to see each other when they reassembled after the break between semesters. They stood and chatted in two small circles far from me and the chair in which I had planted myself. In general, I preferred to sit in the row of extra chairs on the side of the classroom. At the end of my first semester of studies at the Midrasha I had no real friends. There were half-smiles, vague queries, and concise replies. I was an outside observer of the exceptional student intimacy that was based on the women's many years of acquaintance prior to their studies at the Midrasha. But fortunately for me, I had purchased the source book for the class at the beginning of the year, and Aviva didn't have one. This led her to sit close by and lean over the large pages with me. We whispered to each other at times. Aviva had an eight-month old baby daughter and was already thinking of dropping the graduate program. With the encouragement of her husband, who was studying economics at Bar-Ilan, she decided to remain. During breaks between classes she ran home to her apartment, close to the campus. "My husband's mother is taking care of her for me, but you know how it is—I'm nursing, and I'm the worrying type. Still, I'm happy I decided to stay. It fills me up for the entire week, even though I sometimes drowse off in classes. I just don't sleep well at night."

Aviva looked at me, with my uncovered head and my lack of a wedding ring. She had a hard time holding back her question: "Do you have children? What, really? Such big ones, I wouldn't have believed it. You must have already forgotten what it's like. What happened last week? I missed class—I think she's starting to teethe."

"We spoke about different types of faith," I answered her, just before Dr. Weiss herself launched into a summary of the previous session.

Weiss: "We can sum up the selections we have read up until now by saying that Rabbi Kook distinguished between two major types of faith: One, the main part of faith, which is emotional and instinctive and available to all; two, 'figurative' faith."

> The intelligentsia thinks that it can separate itself from the masses, and that will make it healthier in spirit, more noble in its thinking. That is a fundamental error, an error that does not recognize the healthy side of natural insights, of the natural emotions, of the natural senses, that have not been rectified, but also have not been ruined by any kind of cultural influence. (Avraham Yitzhak Hakohen Kook, *Orot Ha-Kodesh* II, 364–65)

Weiss: "Religious truths are devices meant to lead to the reality that lies beyond all these formulations of faith. Thus the 'truths' may well change according to time and place—the main thing is that they advance the cause of faith. There are, of course, devices that are not exchangeable, whose style accords with the structure of man's soul as it is, to the point that they are necessary—for example, the 'necessary faiths' of Maimonides."

Naomi: "Wait just a second. So then halacha is also truth of that type that can be changed."

Weiss: "Sometimes, and that's why I read Rabbi Kook's opinion of Maimonides. Halacha is indeed a necessary truth, but that is a style that turns into a necessity; if we replace it, it will damage the main thing. In order to understand the absolute truth we must translate it into terms comprehensible to us, which have a practical aspect to them—that is the halacha."

Naomi was older than the rest of the students, and her head was not covered. Sometimes she came to the Midrasha dressed in loose-fitting pants. It was easy to read her as someone who was in the midst of a moderate process of searching and of a controlled return to religion.

Naomi: "It's not a matter of getting closer and of truths. It's a matter of conformity. To do something from a position of social fear and not the awe of faith—like wearing or not wearing pants, for instance."

Weiss flashed a broad smile, and the women in the class made themselves part of the intimate atmosphere by smiling or chatting among themselves. They gazed at Naomi, who had not been with them in school or *ulpana*, National Service or Bnei Akiva.

Weiss: "Naomi, I don't want to get into—not even to get close to—the matter of pants."

Naomi: "No. I've got to know once and for all what connection there is between the matter of my conformity and my closeness to God."

Weiss: "I'll try to guess what Rabbi Kook would tell you. He would say that there is something in adhering to the path of a public whose goal is to approach God and the absolute truth."

Leah: "Even when the actions of that public are not necessary?"

Weiss: "That too. This is a case of expropriating the ontological value of religious truths. They don't describe the truth—they are a path of worship and becoming close to God."

Naomi: "Excuse me, I'm going back to that; What about someone who feels close to God in pants?"

Laughter in the class. Weiss smiled, and the women waited.

Weiss: "Yes, Rabbi Kook is not the only person to say that there may well be a gap between where we are and the halacha. He argues that the halacha is not sealed and static; I can refer you to places where he says that explicitly. True, he does not take that to the limit, but there are some pretty radical statements. At least in the matter of the Land of Israel and Zionism."

Michal: "If we return to the question of why halacha is a necessary truth, then I want to answer. Because every time something new comes out it's impossible to know whether it's good or bad, necessary or not."

Weiss: "Right. So in religious life there are also gambles—not like the nonreligious think: that everything is sealed and given. Many questions are resolved after the fact. Shabbateanism, Christianity—their status became clear only after the fact, while decisions have to be made in real time, and there is a certain gamble in them. So they say maybe it's worthwhile to go in the ways of our forefathers."

Leah: "But you're contradicting yourself. After all, Rabbi Kook made halachic innovations."

Weiss: "Yes, he felt that he had to take a chance, because too large a gap had been created between simple faith and the place in which he and most of his generation stood. The sense of loss and diminishment was strong, but Rabbi Kook did not accept the diminishment of the generations. Maybe our forefathers were giants and we are dwarfs, but we are borne on their shoulders and therefore we are higher than they were. Maybe we should read a short passage that describes a part of this problematic system of relations. Racheli, please."

> The sacred must be built on the profane because the profane is the material of the sacred, and the sacred is its form. And the stronger and fitter the material is, its form will be more important. Sometimes it happens that the sacred represses the profane, until the material attenuates. And then a period continues that the material demands its figuration. . . . With usury and interest the profane then takes its debt from the sacred, and insolence overwhelms. (*Great in Holiness, First Things*, in *Sayings of A. Y. H. Kook*, II, 400)

Michal: "I've got a problem with that. Every time he runs into apostasy, he's got some sort of apologetics. I don't like that."

Weiss: "If you want to go in that direction, there are those who say that Rabbi Kook, like a great leader of any generation, is in distress. He can't look at the Jewish people around him and declare them irrelevant, and rule that a majority of the nation is sinning and evil. He has to find himself an intellectual and constructive explanation. Rabbi Kook did not take the path of insularity and look the other way; on the other hand, he did not want to sell his soul to Satan."

Leah: "Practically, what do we do? After all, last year I learned that Rabbi Kook argued that every human activity augments the general good, so it really isn't important at all what you do—all the people around us who take different paths are also really doing good, right? That's also important to me for understanding the Holocaust—for understanding the meaning of human evil."

Weiss: "That is Rabbi Kook's risky point, and he knew it. He did not live long enough to have to try to explain the Holocaust. I think he would have given an explanation that would be hard for you to accept. But in an obligatory sense, the role of every person on earth is to reconstruct the absolute good, by routine diligent labor, according to the concepts he knows."

Michal: "That's tiring."

Naomi: "Life is tiring."

Weiss: "Soon we'll get to 'boring apostasy.' I promise you that when we reach the rabbi's formula, we will become acquainted with another possibility."

CONSERVATISM AS A BOLD GAMBLE:
THE DANCE OF THE OBSERVERS

From the year's halfway point and onward it seemed as if the class had gotten into the rhythm and had assimilated the teacher's approach. Weiss's attempt to present and smudge the dichotomy between primary natural thinking (the main part of faith) and intellectual faith (the figure of faith)—had been successful. The dialectic in class had already adopted a familiar and even pleasant cadence. But when Rabbi Kook's binary clusters developed and reached necessary truths, which were devices for reaching full faith, the dialogue lost its hold on the dialectic trapeze. Naomi led a discussion based on the thesis that halacha was only a necessary truth. Her different status among the women—older than they were and someone who had come from the "outside"—gave her an established role in the class. From time to time she compared the material under study to teachings from the Far East, to other philosophers, or to New Age thinking.

Dr. Weiss treated her with respect and patience, as she treated everyone else, but she reserved a special smile for her—one that hinted at fixed expectations. Naomi's pants, which stood between her and the rest of space, between her and the other women in the Midrasha and the community, and between her and the halacha, became concrete material that clothed the rabbi's thinking. Would he or wouldn't he have allowed me to wear pants? she demanded to know. To what degree is it permissible for a believer to make interpretations for herself? How far can an observer go? After all, the rabbi's words indicate a social structuring of the orthodox code, depicting it as a sociological necessity. If so, Naomi argued, "I/we observe the precepts only out of social fear and conformity."

Naomi's stubborn intrusion from outside caused the internal group (the students and Dr. Weiss) to divest themselves of the luxuries of philosophical discussion and discipline it. "The style," Dr. Weiss said, "there is already style, which is indeed only external form, but which has become necessary. The wall begins to be rebuilt, but it is still full of cracks." Michal volunteered

to close up some of the fissures. It is impossible to give yourself over to
every innovation that appears because you don't know what its quality is.
Paradoxically, and so characteristic of orthodox discourse,[11] the teacher also
took upon herself to mend the cracks. She presented conservatism as a
gamble. Since there is truth in everything and all thought is logical, one
should continue to wear a skirt. Since nonreligious Jews are also holy, and
all the world's theories and religions are good to some extent, one should
adhere to the ways of the forefathers. The same dialectic that challenged
the presumptive, the orthodox, was not enlisted to revive it. Dr. Weiss took
her place beside her students for a few moments, against Naomi. She stuck
to her claim that the halacha is indeed not closed, and showed how Rabbi
Kook broadened (if not to the limit) its openings. But she did not permit any
damage to the form, style, and way of the public she considered holier. Only
when Leah asked what to do in practical terms did Dr. Weiss shake herself
free of conservative discourse. Leah's demand to receive absolute answers
about a good and beneficent God, and her banal connection of this to the
Holocaust, brought Weiss back to a philosophical position—but not before
she had calmed the class by constituting conservatism as the great gamble of
the twentieth century. In this she allowed herself and them to remain within
the modern intellectual experience of this century—even as she recreated
the boundaries of their orthodoxy. In this way she allayed the believers' fear
that observance of the precepts and the halacha might be the wrong gamble.
In order to complete this process, before the end of the year she presented
Rabbi Kook's "formula."

The Formula

The supreme unification is the unification of man and his will with all the universe, in
its whole and in its parts, unification with the divine matter performs this action in
full, and there is no wonder that the righteous who cleave to God then will
change being and their prayer brings fruit. So will all humanity be, of course
through the revelation of Israel's preferable essence, and will spread over all, and
God's grandeur will fill the whole world, and God will rejoice in what he made.
Rabbi Avraham Yitzhak Hakohen Kook, Arpilei Tohar, 13

In the two final lessons, the unifying solution of the dichotomy was made
clear. Rabbi Kook's lexicon was written on the blackboard. The paradigm
had four levels, and the students faced a more or less organized table that
laid out the milestones they had followed through the course of the year.

The final station was "unity." Before parting from her students, Dr. Weiss asked them: "Where will unity lead us?"

Naomi: "To the resurrection of the dead."

Weiss: "That's part of it, but you have to understand the depth of the matter before you speak about the resurrection of the dead. This unity between Messiah/spirit/self-awareness/internal redemption is based on the 'I' reaching the height of its individuality because it recognizes that it is part of a system. The 'I' will gain in force, and there will also be an elimination of the boundaries between morality imposed from outside and inner morality; things will be done out of total willingness."

Naomi: "I've seen people who get stuck with an obligation or who fight it, but I've never seen anyone who internalizes it."

Leah: "What kind of moral forces are you talking about? Where are they? I see separation and self-disorder of individuals and the nation. We are not strong, and we are divided."

Miri: "The feeling is that the world is heading toward destruction. Where does this optimism come from—Rabbi Kook's belief in democracy, in human maturity? Where did he take that from?"

Weiss: "There are those who will say that his theory has a real ontological value that should lead somewhere, and they will pull his words in the political direction—as did Zvi Yehuda Kook—while the Nazarite[12] saw in them eternal philosophical value, a teaching of tolerance, a place for every phenomenon."

Rachel: "That's tolerance with a limit, because in the end the sacred swallows up the profane."

Weiss: "Being swallowed up doesn't mean something disappears. It changes the sacred. Everything comes together and contradictions vanish."

WOMAN AS BELIEVER AND OBSERVER

Efrat, Naomi, Miri, and Leah did not see how contradictions vanished and were replaced by the promised unity. Elimination of binary thinking seemed like philosophical idealism to them—a naïveté out of contact with the reality they saw from the window. The retreat from a single pole in favor of a generalized and holistic position seemed to them an unrealistic exercise waiting for a different solution. Naomi was waiting for the resurrection of the dead, doubtful about the ability to internalize a command so that it become an integral part of the "believer." It was possible, in her opinion, to fight the command or sink into it, but not to become one with it. Leah was doubtful about the unity of public and private morality; to her, society seemed to be falling apart. Miri exchanged her doubt for a prophecy of destruction. It was hard for her to understand where Rabbi Kook got his optimism when the world outside was heading for ruin.

To dispel this dismal atmosphere, Dr. Weiss proposed two possibilities. One was to follow in the footsteps of the rabbi's son, who sought to blaze political trails for his father's theory. The other was to treat Rabbi Kook's teachings as moral philosophy—this being the approach of the Nazarite. The students had no doubt that Weiss preferred the second approach, and that left her far from the binary poles and within the murky unification.

Rachel made one final attempt to challenge this. She argued that tolerance or pluralism does not allow the existence of the sacred next to the profane, because unification means that the former will swallow up the latter. Loyal to the doctrine of force that characterized their side of the dialogue, the students rejected the possibility of unification. There is no synthesis or, in fact, all synthesis is the thesis of the next confrontation. The day of the last battle had not yet come, and it was best to leave the barricades up. It would seem that theirs was not the militancy of soldiers refusing to give up their weapons, but rather a combativeness stemming from despair and doubtfulness, which were evoked by the tension between what was being said in class and what was taking place outside.

That tension was limited to Dr. Weiss's class alone. It is evident in the lessons described here because it is a fixed element in every literacy experience. The gap between students' social reality and the theories, models, or work plans presented to them in any framework is a fixed part of all learning processes. In modern Israeli Hebrew this gap is named by the military term "the field." "I'm talking as someone who comes from the field," a student sometimes said in class, thus separating herself from the public of young students and pointing to a disconnection between what was being studied and what was actually happening outside. "Practically, in the field," another student said, "it doesn't work; here it sounds very nice."

Paulo Friere, the Brazilian pedagogue, focused the major part of his educational research on this gap. As described in more detail in the next part of this book, Friere sought to bring material under study closer to the reality seen from the window. This process did not try to represent reality; rather it was built out of its components for the learners. Relevant learning, that which gathers unto itself the daily reality of the learners, is meant to overcome the alienation between the languages of knowledge built in other places and the local reality of the learners. Only in this way, Friere argues, could the residents of the pueblos in Salvador Bahia learn to read and write—a task that had nothing to do with their other daily functions. Only in this way could the fishermen, for example, gain tools and information that were seemingly useless.

The way in which the gaps between what is studied and what is experienced are built and closed is vital to an understanding of the literacy in the Midrasha. Each of the classes described in this book depicts a different creating/resolving approach to such gaps. Dr. Weiss "pulled" the students "upward," showing them abstract points of view floating above the place where they found themselves. In the other dialogues presented, there was one teacher who pushed her students "down" from where they were—a practical, routine, and unrespected existence—and another who pushed them "out"—into the sociopolitical reality they sometimes preferred to ignore. Dr. Weiss's offer of points above and beyond events derived from her philosophical discipline, the texts she chose to read, and her position as an educator. She exerted a tremendous effort to avoid surrendering to the force of gravity—to make full use of every imaginative moment to elucidate the material. The students pulled the discussion down and brought it closer than any other class did to the dialogue framework.

As explained at the beginning of this part of this book, the dialogue can emphasize the temporary opposition of those who take part in it. However, according to Jauss's approach, a dialogue can also emphasize precisely what is temporarily shared by the people who engage it. Dialogue is always conducted in a context, whose growth it permits and whose borders it marks. A momentary or ongoing rift, like acceptance and participation, depend on the way in which the gap between what is read and said and what is experienced is processed in the lives of the students. In other words, alienation from dialogue or the sense of belonging to it depend on its degree of relevance to the lives of those who take part in it. Thought must thus be given to how the entire literacy process deals with the gap between what is learned and what there is.

Friere hopes that learning will grant the learners tools for thinking and criticism of their social reality. This will enable them to return to that reality empowered with knowledge that allows critique and sociopolitical change.

Toward what can the students in Dr. Weiss's class, or the entire student body at the Midrasha, direct their new knowledge? Can we speak in this case of social change, change in the identity of the students, or both? The scholarly growth that is a fixed element in the development of a Jewish boy, young man, and adult male who engages in sacred studies has an ancient and institutionalized path. The growing tide of knowledge among women is dredging new channels and searching for a drainage basin.

In a study that followed the implementation of Friere's methods in São Paulo, Brazil, the students reported a lack of satisfaction with the method.[13] Many of them, in fact, admitted that the studies had been interesting and that they now felt more self-confident—but they had expected to gain some material benefit. They had expected to receive practical skills that would enable them to put up a lottery stand in the neighborhood, improve their performance in the cigarette trade, or receive a minor civil service position, for example. Their conservative approach, seeking to improve one's position within the system rather than change it, is interesting but not surprising. The correct way to decipher what they said is via the category of "class." By contrast, the situation of the students in the Midrasha could be more accurately deciphered using the concept of gender in its religious Zionist context: that is, in the category of modern believing and observant women.

The categories that structure the community of observers and divide it into different levels were more transparent in Dr. Weiss's class than in any other course at the Midrasha. The division there was not between younger and older women, between scholars and others, between different ethnic groups—and, astonishingly, not even between women and men. Dr. Weiss's class, of all the classes that appear here, was the one least specifically directed at women. It was not a "female" area of study (as is oral law or, to a certain extent, Bible), nor was it a subject of special concern to women. During the course of the year the teacher made almost no reference to her students being women, their enrollment in a women's institution, their being taught by one of the few female teachers in that institution. And the students did not try to divert the course's content into a discussion of their problems as women (with the exception of Naomi's pants, which served as a metaphor) or mothers. The class never discussed the right of women to study, did not go anywhere near the issue of women's status in the community, and did not ask how these students in the graduate program would integrate their new knowledge into their lives.

The only structural division alluded to in this class was the one between religious and nonreligious people. However, the fact that Rabbi Kook sought to see the sublime in all human beings, to sanctify the profane and include the nonreligious in the religious public, blurred this categorical division as

well. Rachel noticed this and tried for a moment to challenge the delight in
this blurriness, saying: "That's tolerance with a limit, because in the end the
sacred will swallow up the profane." It is not, in her opinion, an easygoing
way to link godless modernism and modern Jewish religion; rather it is a
violent act of swallowing up and obliteration.

It is interesting to note how a young student in the Midrasha expressed,
in her own way, the central argument of comprehensive scholarly study.[14]
Dov Schwartz, who traced the history of religious Zionist thinking, showed
that its central task was indeed the creation of a new theology that would
embrace both the old and the new and that would touch all areas of life.
Along the entire spectrum of approaches that sprouted in religious Zionist thinking, the redemptive-Messianic one became dominant—a theology
whose slogan was "the old will be renewed and the new will be sanctified."[15]
Under this canopy, the division between religious and nonreligious becomes
worthless, and there is no place for genuine pluralism.

An immediate, personal atmosphere pervaded the classroom: a woman
facing her God, facing a public she is part of. In a situation where social
categories are transparent, there is a place for all the believers in a community of observers. There they can reconfirm their modern/religious identities without colliding head-on with the religious Zionist lack of tolerance
for secularism and the social/gender inequality that threatens this identity.
The modern identity is reconfirmed by the act of learning, exposure to
new knowledge and universalism, by experiencing a process of questioning,
doubt, broadening of knowledge, and study for the sake of study.

The religious identity is reconfirmed by the attempts to close the gap
between what is studied and what is done, between the "substantial" and
the "practical,"[16] and also by the fact that knowledge is always measured
by its ability to broaden and deepen the range of individual participation
in the community. The link between modernism and religiousness is made
possible by the very description of "going in the ways of the forefathers"
as the great gamble of the twentieth century. Modernism is the choice of
religious Zionist orthodoxy. Such a choice does not challenge science or
undermine its fundamental assumptions. Quite the opposite: It empowers
it. These two components of the women's identities grant them the least
problematic entry ticket into the modern religious community. In this way
they can experience themselves as part of an ostensibly modern community
and part of the community of observers that practically tests its knowledge.
Even though the class was gender-transparent, it may well be that the creative power of the experience described above derived from the fact that

it was created in a place where mostly young women sat and coped with complex texts with the help of a professional and religious woman.

It should be remembered that the central axis in the relation between knowledge and community moves between the creation of learning identities and the creation of a community of observers. The flooding of the community with more and more "knowing identities" who are women is in and of itself a great change that affects the way in which the social space turns into a location of the dissemination of knowledge and activity.[17] The way in which division and coordination between participants is created is a matter of social structure and power.

The way of woman as believer and observer appears here in its private and less problematic dimension because in Dr. Weiss's class the social structure and power relationships were transparent. Still, the learning process exposed a part of this structural relationship, since this is the nature of inquiry. To this private dimension of the believing woman one should thus add the dimensions of nationality and gender that were clearly raised in the previously reported dialogues. The connection between the private, the national, and one's gender reveals the heavy burden and complexity of the effort to weave an identity in which young women act. Their growing devotion to Jewish study increases their identity distress, and they look for an easing of that distress within study itself.

IV

ANTHROPOLOGY AND LITERACY—
FROM CRITIQUE TO PARTICIPATION

LEAH'S TALLIT

During the 1995–96 academic year a discussion group called New Midrash operated in the framework of the Van Leer Institute in Jerusalem. At one of the sessions Leah Shakdiel[1] spoke about her attempt to establish a women's Torah reading group with friends at the Afikim Ba-Negev synagogue in Yeruham.

"I think we forced most of the members of the synagogue to confront a problem they were not prepared for, had not dealt with consciously. We imposed a premature discussion on a heterogeneous collection of people. Some were indifferent to the matter, others left the synagogue because of it, and there were those who remained. After all sorts of discussions among us, conversations and clarifications, we decided to come to the morning service, and at the time of the Torah reading to move over to a nearby house where everything was already prepared for our Torah reading for women. In fact, more or less, that is how it is conducted to this day; we don't read in the synagogue but rather in the home of one of the women."

When Leah Shakdiel finished describing the unique activity of this group of women on holidays, in prayers, and at celebrations, a discussion was held. The half-moon-shaped room at the Van Leer Institute was not crowded, and the people sitting there, the members of the New Midrash group and their guests, were able to conduct a real conversation.

Among the many responses, I remember in particular that of Tova Ilan, a member of Ein Tsurim, a religious kibbutz. Ilan is a long-time public activist and feminist:

"I'd like to see you in this matter the way I've become accustomed to seeing you in political matters. Fighting and not giving in. I want to attack the rabbinate or the establishment with their own weapons, from within the world of Torah, and to do that I have to bring up women who can fight with those weapons. I want, if I study Torah, to be within the male world as part of it and not 'next to it,' as part of me, and to say in a great and clear voice what I have to say. While I understand you, it's hard for me to accept the fact that you need to hide in a private home in order to read from the Torah, and that you need to get permits of all kinds. All those twists and turns in order to remain under the canopy of the halacha. There has to be a halachic change, that's what I would like to see."

"Tova," said Shakdiel, "I admit that in this matter, in contrast with political issues, I have no agenda. It evolved. I have described here a certain development. I was excited about every stage that we went through, and I still find myself excited now in this room. Do you know what it is for me that Rabbi Naftali Rotenberg and Rabbi Dov Berkowitz are sitting here and listing to a story about women learning, and reading from the Torah, and writing new versions of prayers? Do you know what it is for me that they react positively and encourage us to go further? Maybe that doesn't sound feminist; maybe that contradicts my image to some extent. It might sound paradoxical, but the synagogue is important to me, so it is difficult for me to conduct a battle within it. The synagogue has a certain place in my consciousness that I have no desire or emotional ability to expunge."

Shakdiel removed, from a decorated bag, a tallit that she had prepared with her friends. It was made of an off-white shade of linen with blue trim, and embroidered on it were the words of a medieval devotional poem, "Attend to the Soul."

"This is a tallit for women," Shakdiel explained. "It is sewn according to the rules of the halacha, but it is not a man's. Its colors are blue and white, and that is important to me because those are the colors of our flag. Its cut is special and makes it possible to hold the Torah scroll or children in one's hands without it falling. I love my tallit very much. I have no doubt that it is an innovation, for me and for the other members. It is important to us that it be in the framework of the halacha. Within that framework, with creativity and work and study, we want to participate more and more, to do more and more."

The collective biography unfurled before the listeners described the ongoing attempt of a group excluded from the main part of Jewish practice to take up and participate in that practice. Tova Ilan heard in the story reverberations of opposite poles that granted the story a dimension of permanence, a kind of dichotomous social situation that cannot be changed—men versus women, a public sphere versus a private sphere, those who decide the halacha versus those who practice it, social change versus social conservatism. It would seem, however, that this is not the way that Leah Shakdiel wished to read that same biography. By leaving behind the "agendas" that guide her political life and entering the intimate bosom of the worship of heaven, she allowed one major goal to guide the struggle and innovativeness of the members of the group: increased participation. Participation and entry into the circle of practitioners bring about the collapse of the binary system[2] and imbue with new connotations such terms as breakthrough, political struggle, and social change. The private home in which the Torah is read by women turns into a site of public assembly. The "concession" the women have made—not reading the Torah within the synagogue on Shabbat—has distanced them from that synagogue, but it has also, simultaneously, changed the significance of the synagogue as a public place, as well as the significance of the private home into which they have retreated.

Along with the changes that the sites have undergone, the public itself has been redefined. That public, whose halachic definition prevents women from reading from the Torah in mixed company, has changed. It is no longer an active male public with a passive company of women watching it, following or not following the service from the women's section. It is no longer a male public that leads a central religious activity in which there are no roles for women, girls, or small children. Instead, a new public has been created. There are, on the one hand, men who have been abandoned by a public that cannot halachically participate, and on the other hand a public of women that has chosen to act on its own, surrounded by girls watching their mothers read from the Torah, and thinking about their own bat mitzvah ceremonies.

The halachic authorities have remained as they were, and the rules have not changed. But these women have made a range of new decisions regarding their Jewish identity. The pyramid of interpretation and interpreters is broadening. Proprietorship of knowledge, its use, and the empowerment deriving from that are increasing, and their boundaries are becoming blurred. The concept of literacy itself—who are the knowers and what can they do with their knowledge—is being imbued with new meaning.

The system of relations between the concept of literacy as knowledge and as practice, and the social contexts in which it exists, lie at the center of this chapter. It is a dialogue between anthropology as a scientific discipline— seeking to describe and analyze and understand sociocultural states— and the concept of literacy.

The principal emphasis of this chapter is theoretical. At its core is an attempt to explain the quality of the links between anthropology and literacy, and the history of those links. Bringing the two together clarifies the central problems of each of them, aids in the construction of critique, and encourages the creation of new theory.

The first part of this chapter raises three fundamental issues in anthropology that the discussion of literacy brings to the fore. The second part examines the history of the concept of literacy in its sociocultural aspect. The third and last part presents an ethnographic segment from the Midrasha that embraces and advances the entire theoretical discussion.

WHY LITERACY?

The relations between anthropology as a scientific discipline and literacy as a subject of research powerfully highlight three of the fundamental dilemmas of anthropology. The first is the tension between a desire to emphasize similarities between different human cultures and an interest in portraying the detailed differences among them. The second derives from the popularity of binary structures within anthropological theory. And the third is the abiding tension between theoretical critical anthropology and applied anthropology. These three issues are at the heart of every anthropological act, but when anthropology addresses literacy, they are explicit and cannot be ignored.

Between the Similar and the Different

Social anthropology is torn between its desire to demonstrate the equivalent and the common among all human beings, and its appetite for focusing on cultural uniqueness and diversity. Seeking to show that all human cultures are fundamentally similar, traditional anthropological practice tries to challenge the West's prevalent hierarchical ordering of cultures and present them outside the ethnocentric gaze.

At the same time, the desire to learn about differences among societies impels anthropologists to make comparisons. Comparison, by its very nature, is performed according to a set of criteria. It is difficult to choose parameters for comparison without again becoming entangled in ethno-centrism. The choice of technology, mortality rates, years of education, or wages seems to give a clear preference to the Western scale of values. But classical preoccupation with socialization processes, patterns of political decision making, signification, and symbolization is not free of the same ethnocentrism.

In order to grasp the rope at both ends—in other words, to argue for a resemblance between all societies without missing out on the differences between them—anthropologists have tended to peel off layer after layer of social difference while describing each in detail. At the end of this process they arrive at the "fundamental phenomenon," which can easily be compared to a parallel phenomenon in another society.

In this way the immersion of children in a river swarming with alligators can be juxtaposed to washing children in a bathtub, an African initiation rite to the Jewish circumcision ceremony, and shepherds' conversing while sitting in a circle around a campfire to a parliamentary debate. These behaviors symbolize the immanent similarity between human beings, hidden under its local guise. Human beings are presented as fundamentally similar to each other, and culture is described as a context-dependent phenomenon.

Seeking to identify "pure components" of human society that place its members at a single, unranked level, British anthropologist Jack Goody chose to work on literacy. In the introduction to his classic work, *Literacy in Traditional Societies*—which demonstrates the seminal link between anthropology and the study of literacy—Goody explains the motive for his decision.[3] Zoologists study animals, he states with a simplicity that sounds out of place today, anthropologists study speaking people, and sociologists study people speaking, reading, and writing. What is common to all human beings, it turns out, is language and the ability to speak and communicate; the sweeping difference among them is the expression of this ability. In transferring anthropology from the serene field of "people talking" into the clamorous community in which they also write and read, Goody gave up on emphasizing what is common in order to focus on the description and analysis of the different.

Literacy, then, is a basic and important site for unraveling the anthropological dilemma of equal and different. Anthropology contains the element that separates human beings from other living creatures: language. As such, it deals with the essence of human existence, common to all human beings as human beings. Yet it also deals with the entire range of expressions of language, languages, and all the creation associated with them, and these, of course, vary from society to society. This problem of similarity and difference links up well with the question of binary explanation.

The Binary Burden

It is accepted practice to attribute expertise in the creation of binary systems, which elucidate the network of meanings of the society under study, to the structuralist stream in anthropology.[4] Still, it would not be an exaggeration to say that the entire anthropological discourse is swathed in binary clusters, which begin with the fundamental segment of the investigator and the "others"—white man versus the natives, first world versus the rest of the world, the lone researcher versus a foreign and sometimes alienating society, the home versus the research field.

As a science that focuses on human experience and people's attempts to decipher the progress of their lives, anthropology cannot evade the constant tendency to separate heaven and earth, life and death, reality and magic, and to make the rest of the binary divisions that constitute the interpretive process. Yet many researchers have sought to show that binary explanation is principally Western and that anthropology has imposed it on the range of its subjects. The British anthropologist Marilyn Strathern famously used her study among the Hagen tribe in New Guinea as a basis for deconstructing the parallel of nature/culture = woman/man offered by Ortner—but she ended by constructing an alternative binary system.[5]

The history of work on literacy in the social sciences and the body of research it has produced demonstrate this fundamental tension between the creation of binary clusters and unceasing attempts to deconstruct them. In an article that appeared in 1995, James Collins surveys and sums up the output of anthropological research in the field of literacy.[6] Like everyone in the field, he opens with Goody's work. The accusation of binary criticism heads the list of critiques of Goody. He is the one who marked the fundamental axes of the anthropological literacy discourse as moving between the literate and the illiterate, societies with written literacy versus societies of oral literacy, and the era before the invention of printing versus the era after printing. These dichotomies and the periodization they have produced have added further links, such as the difference between myth and history, opinion and truth, traditionalism versus modernism, oppressive versus democratic rule.

The binary substratum Goody and Watt laid in the article that opens *Literacy in Traditional Societies* makes a direct and unambiguous connection between written literacy, printing, and the distribution of written material on the one hand, and bureaucracy, science, and democracy on the other.[7] Goody's concept of literacy joined anthropology to the Western world's vision of enlightenment, progress, and modernism—a vision that, in other cases and at the same time, the discipline has choked on. The practice of intercultural comparison, which assumed a common base for all human beings, tended to glorify simplicity and set it up against the injustices of the new world. The study of literacy has once again distinguished human societies according to rigid criteria that have placed the reading/writing world in a superior position to the world that merely speaks. The construction of binary systems has endowed a fixed and natural character to the dichotomies deriving from them.

However, Goody's work, along with studies by linguists and educational researchers who hold views similar to his,[8] constitute only one facet of the fruits of research. Goody's powerful writing, the productivity of his research, and his stature in the British academy have endowed this facet with great power and influence. Yet they have also encouraged an abundance of research that has contradicted his findings; in particular, this research challenges the binary foundation on which his work is built, along with its ethnocentric implications. When, after his survey of research on literacy, Collins attempts to sum up the problem of binary divisions, he notes that everyone today recognizes that the differentiation between written and oral culture constitutes an obstacle. Nevertheless, he suggests continuing to weigh the place of written literacy in the shaping of individual identity and in articulations of this identity. In this way he directs the major movement that sought to conduct large comparisons between societies and cultures onto the delicate and cautious paths of the constitution of the subject and the identity of the individual.

So as not to give up on the larger anthropological mission, Collins concludes his survey with a practical suggestion that seeks to link the micro level of a given individual in a given culture to the macro level and its generalizations. "Literacy," he argues, "will remain a social problem that will be a site for research in many directions, research that strives for cultural, political, and historical generalizations on the basis of situated accounts" (1995, p.86). It would seem that the binary battle between the global and the local, between the written and the spoken, is all contained within the term "situated accounts" (Collins, 1995, p. 86). Through it, anthropology returns to its classical starting point—speaking from within a place. Except that now the place is a position, deprived of its permanence, its innocence,

its naturalness, and conscious of the system of relations it has with its surroundings. "Situated accounts," Collins says, can embrace cultural, political,
and historical generalizations without being suffocated by them. A situated
account is an account conscious of the positions of the subject speakers and
of the investigating speaker. Such an account does not assume permanence
or naturalness of place; instead, it claims that the local uniqueness it por-
trays is an artifact of the research process.

A village in Africa, a pueblo in Brazil, or an immigrant neighborhood in
a large city cannot "naturally" represent a place of people lacking literacy.
They cannot be automatically contrasted with the first world, the Brazilian
upper class, or the western European bourgeoisie. In order to decipher the
literacy situation of these people, an account conscious of the position of
all those involved must be produced. Such an account can deconstruct assumed binary systems of East versus West, educated versus ignorant, ethical
versus barbarian, and so on.

The deconstruction of the binary explanation, the frustration of its pre-
tensions to universalism, and its presentation as an interpretative restriction
that has political implications bring the study of literacy closer to the question of the application of theoretical knowledge and intervention in the lives
of the subjects.

Between Theoretical and Applied Science

The practice of anthropology would seem to impinge on its status as a critical field of scholarship by constantly reconnecting it with its colonialist
origins. Nevertheless, and despite the low status that some applied anthropologists have earned, practical anthropology has continued to be an organic part of the scholarly community, and the debate over its status on the
intra-disciplinary scale has not been decided. Sectors of the anthropological community who declare a sociopolitical commitment to a particular
issue—such as proper medical care for all citizens of the world, reduction
of the economic exploitation of the Third World, feminism, or ethnic/racial
equality—have difficulty keeping their work within the confines of theory.

Deborah Gordon, a historian of anthropology, claims that during the
course of the attempt to free the discipline of its colonialist image, the applied side of the field was marked as "politically dirty"; by contrast, the
theoretical-critical side was fostered, and it presented itself in reflexive
writing.[9]

Current anthropology, preoccupied with itself and its writers, borders
on literature, cultural criticism, and philosophy, and succeeds, according

to Gordon, in presenting a purer face. She argues for a theoretical value free of dependence on the establishment, ostensibly increasing the difference between the anthropological act (the study and representation of "others") and political manipulation, paternalism, and colonialism. However, she adds, this new writing puts the writer, who is generally male, at the center, celebrates his abilities, embraces his style, and somewhat blurs the human experience he is dealing with.

Most anthropological research on literacy is, in fact, theoretical. Some of the investigators have a penchant for abstract theory in the linguistic and semantic fields,[10] and the most noted anthropologists have not been involved in applied projects. Still, it would seem that the study of literacy brings anthropology closer to the applied-involved pole of education, pedagogy, and cognitive psychology. When describing and analyzing the state of literacy in different societies, it is tempting to color a map of the world with light and dark patches marking areas of literacy and "ignoracy."[11] Such marking would embrace all three of the issues cited above. It would emphasize differences between human societies, base these differences on binary distinctions, and contain an implicit call for intervention.

It turns out that the study of literacy is indeed a busy site of different fundamental assumptions in anthropology—a site no one intends to concede. The endeavor to rescue it and bring it safely from the modern age to the postmodern era must follow a route that passes through three central stations: progress, critique, and participation.

PROGRESS, CRITIQUE, AND PARTICIPATION

The journey through progress, critique, and participation is not a quest through time, and it does not designate a linear development of the concept of literacy. It is an interpretative movement between three foci of meaning, which can be represented as a kind of triangle. Progress and critique are the points at either end of the triangle's base, while participation is at its apex. The triangular structure delineates the relations between these points as manifested in different interpretations of literacy. Differences are especially notable at the poles of progress and critique, because the critical approach has grown as a reaction to the concept of progress.

Deployment of the concept of literacy on the side leading from progress to critique is based on the claim that all ways of understanding and dealing with the concept contain a certain measure of sanctification of knowledge—an assumption that knowledge is power. Since the Enlightenment, the sanctification of knowledge has been decoded, both scientifically and in common usage, as having political and social implications.

This part of the discussion seeks to show that the proposed interpretations for the concept of literacy on the two opposing poles of progress and critique recreate the three fundamental issue with which this chapter began. In other words, the conception of literacy at each of these two poles draws the three fundamental dilemmas of anthropology into a certain extremism, as will be clarified below. Understanding literacy as participation, the third point, provides a way of eluding these issues, at least to some degree.

BETWEEN PROGRESS AND CRITIQUE

In their historical survey of the concept of literacy in the modern age, Friere and Macedo begin with the Enlightenment, because it was then, they claim, that the Western world's concept of knowledge was reshaped.[12] Their survey paved the way for the transition from the concept of literacy as autonomous, in accordance with the spirit of the Enlightenment, to the concept of literacy as an ideological phenomenon, in the critical spirit.

The concept of autonomous literacy detached human knowledge from restrictions of immediate place and context. With the help of printing—a simple and inexpensive technology for its dissemination—knowledge, committed to science, could circulate among all human beings, free of the constraints of the church. Parents, schools, or the state assumed responsibility for training the public to read and bringing this public into contact with the knowledge contained in the pages of the encyclopedias. The outcome of the encounter between readers and knowledge is taken for granted. A rational man who reads the truth will understand and accept it. In any case, this truth will turn him into an enlightened man—an essential component in the formation of the modern state and society.

The humanism at the dawn of the Enlightenment was exchanged for liberal tones in its twilight. Rousseau, Voltaire, and Diderot, who dreamed of the "education of the world," were replaced by professional knowledge-conveyors who merely embody those who have "got" it. Emancipatory enlightening knowledge became a resource with a market value and position. It could be purchased and resold, with added value, to others.

When the autonomous conception of knowledge is placed along side the anthropological dilemmas presented at the beginning of this chapter, it turns out that the concept of autonomous literacy strengthens the binary distinction between those who know and those who do not know, redrawing the boundaries between simple "oral" societies and complex "literate" societies. Autonomous literacy prefers the knowledge of the Western world, encoded and enciphered in European languages, over other kinds of knowledge. Such literacy transpires outside its social context and even in opposition to it. Thus, argue those who adhere to this autonomous conception, tribes with mystic and concrete thinking can exchange this for abstract and rational thinking. Political struggles can be ameliorated with the help of an educational platform common to all, and this will also reduce class, ethnic, and gender gaps. Enabling people to read and write detaches knowledge from the conveyors of knowledge and from the context in which it was conveyed, and allows the development of science.[13]

Autonomous literacy of the Enlightenment and modernist variety believes that differences between human societies can be eliminated. This belief is based on the assumption of the existence of "rational man." But the unitary face of such a man recreates the difference between what he is now and what he is supposed to be. Such a concept inevitably invites intervention in the lives of the subjects in order to turn them into enlightened people. Therefore, those who hold to the autonomous-emancipatory interpretation of the concept of literacy are linked as if by an umbilical cord to an applied anthropology with a modernist ideological commitment.[14]

Apparently it was disappointment in knowledge's emancipatory ability that brought many investigators to examine the autonomous value of literacy. Early in the 1970s, critique began eroding the fundamental terms of modernism, and literacy has not come out clean. On the basis of historical research, Graff argues that literacy is a myth. It is, he maintains, a tool that advances, develops, and liberates when it is examined from a quantitative perspective, but a qualitative study shows that it is a tool for hegemonic manipulations.[15] Literacy, he goes on to argue, has not benefited all those who possess it, and those who do not possess it are not all troubled by its lack. Moreover, its social role is charged with many contradictions. Graff's study shows that school education in the Canadian cities he studied broadened gaps and reinforced the existing social structure. Indeed, literacy constitutes a symbol of gender, age, class, and ethnic distinction.

To Graff's historical test have been added other doubting anthropological voices, who have put the concept of autonomous literacy to an additional test—this time cultural.[16] Brayn Street summed up the results of this review in a book that formulates the critical position toward the study of literacy in anthropology.[17] With a comprehensive theoretical effort and on the basis of ethnography he conducted in Iran before the Khoumeinist revolution, Street calls for a redefinition of literacy as *ideological literacy*. In his judgment, scholars should talk about many literacies, not just one, and understand the significance of literacy within the institutional context on which it depends. Such institutions are political and ideological. The acts of writing and reading are not just technical skills. They should be understood via the social, cultural, and institutional context within which they are produced and maintained. Literacy is always part of a social situation, and therefore it cannot function outside of or in opposition to its context.

The critical approach to literacy depicts a rigid social situation in which there is an almost conspiratorial coordination of intent among a range of social institutions. According to the picture painted by this approach, a person has next to no chance of operating in opposition to the hegemonic institutions. So, for example, the factory in which a woman works has the same social agenda as the school her son attends. The programs she watches on television, the magazines she leafs through, the posters on the street, and everything else in her environment guarantee that she and her family are kept in their places. They allow only small-scale changes that provide a false sense of significant change.

By declaring that literacy has no independent status, the critical approach denies the binary distinction between those who know and those who do not know. Anthropological studies that take a critical position place oral and written literacies side by side, blurring distinctions between them and demonstrating that a transition from one literacy to the other does not obviate social systems. Instead, it organizes them in different ways. This interpretation of literacy takes exception to the intervention of the Western world in the dissemination of knowledge, in the marking of areas of ignorance, and in awarding qualitative marks to different literacies.

Critical literacy, in its extreme form, together with the three fundamental dilemmas of anthropology, lead to the following assertion: Human cultures are different from each other, and any attempt to posit that a "rational man" is a component of them all ends up being paternalistic and colonialist. There is not a state of literacy versus illiteracy, but simply different literacy situations. Therefore, any intervention intended to instill a given type of literacy is an ethnocentric act that will simply fasten the learners more firmly in place.

The critical stance successfully challenged the notion of autonomous literacy and demonstrated the fundamental assumptions on which it is based. Those working on literacy have stopped speaking of a single literacy, of an autonomy of knowledge, and of "class" and "study" as islands with no social context. Cultural diversity has become legitimate and desirable, and intervention, or the transition to applied anthropology, has been put in its insignificant place.

By its nature, critique clarifies, but it can also paralyze. Anthropologists who depict literacy as ideology have generally occupied themselves with critical readings of their predecessors, surveying international projects that have failed and done damage because of their autonomous fundamental assumptions, and supplying ethnographic proof to reinforce their theoretical positions. Those who have accepted this concept of literacy, but worked in the field of education, could not remain in this paralyzed position. They created a theoretical-practical link between their work and their critique, which has been given the name "critical pedagogy."

Critical pedagogy has been woven out of the educational and theoretical work of a small group of people. At its center stood the late Paulo Friere, a Brazilian educator, a local and global politician, and a pedagogical guru. The group has grown as it was joined by teachers, philosophers, ethnographers, and educational researchers—all of whom have seen a need for an alternative practical portrait of the education act as it derives from the modernist-liberal conception.

This depiction can be broadly described if one ignores differences among the members of the group: Literacy is dependent on context and the political world, and it has the power to change human situations on personal, communal, political, and international levels. This literacy grows out of the reality in which it transpires. It begins at the immediate concrete level of its learners, grows into an abstract worldview, and returns to the reality of those who hold it in order to change this reality.

In the Brazilian fishing village where Paulo Friere worked, adults learned how to read and write in straw huts. Their curriculum reflected their world—fishing nets, flimsy boats, fish dinners, the city merchant who came to buy the fruits of their labors. The letters, words, and sentences connected to their familiar reality and transferred it into an abstract text that made it possible to step back from the concrete. This stepping back, Friere argues in his famous book *The Pedagogy of the Oppressed,* enables the growth of awareness, consciousness, and criticism. After these are formed, a social change based on the empowerment that knowledge provides can take place. Such a pedagogy is appropriate for all the powerless people in the world—on the condition that it always grows out of the existence of its learners and within an obligation to change that existence.[18]

The range of studies produced by this group point to some successes en-abled by the application of critical pedagogy. Their work seeks to shift from a merely critical position into a practical process, and as such it has drawn a new round of criticism. This criticism seems to arise from the fact that critical pedagogy has recreated, in its own way, a commitment to the mod-ernistic concept of knowledge. It sees ownership of knowledge as empow-ering, revives the distinction between those who know and those who do not know. Western democracy with a socialist emphasis is presented as the preferred political order, and there is a summons to intervene in the lives of the subjects. Any transition from a theoretical position to educational actu-alization situates literacy at the heart of the three anthropological issues of equal and different, the binary system, and intervention.

A study of the recent work produced by the critical pedagogy group reveals attempts by its members to cope with the postmodern age and with these three issues. Two innovative academic directions became especially influential in the 1980s: cultural studies and feminism.

In advance of the first cultural studies conference, Henry Giroux, the group's theoretician, presented the "border crossing" approach in a 1992 article. This approach seeks to theoretically link critical pedagogy with cul-tural studies and allow, practically, the modernist educational project in the postmodern atmosphere in which it transpires.[19] "I want to cast cultural studies as a political and pedagogical project that provides a convergence between a species of modernism that takes up questions of agency, voice, and possibility with those aspects of a postmodern discourse that have criti-cally deconstructed issues of subjectivity, language, and difference" (Giroux, 1992, p. 201).

The pedagogy of border crossing, Giroux argues, is a dialogic practice. Literacy grows from the position of its learners, and opens and broad-ens toward other learners. It is an attempt to probe the class/racial/gender boundaries of its learners' existence, and to understand the "others" from their own position. This work, he says, seeks to create a multiplicity of lit-eracies and a multiplicity of identities that will challenge the hierarchy of knowledge and minimize the exploitation and oppression of those marked as being at the bottom. Giroux does not reject the value of democracy; rather he describes his method as meant to strengthen its fragments. Relativism of values cannot be absolute; it turns, in an educational process, into a journey of experience meant to bring its travelers home safely.

Another critique of principle that grew out of the critical pedagogy group derived from feminist thinking. Carmen Luke and Jennifer Gore claim that the leaders of critical pedagogy were a coterie of men who developed a gender-blind approach.[20] The ethnographies on which the male writers base themselves are focused on class and cultural differences, but they ignore gender differences and the female experience. An analysis of gender-sensitive ethnographies reveals the patriarchal infrastructure that is still common in most educational frameworks. Empowerment in patriarchal education is directed at an invisible learner who is always an individual, a lone learner. Luke and Gore seek to challenge the existence of this taken for granted individual and to speak of a network of learners, people who are inside a system of relations that is not always based on distinct monads. The empowerment that should be achieved can thus take place in a group, between a couple, between a granddaughter and a grandmother; it is the result of an interactive experience.

Using a similar approach, Debora Gordon constructed a feminist critique of both literacy and ethnography from her study of a literacy project conducted in New York by Puerto Rican women.[21] The women wrote literacy biographies that Gordon treats as ethnographic documents. The group's support of the individuals within it led each of them to recount her unique story, and each biography was also connected to the stories of the other women. The result is a collection of stories constituting ethnography of the literacy of Puerto Rican women in New York. The link Gordon points out between literacy and ethnography broadens both concepts. It distances them from the uniform-canonical focal point, disperses the power of the knowledge of writing and the description of reality among the many and different, and situates them in cultural sites that do not necessarily answer to the value and economic code of the ostensibly unified center.

[F]eminist ethnography as literacy work becomes a compelling model of politically grounded research that does not reduce intellectual acts to political acts and vice versa. Critical literacy creates new notions of women writing culture to fit patterns of global migration under multinational capitalism. . . . Feminist ethnography as a practice of critical literacy situates ethnographic writing within these daily life struggles of women who are pulled away from their homes and toward the United States. (Gordon, 1995, p. 376)

While the aggregate work by the critical pedagogy people is impressive, theoretically challenging, and committed to the practice of teaching, it seems to me that it is necessary to move onward. We should arrive at

another conception of literacy within anthropological practice, in the spirit
of feminist criticism, and in accordance with the life experience of those
who seek it.

LITERACY AS PARTICIPATION

The search for other definitions of the term literacy is also, and perhaps
principally, the concern of those who instill it—those who teach reading
and writing, the disseminators of computer literacy, those occupied with
reading comprehension and the advancement of writing. At the beginning
of the 1980s, scholars in these fields proposed the term "new literacy." Out of
scientific and practical obligation, and together with clear social positions,
literacy was formulated as a social state rather than a collection of abilities.
As Janet Emig states: "Literacy is power . . . . [L]iteracy is a way of ascending,
of going out, of penetrating inside. . . . [W]e know that the lack of literacy
in a culture based on words and built from words means preventing the
enjoyment of one of the most basic human rights."[22] But it would seem
that the most innovative connection between anthropology and literacy
was made elsewhere—far from the skills of reading and writing, outside
the standard school, and much closer to a subject of classic anthropology:
apprenticeship.

In a fascinating work published in 1991, anthropologist Jean Lave and
cognitive psychologist Etienne Wenger use an ethnographic analysis of apprenticeship to grant other meanings to the concept of learning in the community, and to the concept of literacy itself.[23] The process by which a tailor's
apprentice enters the community of professionals, the way in which a girl
learns to participate in the birthing of a baby on her way to becoming a mid-
wife, and the stages a young man goes through on a pilot boat in a port all
constituted an anthropological basis for a new theory. The concept of literacy here returns to the learners and their world. The community of learners
is a community of practitioners. So from this point of view, for example,
the literacy biography of Leah Shakdiel, presented at the beginning of this
chapter, reads as a story of increasing participation in the community of
observers of halacha. The story describes an enormous change for the participating women, aimed at broadening the meanings of their lives within
the community of observers but not aimed at changing the halacha itself.
The desire to read from the Torah on Shabbat, together with the lack of a
need to do this as part of changing the general framework, tell of the extent
to which the women belong to their community. The organic structure of

the community and the positioning of its members receive new meanings from the fact of increased participation of women in Jewish practice. The practice is not part of the learning. Quite the opposite is true: The learning (in this case, how to read from the Torah) is part of an inclusive and comprehensive act.

The title of Lave and Wegner's book is *Situated Learning: Legitimate Peripheral Participation*. The power of the concept of legitimate peripheral participation (LPP) is that it forges an unbreakable link between its three components. One cannot speak about the opposites of each of them as an additional concept, a kind of "lack of illegitimate participation from the center." This is because each of the components of the concept of LPP is not binary. A peripheral position is understood as a position in the field, not as the opposite of the center. Participation is any action, any taking part. And legitimacy is belonging to a community.

Every participant is, in principle, on the way to fuller participation, and their positions can change. The only antithesis of legitimate participation is the lack of relations with the group of practitioners; the group has no meaning for those who do not relate to it. Leah Shakdiel wishes to avoid such a situation, and for this reason she rejects a halachic battle at this point in time. In her answer to Tova Ilan, Leah Shakdiel expresses unaffected and "non-feminist" excitement about the fact that, instead of fighting rabbis, she is sitting together with rabbis who are touched by her words. The fact of wearing a tallit, which is only partial participation, brings the speaker complete happiness because it is a broadening of Jewish practice within the community of practitioners, not outside it. Such participation, despite its partial nature, broadens the practice itself, as well as its meaning.

LPP is not a pedagogical method or ideology. It is a concept intended to decipher the learning process. As such, it relates to the entire set of sociocultural contexts in which learning transpires, school being only one of those contexts. Viewing learning as an ever-growing process of participation in the community of practitioners takes into account all the individual's activities in his world. This prevents the reduction of people to their minds, of mentality to instrumentality, and of learning to the acquisition of knowledge. Participation is not only the assimilation of templates of knowledge or the demonstration of abilities. Participation is always negotiation over meanings in the world, and therefore it is dialogic and critical.

This decipherment of literacy as participation gives some comfort to the anthropological tradition and blunts the force of its three fundamental dilemmas. First, explanatory power returns to the subjects under study, from whom the researchers learn the meaning of learning for them. The literacy world is presented as dependent on culture and free of any comparative criterion, with the exception of the individuals' membership in the community. This blurs the question of similar versus different among cultures with regard to their literacy. Second, learning as participation brings about the collapse of binary dichotomies such as those who know versus those who do not know, abstract and concrete, mind and experience, actor and action, abstention and participation. Learning as participation emphasizes the knowing person, not knowledge itself: the knowing woman in place and in time, under fixed universal knowledge, assimilated permanently among learners. Learning as participation is learning in motion—between new and old, between margins and the center, between generations. This allows the broadening of areas of practice within the community, and the chances for contact and dialogue increase. The areas of meaning and the power of the community also broaden. The third release is from the fear of intervention. Elitist abstention from practical anthropology is no longer relevant, because the practice is always the practice of the learners themselves.

Thus, the decipherment of literacy as a type of belonging, practice, and socially active participation is more comfortable for anthropology. Such decoding invites ethnographic work. Its interpretive center of gravity lies among the subjects under study, and it enables an easy connection between theory and practice. It would seem that the only stumbling block in the path of anthropologists who decide to interpret literacy as participation is the innocent acceptance of belonging to a community. This link between community belonging, social power, and the meaning of knowledge raises several questions that will be addressed subsequently.

The discussion of situated learning necessarily entails a description of place and position. Such a description is available in a segment from the class on halacha and morals, given at the Bar-Ilan Midrasha in the 1994–95 academic year. I have excerpted this segment from the whole in order to demonstrate the concept of literacy as participation, even though, like all anthropological material, it can serve to provide many other insights that will not be stressed here.

NOT OBLIGATED BUT ABLE

It looks as if all the carefully crafted lesson plans of Rivka Sternberg are on subjects that "get women angry." Sternberg gives a course at the Midrasha called "Halacha and Morals" (presented in detail in chapter 1). As a skillful veteran teacher, Sternberg follows the compass of relevance. She takes upon herself to confront burning issues in the lives of those who seek to continue to be part of a religious community that excludes them from many activities and restricts their participation.

At the end of December 1994, on an especially rainy day, Sternberg resumed discussion of whether women may and should observe mitzvot from which they are exempt.[24] She maneuvered carefully between the ruling by halachic authorities that observance of such mitzvot is elective, and the ruling of certain key authorities that a person should not observe a mitzvah from which he or she is exempt. Her intention was to demonstrate a general principle (which she called the Torah principle) that applies to both men and women, and then to trace the range of behaviors available to women in particular.

"So, after we've read those that forbid and those that permit, it is clear that there is no disagreement that 'he who is commanded and performs is greater than he who is not commanded and performs.' In other words, the reward of the person who is commanded and who performs is greater than the reward of the person who is not commanded and performs. The halacha has been decided according to Rabbi Yose, who allows observing mitzvot that one is not commanded to observe. Jewish communities from the Islamic world rule according to the opinion of Rabbi Yehuda, who forbids this. And Rabbi Ovadiah Yosef [considered by many to be the greatest Sephardi halachic authority], for example, rules that women should not make a blessing.[25] Still, you should know that there was a great [Sephardi] halachic authority in Jerusalem, Rabbi Hida, who ruled that it was permitted, so there is an authority to be cited on either side.

"It is said, for example, regarding a woman who brought a sacrifice to the Temple, that she is permitted to lay her hands on the animal[26] in order to give her gratification. Now I know that there are those who interpret this as a kind of paternalism, as if they're doing her a favor, but I see it as sensitivity, as consideration. A woman has brought a sacrifice to the Temple and they won't let her lay her hands on it? They allowed her, yes, in order to gratify her, but understand, that is a custom, that is a social situation, it is not a Torah law. Whoever wants to interpret that today out of a sense of inferiority or a feeling of discrimination—go ahead, interpret it that way. It's also possible to interpret it as sensitivity toward the woman in a given social situation. What's important to know is that women did bring sacrifices and that they did lay their hands on them."

Adina: "It's hard for me here regarding positive time-dependent mitzvot. What you put into the schedule you find time for, and what doesn't fit in doesn't get in. That is, if a woman decides she's going to do something she'll do it, and she'll manage with it, and what she doesn't want to do, or what they in advance don't expect her to do, she won't do. They shouldn't decide for her."

Sternberg: "You're correct in principle, but not in practice. When you've got a baby at home, even one baby, and you try to act like someone who doesn't have one, you are fooling yourself; and if you ignore this fact you will be frustrated. In my opinion, women take too much on themselves. For example, prayer. If someone asks me whether to take upon herself the obligation of saying the Shma Yisrael prayer at its appointed times,[27] I advise against. It's a private matter, and it's possible, but they don't get up on time—they can't always do it. If you are in a classroom or in a class with boys, why not? Fine. But afterward, as adult women, it's not simple."

Adina: "About what we said here on the laying on of hands: That's not a positive time-dependent mitzvah, so why are you saying it in this context? Are you saying that women were in the Temple less and made fewer sacrifices? That's not right. Why is it necessary at all to say a sentence like 'to give gratification to the women'?"

Sternberg: "You can argue with me. I'm trying to point out the source here and show you that it's pure."

Adina: "I think this whole matter of positive time-dependent mitzvot is wrong. What does that say? After all, our life is religion, and in that way you push people away from public life. Synagogue is a bunch of men, so we [women] grow distant from religion. In my synagogue they say after the services 'there is a kiddush for the public, including the women.[28] What does that mean? There's a public and then there's women?"

Sternberg: "That's a social matter, not a religious matter."

Adina: "Yes, but it relies on the rejection of women from time-related mitzvot. That's the religious basis that allows the social distancing of women."

Sternberg: "A priest also does more than a layman, and a person who lives in Israel does more than a person who lives in the Diaspora, and a person who lives in Jerusalem more than one who lives far away—so there will always be differences among people."

Adina: "But what's this thing with the sacrifice—they give her gratification? This is my language, this is my worship of heaven, this is my speech with God—and they keep me at a distance?"

(Sternberg looks angry. Adina's rhetorical and emotional vehemence dis-
turbs her. She quotes verses that downplay the importance of sacrifices, and
the importance of the Temple service, in the mode of "who really needs it?"
Then she recovers and responds to Adina.)

Sternberg: "You were educated in an English-speaking society, and there
Jewish life is carried on around the synagogue. That's why the public issue
is so important for you."

Adina: "And it isn't?"

Sternberg: "I'm in favor of more study, more *batei midrash* for girls that
will really be parallel to *kolelim*, and of women studying more Torah and
improving themselves more, but not because it's an obligation—because
it is now possible. Today there's time. I say that the difference between the
way I raised my older and younger children is huge. So let's acknowledge
that there is more time. But society today works on the external, on what
you see, and fast. There's enough to work on inside yourself. There's enough
mitzvot and service of the Creator that it is possible to do within what you
are commanded, and they won't always see that outside."

Efrat: "You're telling her to search through her small actions, and that
can always be done, but what if someone wants to go far, in spiritual, public
nature? What do you have to answer to that?"

Sternberg: "Whoever wants to achieve what the men achieve—she'll
always feel discriminated against. And this is not a matter for discrimination
or a sense of inferiority, because it derives from a desire to become equal to
something that is different from me—that will always be accompanied by
a sense of inferiority."

Osnat: "But those who ruled against commanding women thought that
women don't have minds—like Maimonides, for example, who everyone
knows didn't think very highly of women. And for all the quotes you bring
me, I'll give you other quotes that show that they thought women don't have
minds. That was, after all, the way of thinking in the Middle Ages."

Sternberg: "I'm not afraid of quotes, and I'll show you Maimonides'
language. And besides, they did not rule according to his feelings about
women."

Osnat: "Maybe not, but it had an effect. Things that are said by a man
like him have an effect."

Shirli: "After all, there are things that really were ruled in the spirit of
Maimonides. I know there's a difference between social conventions and
God's and the Torah's conventions. It was given at a particular time and in
a particular place. But society then and now is latching on to that in order

to discriminate against women, like in Maimonides' time. Even in *haredi* society they didn't teach women at one time, and now they do. It's society that decides and nothing else, so it is possible to change in the spirit of the Torah."

Sternberg: "The Torah protected women from social conventions. The status of women among the other nations was always worse than in Israel."

Naomi: "I think you are running away from the subject. When we say something you say that it's not in the Torah, when it's in the Torah you say that in other nations it was worse. That's running away from the issue. The question is, what do we do today so that we can do more, not what they did in Maimonides' time?"

Sternberg: "You know what? Maimonides himself, in his introduction to the *Mishneh Torah*, says of Torah study for women: 'until their mind is completed.' So, yes, let's go to the subject of the sanction for women studying Torah. Study seems to me to be an important arena today."

STUDY, PARTICIPATION, AND
THE COMMUNITY OF PRACTITIONERS

*Rabbi Papa said: The Torah says "and you learned and you did"—all that there
is in deed there is in study, all that there is not in deed there is not in study.*
Babylonian Talmud, Yebamot, 109b

Undoubtedly Rabbi Papa's interpretation of the verse "and you learned and you did" would be happily adopted by Lave and Wegner, the originators of LPP. Study, in their view, is part of practice and participation, and depends on them. Rivka Sternberg, who taught the course on halacha and morals, and who prepared a reading list of sources for it, chose to quote Rabbi Papa in large letters on the page dealing with "women's obligations in mitzvot." Hence the choice of the approach of "situated learning" for the reading and analysis of this ethnography.

The young women studying at the Midrasha at Bar-Ilan are part of the community of practitioners. This is a community in which participation in religious practice is the fundamental platform for the life of its members. In this community, in which there are those who know and those who know more, everyone practices. Their practice, not their information about the practice or their status, is the decisive factor in their belonging to the community of practitioners. In this community the women are always in a situation of participants-members. Despite the fact that all literacy studies do not treat LPP theory as another theory of literacy, and even though the authors of the theory chose to demonstrate it in the world of apprenticeship, it seems extremely appropriate for the analysis of a religious community and religious practice, especially in the anthropological context. The power of understanding of the accepted participation in the field approach grows out of the words of Leah Shakdiel, who participates in reading from the Torah, from the critical voice of Adina on her exclusion from the participating public, and from the voice of Shirli, who points out the social manipulation regarding the desire of the members of the community to participate.

Study as an act located within current experience with a history and a future points to its relevance for its owners. Any attempt to abstract this study beyond experience, whether on the part of the teacher or on the part of the researcher, effaces the lives of the learners, distances them from themselves, and alienates them from the material under study.

The ethnographic excerpt reported above is charged more than anything else with questions of participation—the extent of participation, its quality, its depth, and its personal and social meaning. The teacher herself built the framework of the discussion around the sanction to observe mitzvot, or, more accurately, around the sanction to practice. In her opening words, Sternberg dealt with the debate among medieval halachic authorities over the right to practice a mitzvah that one is not required to perform, and she explained the reasoning behind the halachic decision to allow such practice. She also noted the tendency in Sephardi Jewish communities (a third of the students are from such communities) not to observe mitzvot that are not required, and the ruling of Rabbi Ovadia Yosef forbidding women to do more than what is required of them. She cited Rabbi Hida, who permitted women from Sephardi communities to broaden their participation. This move by the teacher formulated the boundaries of the discourse on practice around two elements. One of them is straightforward: The reward given to a person performing a mitzvah he or she is required to perform is greater than that given to a person who performs a mitzvah she is not required to perform. This makes it clear that the reward given to men who study Torah and pray at the appointed times is greater than that given to women.

The second element is more ambiguous. Women may broaden their circle of participation; even those who are, on the face of it, forbidden to do so—such as Sephardi women—can, if they wish, find a way around the prohibition. The example Sternberg chose to begin with describes a participating woman, one who brought a sacrifice to the Temple and who is allowed to lay her hands on the sacrifice. This example is located at a central site at which the acme of Jewish practice took place. But the Temple no longer exists, and the practice of sacrifice, which has been removed from Jewish practice, becomes a problematic site. On the one hand, it is a coveted place, where women walked through its courts and participated in rituals; on the other, it is an absent, irrelevant place, where, as it turns out, women were allowed to participate out of compassion for them. The double meaning created by the unclear boundaries of the range of participation, and the woman who participates because the men wish to "gratify" her, provoked the class of learners. "This is my language, this is my worship of heaven, this is my speech with God, and they keep me at a distance," Adina says. "Why is it necessary at all to say a sentence like 'to give gratification to the women'? . . . After all, our life is religion, and in that way you push people away from public life. . . . In my synagogue they say after the services, 'there is a kiddush for the public, including the women.' What does that mean? There's a public and then there's women?"

Adina's words, which can sound like denunciation, critique, or anger, are first and foremost a confession.[29] Adina apparently differed from the others in the room in her strong desire to participate, to take part. Such a confession, like Shakdiel's confession reported at the beginning of this chapter, should be decoded cautiously. In order to extract the power of the critique from this confession, as well as its ability to reveal social structures that prevent participation, it is necessary to understand it in its context. This confession involves taking a risk, and Adina may yet be hurt by it. Her desire to be like the others (the men), her desire that something of them be transferred to her in terms of participation, cannot be translated into the regular words of learning, goals, methods, and the application of tools — or what Shakdiel called "agenda." The language describing her desires, like the language Shakdiel used to describe her feelings upon wrapping herself in her tallit and in prayer, is full of pathos. To an outside ear it sounds romantic, overwrought, sometimes heroic, generally "irrational." To the ears of teacher Rivka Sternberg, who is on the inside and who is preoccupied with the impossible work of blurring boundaries and markers, Adina's words sound different.

Sternberg located the voice of the speaker within two contexts that pushed Adina out of the community of practitioners; she labeled her foreign and frustrated. (Jules Henry said long ago that a student should never express real emotions or confess to his teachers, because the latter will exploit his vulnerability and accessibility in order to enslave him to the system.[30]) Adina felt sure of herself among women similar to herself, but her American

accent allowed Sternberg to cast doubt on her membership in the community and thus challenge the quality of her arguments. "You were educated in
an English-speaking society, and there Jewish life is carried on around the
synagogue. That's why the public issue is so important for you." Adina's clear
voice, her demand for recognition as a religious-practicing woman speaking
in the name of all the women, and her challenge to the definition of the term
"public" were all rejected because of her foreignness. This young woman,
who moved to Israel at the age of seven, who studied in a girl's religious
school and performed National Service, became the spokeswoman for the
Western Diaspora. The desire to participate and increase participation must
always, in the discourse of Sternberg and of the majority of the women's
educators in the national religious public, come from a "pure" place—not
from outside, not from secular feminism, not from pride and competition,
not from anger, and not from frustration. The burden of proof of "purity"
lies always on the one being educated.

The participation dialogue that unfolded between Adina and her teacher
needs to be interpreted in this context of the burden of proof. This is a dialogue on the legitimacy of demanding participation within the inclusive experience of Adina as a woman in Israeli society (even if she was educated in
an English-speaking home—a fact that is not without importance). Sternberg strove to expunge experiences that do not derive from the Torah (but
which do not in any way contradict her) and to ignore the social context of
her students, their experience as modern women, and especially their experience as religious women. "Whoever wants to interpret that today out of
a sense of inferiority or a feeling of discrimination—go ahead, interpret it
that way. It's also possible to interpret it as sensitivity toward the woman in
a given social situation."

Sternberg proposes understanding "gratification for women" as a sociological matter, but she dares not to include the social situation of her students today, here and now, as part of the same explanation. Their situation
is always one of feelings of inferiority to which no understanding should
be offered—except for the same paternalism that priests at the Temple displayed to the women who brought sacrifices. Students who seek to broaden
the range of their participation in the religious world beyond that of their
mothers do not want to break out of this world. They want to remain within
it, but to plumb its depths. They seek to turn from those who know to
those who know more, and this request always depends on the broadening
of practice. The broadening that they have already accomplished, and that
which they see before them, turn the world of religious practice around,

turn its gates and gatekeepers from invisible to visible. The systems that channel the quality and quantity of participation turn from transparent and generally understood into a bare social structure about which questions may be asked.

Apparently this fact threatens the gatekeepers of participation. "I think this whole matter of positive time-dependent mitzvot is wrong. . . . [T]hat's the religious basis that allows the social distancing of women," Adina said. She pointed an accusing finger at the halachic law exempting women from activities that are to be done at an appointed time, did not accept the "consideration" it implies, and chose to call it a social law—an arrangement for dividing work according to gender that constitutes the basis for excluding half of the Jewish public from participation in the prestigious practice of their culture. "What you put into the schedule you find time for," she insisted; that is a personal decision with personal responsibility. The discussion's focus on the law, on the halachic system, on those who have written and rewritten it, challenges what is taken for granted. It turns the religious system from a system of divine, uncontested values to a social system of power with interests, preconceptions, and a conservative instinct that can be identified, as Shirli did: "I know there's a difference between social conventions and God's and the Torah's conventions. It was given at a particular time and in a particular place. But society then and now is latching on to that in order to discriminate against women, like in Maimonides' time."

The students insisted on linking the religious level with the social system that operates it. Sternberg, for her part, navigated between distant social systems without returning home to the relevant site that she chose to deal with a priori. But Naomi didn't let her get away with this: "I think you are running away from the subject. When we say something you say that it's not in the Torah [that is, it is a social matter and not from a 'pure' source], when it's in the Torah you say that in other nations it was worse [that is, in our society then, it was better than in other societies]. . . . The question is, what do we do today . . . ?" Naomi was not prepared to separate Torah from society, nor was she prepared to place herself today in the situation of a woman in the Middle Ages.

When the learners run into a brick wall that represents itself as a window, this raises the issue of their ability to participate in the community of practitioners. A person can observe his or her mitzvot on different levels of transparency and visibility. These levels are linked to the person's location in the space of practitioners and, of course, to social categories. A child is supposed to fulfill his mitzvot from a position of innocence, to take them for granted, with no sense of the social structure. An adult reaches the same point of "taking for granted" because when he runs into the wall, he interprets it and grants it meaning (the reason for the mitzvah, its history, the reward it brings), making the action unproblematic and the social structure transparent. This is, of course, a different transparency from that of the child or the innocent observer (for example, a woman or a layman). The question of which is the superior observance—that of the innocent who is not aware of structures, or that of the person who is aware and the knower who turns his understanding of the structure transparent—preoccupies the community of practitioners. Many women at the Midrasha have learned in classes on the philosophy of Rabbi Kook that the present age no longer allows innocent observance. Innocent observance is lost observance. The transparent windows have become covered with specks of doubt, dissatisfaction, cynicism, and despair. This generation, men and women, children and adults, must study and know in order to practice. This broadens the circle of practitioners, and the meanings given to their actions are altered.

It is this broadening that the teacher Rivka Sternberg is working on. She herself is an example of a learned and educated woman who devotes herself to educating generations of women who participate more and more. Yet this broadening also frightens her, and she tries to divert it into side channels. In one of her responses to Adina, she said: "[S]ociety today works on the external, on what you see, and fast. There's enough to work on inside yourself. There's enough mitzvot and service of the Creator that it is possible to do within what you are commanded, and they won't always see that outside." The furor created in the class in this lesson, similar to the reaction Sternberg got from the class all year, caused her to use the ultimate mode of exclusion: connecting that response to frustration and feelings of inferiority. This method reflects the training or the subalternization of the student.

In Lave and Wegner's book, in a chapter that addresses the difference between surrender to systems of knowledge and knowledge for the sake of participation, they discuss the subject of training. When the ethnography indicates learning that does not have increased participation as a basis, this is a sign, so the writers argue, that "didactive caretakers" are active. Didactive caretakers work to shape the motivation of the students. In such cases, learning for the purpose of participation is replaced with learning for the purpose of changing the person—reshaping him or her as a value goal and as training. This happens instead of creating a new identity, which is, in any case, created in the transition from partial participation to fuller participation. In such cases there is a commodification of knowledge, which stands separately from the women practitioners, between them and their community. Sternberg claims that she favors learning, but learning that is separate from the wishes of the student, learning that is "pure." Such learning does not exist, so every demand to study or participate turns into an exhibitionist whimsy of a woman looking to impress those around her.

Efrat tried to find a way out of Sternberg's moralistic grip, saying: "You're telling her to search through her small actions, and that can always be done, but what if someone wants to go far, in spiritual, public nature? What do you have to answer to that?" The message of returning the motivation to the arena of participation, and locating it around sublime goals did not reach the teacher's ear. She was not prepared to think at that moment (in other contexts she behaved differently) about expanding the circle of practitioners, only about inclusion and exclusion. A woman who wants to do, wants to do like a man. And a woman who wants to be like a man will, in the end—as has already been learned—be frustrated.

Placing knowledge between the learners and their community as an obstacle to participation ("until their mind is completed") cannot succeed. Religious women are always participants, even if this participation appears partial and inferior from the outside. Their lives provide them with relevant fields in which to check their knowledge. Within the family and the community, with spouses, with female and male friends, these young women find arenas for practice and participation. As was demonstrated in the ethnographic selection, during their studies at the Midrasha the teaching shifts between increasing participation and the direction of policing and subalternization. It often seems as if instruction is intended to persuade the learners to fully accept their partial participation, to relate to the transience of their lack of knowledge as a fixed condition, to shape their partial identity in a compensating moral religious system. These compensations, like the construction of the image of the "new mother" (discussed in chapter 5), do not, however, satisfy the learners. They continue to create for themselves and their teachers a disquiet that demands more.

LITERACY ON ANTHROPOLOGY AND
VICE-VERSA — CONCLUSION

Anthropology's enlistment in the study of literacy and its contribution to shaping it have brought to the fore with even greater force the three fundamental issues of this discipline: the ambivalence between emphasizing the equal and documenting the differences between people, the difficulty of breaking free of binary explanatory systems and the dichotomies that these create, and the connection between theoretical critical anthropology and practical and committed anthropology.

In this part of the book I have presented a theoretical triangle of progress, critique, and participation—a triangle with a different model of literacy at each corner. The progress model describes a transition from society A to society B, a movement from a society with simple literacy to a society with complex literacy. The critical model seeks to turn A into B—that is, not to progress toward a new and different society but rather to grow within a given society, to develop a critical faculty toward it, based on a certain measure of alienation and distance, with the intention of then returning to that society and repairing it. The participation model could be graphically described as the circular ripples created when a stone is tossed into a pool of water—a series of circles open and expand until the point at which the stone touched the water is no longer discernible, and the surface of the entire pond is disturbed.

Literacy as participation has been presented as offering one solution to these three fundamental dilemmas. The model provides a theoretical framework that prefers to observe the cultures it studies via people's desire to participate, to belong, and to be relevant. In this it avoids the ethnocentrism and paternalism of the critical models. Putting the literacy *process*, rather than the result, at the center brings the theory of participation another step closer to anthropology. Neither the goal, the result, nor the social revolution is the major interest, but rather the measure of belonging and relevance achieved at each given moment. This emphasis is appropriate to the way anthropological work is carried out, especially for the writing of ethnography.

Ethnography has been presented as an additional type of literacy. A group that writes itself in a literacy-biographical project in New York; a young woman in this study who responds to the request "tell me your literacy biography"; Shakdiel making the literacy history of the group of women to which she belongs into a "new midrash"—all these are creators of literacies. Writing from different positions, in different human combinations, challenges the autonomous value of knowledge and places some constraints on the heroics of the lone writer.

This form of ethnography mitigates the concern that the theory of participation might produce a syrupy romanticism reminiscent of the old anthropology. The cross-pollination of anthropology and the theory of participation breeds a critical faculty that accords with the desire of individuals to belong (not to dismantle, rebel, change, and so on), which directs the process of interpretation. The matter of transparency and visibility, discussed in the final part of the chapter, is a good example of this critical power. During the process of broadening participation, the factors that sought to prevent this are exposed and their illusory transparency becomes evident. It is precisely this yearning to belong and the desire to participate that bring to the fore the guardians of the gate and the treasures they protect. The presentation of the students at Bar-Ilan University's Midrasha for Jewish Studies as part of a community of practitioners ratifies their supervised position within it. At the same time a critical negotiation is opened over the questions of this position, the ability to maintain it, the position that women imagine for themselves, and the range of new positions they are already creating. All these point to an intra-community revolution deriving from an intense desire to participate in that community.

An anthropological look at the investigators of literacy shows that they deal largely with how literacy is inculcated. Their view of anthropology shows that the anthropologists have largely occupied themselves with describing literacy projects that have failed. But combining the anthropological and the literacy perspectives demonstrates that neither group has been liberated from the sanctification of knowledge. Knowledge returns in different forms: oral, in religious guise, sectioned off by ethnicity or gender, or obscured under a multicultural fabric. The seeds of the Enlightenment can be found in this discourse. They create an equivalence between the object of the study and its subject. This is summed up in the motto of critical sociology, which has become an American highway billboard slogan, thanks to funding from educational agencies: Knowledge Is Power.

~

EPILOGUE:
IS IT A REAL REVOLUTION?
THREE STATIONS

*1. At the Gates of the Institute for
Advanced Studies at the Hebrew University*

At the end of October 1997 a group of scholars began a year of work at the
Institute for Advanced Studies of the Hebrew University of Jerusalem. The
field of research that brought them together was "Jewish Orthodoxy." The
opening lecture was given by the late Professor Ya'akov Katz, a leading historian and sociologist whose studies opened up new horizons in this field.
This was followed by a series of additional lectures—historical, theological, political, and philosophical surveys that covered the last two centuries.
Among the scholars was one woman, and over the course of the group's
eighteen meetings, a single lecture, half-way through the year, was devoted
to the subject of gender. That lecture was given by Dr. Deborah Weissman,
a feminist historian and religious woman, who was invited as a guest lecturer. On that occasion I sat close to her and looked around me. Lectures
on gender generally draw a mostly female crowd. This time the room was
packed with men, most of them members of the group. They had known
one another before the sessions began, and their work together that year
added something to the rapport among them. I felt alien—alien to the language in which they addressed each other, alien to the *kippot* many of them
wore on their heads, of different gender—but very close to the subjects that
preoccupied them.

Dr. Weissman surveyed the historical developments that led to the revolution in religious education for women and concluded with fresh impressions she had brought with her from the recent Conference on Feminism and Orthodoxy held in New York in February 1998. In the discussion that followed her lecture it seemed as if everyone agreed with her that a revolution was underway in religious education for girls and women, and that it bore within it a huge potential for other changes that would take place in the nature of Jewish orthodoxy in the years to come. The audience, I found out, had already heard such arguments from Dr. Moshe Samet, who had lectured the week before and claimed that gender relations were the most dynamic site in the current lives of orthodox communities.

The sweeping theoretical consensus made the gap between the participants and the events in the room all the larger. Many of those who responded to the lecture related anecdotally to the subject via their mothers, spouses, and daughters. They passed easily and unproblematically from the academic level to their own homes in order to confirm, out of their own life experiences, that "something significant is really happening." Nevertheless, the institutional reality they created and within which they acted evinced no signs of the progress they remarked on. They had not bothered to involve a feminist scholar (e.g., a historian, philosopher, or sociologist) in their research group. They fenced off the subject of gender as a separate topic that was not an integral part of the general process—that was, in fact, presented by a guest lecturer. The religious feminist revolution was accepted, on the one hand, as inevitable and, on the other, as an academic curiosity.

However, what may be held back at the gates of the establishment is nevertheless penetrating into the lives of the believers-observers. In the community, synagogue, school, and inside the house it is much harder to ignore what is happening.

2. EFRATA WAY

The orthodox synagogue Kehilat Yedidya operates out of a basement room in the Efrata elementary school in the Baka neighborhood of Jerusalem. Dr. Weissman is an active member of the community. At the beginning of March 1998, some three weeks after her lecture at the Institute for Advanced Studies, she organized a panel discussion at the synagogue in order to report on the Feminism and Orthodoxy Conference she attended in New York. I went to Efrata to hear the discussion, and on my way there I thought about gatherings of this type that used to take place in foreign lands, where people who had been to the Holy Land related what they had seen. Here was a modern orthodox community gathering in Jerusalem in order to hear the reports of four women about what had been said "there."

The room was packed with women, and no few men, who were anxious to hear, at home, what had been said overseas about relations between the genders in observant Judaism. The "here" and the "there" drew out and impressed themselves on the discussion, since most members of Kehilat Yedidya were born in English-speaking countries. Three of the four speakers who described the conference spoke Hebrew with an Anglo-Saxon accent. Debbie Weissman recalled that the first such conference was held eleven years previously in Jerusalem, and that the conference in New York ended with the declaration "next year in Jerusalem."

Shira Breuer, principal of the Pelech high school for girls and the only Israeli-born member of the panel, said, "I came home and I told myself: Huge things are happening among us and we don't need to look to America as if the Torah will come from there, because we are already far ahead of them. We will continue to pave the way and to build our agenda, here in Israel."

Many women in the room did not agree with Breuer's optimistic description. During the discussion period, one of them said: "I grew up on the values of freedom and democracy, individualism, and equality. When I came here, to Israel, I saw that those things could not be taken for granted. I have to tell you, Shira, that the situation there is much better than it is here." "For that reason," added another member of the audience, "I am one of the few Israelis in Kehilat Yedidya. It's no wonder that most of the members here are Americans. It's a different mentality."

To a large extent, the origin of the speakers organized the nature of what they said and gave the social context greater significance than the halachic or theological context. This fact presents orthodoxy first of all as a sociocultural organization, challenged in this case by feminism.

It is no wonder, then, that the talk by Dr. Tamar Ross was the center of attention that evening. She suggested it would be best not to import the American fighting spirit to Israel, not to rouse the rabbinical establishment's hostility, but to keep up the relaxed style that had been used so far. Yet under the protection of her American accent Ross read a bold document on orthodoxy and feminism that crossed the boundary of the relaxed style and marked a theoretical, halachic, moral, and theological avant-garde.

The feminist revolution, she said, was also a spiritual revolution that offered new ways of understanding God, humanity, and history. Awareness of the patriarchal infrastructure of the religion eroded the very foundations of faith. A feminist reading was liable to end with an absolute refusal to maintain a text that itself maintains and reinforces such a patriarchal existence. She also said that in her opinion there were intellectual and halachic solutions to these problems. Ross presented these solutions in an article that appeared about a month after the talk at Yedidya, in the first issue of a periodical called *De'ot*. The central focus of these solutions was her reading of divine revelation as an ongoing revelation, heard through history as well: "[T]o see . . . these new egalitarian insights, despite their non-Jewish origin in Western culture, as actually being an impetus from heaven to broaden women's participation in public life, including among observers of the Torah and the commandments—in study, in observance of the commandments, and in spiritual leadership."[1]

According to Ross, this still constitutes a threat to the rabbinical establishment. By beginning with a call to avoid conflict and ending with the necessity of such conflicts, she was demonstrating the nature of the religious-feminist struggle in Israel, or at least at Yedidya.

The religious-feminist revolution taking place in the U. S. has "come on aliya"—immigrated to Israel. In Israel it must deal with a different local gender culture and, even more importantly, with a society that has not separated religion from the state. My final stop will thus be in one of the more local organizations—far from New York, but not far from Efrata—at Kibbutz Migdal Oz in the Gush Etzion settlements, near Jerusalem.

3. Maybe at the Kibbutz

The academic pursuit of events in the "field" is both frustrating and enjoyable. On the one hand, I am sorry that I cannot in this work address all the relevant articles, conferences, curriculum innovations, and openings of new midrashot. On the other, I was happy to see that the "field" is stirring with indications that confirm the trends of change shown in my research and which present new questions about the rate at which the orthodox community is assimilating the gender revolution, and about the quality of that change.

I could imagine myself visiting the new midrasha established by Esti Rosenberg at Kibbutz Migdal Oz and weaving the ethnography I could produce there into the final lines of this book. In fact, all the midrashot are in a process of self-renewal, offering fresh programs, growing, professionalizing, adopting a language that addresses a specific audience within the religious Zionist public; each takes on a unique look. The midrasha at Migdal Oz was, however, at that time, the newest institution for higher religious studies for women.

In the end I was not able to visit the kibbutz. Instead, at the beginning of May 1998 I had a long conversation with Esti Rosenberg in Jerusalem. A summary of what Rosenberg told me traces the future of the phenomenon surveyed here—the hopes, the apprehensions, the range of choice, and the boundaries.

"The challenge of the midrasha at Kibbutz Migdal Oz is breaking out of the framework of a single year of studies of *Torah le-shma*, the creation of an institution that is a living space, something ongoing, in which women can remain at their studies. In the future I would like to institutionalize a five-year program that integrates National Service or military service and studies. The girls will begin with a year of study, continue as a group in National Service in an underprivileged community, integrate an additional year of service with studies, and then conclude with two years of study that will grant them a teaching certificate with professional qualification in one of the fields of sacred studies. I would like to accept only those girls who commit themselves to this full sequence. In such an institution I could integrate teachers from the inside, women who have studied at midrashot rather than those who come from an academic background. I would like it to be possible for a woman who marries or even has children to continue, and that there be the possibility of a female *kolel* [a yeshiva for married women with families].

"The problems I see myself facing lie first of all in the connection between study at the midrasha and the teaching profession. The fact that the studies lead only in that direction restricts my target population. While the Torah world of today is developed enough that some of the graduates could be integrated as teachers in the developing and burgeoning midrashot, the women still think that if they study law they can in principle reach the rank of a Supreme Court justice, while if they study at a midrasha they'll end up being just another elementary school teacher. Many of them want academic knowledge, acquaintance with the secular world of knowledge, with the tools that the academy offers. They don't want to shut themselves up in the religious world; they also want a link with the surrounding culture, people, to ideas outside the religious world. At present we integrate the two frameworks and some of them study both at the midrasha and at the university. But it's difficult for them; they are split; each place has its own demands, and they expect high performance from themselves.

"Perhaps in the future there will be a minority that will devote itself only to sacred studies and which will constitute a cadre, a kind of avant-garde, while the majority studies only a year or two at the midrasha and then goes on to other studies.

"At this point I am not including feminist material, academic feminist texts, or such approaches to sacred studies. But who knows, perhaps in the future that will come; we have to progress slowly. I choose women for the faculty but not at the expense of the level of studies and not with the intention of excluding men. It is very important that there be male rabbis and teachers. The concerns voiced around us about damage to the students' families, about an anticipated decline in the number of children they have, or about them putting off the age of marriage are still strong, but those are also things that will be worked out in the future.

"Think about it: A young woman who marries or has a child will want in the future to give honor to her teacher, to the spiritual figure who influenced her. We'll see women honored with [roles currently reserved for males, such as] holding the baby at circumcision and reciting the wedding blessings under the wedding canopy. Even though it's not a simple matter, apparently it will happen. Everything happens in the end; after all, ten years ago no one foresaw what is happening now, and all that almost without the students themselves using terms such as revolution or feminism. As far as they're concerned, they just do it."

A BLOODLESS REVOLUTION

"The radical will become normal. Get excited! We are seeing it with our own eyes, experiencing it ourselves, a bloodless revolution."

So said Ms. Gail Hammer of Australia to the participants in the International Conference on Feminism and Orthodoxy, held in New York in February 1998. Leah Shakdiel chose it as a motto for the report she prepared for the periodical *De'ot* when she returned from the conference.

It is doubly rare to be able to observe a feminist revolution in real time and to experience it as nonviolent change. If we add to that the orthodox religious context in which the revolution is taking place, it becomes triply rare.

A nonviolent revolution is a rare thing. The attempts to describe feminism as revolutionary, or to organize it in those terms, have created no few dilemmas. First, the great majority of feminists have denounced violence of all types. Second, the barricades of the struggle have often positioned feminists against fathers, brothers, sons, friends, and lovers. In retrospect it looks as if most of the feminist movement's achievements were not attained through violence but rather through a multi-level struggle over time.

Religion has not been perceived as an amenable field for change—indeed, quite the opposite. It has remained in the rear while the struggle has concentrated on politics, economics, health, and the family. Perhaps its time has come. The feminist way of thinking has been assimilated into Western culture and has become an additional language within it, crossing boundaries of class, race, gender, and nationality, and taking on many different aspects. Within this mosaic, which also contains contradictions and conflicts of interest among feminists, the religious field turns out to be a cultural site that is not immune to change.

Gail Hammer thus reminded her audience that they ought to be excited. They should be excited that feminism can indeed accomplish a nonviolent revolution, excited that despite anxieties about exposing religion to this revolution it is in fact able to take it in.

"How could it be that I'd know next Pesach exactly what I knew about the holiday last Pesach," Miri told me when I asked her why she engaged in sacred studies. Her refusal to find herself next Pesach in the same place she was the previous Pesach had no radical ring to it. It may well be that to say that she and her friends are experiencing and carrying out a revolution would be an expression foreign to her. The tone of her voice indicated that it was obvious to her that a woman should seek to broaden her participation in areas important to her, and to go onward.

That, apparently, is how the radical becomes normal.

~

NOTES

PRELUDE

1. The choice of the word midrasha (midrashot is the plural, midreshet the combining form) to denote a postsecondary school for the study of Judaism specifically
for women is an interesting one. The word is taken from the term *beit midrash*,
which literally means "house of study." Traditionally, the *beit midrash* was a place
where men studied Talmud and prayed. At the beginning of the nineteenth century
the term *beit midrash* was appropriated to name new institutions of Jewish studies
that differed from the traditional yeshivot. These new institutions integrated critical scholarly approaches with Jewish tradition. Later the term was used to refer
to teachers' colleges. Today, in the United States, institutions of Jewish studies for
women are called women's or girls' yeshivot, but in Israel the term "yeshiva" is reserved for men only. Hence postsecondary institutions for women have a name that
puts them into the category of more "modern" institutions of Jewish studies.

While some of the institutions surveyed in the next section do not call themselves
midrashot, among religious Zionists the term serves as a generic designation for
these institutions.

2. On the significance of anthropological fieldwork as "home work" or "home
research," see chapter 2.

3. See El-Or, 1994.

4. Rabbi Avraham Yitzhak Hakohen Kook (1865–1935), known in Israel as Rav
Kook, was the first Ashkenazi Chief Rabbi of Palestine and a seminal thinker in the
evolution of religious Zionism. His theology, which viewed the Jewish return to the
Holy Land as a step toward the Messianic era, provided a way for religious Zionists

to work together with secular Zionists—even though in religious terms the latter were heretics. Rabbi Kook founded the Merkaz Ha-Rav Yeshiva, which has produced generations of eminent religious Zionist rabbis strongly influenced by Kook's messianism, especially as interpreted and refined by his son and successor as head of the yeshiva, Rabbi Zvi Yehuda Kook. Graduates of Merkaz Ha-Rav are prominent in the ideological leadership of the National Religious Party and of Gush Emunim, the nationalist movement known for its establishment of Israeli settlements in the West Bank and Gaza Strip.

CHAPTER 1

1. On this, see Ravitzky, 1993; Schwartz, 1996.

2. Weissman, 1976, pp. 139–48; Weissman, 1993; El-Or, 1994; Oryan, 1994.

3. For a detailed and broad description of Bruria (or, its later name, Lindenbaum), Matan, and Nishmat, see Granite, 1995, pp. 98–123.

4. Gemara *al ha-seder* is the methodical study of the Gemara tractate by tractate, as opposed to studying a specific subject and texts taken from different tractates of the Gemara which address that specific subject.

5. There is still not a comprehensive study of the history of feminism in Israel, but parts of this history may be learned from the following books and collections: Rapoport and El-Or, 1997; Azmon and Izraeli (eds.), 1993; Bernstein (ed.), 1992; Swirsky and Safir (eds.), 1991; Special issue on Women in Israel, *Israeli Social Studies Research* 12/1 (1997).

6. From an article by Yair Sheleg, "Seder Nashim," *Kol Ha'ir,* 6 June 1997.

7. For a discussion of this subject and references for further reading, see El-Or, 1994, pp. 91–96; also part IV of this book.

8. The consolidation of *haredi* society as a society of learning men has been widely addressed by sociologist Menachem Friedman. A summary of his insights is collected in Friedman, 1991.

9. On this, see Ravitzky, 1993; Schwartz, 1996; Sagi (ed.), 1996; Peleg, 1997; Aran, 1991, pp. 265–344.

10. From a religious point of view, the gatekeepers find it difficult to send away those seeking knowledge because it is the central part of the Jewish experience. In the *haredi* world (as I show in my previous book [El-Or, 1994]), criteria such as community and gender may still be used to keep out new members and to manifestly compartmentalize those areas of knowledge suitable for them. In the religious Zionist community this option is becoming more and more problematic, as will be demonstrated below. There are those who tend to attribute the relative weakness of the knowledge link and the breaking of the chain in this community to the fact that educators want to strengthen women students so they can confront secular society, or to their difficulty in telling a woman who is studying physics or law that she cannot study Gemara. These are no doubt important possible explanations—indeed, members of the community themselves express them.

11. El-Or, 1994, p. 65.

12. From Sheleg, "Seder Nashim," *Kol Ha-Ir*, 6 June 1997, p. 74.

13. The intention is not to ignore the woman learner's gender. Daniel Boyarin's extensive work shows that it is actually the uncompromising attempt to find a comfortable way for any gender to study Gemara that contains a force for creativity and interpretation (1993, 1995).

14. This is dealt with at length in chapter 3.

15. On Merkaz Ha-Rav and "spirituality," see Aran, 1987.

16. Men before and after military service are also perceived as vulnerable. They have recently been offered Torah frameworks to "reinforce" them, such as the preparatory boarding program in the settlement of Eli in Samaria.

17. Klein, 1998.

18. Aran shows, for example, how a change has occurred in the literacy status of the teaching of Bible in religious Zionist yeshivot, following changes in political ideology (1991, pp. 101–32).

19. On this, see Shamir, Shtai, and Elias, 1997, pp. 313–48.

20. *Drash* is the explication of Torah text in a broad way that seeks to explain its underlying intention, making use of external, often rabbinic, sources. *Pshat* is the method of explaining the clear meaning of the Torah text itself.

21. *Rabbanit* is the title given to the wife of a rabbi. (Orthodox Judaism does not [[yet] ordain women.) The title also often serves, however, to designate a woman holding public and educational positions within the community (even if she is not married to a rabbi). At other times the term is used with a trace of derision—and then it is usually pronounced as in Yiddish, *rebbetzen*—to denote a self-important or sanctimonious woman.

22. *Mar'ot*, June 1996.

23. Some of the recent research in these fields: Rudavsky (ed.), 1995; Buchmann and Spiegel (eds.), 1995; Levitt, 1997; Peskowitz and Levitt (eds.), 1997.

24. So, for example, in Granite, 1995, above.

25. It is possible to argue, of course, that changes in patterns of parenthood and child rearing contradict private memory. A career woman labors to develop new ways of raising her children that are not necessarily similar to those of her mother, who may not have worked outside the home. But these changes are not connected to faith in a higher power.

CHAPTER 2

1. In this context, see the dialogue between the Israeli anthropologist Moshe Shokeid and the American anthropologist Ted Swedenburg. Also see Shokeid, 1992, pp. 464–77; and Swedenburg, 1992.

2. Lavie and Swedenburg, 1995, p. 80.

3. Jewish law requires married women to cover their hair, and the various kinds of covering are good indicators of where women place themselves within the

religious community. Wigs are worn primarily by *haredi* women. Colorful kerchiefs that completely cover the hair are a badge of religious Zionist women who consider themselves more pious and, often, more right-wing in their politics. Hats or kerchiefs that leave some hair showing tend to be signs of modernity and openness.

4. Two students from the Midrasha decided to call me, and we subsequently met. As had happened in the past, it turned out that the women had complex, mostly personal problems, and they regarded me as an insider/outsider figure whom they could consult.

5. See Geertz, 1973.

6. *Ehud Banai and the Fugitives*, 1986.

7. On the gap between the way the "other" experiences himself and the way he is perceived by the majority, see Young, 1990, p. 148.

8. A great deal of theoretical material points to these trends. Three representative ones are: Clifford and Marcus (eds.), 1986; Marcus and Fisher (eds.), 1986; Behar and Gordon (eds.), 1995.

9. Our brief conversation about this characterization is cited in chapter 6.

10. This figure appears in chapter 5.

11. On dialogue and polyphony, see El-Or, 1994, pp. 54–60. For an example of polyphonic feminist writing, see Gordon, 1995.

12. Ordinarily, anthropologists are inclined to talk with "marginal" people (at both ends of the spectrum), and the text problematizes this fact. In this case, there was a greater number of "mainstream" types among the forty women we interviewed. Chapter 3 features six biographies; two of them (Michal and Raya) reflect the mainstream type. The rest of the chapter builds on many biographies and includes different types of personalities, cultural choices, and sociological paths. It depicts myriad ways of life and, at the same time, the structured path of "growing up" and "becoming a woman" in Israeli society. Almost every interviewee declared "I am not representative," but this doesn't mean that they felt marginal. Being chosen by a researcher to speak for your culture objectifies a subject and puts her in a situation where she is not entirely comfortable. Regardless of their "type," all the interviewees emphasized, in one way or another, their uniqueness and individuality. I write further about this in the opening of both chapters 3 and 4, and frequently allude to the delicate movement between the private and public, critical and conservative, overt and hidden worlds.

13. Wolff, 1995, pp. 88–134.

14. In this context see Rachel Wasserfall's essay discussing the loss of her reflexive ability during fieldwork; Wasserfall, 1997, pp. 150–68.

15. Glaser and Abu-Ras, 1994, pp. 269–88.

16. See, for example, Minister Uzi Baram's statement on election night, when it seemed that Shimon Peres would win. Baram said he would be happy to form a coalition with the Arab parties and incorporate them into the government—for the first time in history—as an alternative to the NRP and the *haredi* parties.

17. No wonder, then, that one pro-Netanyahu slogan was "Either Bibi or Tibi." Bibi is Netanyahu's nickname; Tibi is Ahmed Tibi, an Israeli Arab who served as an adviser to Arafat and was a frequent guest on television and radio talk and news shows, where opponents of the Oslo accords had difficulty gaining access. Tibi was elected to the Knesset in 1999.

18. See chapter 6 for elaboration of this issue.

19. The attempt to decode the Rabin assassination as a "murder for national honor" analogous to a "murder for family honor" is not taken from the discourse that accompanied the event in Israel. The analogy offers me a critical language developed in feminist research (Palestinian and other) that may shed new light on the reasons for the assassination. It uses the term "murder for family honor" to describe a practice that enhances patriarchal hegemony over weaker members of society. Protecting "the family," like protecting "the nation," allows disregard or abandonment of others (women in the first instance, non-Jewish citizens in the second). For a discussion of this topic between Dani Rabinowitz and John Simmons, see *Te'oria U-Vikoret*, 7, 1995.

20. In parallel, the oriental *haredi* public coined and publicized its own slogans: "Peace begins between the Jewish people and its God" and "An entire generation demands a return to religion."

CHAPTER 3

1. Sarit Barzilai Ben-Yakar, 1996.

2. The philosophical-theological works of the Maharal (Rabbi Liva Yehuda of Prague, seventeenth century) and the *Kuzari*, a work by the medieval Spanish rabbi and philosopher Yehuda Ha-Levy, are part of the curriculum in most religious Zionist yeshivot.

3. This claim runs counter to the conclusion reached by Granite (1995), who saw in the act of women's study a kind of mediation between the traditional and modern worlds.

4. The Merkaz Ha-Rav [Kook] Yeshiva, colloquially called "Merkaz," is the central Torah institution of religious Zionism. On its place in religion and nationalism, see Aran, 1987.

5. "From the inside" — that is, from the book itself, rather than from a quotation of the text or its interpretation in another source, from an anthology, or from photocopied pages from the book.

6. "*Ulpana* girl" — Michal is referring to the stereotype of the girl educated in the intensive framework of an *ulpana* boarding school. The *ulpana* girl is depicted as uncritical, sticking to the path laid out for her, and remaining within the insular religious Zionist world.

7. Such a situation is described in part IV, in the ethnographic segment.

8. Orian, 1994.

9. The Nachal is a division of the Israeli army created to offer young people the possibility of combining military service with settlement and agricultural activity, but under recent reforms the unit has largely lost its special character. Groups made up of both boys and girls were formed during high school, often in the framework of a youth movement. A group would then enlist in the army together and serve a preliminary period of labor on a kibbutz or at some other settlement. Subsequently boys and girls engaged in separate military training and duties, but the military service was broken up by periods of further settlement activity when the boys and girls would come together again. Nachal was one of the few army frameworks considered appropriate for a religious girl—at least by a part of the religious community. Some religious Nachal groups are categorized as "Torah" groups, and in these a part of the agricultural and settlement activity is replaced by religious studies.

10. Kehilat Yedidya is an orthodox synagogue in Jerusalem that endeavors to maximize women's participation in ritual within the framework of the halacha. Among other things it conducts separate Torah readings for women. See the epilogue.

11. This section conducts a dialogue with an article written by Paul Roth and entitled "Ethnography without Tears" (1989). The article criticizes a type of writing that was then considered innovative: reflexive writing that uses the author and her feelings as a source for producing research knowledge. The source of the tears is the description of personal mourning as a basis for understanding the anger of others that appears in an article by Renato Rosaldo, with whom, among others, the writer of the article argues.

12. Boyarin, 1997.

CHAPTER 4

1. For a more extensive discussion of this, see chapter 2.

2. On the history of the *ulpanot,* see Bar-Lev and Rozner (eds.), 1987. For a critical analysis of the education offered by the *ulpanot,* see Rapoport et al., 1995.

3. On this image and the change it has undergone, see chapter 1.

4. In my study of a *haredi* community I found that in public discourse the term "the home" is preferred to the term the family—a phrase used in the discourse of the nonreligious community. "The home" appears in the religious community's discourse as a value institution, an idea, a concept that embodies the complexity of the family with all the relations it comprises.

5. On "the home" as a place where a woman seeks her complex identity, see Levitt, 1997.

6. "The home" and motherhood are dealt with at greater length in chapter 5.

7. Belenky et al., 1986, pp. 191–92.

8. Lave and Wenger's book (1991) develops the subject of participation and study as practice as located within the community. This approach is discussed at length in chapter 4.

9. See chapter 3, note 6.
10. Lave and Chaiklin (eds.), 1993.
11. See chapter 1, note 4.
12. On the philosophical aspect of women's ways of knowing, see Code, 1991. On the pedagogical aspect, see Luke and Gore, 1992; also Luttrel, 1997.
13. This is a kind of sing-song mode characteristic of the Talmudic study discourse, especially in the presentation of an argument.
14. On the opportunity given to male teachers who are teaching women to go beyond conventions, see chapter 1.
15. Dumont and Was, 1967.
16. On this distinction, see El-Or, 1994, pp. 89–135.

PART III

1. Calling the collections of discourses presented below "dialogues" follows several trends. In pedagogical-critical literature, dialogue is understood as a correct replacement for a teacher's lecture. Friere, for example, says: "Through dialogue, the teacher of the students and the students of the teacher cease to exist. Instead a new concept is born: a teacher student with student teachers"(1972, p. 67). An additional positive image, if less ideal, comes from the study of the processing of texts. A dialogue takes place between the text and its readers—the way of reading and the reality of the readers' lives—that grants meaning to the entire process. Between Bakhtin, who emphasizes difference and multiplicity as unsolvable essences in dialogue, and Jauss, who emphasizes the momentary partnership created within it, dialogue—what is between the speakers and the text and beyond them—is depicted as the central arena of events (Krinsky, 1995, pp. 118–40). Marcus and Fisher describe the ethnographic text in the same way (1986, pp. 67–69). This description is meant to challenge the illusion of the unity of voices that characterized classical ethnography. The anthropologist and her research subjects are no longer considered objective: She is not an objective listener, and they do not portray reality. A complex discourse is constructed among them, with tensions, internal contradictions, sublimated and open interests, as well as agreements. Peled and Blum Kulka have made enlightening distinctions between "conversation," "literacy discourse," and different types of dialogue (1997, pp. 28–60).

CHAPTER 5

1. Bruner, 1993.
2. The products of this research are presented in the studies of Adams, 1995; Ross, 1995; Bassin, Honey, and Kaplan (eds.), 1994; Kaplan, 1992; Langer, 1992; Rosenzweig, 1993; Walters, 1992.

3. On maternity as a basis for demanding rights, see Ladd-Taylor, 1994; also Bursh, 1996.

4. A part of this research is noted in chapter 1, note 23. To this may be added Biale, 1984.

5. From all of Boyarin's work, I will refer here specifically to two of his articles, from 1993 and 1995, and to his books of 1993 and 1997. A critical examination of Boyarin's interpretation of the sages' approach to gender can be found in Hazan-Rokem, 1995.

6. In addition to the booklet, which provided the source for each selection, the instructor also published a book on the subject, which went through several editions.

7. On these transitions and their pedagogical power, see Rapoport, Panso, and Garb, 1995.

8. On the place of the midrashim dealing with the generation of the Israelite women in Egypt as a feminine-religious discourse today, see El-Or, 1993.

9. Walkerdine, 1992, p. 21.

10. On the difference between what is said in private conversation and what is voiced in public, see chapter 3.

11. Ruddick, 1994, p. 30.

12. This demand is consistent with the approach of feminist philosopher Susan Bordo, who opposes the postmodernist position that rejects any type of recognition of gender as a social essence. Bordo calls for drawing the boundaries of the "I" so that they can contain feminine identity—not in order to grant it recognition as an inflexible essence, but the opposite. Only familiarity with and recognition of the "female experience" (such as motherhood) can bring about changes in sociopolitical arrangements (Bordo, 1990, p. 138).

13. In one of the aggadot Hannah threatens to act as if she is unfaithful to her husband. Then she will be required to undergo the trial of the bitter waters that the Torah prescribes for women suspected of adultery. When the test proves her innocent, she will become pregnant, since this is God's promised reward to a woman who has been wrongly accused of adultery.

14. Rapoport, Panso, and Garb (1995) address this subject; also El-Or, 1993.

CHAPTER 6

1. In my own mind, I called this way of dressing "the American style": Keds sneakers, floppy white socks, a narrow denim skirt, and a classy shirt. It was more characteristic of women from the cities than of those who lived in the territories or in Jerusalem, and it was copied from the many American girls they had met during their years in school and in their youth groups. During my time at the Midrasha I encountered groups of young women from overseas who had come to study in special programs there. They brought with them a new and bold fashion that caught my eye. On the face of it everything was kosher—long and covering everything that

should be covered. But the shoes were black—high-soled Dr. Martens—and black cotton tights showed under the skirts, which came down to just above the ankle and shoe. They also had a taste for colorful flannel shirts and baseball hats worn with the brim in back, looking much like a rap group from the streets of New York or MTV. They looked a lot like nonreligious Tel Aviv girls and not at all like their colleagues at the Midrasha.

2. In my initial meeting with Rabbi Cohen I told him about my book on Gur Hasidic women. I asked him to leaf through it in order to get an impression of how I presented the women and to understand my scholarly and ideological approach. He apparently did so, since he said he was afraid of coming out like the *rebbetzin* (see note 8).

3. Rabbi Shach was at that time the leader of the Lithuanian ultra-orthodox community, which rejects Zionism. The rabbi's "woman in the Knesset" is Yael Dayan of the Labor Party, who has been active in promoting equal rights for homosexuals.

4. During this period the Habad Hasidic sect was papering the country with billboards and signs emblazoned with the slogan "Prepare for the coming of the Messiah."

5. Giróux, 1991, p. 12.

6. The work on social difference done at the margins of power strongholds and within them has crystallized into a fascinating theoretical-political discourse based on postmodernist philosophy and feminism. Some of the prominent voices in this discourse are Anzaldua, 1987, Chambers, 1990, and the article on this discourse by Lavie and Swedenburg, 1995.

7. Paradoxically, in the 1990s, especially after the assassination of Prime Minister Yitzhak Rabin, there have been calls to dismantle the state-religious educational system. These proposals, which have come from the secular center, have argued that the state-religious system (like the *haredi* system) benefits from the protection of democracy as it educates its students in undemocratic values. This is a familiar dilemma and will be addressed later in the chapter. It also teaches something about the boundaries of tolerance for these "different others."

8. His choice of the Yiddish inflection "*rebbitzen*" instead of the Hebrew "*rabbanit*" was meant to stress the negative connotation of the term. *Rabbanit*, the female form of the word *rav* (rabbi), is not a formal title (there being no female orthodox rabbis); it is generally used to refer to a woman who is a rabbi's wife. In the religious Zionist community the term is one of respect (as in its application to Rabbanit Esther Lior). For this reason, the rabbi used the Yiddish inflection to conjure up the connotation of the rabbi's wife in the Diaspora, a role he clearly has little regard for.

9. Regarding the hierarchy of texts, see chapter 1.

10. Study *al ha-seder* is the study of Talmud by complete tractates, the traditional way in which men study. On the matter of Talmud instruction for women in general, the way it is taught, and the importance of this teaching for the women themselves, see chapters 1 and 4.

11. It should be noted, nevertheless, that the rabbi was perceived by the students

as someone who had opened their minds, shaken the foundations of their thinking, and caused them to change their approach to texts and their interpretation. On this, see chapter 3.

12. On this change and its nature, see Bartal, 1994.

13. On this ethos, see Zerubavel, 1995.

14. On Holocaust discourse in orthodox Judaism and in religious Zionism, see Ravitzsky, 1993, pp. 89–93.

15. One of the more notable changes in *haredi* life in Israel in the 1990s has been the movement from the passive margins, fenced in behind strictly religious concerns, into involvement in the full range of national political issues. I took note of this in my earlier study (El-Or, 1994, pp. 207–10).

16. On activism and Messianism, see Ravitzsky, 1993, and Peleg, 1997.

17. On this group, see part IV.

18. On the changes in the anthropological discipline, see chapter 2.

19. On the cafeteria, see chapter 1.

20. McLaren, 1992, p. 86.

21. On the internal failures of Giroux's border crossing theory, see Gur Ze'ev's article "Critical Pedagogy?" [in Hebrew], in Gur-Ze'ev (ed.), 1996.

22. Young, 1990, p. 148.

23. On this, see Schwartz, 1996, pp. 215–28 and 268–78; Ravitzsky, 1993, pp. 111–200.

24. McLaren, 1992, p. 85.

25. On multiculturalism, hybrid democracies, nationalism, and nation states, see Lavie and Swedenburg, 1995; also Appadurai, 1991.

26. On the connection between gender and political activism, see El-Or, 1993.

Chapter 7

1. For a breakdown of the Midrasha faculty by training and gender, see chapter 1.

2. "Kookism" is a word coined by Gideon Aran to describe the set of beliefs and religious views of Gush Emunim, the radical activist and largely religious movement for a Greater Israel that, in the two decades after the Six Day War, worked to establish Israeli settlements in the occupied territories. Aran saw Kookism as a later incarnation of Rabbi Kook's original thought—a version of his philosophy that went beyond it and took on its own unique and independent character. In his work, Aran relates how the subjects of his research, the members of Gush Emunim, were originally leery of the term, but that they slowly adopted it into their vocabulary (1987).

3. All three were Rabbi Kook's contemporaries in the early period of Zionist settlement in Palestine. Yosef Chaim Brenner was a Zionist activist, journalist, and short-story writer who strove to create a Hebrew culture tied to the land and independent of religion. Joseph Klausner was an antireligious Zionist literary historian.

Shmuel Yosef Agnon, considered the greatest modern Hebrew fiction writer, went through a nonreligious period but later returned to orthodoxy.

4. These four great branches are the four subject categories that comprise Jewish studies in most religious Zionist frameworks: Bible, Jewish law (for women the term will generally be "oral law"), Jewish philosophy, and Jewish history. The Midrasha does not have a history category, even though Jewish history courses were part of the general Jewish studies courses offered by Bar-Ilan to the general student body. For more on this subject, see chapter 1.

5. The order of importance of the categories of knowledge is a central factor in understanding the connection between text, literacy, and the literate. Jewish law is generally accepted as taking first place in the central corpus of sacred knowledge. Deriving from this placement are the remunerations and positions of power of those who have mastered the literacy of halacha. Any change in the hierarchy of texts (how many study it, when, in what context, with whom, and so forth) or in the community of learners (women, men, children, religious scholars, lay people, and so on) signals an important message. Aran has argued, for example, that in some of the *hesder* yeshivot and in some of the higher religious Zionist yeshivot the study of Bible has been given a higher place than it enjoys in *haredi* yeshivot (that is, higher than its traditional position). The first two groups regard the Bible as a central text in developing a nationalist Greater Israel outlook (Aran, 1994).

6. On the attitude toward tests and exams in the Midrasha, see chapter 1.

7. On Midreshet Bruria, see chapter 1.

8. On the *haredi* attitude toward modernism, and on the way in which social studies addresses this attitude, see El-Or, 1994, pp. 135–39.

9. On participation as a theoretical concept, see part IV.

10. Feminist literature emphasizes the disconnection between "scientific truths" and the audience of women that discusses them. The disconnection is caused by the constitution of science and its tools on male, Western, and white standards (Harding, 1986; Belenky et al., 1986). The major force of this criticism is directed at science's "natural" aspects, but a large number of insights can be derived from it about pedagogical power over the lives of female students.

11. On the centrality of paradox in (ultra-)orthodox discourse and on the way it is flattened in order to confirm a preferred reality, see El-Or, 1994, pp. 135–206.

12. The Nazarite (*Ha-Nazir*), or the Nazarite Rabbi, was the name given to David Cohen (1887–1972), Rabbi Kook's student and the editor of some of his writings. On his teachings, see Schwartz, 1996, especially pp. 48–53.

13. Pilar, O'Cadiz, and Torres (1994) report on a literacy project they conducted in São Paulo, Brazil, in which they sought to implement Paulo Friere's method.

14. It is worth considering that sometimes one gets better insights proceeding from sociology and praxis to philosophy than going the other way. What Schwartz found through a long scholarly process was sensed intuitively by those living under the ideology derived from the theology he studied. Schwartz himself said that Arieh Fishman's sociological study of the Religious Kibbutz Movement and Ehud Luz's

study of the ideologies that contributed to religious Zionism came close to the findings of his study long before he did (1996, p. 10).

15. Rabbi Avraham Yitzhak Hakohen Kook, Letters, I, 214.

16. These are the two terms given by the Gur Hasidic women I studied to the worlds of knowledge. The "substantial" was knowledge less relevant to their lives, the "practical" more relevant. This dichotomous division does not necessarily co-incide with abstract and concrete, male and female, theoretical and utilitarian. The major determinant was the ability to actualize the knowledge in their existence (see El-Or, 1994, pp. 89–135).

17. On the connection between the creation of "learning identities" and social power, more may be found in Lave and Wenger, 1991, p. 55.

PART IV

1. Leah Shakdiel, an orthodox feminist, was the first woman elected to serve on a religious council; such councils are the statutory bodies responsible for ᵗʰe provision of religious services in each Israeli town and city. She was elected in January 1986, but she was seated only after the intervention of Israel's High Court of Justice, which rejected the objections of the Chief Rabbinate. She served in that role for five years, between 1988 and 1993. Since then, seventeen other women have served on religious councils.

2. Binary system: the use of a binary term—that is, in its regular sense of bipolar divisions of a thing and its opposite. In many cases a binary division turns into a cluster system built on dichotomies that string out from one another—nature and culture, woman and man, emotion and mind, pure and impure, and so on.

3. Goody and Watt, 1968, pp. 27–68.

4. Douglas, 1973; Levi-Strauss, 1966 (1962).

5. Strathern, 1980, pp. 174–222; Ortner, 1974.

6. Collins, 1995, pp. 75–93.

7. It is interesting to note that most of the articles collected by Goody in this book employ a contradictory approach to the method he describes, together with Watt, in the book's introductory article. Many writers present a complex situation that does not answer to the code that equates written literacy to democracy, social justice, and "progress."

8. Hildyard and Olson, 1978.

9. Gordon, 1995, pp. 373–89.

10. Berstein, 1971.

11. "Ignoracy," a translation of the Hebrew boryanut, denotes the inability to achieve power and strength from knowledge. The Hebrew term was coined by Tzvia Valdan (1996, pp. 263–80). It is interesting to note that although current anthropology does not divide the world into "enlightened" and "primitive" zones as classical anthropology did, it employs a different kind of division. Many anthropologists now

mark "zones of suffering" in the world, places in which the individual is (largely) exposed to spiritual and physical anguish at different levels because of an unsound political system. In general, this lack of soundness is explained as a late incarnation of colonialism, the influence of the West on the Third World, and economic, military, and ideological exploitation. The exchange of "primitive" for "touched by suffering" allows a continuation of the superiority of the Western democratic Christian world over other places, while ostensibly accepting responsibility for the situation. See Crapanzano, 1985; Kleinman, 1985; Scheper-Hughes, 1979 and 1992.

    12. Friere and Macedo, 1987.

    13. Goody, who is perceived as formulating autonomous literacy, was indeed aware of the social contexts in which literacy receives actual meaning. In his first book he had already described certain situations (largely in the religious context) that do not allow full expression of literacy. These situations did not prevent him from seeing literacy as an autonomous resource, whose force is sometimes restricted. For this reason, he coined the term "restricted literacy." See Goody, 1968, introduction, p. 11; also Goody, 1988.

    14. Greenfield, 1972; Olson, 1977, pp. 257–81; UNESCO, 1975.

    15. Graff, 1979.

    16. Bledsoe and Roby, 1986, pp. 121–43; Bloch, 1977; Bloch, 1993, pp. 87–109; Bourdieu, 1967; Bourdieu and Passeron, 1977; and Henry, 1972.

    17. Street, 1984.

    18. Friere, 1972.

    19. Giroux, 1992, pp. 199–212.

    20. Luke and Gore, 1992, pp. 1–14.

    21. The example of the El Barrio women, whose story Gordon recounts, is taken from an adult education project in New York implemented in cooperation with Hunter College. The women—of Puerto Rican origin—wrote, among other things, biographies describing their literacy histories. This method of self or group writing is a tool accepted by researchers of both theoretical and applied literacy. This life story, like Leah Shakdiel's story at the beginning of the chapter—or, like the stories the women in the Midrasha told when I asked them in interviews "What is your literacy biography?"— produces ethnography. The uniqueness of this ethnography is that it is stitched out of a personal, sometimes reflective story, rooted in its culture. From it many of the learning contexts of the speakers become clear. See Torrullas, Benmayor, Goris, and Juarbe, 1991, pp. 183–220; and Gordon, 1995, pp. 373–89.

    22. Emig, 1993, pp. 11–16.

    23. Lave and Wenger, 1991.

    24. Women are exempt from positive time-dependent mitzvot—mitzvot that require that a specific action be done, as opposed to those which prohibit something—whose observance is required at a particular time. It should be noted that there are time-dependent mitzvot that women are required to perform: sanctification of Shabbat; the eating of matzah and bitter herbs on the first night of Pesach, as well as drinking four cups of wine that same night; the reading of the Megillah,

or Book of Esther, on Purim; the lighting of Hanukah candles; Hakhel (the public reading by the king of a part of the book of Deuteronomy); and hearing the shofar on Rosh Hashanah. The two central mitzvot of public prayer and Torah study are included among those from which women are exempt.

25. According to Jewish law, most observances are accompanied by a blessing, in which the observer declares that God has commanded the Jewish people to perform this observance. Rabbi Yosef rules that a person, in particular a woman, who is exempt from a particular observance but who nevertheless observes it should not recite the associated blessing.

26. A person who brought a sacrifice was required to lay his hands on the animal before it was slaughtered, as prescribed in Leviticus 1:4: "And he shall put his hand upon the head of the burnt offering; and it shall be accepted for him to make atonement for him."

27. *Shma Yisrael* is to be said in the mornings and in the evenings. As such, it is time-dependent, and women are not required to perform this observance.

28. Kiddush is the blessing of Shabbat or festivals with wine. While generally done at home, many synagogues have the custom of reciting the blessing in public, following the morning services, after which refreshments are served. Adina is pointing out that in her synagogue, when kiddush is announced, it is done in a way that implies that the women present are not part of the public at the synagogue, and therefore they need a special invitation to attend. This practice is presumably based on the fact that men are required to pray in public—with a quorum of a minimum of ten men—while women are not.

29. Don Seeman deals with a similar confession at another time. He reread the chapter "The Wisdom of Women" written by Rabbi Barukh Epstein (who is known as the Makor Baruch). In the center of his reading is the figure of Rayna Batya, the Makor Baruch's aunt, as she is portrayed in the memory of her nephew at the end of the nineteenth century. The two of them had long and complex conversations in which Rayna Batya expressed her pain, frustration, and helplessness, derived from her exclusion from the world of Torah. Rayna Batya was an unsuccessful but book-reading housewife. She sought relief from her pain among her books and among Torah scholars. It is interesting to note that the focus of the discussion between the two was also the exemption from positive time-dependent mitzvot. The confessions of Rayna Batya to her young nephew turned in time to ever longer silences that contained her strong desire to belong to the community and her pain that this desire could not be fulfilled. See Seeman, 1996, pp. 91–127.

30. Henry, 1972.

EPILOGUE

1. T. Ross, "Feminist Implications for Orthodox Jewish Theology," *De'ot* 7(1998): p. 9.

~

LIST OF REFERENCES

WORKS IN HEBREW

Aran, Gideon, 1987. "From Religious Zionism to Zionist Religion: The Roots of Gush Emunim and Its Culture." Ph.D. dissertation, The Hebrew University.

Bar Lev, Mordechai, and Shmuel Rozner (eds.), 1987. *The Jubilee: Fifty Years of Bnei Akiva in Israel 1929–1979* (Tel Aviv: Bnei Akiva).

Barzilai Ben-Yakar, Sarit, 1995. "Free and Fearful (*Hared*): The Stories of Newly Non-Religious People from *Haredi* Society." Master's thesis, The Hebrew University.

Bialik, Chaim Nachman, and Y. H. Rabnitzki, 1930. *Sefer Ha-Aggadah* (Tel Aviv: Dvir).

Boyarin, Daniel, 1993. "Paul and the Genealogy of Gender." *Zemanim* 46–47 : 46–65.

———, 1995. "Rabbis and Friends — Are there Jews in the 'History of Sexuality'?" *Zemanim* 52: 50–66.

Bruner, José, 1993. "Mother's Voice: Dialectics of Feminist Self-Consciousness." *Zemanim* 46–47: 14–17.

El-Or, Tamar, 1992. "'From Shilo You Can't See Iceland': The Rachelim Incident." *Alpayim* 7 (1993): 59–81.

Friedman, Marsha, 1991. *Exile in the Promised Land* (Tel Aviv: Breirot).

Friedman, Menachem, 1991. *Haredi Society: Sources, Trends, and Processes* (Jerusalem: Jerusalem Institute for Israel Studies).

Gur Ze'ev, Ilan (ed.), 1996. *Education in the Age of Postmodernist Discourse* (Jerusalem: Magnes).

Hazan-Rokem, Galit, 1995. "The Threefold Thread: On Sexuality, Relationship, and Femininity in Rabbinic Works." *Te'oria U-Vikoret* 7: 255–64.

Kashti, Y., M. Arieli, and Sh. Shlasky, 1997. *Lexicon of Education and Teaching* (Tel Aviv: Ramot).

Krinsky, Aviva, 1995. "The Theory of Acceptance as Dialogue." *Helkat Lashon* 19–20: 118–41.

Lavie, Smadar, and Swedenburg, Ted, 1995. "Between and within the Boundaries of Culture." *Te'oria U-Vikoret* 7: 67–86.

Mar'ot: A National Magazine for the National Service Girl and Young Religious Woman. June 1996.

Orian, Shlomit, 1994. " 'You Have Nothing Better than Modesty' ": Patterns of Communication in the Socialization of *Haredi* Girls." Master's thesis, University of Haifa.

Peled, Nurit, and Shoshana Blum Kulka, 1997. "Dialogues of the Classroom Discourse." *Helkat Lashon* 24: 28–60.

Peleg, Moly, 1997. *To Spread God's Anger: From Gush Emunim to Rabin Square* (Tel Aviv: Ha-Kibbutz Ha-Me'uhad).

Rabinowitz, Dani, 1995. "The Twisted Quest to Save Brown Women." *Te'oria U-Vikoret* 7: 5–19.

Rapoport, T., A. Panso, and Y. Garb, 1995. " 'It Is an Important Thing to Give to the Public': Zionist-Religious Girls Contribute to the Nation." *Te'oria U-Vikoret* 7: 223–34.

Ravitzky, Aviezer, 1993. *The Revealed End: Messianism, Zionism, and Religious Radicalism in Israel* (Tel Aviv: Am Oved).

Ross, Tamar, 1995. "The Implication of Feminism on the Jewish Orthodox Theology." *De'ot*, Vol. 1, pp. 5–11.

Sagi, Avi (ed.), 1996. *Faith in Changing Times: On the Teachings of Rabbi Joseph Dov Soleveitchik* (Jerusalem: Elinar).

Schwartz, Dov, 1996. *Faith at the Crossroads: Between Idea and Practice in Religious Zionism* (Tel Aviv: Am Oved).

Shamir, Ronen, Michal Shati, and Nelly Elias, 1997. "Calling, Feminism, and Professionalism: Women Rabbinic Pleaders in the Orthodox Religious Community." *Megamot* 38 (3): 313–48.

Simmons, John, 1995. "The Feminist Coalition in the Border Region." *Te'oria U-Vikoret* 7: 20–30.

Valdan, Tzvia, 1996. "The Buds of Literacy: Literacy and Ignoracy." In Nurit Peled (ed.), *From Speech to Writing* (Jerusalem: Carmel Publishing), I: 263–80.

Weissman, Deborah, 1993. "The Education of Religious Girls in Jerusalem during the British Mandate Period: The Institutionalization and Consolidation of Five Educational Ideologies." Ph.D. dissertation, The Hebrew University of Jerusalem.

WORKS IN ENGLISH

Adams, Alice, 1995. "Maternal Bonds: Recent Literature on Mothering." *Signs.* vol. 20, no. 21, pp. 414–427.

Anzaldua, Gloria, 1987. *Borderlands/La Frontera: The New Mestiza* (San Francisco: Spinsters/Aunt Lute).

Appadurai, Arjun, 1991. "Global Ethnoscapes: Notes and Queries for Transnational Anthropology." In Richard G. Fox (ed.), *Recapturing Anthropology: Working in the Present* (Santa Fe: School of American Research), pp. 191–210.

Aran, Gideon, 1991. "Jewish Zionist Fundamentalism." In M. E. Marty and R. S. Appleby (eds.), *Fundamentalism Observed* (Chicago: University of Chicago Press), pp. 265–344.

———, 1994. "Return to the Scripture in Modern Israel." In Evelyne Patageon and Alain Le Boulluec (eds.), *Les Retours aux écriptures fondamentalismes* (Paris: Presents et Passes), pp. 101–32.

Azmon, Yael and Dafna N. Izraeli (eds.), 1993. *Women in Israel* (New Brunswick, N.J.: Transaction).

Badinter, Elisabeth, 1981. *Mother Love: Myth and Reality* (New York: Macmillan).

Bartal, Israel, 1994. "Knowledge and Wisdom: On the Orthodox Historiography." *Studies in Contemporary Jewry* 10: 178–92.

Bassin, Donna, Margaret Honey, and Meryle Kaplan (eds.), 1994. *Representations of Motherhood* (New Haven: Yale University Press).

Belenky, Mary et al., 1986. *Women's Ways of Knowing* (New York: Basic Books).

Bernstein, Basil, 1971. *Class, Codes and Control Vol. 3* (London: Routledge).

Bernstein, Debora (ed.), 1992. *Pioneers and Homemakers: Jewish Women in Pre-State Israel* (Albany: State University of New York Press).

Biale, Rachel, 1984. *Women and Jewish Law: An Exploration of Women's Issues in Halakhic Sources* (New York: Schocken Books).

Bledsoe, Y., and K. Roby, 1986. "Arabic Literacy and Secrecy among the Mende of Sierra Leone." *Man* 21 (2): 121–43.

Bloch, Maurice, 1977. *Language and Oratory in Traditional Societies* (London: Academic Press).

———, 1993. "The Uses of Schooling and Literacy in Zafimaniry Village." In Brayn Street (ed.), *Cross-Cultural Perspectives on Literacy* (Cambridge: Cambridge University Press), pp. 87–109.

Bordo, Susan, 1990. "Feminism and Gender Skepticism." In Linda Nicholson (ed.), *Feminism/Postmodernism* (New York: Routledge), pp. 133–56.

Bourdieu, Pierre, 1967. "Systems of Education and Systems of Thought." *International Social Science Journal* 19 (30): 338–358.

Bourdieu, P., and J. Passeron, 1977. *Reproduction in Education, Society and Culture* (London: Sage).

Boyarin, Daniel, 1993. *Carnal Israel: Reading Sex in Talmudic Culture* (Berkeley: University of California Press).

———, 1997. *Unheroic Conduct: The Rise of Heterosexuality and the Invention of the Jewish Man* (Berkeley: University of California Press).

Buchmann, Christian, and Celina Spiegel (eds.), 1995. *Out of the Garden: Women Writers on the Bible* (New York: Fawcett Columbine).

Bursh, Lisa D., 1996. "Love, Toil and Trouble: Motherhood and Feminist Politics." *Signs: Journal of Women in Culture and Society* 21 (2): 429–440.

Chambers, Ian, 1990. *Border Dialogues: Journeys in Postmodernity* (New York: Routledge).

Clifford, James, 1989. "Notes on Travel and Theory." *Inscriptions* 5: 177.

Clifford, James, and George Marcus (eds.), 1986. *Writing Culture* (Berkeley: University of California Press).

Code, Lorraine, 1991. *What Can She Know* (Ithaca: Cornell University Press).

Collins, James, 1995. "Literacy and Literacies." *Annual Review of Anthropology* 24: 75–93.

Crapanzano, Vincent, 1985. *Waiting: The Whites of South Africa* (New York: Random House).

Douglas, Mary, 1973. *Rules and Meaning* (Harmondsworth: Penguin).

Dumont, R., and M. Was, 1967. "Cherokee School Society and the Inter-Cultural Classroom." In Jhon I. Roberts and Sherrie K. Arkinsanya (eds.), *Schooling in the Cultural Context* (New York: David McKay).

El-Or, Tamar, 1993. "The Length of the Slits and the Spread of Luxury: Reconstructing the Subordination of Ultraorthodox Jewish Women through the Patriarchy of Men Scholars." *Sex Roles* 29, 9–10 (1994): 585–98.

———, 1994. *Educated and Ignorant: Ultraorthodox Jewish Women and Their World* (Boulder, Colo.: Lynne Rienner).

Friere, Paulo, 1972. *The Pedagogy of the Oppressed* (London: Penguin).

———, 1985. *The Politics of Education: Culture, Power, and Liberation* (South Hadley, Mass. : Bergin and Garvey).

Friere, P., and D. Macedo, 1987. *Literacy: Reading the Word and the World* (London: Routledge and Kegan Paul).

Geertz, Clifford, 1973. "Deep Play: Notes on the Balinese Cockfight." In *The Interpretation of Cultures* (New York: Basic Books), pp. 412–53.

Giroux, Henry A., 1983. *Theory and Resistance: A Pedagogy for Opposition* (South Hadley, Mass.: Bergin and Garvey).

———, 1992. "Resisting Difference: Cultural Studies and the Discourse of Critical Pedagogy." In L. Grossberg, C. Nelson, and P. A. Treichler (eds.), *Cultural Studies* (New York: Routledge), pp. 199–212.

Glaser, Ilsa M., and Whaiba Abu-Ras, 1994. "On Aggression, Human Rights, and Hegemonic Discourse: The Case of a Murder for Family Honor in Israel." *Sex Roles* 30 (3/4): 269–88.

Goody, Jack, 1988. *The Logic of Writing and the Organization of Society* (Cambridge: Cambridge University Press).

Goody, Jack, and Ian Watt, 1968. "The Consequences of Literacy." In Jack Goody (ed.), *Literacy in Traditional Societies* (Cambridge: Cambridge University Press), pp. 27–68.

Gordon, Debora, 1995. "Border Work: Feminist Ethnography and the Dissemination of Literacy." In R. Behar and D. A. Gordon (eds.), *Women Writing Culture* (Berkeley: University of California Press), pp. 373–89.

Graff, Harvey J., 1979. *The Literacy Myth: Literacy and Social Structure in the 19th Century City* (London: Academic Press).

Granite, B. Lauren, 1995. "Tradition as a Modality of Religious Change: Talmud Study in the Lives of Orthodox Jewish Women." Ph.D. dissertation, Drew University.

Greenfield, Patricia M., 1972. "Oral or Written Language: The Consequences for Cognitive Development in Africa, U. S. and England." *Language and Speech* 15: 169–178.

Harding, Sandra, 1986. *The Science Question in Feminism* (Milton Keynes: Open University Press).

Heilman, Samuel C., 1983. *The People of the Book* (Chicago: University of Chicago Press).

———, 1984. *The Gate Behind the Wall* (New York: Summit Books).

Henry, Jules, 1972. *On Education* (New York: Vintage).

Heschel, Susannah (ed.), 1983. *On Being a Jewish Feminist* (New York: Schocken Books).

Hildyard, A., and D. Olson, 1978. "Literacy and the Specialisation of Language" (Ontario Institute for Studies in Education).

Hyman, Paula, 1983. "The Jewish Family: Looking for a Usable Past." In Heschel (ed.), *On Being a Jewish Feminist*, pp. 19–26.

Kaplan, Ann E., 1992. *Motherhood and Representation: The Mother in Popular Culture and Melodrama* (New York: Routledge).

Kleinman, Arthur, 1985. *Culture and Depression* (Berkeley: University of California Press).

Ladd-Taylor, Molly, 1994. *Mother-Work: Women, Child Welfare, and the State, 1890–1930* (Urbana: University of Illinois Press).

Langer, Marie, 1992. *Motherhood and Sexuality.* Trans. Nancy Caro Hollander (New York: Guildford Press).

Lave, Jean, and Seth Chaiklin (eds.), 1993. *Understanding Practice: Perspectives on Activity and Context* (Cambridge: Cambridge University Press).

Lave, Jean, and Etienne Wenger, 1991. *Situated Learning: Legitimate Peripheral Participation* (Cambridge: Cambridge University Press).

Levi-Strauss, Claude, 1966 (1962). *The Savage Mind* (London: Weidenfeld and Nicolson).

Levitt, Laura, 1997. *Jews and Feminism: The Ambivalent Search for Home* (New York: Routledge).

Luke, Carmen, and Jennifer Gore, 1992. *Feminism and Critical Pedagogy* (New York: Routledge). Introduction, pp. 1–14.

Luttrel, Wendy, 1997. *School Smart and Mother Wise* (New York: Routledge).

Marcus, G., and M. Fisher, 1986. *Anthropology as Cultural Critique* (Chicago: University of Chicago Press).

McLaren, Peter, 1992. "Collisions with Otherness: 'Traveling' Theory, Post-colonial Criticism, and the Politics of Ethnographic Practice—the Mission of the Wounded Ethnographer." *International Journal of Qualitative Studies in Education* 5: 77–92.

O'Cadiz, Marta del Pilar and Carlos Alberto Torres, 1994. "Literacy, Social Movements, and Class Consciousness." *Anthropology and Education Quarterly* 25 (3): 208–25.

Olson, David, 1997. "From Utterance to Text: The Bias Language in Speech and Writing." *Harvard Educational Review* 47: 257–81.

Ortner, Sherry, 1974. "Is Female to Male as Nature to Culture." *Woman Culture and Society* (Palo Alto: Stanford University Press). pp. 67–87

Peskowitz, Miriam, and Laura Levitt (eds.), 1997. *Judaism Since Gender* (New York: Routledge).

Rapoport, Tamar, and Tamar El-Or, 1997. "Cultures of Womanhood in Israel: Agencies and Gender Production." *Women Studies International Forum* 20 (5/6): 573–580.

Rosenzweig, Linda W., 1993. *The Anchor of My Life: Middle-Class American Mothers and Daughters, 1880–1920* (New York: New York University Press).

Ross, Ellen, 1995. "New Thoughts on 'The Oldest Vocation': Mothers and Motherhood in Recent Feminist Scholarship." *Signs: Journal of Women in Culture and Society* 20: 397–413.

Roth, Paul, 1989. "Ethnography without Tears." *Current Anthropology* 30 (5): 555–61.

Rudavsky, T. M., (ed.), 1995. *Gender and Judaism: Transformation of Tradition* (New York: New York University Press).

Ruddick, Sara, 1989. *Maternal Thinking: Toward a Politics of Peace* (Boston: Beacon Press).

———, 1994. "Thinking Mothers/Conceiving Birth." In Bassin, Honey, and Mahrer (eds.), *Representations of Motherhood*, pp. 29–45.

Scheper-Hughes, Nancy, 1979. *Saints, Scholars and Schizophrenics: Mental Illness in Rural Ireland* (Berkeley: University of California Press).

———, 1992. *Death without Weeping; The Violence of Everyday Life in Brazil* (Berkeley: University of California Press).

Seeman, Don, 1996. "The Silence of Rayna Batya: Torah, Suffering, and Rabbi Baruch Epstein's 'Wisdom of Women.'" *Torah v Madda Journal* 5: 91–127.

Shokeid, Moshe, 1992. "Commitment and Contextual Studying in Anthropology." *Cultural Anthropology* 7 (4): 464–77.

Strathern, Marilyn, 1980. "No Nature, No Culture: The Hagen Case." In M. Mac-Cormack and M. Streathern (eds.), *Nature, Culture, and Gender* (Cambridge: Cambridge University Press), pp. 174–222.

Street, Brayn, 1984. *Literacy in Theory and Practice* (Cambridge: Cambridge University Press).

Swedenburg, Ted, 1992. "Occupational Hazards Revisited: Reply to Moshe Shokeid." *Cultural Anthropology* 7 (4): 478–495.

Swirski, Barbara, and Marilyn P. Safir (eds.), 1991. *Calling the Equality Bluff: Women in Israel* (New York: Pergamon Press).

Torruellas, Rosa, Rina Benmayor, Anneris Goris, and Ana Juarbe, 1991. "Affirming Cultural Citizenship in a Puerto Rican Community: Critical Literacy and the El Barrio Popular Education Program." In C. E. Walsh (ed.), *Literacy as Praxis: Culture, Language and Pedagogy* (Norwood, N.J.: Ablex), pp. 183–220.

UNESCO, 1975. *Women, Education, Equality.*

Walkerdine, Valerie, 1992. "Progressive Pedagogy and Political Struggle." In Luke and Gore (eds.), *Feminism and Critical Pedagogy*, pp. 15–24.

Walters, Suzanna D., 1992. *Lives Together/Worlds Apart: Mothers and Daughters in Popular Culture* (Berkeley: University of California Press).

Wasserfall, Rachel, 1997. "Reflexivity, Feminism, and Difference." In Rosanna Hertz (ed.), *Reflexivity and Voice* (Thousand Oaks, Calif.: Sage), pp. 150–68.

Weidman-Schneider, Susan, 1985. *Jewish and Female* (New York: Simon and Schuster).

Weissman, Deborah R., 1976. "Bais Ya'akov: A Historical Model for Jewish Feminists." In Elizabeth Koltun (ed.), *The Jewish Woman* (New York: Schocken), pp. 139–48.

Wolff, Janet, 1995. *Resident Alien: Feminist Cultural Criticism* (New Haven: Yale University Press), chapters 6 and 7, pp. 88–134.

Young, Iris M., 1990. *Justice and the Politics of Difference* (Princeton: Princeton University Press).

Zerubavel, Yael, 1995. *Recovered Roots: Collective Memory and the Making of Israeli National Tradition* (Chicago: University of Chicago Press).

~

INDEX

Torah scroll, 11
Torah study, for women. *See* Literacy, religious, for women
"Trivializing the Torah," 97
Tzimtzum, 247–48
Tzitzit, 10

Ulpana, 11, 26, 27, 31, 117, 217; versus high school, 134–35; as mark of strict religious observance, 135; *ulpana* literacy, 93–94, 150, 220–21, 305 n.6
Ulpanit, 11, 27, 93–94, 117, 134

Valdan, Tzvia, 312 n.11
Van Leer Institute, 263

Walkerdine, Valerie, 191, 197
Wandering gaze, 74–75, 76
Watt, Ian, 268–69
Weissman, Deborah, 293–95
Wenger, Etienne, 149; *Situated Learning: Legitimate Peripheral Participation* (with Jean Lave), 278, 279, 289
Wigs, 303 n.3
Wolf, Rabbi Avraham Yosef, 30
Wolff, Janet, 74–75, 76
Women's College, Bayit Ve-Gan, 123
Women's literacy, 220–21
Women's Midrasha, Bar-Ilan University, 17, 21, 41–44; admission criteria, 58; *beit midrash* program, 45–46, 155, 241; border-crossing exercises, 217, 225–27; classroom observation, 173–74; curriculum, 44–47; difficulties of women in realizing expectations for, 152–54; discontinuity between students'

lives and representations offered in classes, 192–93, 258–59; growth of course offerings over time, 45; *havruta*, 18, 233, 235, 241; as home on campus for women, 43–44, 104, 152; independent study framework, 241; learning preferences of women, 155–58, 161–66; literacy as participation, 280–90; new literacy experiences, 163–64, 250–51; oral law classes, 44, 47; perceived as close-minded and limited, 115, 125–26; perceived as enlightening, 110; rabbinic advocates program, 45, 46; shift in teaching from encouragement of particpation to policing, 290; struggle by women to broaden participation, 193–95, 196, 197, 198, 199, 232, 285–86; teachers and teaching methods, 45, 47–49, 158–61; women as part of community of practitioners, 284–85. *See also* Literacy biographies, of women at Bar-Ilan Midrasha
Women's Ways of Knowing (Belenky), 148, 157

Yadid, Rabbi, 104–5, 110, 125, 159–60
Yedidya synagogue, Jerusalem, 116
Yehuda Ha-Levy, Rabbi, 13
Yeshiva high school, 217
Yeshivat hesder, 11
Ye'ud, 38
Yose, Rabbi, 281
Yosef, Rabbi Ovadiah, 281, 285, 314 n.25
Young, Iris M., 228

www.ingramcontent.com/pod-product-compliance
Lightning Source LLC
Chambersburg PA
CBHW070439100426

42812CB00031B/3336/J